Amnesties, Pardons and Transitional Justice

In a consolidated democracy, amnesties and pardons do not sit well with equality and a separation of powers; however, these measures have proved useful in extreme circumstances, such as transitions from dictatorships to democracies, as has occurred in Greece, Portugal and Spain. Focusing on Spain, this book analyses the country's transition, from the antecedents from 1936 up to the present, within a comparative European context. The amnesties granted in Greece, Portugal and Spain saw the release of political prisoners, but in Spain amnesty was also granted to those responsible for the grave violations of human rights which had been committed for 40 years. The first two decades of the democracy saw copious normative measures that sought to equate the rights of all those who had benefitted from the amnesty and who had suffered or had been damaged by the Civil War. But, beyond the material benefits that accompanied it, this amnesty led to a sort of wilful amnesia which forbade questioning the legacy of Francoism. In this respect, Spain offers a useful lesson insofar as support for a blanket amnesty – rather than the use of other solutions within a transitional justice framework, such as purges, mechanisms to bring the dictatorship to trial for crimes against humanity or truth commissions – can be traced to a relative weakness of democracy and a society characterised by the fear of a return to political violence. This lesson, moreover, is framed here against the background of the evolution of amnesties throughout the twentieth century and in the context of international law. Crucially, then, this analysis of what is now a global reference point for comparative studies of amnesties provides new insights into the complex relationship between democracy and the varying mechanisms of transitional justice.

Roldán Jimeno is a Senior Lecturer in Legal History at the Public University of Navarre, Spain.

Transitional Justice

Series Editor: Kieran McEvoy
Queen's University Belfast

The study of justice in transition has emerged as one of the most diverse and intellectually exciting developments in the social sciences. From its origins in human rights activism and comparative political science, the field is increasingly characterised by its geographic and disciplinary breadth. This series aims to publish the most innovative scholarship from a range of disciplines working on transitional justice-related topics, including law, sociology, criminology, psychology, anthropology, political science, development studies and international relations.

Titles in this series:

The Reparative Effects of Human Rights Trials
Lessons from Argentina
Rosario Figari Layus (2018)

Rape, Sexual Violence and Transitional Justice Challenges
Lessons from Bosnia-Herzegovina
Janine Natalya Clark (2018)

Amnesties, Pardons and Transitional Justice
Spain's Pact of Forgetting
Roldán Jimeno (2018)

Forthcoming titles in the series:

The Judiciary and the Politics of Transition
Police Brutality Cases in Chile, Northern Ireland and South Africa
Marny Requa

The Trouble with Truth
Dealing with the Past in Northern Ireland
Kieran McEvoy

Amnesties, Pardons and Transitional Justice

Spain's Pact of Forgetting

Roldán Jimeno

Translated by
Owen Harrington Fernández

Routledge
Taylor & Francis Group
LONDON AND NEW YORK

First published 2018
by Routledge

2 Park Square, Milton Park, Abingdon, Oxfordshire OX14 4RN
52 Vanderbilt Avenue, New York, NY 10017

a GlassHouse book

Routledge is an imprint of the Taylor & Francis Group, an informa business

First issued in paperback 2019

British Library Cataloguing in Publication Data
A catalogue record for this book is available from the British Library

Library of Congress Cataloging in Publication Data
Names: Jimeno Aranguren, Roldáan | Harrington-Fernáandez, Owen, translator.
Title: Amnesties, pardons and transitional justice : Spain's pact of forgetting / by Roldáan Jimeno ; translated by Owen Harrington Fernáandez.
Description: Abingdon, Oxon ; New York, NY : Routledge, 2017. |
Series: Discourses of law | Includes bibliographical references and index.
Identifiers: LCCN 2017028477 | ISBN 9781138091603 (hbk)
Subjects: LCSH: Political crimes and offenses--Spain--History. |
Transitional justice--Spain--History. | Amnesty--Spain--History.
Classification: LCC KKT4415 .J56 2017 | DDC 345.46/077--dc23
LC record available at https://lccn.loc.gov/2017028477

ISBN: 978-1-138-09160-3 (hbk)
ISBN: 978-0-367-23236-8 (pbk)

Typeset in Baskerville
by Taylor & Francis Books

To my son Beñat

Contents

Acknowledgements

The study presented here was mostly carried out in the academic year 2015/2016 while I was affiliated to the Irish Centre for Human Rights in the National University of Ireland, Galway (NUI Galway). I would like to extend my gratitude to the two directors who led this institution during my stay, Michael O'Flaherty, currently the director of the European Union Fundamental Rights Agency, and Ray Murphy.

My stay was funded by the Salvador de Madariaga Mobility Grant awarded by the Ministry of Education in Spain.

I would like to express my gratitude to Shane Darcy and Thamil Venthan Ananthavinayagan for inviting me to present my main findings at a seminar held in the Irish Centre for Human Rights in NUI Galway. I would also like to thank Begoña Sangrador-Vegas for inviting me to present at a conference organised by the School of Languages, Literatures and Cultures in the same university. Lastly, I would like to thank Alan John Cusack and Olateju Oluwabunmi Taiwo for inviting me to present my findings at a seminar in the Centre for Criminal Justice and Human Rights in University College Cork.

I would also like to personally acknowledge and thank my colleagues at the Irish Centre for Human Rights, Kathleen Cavanaugh, Aoife Duffy, Anita Ferrara and Zoi Aliozi, as well as my Irish friends, Jane Tottenham, Tom Liddy, Milma Urroz, Michele Horgan and Sally O'Halloraw.

This book was originally written in Spanish. The translation into English was carried out by Owen Harrington Fernández, who currently lectures on Spanish and Translation Studies at the University of Glasgow.

I would like to extend my gratitude to Kieran McEvoy, Transitional Justice series director, and Colin Perrin, editor of Routledge, as well as the two reviewers for their interesting observations.

In closing, I would like to thank my wife, Ainhoa, and my three children, Maider, Jakes and Beñat, who accompanied me during my Irish adventure.

Abbreviations

ADMA	Asociación Democrática de Mujeres Aragonesas (Democratic Association of Aragonese Women)
AEDIDH	Asociación Española para el Desarrollo y la Aplicación del Derecho Internacional de los Derechos Humanos (Spanish Association for the Development and Application of the International Law on Human Rights)
AGE	Archive of War and Exile
AI	Amnesty International
ANV	Acción Nacionalista Vasca (Basque Nationalist Action)
AP	Alianza Popular (Popular Alliance)
APDH	Permanent Assembly for Human Rights (Argentina)
ARMH	Asociación para la Recuperación de la Memoria Histórica (Association for the Recovery of Historical Memory)
AWOL	Absent without leave
BND	Bundesnachrichtendienst (German secret service)
BNG	Bloque Nacionalista Gallego (Galician Nationalist Bloc)
CEAQUA	Coordinadora Estatal de Apoyo a la Querella Argentina (Public Co-ordination of Support for the Argentinian Lawsuit)
CIA	Central Intelligence Agency (USA)
CIC	Candidatura Independiente del Centro (Independent Candidacy of the Center)
CiU	Convergència i Unió (Convergence and Union)
CCOO	Comisiones Obreras (Workers' Commission)
CMDPDH	Comisión Mexicana de Defensa y Promoción de Derechos Humanos (Mexican Commission for the Defence and Promotion of Human Rights)
COPEL	Coordinadora de Presos Españoles en Lucha (Organising Committee of Spanish Prisoners in Struggle)
EA	Eusko Alkartasuna (Basque Unity)
EEC	European Economic Community
EE	Euskadiko Ezkerra (Basque Left)
EGB	Educación General Básica (Basic General Education)

EHAS	Euskal Herriko Alderdi Sozialista (Basque Socialist Party)
EIA	Euskal Iraultzarako Alderdia (Basque Revolutionary Party)
EKA	Euskalherriko Karlista Alderdia (Basque Country Carlist Party)
EPOCA	Exèrcit Popular Català (People's Army of Catalonia)
ERC	Esquerra Republicana de Catalunya (Republican Left of Catalonia)
ESB	Euskal Sozialista Biltzarrea (Basque Socialist Assembly)
ESEI	Euskal Sozialistak Elkartzeko Indarra (Force to join the Basque Socialists)
ETA	Euskadi Ta Askatasuna (Basque Country and Freedom)
ETA-M	ETA-Militar (Military ETA)
ETA-PM	Political-Military ETA
FAGC	Front d'Alliberament Gai de Catalunya (Catalan Gay Liberation Front)
FET-JONS	Falange Española Tradicionalista y de las Juntas de Ofensiva Nacional Sindicalista (Spanish Fascist Party)
FIDH	Federación Internacional de los Derechos Humanos (International Federation of Human Rights)
FRAP	Frente Revolucionario Antifascista y Patriota (Patriotic Anti-Fascist Revolutionary Front)
GRAPO	Grupos de Resistencia Antifascista Primero de Octubre (Antifascist Resistance Groups First of October)
IACHR	Inter-American Court of Human Rights
ICV	Iniciativa per Catalunya Verds (Initiative for Catalonia Greens)
IU	Izquierda Unida (United Left)
LAIA (bai)	Langile Abertzale Iraultzaileen Alderdia (bai) (Revolutionary Patriotic Workers Party (yes))
MIL	Iberian Liberation Movement
NATO	North Atlantic Treaty Organization
OAS	Organisation de l'Armée Secrète (Secret Army Organisation) (Algeria-France)
PCE	Partido Comunista de España (Spanish Communist Party)
PCE (i)	Partido Comunista de España (Internacional) (Spanish Communist Party (International)
PDC	Pacte Democrátic per Catalunya (Democratic Pact of Catalonia)
PIDE/DGS	Policía Internacional da Defesa do Estado/Direccão Peral de Segurança (International and State Defense Police) (Portugal)
PNV	Partido Nacionalista Vasco (Basque Nationalist Party)
PP	Partido Popular (Popular Party)
PREC	Proceso Revolucionario en Curso (Ongoing Revolutionary Process) (Portugal)
PSC	Partido Socialista de Cataluña (Socialist Party of Catalonia)
PSOE	Partido Socialista Obrero Español (Spanish Socialist Workers' Party)

PSP-US	Partido Socialista Popular-Unidad Socialista (Socialist People's Party-Socialist Unity)
PSUC	Partido Socialista Unificado de Cataluña/Partit Socialista Unificat de Catalunya (Unified Socialist Party of Catalonia)
RUF	Revolutionary United Front (Sierra Leone)
SECED	Servicio Central de Documentación de la Defensa (Central Information Service of Defence)
SPD	Sozialdemokratische Partei Deutschlands (Social Democratic Party of Germany) (Germany)
TUC	Trade Union Congress
UCD	Unión de Centro Democrático (Union of the Democratic Centre)
UGT	Unión General de Trabajadores (Workers' General Union)
UK	United Kingdom
UMD	Unión Militar Democrática (Democratic Military Union)
UN	United Nations
UPyD	Unión, Progreso y Democracia (Union, Progress and Democracy)
USO	Unión Sindical Obrera (Workers Syndical Union)

Introduction

This study analyses Spanish transitional justice through the perspective of amnesty and pardons. As is well known, transitional justice research focuses on the theoretical and practical aspects of how nations confront the legacy of human rights violations during transitions from dictatorial regimes – as was the case in Spain – or armed conflicts against democratic States or in times of peace.[1] Every country has its own way of implementing transitional justice. Some countries opt for granting amnesty to facilitate the democratic reforms of their institutions, economic and moral reparation for the victims, prosecuting those responsible for violations of human rights, truth commissions, etc.[2]

Spain opted for a blanket amnesty that occasioned impunity. It is, as John Elster says, a unique model of transitional justice in the context of transitions towards a democracy because a deliberate decision was made by the majority to avoid implementing a transitional justice system.[3] Such is the unique character of the situation in Spain that Bartolomé Clavero believes that it is inaccurate to describe it as transitional justice as such.[4] Those who opposed the dictatorial regime were granted amnesty, but a peculiar situation emerged when the amnesty was extended to members of the regime who had committed human rights violations, essentially granting impunity for crimes committed by the dictatorial regime. The law ignored, and then forgot, the victims of the Civil War and the dictatorship,[5] including those who had suffered from the repression of the latter years of Francoism and during the first stage of the transition – in other words, those whose pain was most recent in memory. This wilful amnesia of the past meant that there was no legal will to find out the truth or to punish the perpetrators. There were no trials, truth commissions or purges of repressive institutions, such as the police force that had tortured victims, judges who had handed death and life sentences to those who had opposed the regime, or lawyers who

1 *The rule of law and transitional justice in conflict and post-conflict societies: report of the Secretary-General.* UN: S/2004/616. 23 August 2004.

2 Mallinder, 2008a.

3 Elster, 2004.

4 Clavero, 2014, p. 166.

5 On the links between forgetting and the law, see Poole, 2009, pp. 149–157.

had practised their profession with the same disregard for those oppressed by the regime. Moreover, important archives were destroyed, thus eliminating the only official record of criminal responsibilities, and it took years to open the remaining public archives. But even today, access is not easy. There was no moral or symbolic rehabilitation of those who had been defeated in the Civil War and punished by the Francoist regime, not even a simple condemnation of the dictatorship. It is no surprise, then, that the Spanish transitional model is defined in terms of impunity.[6]

This notwithstanding, it is important to acknowledge that at the time, during the 1970s, purges and trials were only carried out in transitions in which the authoritarian regimes were defeated externally and internally, or when regimes suffered a considerable institutional crisis. When the Spanish transition began, only one truth commission existed. It would be a mistake to judge the Spanish transition with the benefit of hindsight, from our new perspective informed by the current doctrine on transitional measures. The situation in the 1970s was very different.

There are no clemency measures around Europe that can be compared to the amnesty in Spain, except maybe the case of Austria,[7] where the past has been silenced, ignoring the repression of 1934 and their criminal involvement after 1938.[8] Spain repeated the same tragic irony that is common to countries with weak democratic institutions and traditions; in other words, the countries least prepared to implement adequate policies to reconcile the past. It is these countries where repression and suppression has been most widespread, and where the number of victims is greatest – the countries, in fact, where the need for transitional justice policies is most pressing.[9]

Legal amnesia gave way to economic reparations, which were almost always distributed late, incomplete, and of little economic consequence for Republican soldiers and civil servants (and years later, for those who had been imprisoned by the regime for political reasons). The first two decades of the democracy saw copious regulations that tried to equate the rights of all those who had been granted amnesty and who had been damaged by the Civil War or the immediate post-war. But beyond these reparations, institutional amnesia prevented inquiries into the legacy of Francoism which was still palpable in the newly established democracy, and there was no attempt to reconcile human rights and the democratic values of the Second Spanish Republic.

The fundamental characteristics of the two concepts which are central to this study must be defined in accordance with Spanish legislation. Amnesty and pardons correspond to what is called a right or grace prerogative – to use the words

6 Gil Gil, 2009a, p. 22. González Vega, 2009, pp. 67–84. Sáez Valcárcel, 2011, pp. 63–69.
7 Navarro, 2002, p. 25.
8 Historical Commission of the Republic of Austria: http://www.historikerkommission.gv.at/english_home.html (accessed on 30 July 2016).
9 Barahona de Brito, González-Enríquez and Aguilar, 2001, p. 17.

in the Spanish 1978 Constitution[10] – or a right to clemency, as it is called in studies in this subject area. The right to grant pardons is based on the clemency of those who have power to grant it, which is why we speak of grace measures or acts of clemency. It is, as Enrique Lindo stated, "the residue of absolute power that subsists in a constitutional state".[11] As the doctrine constantly reminds us, these measures of the past are incompatible with the devolution of power that a democracy requires.[12] It would be simplistic to analyse the amnesty from our current situation, because acceptance and rejection of the amnesty has continued to evolve through time.[13] The criteria through which we analyse this phenomenon in the twenty-first century has shifted and changed from the criteria of the previous century.

The idea of amnesty is formalised by criminal law, and administered by public institutions to address a specific political circumstance, as a way of extinguishing sentences and all their effects. In other words, amnesty is an arbitrary measure that is legally illogical, and which can only be justified in political terms.[14] Sentences are extinguished because they were imposed for a crime that the Amnesty Law in Spain no longer considers a criminal offence, at least within the timeframe stipulated by the law. Any criminal activity which did not correspond to the categories delineated were not eligible. An amnesty – which comes from the Greek word αμνησια, meaning "to forget" or "to be without memory" – implies *forgetting* the offence, invalidating criminal proceedings and, ultimately, questioning the legitimacy of the sentence. Amnestied acts are no longer punishable, which grants impunity to those who committed the offence. The amnesty also covers criminal proceedings, declaring a stay of the proceedings pending for crimes covered under the Amnesty Law.[15]

But amnesty in Spain does not belong solely to criminal law; as will be discussed in the book, workers who had exercised their right to strike were also granted amnesty in 1977,[16] which is why, in 1980, the Supreme Court interpreted that:

> It is not accurate to say that the amnesty belongs to criminal law exclusively, as it can be adapted to any branch of our legal order where there is a system of punishable conduct, disciplinary procedures, government sanctions or any

10 Article 62.i of the Constitution alludes to the "right to clemency", while articles 87.3 and 102.3 mention a "clemency prerogative".

11 Linde Paniagua, 1998, p. 1413.

12 In relation to the Spanish doctrine, the following are particularly noteworthy: Lozano Cutanda, 1991. Martín Pallín, 1992. López Aguilar, 1996. Zúñiga Urbina, 1996. Llorca Ortega, 1997. Linde Paniagua, 2000. Aguado Renedo, 2001. Pérez del Valle, 2001. García Mahamut, 2004.

13 Teitel, 2003, pp. 69–94. Mallinder and McEvoy, 2011, pp. 107–128.

14 In relation to this arbitrariness, José Antonio Martín Pallín's words are appropriate here: "any members of the doctrine and jurisprudence who have tried approaching amnesty from a legal perspective has been left confused". Martín Pallín, 2011, p. 59.

15 Vallès Muñío, 2004, p. 9.

16 There is also a tax amnesty, but its application is not related to transitional justice, and is therefore not part of this study.

type of limitation of rights that could be forgotten and the various effects cancelled.[17]

For its part, pardon, which can be handed out for any type of crime, does not presuppose forgetting the offence because it does not extinguish criminal records or discredit criminal proceedings. It simply pardons the sentence, completely or partially, or transmutes it to another type of sentence, but it does not forgive the crime. In Spain, pardons are regulated by the Law of 18 June 1870,[18] which is still in force in its revised version, as per the Law of 14 January 1988.[19]

Blanket pardons could be dictated right up until the promulgation of the 1978 Constitution. Pardons were used profusely during Franco's dictatorship; the number of individuals who benefitted from these pardons is difficult to determine, but regardless, this type of clemency measure was banned in the 1978 Constitution. Only individualised pardons are possible in Spain today, and even these are reserved for exceptional circumstances.[20]

The current doctrine is very critical of pardons, as it considers them antithetical to the separation of powers that is an inherent aspect of every democracy. A pardon granted by the executive power presupposes usurping the functions of legal institutions. It is, furthermore, an arbitrary measure, as governments are under no obligation to justify their decision. It is this arbitrariness which, ultimately, violates principles of equality and legal equity.[21]

17 Sentence dictated in the 4th Chamber, Social Division of the Supreme Court, 677/1980, 24 March.
18 Law of 18 June 1870, Regulation for the implementation of pardon as a clemency measure. *Madrid Gazette*, 24 June 1870, p. 1.
19 Law 1/1988, 14 January, to modify Law of 18 June 1870, establishing regulation for the implementation of pardon as a clemency measure. *Official State Gazette*, no. 13, 15 January 1988, p. 1386. Specifically, it modified articles 2, 3, 9, 11, 15, 20, 22, 23, 24, 26, 29 and 30. The legislation on pardons is complemented by the Criminal Code (articles 4 and 130.3, and the sixth transitional provision); the Criminal Procedure Law (articles 666.4, 675, 676 and 902); the Ministry of Justice Order of 10 September 1993, on guidelines for the administration of applications for pardon; article 6 of Royal Decree 1879/1994, 16 September, approving specific procedural regulations in relation to Domestic and Legal Affairs; and the 29th additional disposition, second regulation of Law 14/2000, 29 December, on tax, administration and social order measures.
20 Sobremonte Martínez, 1980, pp. 239–242. Llorca Ortega, 1997, pp. 37–43.
21 For this reason, Judge José Antonio Martín Pallín said that pardon is a "not very common in the legal framework of constitutional states. It is a legally subjective prerogative, and it is the responsibility of the judiciary to vouch for this subjectivity, precisely because it presupposes contravening the criminal law principle of generality, and the jurisdiction principles of independence and exclusivity. Once it is admitted by the constitution, its implementation is safeguarded by prudence measure in order to minimise its disturbance of the normal legal order." Sentence of the 2nd Chamber for Criminal Cases in the Supreme Court, 18 January 2001. Presiding judge: José Antonio Martín Pallín.

Pardons and amnesty do not sit well with equality and a separation of powers in consolidated democracies. As José Antonio Martín Pallín says, amnesty is more of a feature in authoritarian states. Democratic states tend to restore justice through different mechanisms, especially when it comes to transitioning from a dictatorship to a democracy, because amnesty "does not align with the principles of a constitutional system which foregrounds justice and values it above everything else". Whilst I concur with this claim, I disagree with Martín Pallín when he says that "the constitutions promulgated after the Second World War are opposed to integrating amnesty as a formula that conforms to the governing principles of their democratic model".[22] The precedents set in the States neighbouring Spain contradict this claim. France integrated amnesty in article 34 of its 1958 Constitution, which proved crucial when it came to finding a solution to events in Algeria; France offers a salient point of comparison for Spain, given that the Algerian amnesty was a precedent that Spain considered when it came to promulgating the first blanket amnesty of the transition. For its part, Portugal included amnesty in article 161f of the 1976 Constitution, although the measure was not implemented during the Portuguese transition. Added to these, we must also take into consideration the amnesty specified in article 29 of the 1947 Italian Constitution.[23]

These constitutions include amnesty as a preventive measure for extraordinary circumstances, such as transitions from a dictatorship to a democracy. The amnesty granted in Greece, Portugal and Spain was a quick solution that saw the release of political prisoners, but on the other hand, in Spain, amnesty also granted impunity to those responsible for the grave violations of human rights which had been committed for 40 years. This books aims to transcend the geographical limits of focusing solely on Spain by carrying out a comparative analysis that includes the amnesties in Italy, Algeria-France, Greece and Portugal. Although these cases bear striking similarities, they are also profoundly different.

Twenty-five years after the Spanish transition, and dovetailing the resurgence of historical memory at the beginning of the century, the associations for victims of the Civil War and Francoism began using legal, political and social mechanisms to put pressure on the authorities to remove the Amnesty Law so that Francoist crimes could be prosecuted, so that truth could be restored and so that adequate reparations could be made.

The 2007 Historical Memory Law failed to satisfy the demands of the victims in full, among other reasons because it vindicated the Amnesty Law and therefore legitimised the impunity of Francoist criminals. Spain's post-transitional justice repeated the mistakes that were made in other European and American transitions and post-transitional processes by not taking into consideration the views of the various pro-memory associations.[24] The Historical Memory Law, as well as

22 Martín Pallín, 2011, p. 58.
23 Linde Paniagua, 1976b, pp. 457–486.
24 McConnachie and Morison, 2008, pp. 75–98. Lundy and McGregor, 2008, pp. 99–120.

the different regulatory measures through which it was developed, did not answer the calls for the truth, for justice and for the reparation of the victims whose human rights had been violated during the Civil War and the dictatorship. The pro-memory associations decided to take legal action and began proceedings in the cases where they had the best chance of seeing the rights of the victims recognised. The victims dived in at the deep end into an ocean of international criminal law, Spanish criminal law, human rights law and more, but they were always swimming against the tide, unable to fight against the 1977 Amnesty Law, fervently defended by the main political powers in Spain as a symbol of the "exemplary" Spanish transition.

The common denominator of all the cases brought by the Pro-Memory groups was the demand that Spain comply with its international duty on human rights, something which, to this day, it refuses to do. Some cases even reached the Supreme Court and the Constitutional Court, where the associations requested the annulment of sentences passed by Francoist courts against individuals who opposed the regime. These legal proceedings reached a landmark when Judge Baltasar Garzón opened an investigation into Francoist crimes. In the capacity of National High Court judge, he interpreted that the Amnesty Law did not represent closure, and should therefore not obstruct the prosecution of crimes or the search for the truth about the events. The judge was more than aware that, after so many years, there was no one to prosecute, as most of the individuals concerned had passed away. But the judge could find some justice by providing families with the legal mechanisms they needed to find disappeared members of their family. Baltasar Garzón was charged with prevarication – a manoeuvre to subvert the Courts of Justice – which culminated with the sentence passed on 27 February 2012 by the Supreme Court which blocked Spanish Courts from investigating Francoist crimes. The sentence maintained that Baltazar Garzón made the mistake of classing the charges brought by the pro-memory associations under the Amnesty Law, which is still in force.[25] The Spanish Supreme Court based its decision on the Amnesty Law and rejected the possibility of initiating legal investigations into the crimes against humanity committed during the 1936 coup d'état and the subsequent Francoist dictatorship.

The Amnesty Law was central to the debate on the recovery of historical memory which emerged after 2004. The debate got a second wind from the sentence that removed Baltasar Garzón from the National High Court. Human Rights Watch, Amnesty International and the Spanish Society for the Advancement of International Human Rights Law were among the first dissenting voices critical of the impunity bestowed by the law; soon they were joined by various branches of the UN, such as the Human Rights Committee, the Committee Against Torture, the Office of the High Commissioner for Human Rights, the Working Group on Enforced or Involuntary Disappearances, and the Special Rapporteur

25 Sentence dictated in the Criminal Division of the Supreme Court, 101/2012, 27 February.

on the promotion of truth, justice, reparation and guarantees of non-recurrence; the number of critics that demand the derogation or modification of the Amnesty Law is as numerous today in the Spanish legal doctrine.

When Spain closed the door to its legal system, the victims adopted a two-pronged approach to delegitimise the status of the Amnesty Law as a *Ley de punto y final* (End of Story Law). The first aspect of this approach was initiated in 2010, when more than a hundred associations of victims of the Civil War and Francoism sought recourse in universal jurisdiction. This move led to the Argentine lawsuit against Francoist crimes on the ground that Spain is failing to comply with signed international agreements obliging the democratic state to investigate Francoist crimes, regardless of the 1977 Amnesty Law. Judge María Servini leads this investigation, and has thus far called 19 ex-officials and members of the forces and security corps during the dictatorship and the first transition to declare. The second aspect of the two-pronged approach consisted of bringing different cases to the European Court of Human Rights with the aim of using this platform as a way of forcing Spain to comply with its international duty on human rights.

This study is framed with a historical-judicial perspective[26] and founded on a multidisciplinary approach,[27] making this a socio-legal study which integrates contributions from other fields, thus falling in line with Méndez's claim that transitional justice should be analysed through its three pillars: the ethical, the political and the legal.[28] The arguments put forward in this book are based on the close reading of transitional justice research carried out by judges, historians, political scientists, sociologists, theologians and, ultimately, by any authority that has contributed to this research area.[29]

As mentioned previously, this study is comparative in nature. Amnesty and pardons in Spain cannot be looked at in isolation without considering earlier transitions in Greece and Portugal, as well as the amnesty and pardons granted by the French government in Algeria. It is worth noting that there are excellent comparative studies on amnesty and clemency undertaken by academics. Brian Gormally and Kieran McEvoy (1995) pioneered comparative studies into amnesty,[30] followed by the work of Louise Mallinder, who is responsible for an

26 This issue is dealt with extensively from a judicial perspective. Santiago Ripol has recently taken up this issue, taking into consideration the existing debates on scientific aspects. First, he collected the most significant works on the conceptualisation and the foundations of transitional justice, as well as works on the mechanism through which it operates and the experiences of different states. Second, he put together a bibliography relative to the case of Spain, followed by a selection of UN-approved fundamental texts about transitional justice, both general and specific to Spain, as well as important documents on legal and judicial practices in Spain. Ripol Carulla, 2014, pp. 76–107.

27 See Bell, 2009, pp. 5–27.

28 Méndez, 1997.

29 On the evolution of the transitional justice doctrine, see the eminent work of Teitel, 2003, and, more recently, Benavides Vanegas, 2011.

30 Gormally and McEvoy, 1995.

extensive database – containing 506 amnesty processes from 130 countries between the end of the Second World War and January 2008 – which has facilitated comprehensive comparative analyses.[31] This database, developed as part of a project at Queen's University Belfast, includes a search engine that gives access to amnesty laws according to country, which is of great benefit to furthering our understanding of the fundamental characteristics of amnesty laws throughout the world.[32] The invaluable work of Canadian lawyer, Mark Freeman,[33] and the volume edited by Francesca Lessa and Leigh A. Payne[34] are important precedents to this study. In this latter volume, the work of Paloma Aguilar[35] is of particular relevance, as well as other comparative studies that she has carried out exploring Spain's Amnesty Law in relation to other amnesty processes, especially in the Latin American context.[36] As well as the work of Paloma Aguilar, the work of Alicia Gil, which compares the Spanish transition with the analogous process in Brazil with its corresponding laws and amnesties, is also of particular importance.[37]

The history of transitional and post-transitional justice goes beyond the confines of the legal framework and the judicial-political and socioeconomic strategies implemented by the institutions of power as reparation for past human rights violations. The Spanish amnesty during the transition would not have been granted had there not been an intense public outcry that pressured the government. For this reason, it is also important to approach this topic from a perspective that takes into consideration the role played by civil society[38] or, as Kieran McEvoy and Lorna McGregor[39] put it, a "from below approach". Thus, we explore the important role played by the popular socio-political movements and organisations and the social currents around the calls for a labour amnesty and an amnesty for political prisoners during the transition, and those that currently call for the abolition of the amnesty for Francoist criminals. What the events in Spain demonstrate is that civil society and the victims have been the main artifices of extending the discourse of transitional justice, instigating grassroots processes that have created an alternative space where the truth, justice and reparation can exist, and where the victims themselves take centre stage.[40]

31 Because of its comparative nature, we must highlight the work of Mallinder, 2008a, Mallinder, 2008b, Mallinder, 2010, and Mallinder, 2014.
32 *The Amnesty Law Database*, Queen's University. http://incore.incore.ulst.ac.uk/Amnesty/about.html
33 Freeman, 2009.
34 Payne and Lessa, 2012.
35 Aguilar, 2012.
36 Aguilar, 2008, pp. 413–479. Aguilar, 2013, pp. 245–266. Aguilar, Bacells and Cebolla, 2011, pp. 1397–1430. Aguilar and Hite, 2010, pp. 119–168.
37 Gil Gil, 2012a, pp. 77–108.
38 See Gill, 2004.
39 McEvoy and McGregor, 2008.
40 Gómez Isa, 2012, p. 184.

We also consider it important to complement theory with practice, which is why we pay special attention to individual cases in order to explore how amnesty was applied and the problems the victims faced when it came to exercising their rights. This particular aspect of our study is mainly based on personal interviews and testimonies.[41]

41 The advantages of adopting this methodology for transitional justice studies can be seen in González, 2009, pp. 295–312.

Chapter 1

Background to Francoist Spain

Granting pardons to the defeated in the war and enemies of the regime

1 Amnesties and pardons after the war

It is a well-known fact that the democratic government of the Second Spanish Republic suffered a coup d'état in July 1936. The Popular Front, a coalition made up of different left-wing parties (the Republican Left, the Republican Union Party, the Communist Party of Spain, the Spanish Socialist Workers' Party and the Republican Left of Catalonia), had secured an overall majority in the election held on the 16 February 1936. The government was led by Manuel Azaña, of the Republican Left. The military uprising that led to the Civil War, from which the nationalist faction emerged as victors, was led by Francisco Franco.

Franco's government abolished legislation introduced by the Second Spanish Republic, beginning with the Spanish Constitution[1] that was brought into law on 9 December 1931, wherein article 102 determined that pardons could only be sanctioned by Parliament, and that a blanket amnesty should not be granted. The doctrine of the time viewed amnesties and pardons indiscriminately given that it did not allow for case-by-case sentencing.[2] The addition of this prohibition owes its origins to the agreement reached in the pre-constitutional debate that a one-off blanket amnesty would be granted when the constitution came into effect, and that, furthermore, it would serve as reparation for past injustices.[3] The Republican Constitution did, however, foresee the possibility of individual pardons being granted by the Supreme Court upon the recommendation of a

1 As Carlos Jiménez Villarejo recalls, as soon as the military uprising began to gain substantial power in areas where the control of the Occupation Army continued to grow, the necessary decisions were taken to dissolve the legality and effectiveness of the Constitution in those areas, and, in particular, the legality of laws dictated post-18 July. Article 2 of the Decree issued on 1 November 1936 entrusted the Justice Commission of the State Technical Council to "examine all laws, decrees, orders, regulations and circular letters that preceded the uprising and are considered in their enforcement contrary to the national interests, for their immediate abolition by General Franco" (Jiménez Villarejo, 2007, pp. 9–10).

2 Jiménez de Asúa, 1932, pp. 419–421.

3 Requejo Pagés, 2001, pp. 96–99.

particular judge, the Attorney General, the prison boards, or at the request of an interested party.[4] This crucial modification forced the abolition of parts of the 1870 Law (18 June 1870).[5]

The perpetrators of the coup did not need to abolish the Criminal Code of 1932,[6] whose article 115 included pardons as a cause for the absolution of criminal responsibilities. Neither did they abolish the 1882 Criminal Prosecution Act (14 September 1882),[7] wherein articles 666.4 and 902 legislated on amnesties and pardons. Neither of these pieces of legislation covered the practical application of amnesty for political crimes, which were tried in military courts.

On 13 September 1936, the National Defence Council[8] published Decree number 109 that determined that any military personnel who had taken part in the insurrection against the Spanish Republican Government on 10 August 1932 should be reinstated in their post upholding all their previous rights, namely to the military personnel who played a major part in the coup prior to Sanjurjo's coup, and to those of the garrison of Alcalá de Henares, who rose up in the spring of 1936, these failed revolts against the Spanish Republic being exalted in the preface to the legal text:

4 The only precedent in Spain was the Spanish Constitution of 1 June 1869, article 74.5 therein indicating that the King needed a special law to give him the authority to grant amnesties and general pardons. For a discussion on article 102 of the Second Spanish Republic Constitution, see Linde Paniagua, 1976a, pp. 40–42, Requejo Pagés, 2001, p. 22, and Herrero Bernabé, 2012a, pp. 97–107.

5 *Madrid Gazette*, no. 175, 24 June 1870, p. 1. The modification was decreed by the Ministry of Justice on 4 February 1932, in relation to the administration of pardons (*Madrid Gazette*, no. 36, 5 February 1932); it specified the procedures that the petition and the subsequent concession had to follow. The petitions for pardon had to be submitted to the president of the Supreme Court, who received the case file formed by the court that handed out the sentence. All petitions for pardon had to be referred to the court that handed out the sentence, which had to issue the corresponding mandatory report. The case file had to contain the documents and requirements as per articles 24 and 27 of the 1870 Law. But, unlike in this law, no consultation with the State Council was required. For its part, the Administration Division of the Supreme Court would agree, when appropriate, to the concession of court-ordered pardons; this agreement would be added in the *Madrid Gazette* (which preceded the *Official State Gazette*). The petition could only be filed in cases of extreme gravity, both on the initiative of the Government or the Courts, as well as at the request of an interested party. The administration of these pardons for crimes of extreme gravity, was, in any case, the responsibility of the Ministry of Justice. The Decree of 1932 also introduced a clause that gave the Ministry of Justice the power to resolve the claims and incidents that could be presented in relation to a blanket amnesty and pardons previously granted by the Constitution. Therefore, although the Decree circumscribed pardons, its reach widened to deal with issues regarding previous amnesties.

6 The validity of this text was aided by the ubiquity of military legislation, which was the legislation applied to the political enemy, lest it should be forgotten that a state of war lasted until 7 April 1948, different jurisdictions of special political control, complementary criminal codes, and exceptional measures such as the death penalty.

7 *Madrid Gazette*, 17 September 1882.

8 *National Defence Council of Spain Gazette*, no. 22, Burgos, 16 September 1936.

> Notorious were the patriotic ideals that inspired the movement originating in Madrid on the tenth of August nineteen thirty-two, that although those who unlawfully held Power during that time using draconian measures, procedures and campaigns in a subservient press, have managed for the time being to block the externalization of the deep-rooted and true feelings of the healthy masses of our Country in relation to that ideal, they had such clout and strength that were revealed whenever opportunity arose to freely express it, and especially in the behaviour that, in the first instances, they directed towards those punished for said movement.
>
> Add to this the courage, high spirits and nobility which, from the very first moment, was part of the liberation movement of those who, from within the referenced personnel, have been able to reincorporate to our ranks.
>
> For all of this, and with the National Defence Council mindful of the needs of the Country, the Council considers it appropriate to bring into effect, for all intents and purposes, the amnesty that the nation, despite all the compelling evidence, granted to them in a restricted sense, or, more appropriately, in an unreal sense.
>
> The acts relating to the garrison in Alcala de Henares last Spring are characterised in the same way, which, although they developed differently, they involved the same ideals. For this reason, the same decisions are taken in this instance, notwithstanding differences between one case and the other.

This amnesty – though it would be more appropriate to call it a "self-amnesty" – was administered to a large extent by the National Defence Council.

On the other hand, Franco's government did not decree any general pardons during the first 18 months of the war; for this reason the government did not bring in any new legislation until 1938. As Juan Luis Requejo has said, in the new fascist regime, "clemency once again had, after the transient republican phase, the opportunity of developing in a natural way".[9] Instead of granting general amnesty, the dictatorship granted pardons to the opposition, which meant that their crimes and criminal records still stood. A Decree dictated by the Ministry of Justice on 22 April of the same year re-established the legitimacy of the 1870 Law,[10] wiping out all the innovations of the Second Spanish Republic that did not sit well with the new dictatorial spirit of the government. In order to avoid any ambiguities, article 5 abrogated any measures that conflicted with the decree. The first article bestowed upon the Head of State the power to grant pardons. The second article indicated that in order for petitions for pardon to be successful, they would have to be administered by the Ministry of Justice in accordance with the norms and processes established by the 1870 Law. Furthermore, it eliminated the minimal controls in the 1870 Law in relation to a report from the State Council (article 3 of the Decree). To project concern for the respect of civil

9 Requejo Pagés, 2001, p. 100.
10 *Official State Gazette*, no. 550, 24 April 1938.

liberties, article 4 indicated that all types of pardons would be granted by a specific decree, after deliberation by the Council of Ministers and at the behest of the Minister for Justice. The decrees for pardons would be included in the *Official State Gazette*.

Months later, the 1938 Law, 2 November 1938,[11] established new timescales for the mandatory declaration of the possession of gold, money and certain other objects. This was mainly an amnesty directed at Spaniards whether or not resident in Spain. Enrique Linde believed it to be an unusual type of amnesty because it was directed at people who had not been prosecuted or who were unknown to the administration, because there was no case file, and because it was not applicable to people who had been accused, prosecuted, and convicted.[12] This amnesty encompassed an important political component: although its main objective was to bring to the surface hidden wealth, it did not close the door on wealth that came from exiled people. The ambiguity of the text, notwithstanding, did not motivate any exiled people of wealth to return to Spain at a time in which, crucially, the country was steeped in the harsh realities of the war.

2 The first pardons in post-war Spain

The post-war years were marked by the amnesty[13] the victorious faction self-administered with the 1939 Law, 23 September 1939. Although it avoided using the term, the Law was a *de facto* amnesty.[14] Specifically, article 1 established that the following would not constitute crimes:

> the events that would have been the object of criminal proceedings given their nature as constitutive of crimes against the constitution, against public order; infringement of the law against the possession of firearms and explosives; homicides, injury, intimidation and coercion, and as long the same were carried out between the 14th of April, 1931 and the 18th of July, 1936 by people whose ideology aligns with the National Movement and as long they were socio-politically motivated and are considered protests against the anti-patriotic sentiments of organisations and governments who, with their conduct, justified the Uprising.

11 *Official State Gazette*, no. 153, 30 November 1938.
12 Linde Paniagua, 1976a, p. 89.
13 This term has already been used by José Enrique Sobremonte to refer to this Act (Sobremonte Martínez, 1980, p. 97).
14 Specifically, this preamble points out *a priori* that it refers to those who "before the National Movement, were already up for trial in the Spanish tribunals for actions carried out by people who, removed from criminal intent, were motivated by the thrust of their patriotic fervour in defence of the ideals that brought about the Glorious Uprising against the Popular Front". *Official State Gazette*, no. 273, 30 September 1930.

In fact, the Law helped the heirs of amnestied soldiers who had been killed to solicit the cancellation of criminal records. As José Antonio Martín Pallín has pointed out, this was a self-amnesty that set a precedent that would be followed, decades later, by the military dictatorships in Argentina and Chile.[15]

The defeated side continued to be harshly repressed by the totalitarian State, which, moreover, was in complete control of "pardons" for the victorious faction through clemency measures. When the war ended in April 1939, one of the first issues that the new dictatorship had to resolve was overcrowding in prisons. Between April 1939 and January 1940 there were around one million prisoners – an exorbitant figure considering that in 1940 the population of Spain stood at 25,877,911. Of the one million prisoners, 500,000 were imprisoned in concentration camps, 90,000 in Workers' Battalions, 47,000 were part of the Disciplinary Battalions of Worker-Soldiers[16] and only 300,000 were kept in prisons. Added to this are the 150,000 prisoners who died in prison (50,000 of whom were executed). Franco's dictatorship was, therefore, the second most brutal of Western Europe behind Nazi Germany, the most brutal by a long distance. However, it is worth noting that Hitler's Germany also held prisoners from countries they invaded; Spain, on the other hand, only imprisoned those from within its State.[17]

The problem of overcrowding in prisons during the years after the post-war was partially alleviated with the above-mentioned firing squad executions and with the thousands of illness-related deaths brought about by the terrible conditions in the prisons. But the spaces left by the Civil War prisoners were taken up by new inmates, as the post-war brought mass arrests, carried out by the police and the militias of the FET-JONS, which resulted in imprisonment in detention centres.[18]

There was no place for an amnesty or for pardons in the tough repression of the enemy; totally the opposite, in fact. The State decreed an amnesty that fomented harassment of those defeated in the war: the 1939 Decree, 30

15 Martín Pallín, 2008a, p. 31.

16 The so-called "Franco's slaves" who made up the various Workers' Battalions were regulated by the Decree of 28 May 1937, in which the Board for the remission of sentences in exchange for work was created. The "workers" reduced their sentence by one day for every two worked. The main Board was created on 7 October 1938. *Official State Gazette* no. 105, 11 October 1938.

17 Gómez Bravo and Marco, 2011, p. 85.

18 There was no time limit to this deprivation of freedom, despite articles 489 and 496 of the 1882 Criminal Prosecution Act, which was still in force, and dictated that temporary detentions were limited to the duration stipulated in the law. In this way, if the arrest was carried out by the judicial police, the detained party had to be brought in front of the judge after 24 hours. However, these time limitations were consciously flouted by the authorities. It must be noted, furthermore, that the duration of custodies could last up to a month, and sometimes even longer. It must also be noted that, when the detainees were sent to prison, months could pass before they were called to declare in front of the military criminal judge. Carrillo, 2006, pp. 511 and 521–522.

December, abolished the Republican 1937 Decree-Law, 22 January 1937,[19] which the Minister for Justice of the Republican government had used to grant amnesties to those who had been prosecuted and convicted for common, war, political or social crimes committed before 15 July 1936.

A later, apparently favourable measure also sought the repression of those who were imprisoned: the Ministerial Order of 10 June 1940 on Parole, which was only granted to those with "impeccable behaviour". This, however, was a euphemistic term that masked a promotion for inmates who snitched on their fellow prisoners, creating an atmosphere of fear and distrust amongst the community of prisoners.[20]

But overcrowding in prisons in 1940, and its elevated cost in weak and impoverished post-war Spain, encouraged the government to put in motion a series of pardons that would free the prisoners who posed the least risk to the regime. These have been studied by Enrique Linde[21] and, more recently, Mirta Núñez,[22] Domingo Rodríguez Teijeiro[23] and Ireneo Herrero Bernabé,[24] among other authors.

This new policy of releasing prisoners was set out in the Provincial Sentencing Courts, created by the 1940 Order of 25 January 1940,[25] whose *ex officio* function was to examine the sentences dictated by the tribunals and to propose the commutation of sentences to lesser ones.[26] For this policy to be effective, legal measures that allowed the release of prisoners were needed. These measures were set in motion with the 1940 Decree of 5 April 1940,[27] which granted parole to prisoners who were over 60 years of age, who had been sentenced to fewer than 20 years and a day, and who had served one-quarter of their sentence. The measure was justified along humanitarian lines, given that the prisoners who qualified for this pardon did not have recourse to the system for the redress of their sentences for reasons of work, and for whom sentences, because of their age, equated to life sentences.

Three months later, the Law of 4 July 1940[28] granted parole to prisoners sentenced to between six and 12 years and who had served half of their sentence. To avoid any ambiguity, the law explained that the recipients of this pardon had to be political prisoners who were not sentenced for common crimes. The granting of pardons through this legal mechanism depended on the authority that this law bestowed upon the government to apply articles 101 and 102 of the Criminal

19 *Madrid Gazette*, no. 25, 25 January 1937.
20 Carrillo, 2006, pp. 526–527.
21 Linde, 1976a.
22 Núñez Díaz-Balart, 2010.
23 Rodríguez Teijeiro, 2011.
24 Herrero Bernabé, 2012a.
25 *Official State Gazette*, no. 26, 25 and 2 January 1940.
26 Núñez Díaz-Balart, 2010, pp. 184–186.
27 *Official State Gazette*, 14 April 1940.
28 *Official State Gazette*, no. 158, 6 June 1940.

Code to people sentenced in the "military jurisdiction, with sentences shorter than 6 years and a day". The law also left open the possibility of its application to prisoners who had served half of sentences up to 12 years, even though, as Daniel Rodríguez Teijeiro observes, at the time no prisoner sentenced to 12 years could have served half of the sentence, not even if the sentence had been imposed at the beginning of the war.[29] The prisoners eligible for pardon had to have a record of excellent behaviour and be able to demonstrate that they had addressed and resolved the reasons for their conviction. They had to have favourable reports from the mayor of the municipality in which they resided prior to their conviction, from the local head of FET-JONS, and the head of the Civil Guard of the same municipality. The final decision on whether the pardon was granted fell on the corresponding Sentence Review Board after consideration of all the above requirements.

The subsequent Law of 1 October 1940 modified article 2 contained in the previous Law of 4 July 1940 and extended its application to prisoners who had served half of their sentence of 12 years and one day. It did not prescribe any type of requirement.[30] For its part, the Decree of 23 November 1940 dictated that prisoners would be released while the case file was being processed.

Given that the sentences, handed out by the tribunals and included in these measures, were minor, only a limited number of prisoners were set free. Added to this, the authorities tended to be unfavourable in their reports, all of which conspired against the prisoners who applied for pardons. In order to solve this problem, the Law of 1 April 1941 gave the Sentence Review Board the authority to grant provisional parole to prisoners who had been sentenced to 12 years and one day, without the caveat of having to serve time in the future. Furthermore, reports from local authorities would no longer be required. Their sole purpose would be to indicate whether prisoners could take up residency in their local community upon their release.[31] A Circular Letter from the General Directorate of Prison Administration, dated 15 April 1941, dictated that if the letter from the authorities was not favourable and denied prisoners residency in their local community, it would be the prisoners themselves who would decide where they would be relocated, as long as it was 250 kilometres from their previous residence. In the years that followed, this type of exile became the mechanism that was commonly used by the penitentiary authorities to set free political prisoners who did not have the consent of their local authorities. For their part, the local authorities came to play an increasingly important role in the repression and control of the defeated. In any case, an earlier agreement by the Central Board for the Redemption of Sentences through Work specified that prisoners could return to their locality of origin "if the governing authorities stated so".[32]

29 Rodríguez Teijeiro, 2011, p. 5.
30 *Official State Gazette*, 1 October 1940.
31 *Official State Gazette*, 1 April 1941.
32 Rodríguez Teijeiro, 2011, pp. 6–7.

Official statistics showed that between January 1940 and June 1941 a total of 28,787 prisoners were granted release. This figure was still low, and prisons remained overcrowded. To expedite the release of prisoners, the regime published the Decree of 2 September 1941[33] to clarify the procedure to follow. This regulation must, nevertheless, have generated doubts, as the General Directorate of Prison Administration, on 2 January 1942, had to specify that legislation on parole related only to crimes committed between 18 July 1936 and 1 April 1939.[34]

Due to the continued failure to expedite the mass release of prisoners, the Defence Ministry was forced to decree an Order on 28 September 1942 directed at the Provincial Sentence Review Boards. The Boards had to review all the death sentences handed out up to that time that had been downgraded to the next most severe sentence "as a consequence of a pardon being granted". The new proposals would be passed up to the Central Sentencing Review Board, which was dependent on the Advisory Board of the Defence Ministry, which would then dictate the definitive resolution.[35]

Weeks later, the Office of the Head of State introduced the 1942 Law of 16 October 1942 to extend the legislation on parole to prisoners who had been sentenced up to 14 years, eight months and one day for military rebellion.[36] This time the measures brought about a greater number of releases. According to official statistics, up until October 1942, there was an average of 2,000 successful applications for pardon per month; however, with the limitations extended to prisoners with sentences up to 14 years, eight months and one day, the figure rose steadily to 7,325 successful applications per month by December 1942.[37]

The Law of 16 October 1942 was modified by the new Law of 13 March 1943,[38] which granted parole to prisoners sentenced to up to 30 years under the same conditions as the previous Law of 16 January 1942. It therefore allowed those who had not been sentenced to more than 20 years to be covered by this measure "without prejudice to the original verdict", the ambiguity designed so that the regime could keep the more dangerous prisoners behind bars. The new legislation excluded those who had reduced sentences on account of their being under the legal age. The law sustained the need for mandatory reports from local authorities, which, were they to be unfavourable, would deny prisoners from returning to their local community. This latter measure, however, was relaxed in the Order of 31 July 1943, which dictated that the written report would be issued by the provincial Parole Board. If the reports were unfavourable, the prisoners would still need to be relocated 250 kilometres from their local community, but it was envisioned that the reports from this authority would be more objective.[39]

33 *Official State Gazette*, 5 September 1941.
34 Rodríguez Teijeiro, 2011, p. 8.
35 Rodríguez Teijeiro, 2011, p. 8.
36 *Official State Gazette*, 22 October 1942.
37 Rodríguez Teijeiro, 2011, p. 9.
38 *Official State Gazette*, 1 April 1942.
39 *Official State Gazette*, 5 August 1943.

This prediction was proved right in light of the 1,087 prisoners who were set free in the first ten days of August 1943; of these, 311 were relocated and 776 were allowed to reintegrate in their local communities.[40]

Aiming to expedite the mass release of prisoners, the General Directorate of Prison Administration issued a Circular letter on 7 September 1943, ordering, with immediate effect, the release (and exile 250 kilometres from their local community) of all the prisoners serving sentences of up to 12 years who had been denied parole on grounds of an unfavourable report from local authorities, and who "had no other unspent criminal charges". Prisoners who were denied parole under previous legislation for attempting to escape were excluded from this measure.[41]

A Decree issued the same month (29 September 1943) facilitated pardons for prisoners who were aged 70 or older, and who had been imprisoned because of the Civil War, regardless of the sentence that had been imposed.[42]

Finally, the Decree of 17 December 1943[43] granted the last pardon in the form of parole for prisoners who had been sentenced to 20 years and one day, and for those with longer sentences in specific circumstances. Following the protracted period of decrees and modifications described here, this last decree was issued with a view towards stability, borne out by the fact that within the mandatory requirements there were a series of conditions that could not be ignored: apart from traditionally observing excellent conduct, the decree added the caveat that prisoners could not have been sentenced for "homicide, cruelty, or other analogous crimes, either as perpetrators, instigators or commanding authorities". Another condition that this decree imposed was that prisoners had to have served at least five years of their sentences, and in cases where prison sentences had been redeemed for work, the time spent at work would be taken into consideration. This decree also took into account excellent conduct or other exemplary merits, under the same conditions as before and taking health reasons into consideration, when deciding whether to grant parole for prisoners who had been sentenced to more than 20 years and one day.

The modifications of laws and decrees that took place between 1940 and 1943 finally achieved the much-awaited mass release of prisoners. The official figures showed that on 7 January 1940 the number of prisoners stood at 270,719, but by 10 April 1943 this number was reduced to 114,958. Of these, 22,481 were prisoners sentenced for common crimes, while 92,477 had been "imprisoned as a consequence of the uprising".

40 Rodríguez Teijeiro, 2011, p. 10.
41 The Order also included prisoners whose sentences had been commuted under the recommendation of the corresponding provincial Review Boards; it asked the prison director to forward the proposal even in cases where someone remained imprisoned as a result of having their parole revoked. Rodríguez Teijeiro, 2011, p. 10.
42 *Official State Gazette*, 3 October 1943.
43 *Official State Gazette*, 20 December 1943.

In 1944 no new amnesty measures were decreed, but in July of that year a new Criminal Code was brought into force,[44] characterised by a deep-seated authoritarianism that was more in line with the codes of other totalitarian regimes of the time.[45] Pardons were legislated for in articles 122.2 and 122.4. Based on the legislation described above and the Criminal Code, the number of releases steadily increased and, in this way, the number of prisoners who "had been imprisoned as a consequence of the civil war" up to 1943 was reduced from 92,477 to 33,267 by June 1945, the vast majority of the total number of prisoners, which stood at 51,300.[46]

3 Pardons in 1945 and the need for Spain to reposition itself after the Second World War

The Spanish dictatorship was progressively ostracised by the Allied forces in the years after the Second World War. The conferences in San Francisco (June 1945), Potsdam (July–August 1945) and London (September 1945) condemned Franco's regime and reached the decision that as long as the regime was in power, Spain would not be allowed to join the UN.[47] The decision was taken around the same time as various news stories from the international press began to appear, condemning the treatment of inmates in Spanish prisons, replete, they claimed, with innocent prisoners.[48]

The international veto forced the regime to change strategy, increasing the presence of its governmental propaganda outside its borders to disseminate its legislation on pardons during the second semester of 1945. The strategy was meant to cast the regime in a more favourable light.[49] Specifically, fundamental laws were issued on 17 July 1945 in an attempt to seem more sensitive to human rights considerations.[50] Among these measures aimed at making the regime

44 *Official State Gazette*, no. 204, 22 July 1944.
45 Ferré Olivé, 2006.
46 Carrillo, 2006, p. 510. Gómez Bravo, 2007, pp. 70–71.
47 By then the Charter of the United Nations, signed on 26 June 1945 in San Francisco, had been approved. Article 55c called for universal respect for human rights and fundamental freedoms without distinction as to race, sex, language or religion.
48 Gómez Bravo, 2007, p. 86.
49 Núñez Díaz-Balart, 2010.
50 The Charter of Rights of 1945 stood out, an apparent declaration of the rights of Spanish people that recognised rights such as freedom to congregate, to associate, of expression, as well as different types of civil, procedural and penal guarantees. However, all these freedoms were limited given that they could not go against the principles of the regime. For example, the freedom of expression of ideas was recognised, so long as they were not contrary to the fundamental principles of the State. Specifically, article 18 established that no Spanish person could be arrested "unless in cases and in the manner prescribed by law", and added that "after a period of 72 hours, all detainees would either be set free or handed over to the authorities". But the declaration of these rights was merely cosmetic, the text was ineffective and could not be used in front of the tribunals. Carrillo, 2006, p. 513.

appear more open, the general pardons – from 12 September and 9 October 1945, respectively – stand out.

The former granted either a full pardon to members of the navy, air corps or ground division, or required them to serve additional time in military service for committing crimes or for facing serious charges for desertion. It included all those who were in the ranks on the date of issue and those who reappeared before 1 January 1946. The pardon was applicable to the penalties that had been, or could be, imposed on AWOL soldiers missing until 25 August 1945, as long as they reappeared before 1 January 1946. An addendum to this measure broadened pardons to also include penalties imposed, or to be imposed on, soldiers who were AWOL until 25 August 1945, but only if they reappeared before 1 January 1946.

This pardon had two objectives. First, it sought to bring exiles back to Spain, given that it was the group that exerted the most political pressure outside the country and kept the fight against Franco alive throughout the world. Second, it sought to exonerate those who deserted the Blue Division – that collaborated with the Nazi Army against the Russian front – and defected to the Soviet Army. This pardon was a way of appeasing the Allied forces, but the measure lacked traction, given that the majority of soldiers who had defected from the Blue Division to the Soviet Army until the end of the war had not been set free. The majority of soldiers who were set free between 1945 and 1949 remained in the Soviet Union or went to the German Democratic Republic. For the most part, deserters were kept in *gulags* because Stalin distrusted them and viewed them as potential enemy spies. These forced labour camps were shared by Falangist soldiers and soldiers of communist or republican ideologies.[51]

The pardon decreed by the Ministry of Justice on 9 October 1945[52] was the only one to be officially named as a pardon. With this measure, the Francoist regime believed that it was bringing to a definitive end the problem of overcrowding in prisons. But the dictatorship found itself in a paradox: it needed to portray overseas an image of benevolence in relation to its policy on political prisoners, but it had no prisoners left to set free, given that the pardons granted between 1940 and 1943 set free the prisoners who were less "dangerous" to the dictatorship, and it was in no way willing to set free prisoners who posed a greater risk politically speaking, or had been charged for crimes resulting in death and other grievous crimes. Thus the pardon of 1945 took into account convictions for the military uprising against the State and public order offences committed before 1 April 1939, except in cases of cruelty, death, rape, theft and other related crimes that "repulse honourable men".[53] Obviously, cases of cruelty, death, rape,

51 Months after the death of Stalin (March 1953), the Supreme Soviet granted amnesties to 253 prisoners, who then returned to Spain in the *Semíramis* boat. Only five of those granted amnesties remained in Odessa. Rodríguez Jiménez, 2007. Arasa, 2005.

52 *Official State Gazette*, 19 and 21 October 1945, p. 1569.

53 The pardon did not contemplate secondary crimes, nor crimes that would have been considered repeat offences. All in all, this decree, apart from some exceptions, did not open the door to new cases that were not already contemplated in the previous measures.

theft and other related crimes committed by the Nationalist group did not repulse the "honourable men" of the regime.

On the other hand, this pardon had great potential to attract exiles who would be able to reap the benefits, as we will see with the following point. The regime, thus, focused on attracting exiles. The measure was not only a nod to those exiled in Allied countries, but also to the close to 9,000 Spanish Republicans who ended up in Nazi concentration camps, and who, at that moment, had the empathy of the Allied forces.[54]

The Decree of 9 October 1945 contained a procedural peculiarity: in cases where a verdict had not been reached, and in which the defendant and his counsel were in agreement with the fiscal assessment and the proposed sentence, the sentence would be passed without the need to go through the whole process, implementing a pardon as long as the Department of Public Prosecutions delivered a positive report.[55]

The pardons of 1945 and before were concluded by a decree (13 September 1945[56]) from the Department of Justice, which entrusted the Parole Board with the responsibility of monitoring the prisoners who had been pardoned. The prisoners, on their part, had to notify the Board of their residence and any other changes to this effect.

4 Pardons to instigate the return of exiles (1946–1949)

The measures adopted in 1945 failed to silence the international outcry against Spain. The UN published a resolution on 9 February 1946 recommending that UN members act in the spirit of, and in accordance with, the declarations from San Francisco and Potsdam. At this juncture, the Spanish government was forced to make another attempt at mollifying the Western powers. A Decree from the Department of Justice on 27 February 1946 allowed Spaniards who returned from their exile within six months of the publication of the decree to apply for pardons under the conditions set out in the Decree of 9 October of the previous year. The measure was not received positively by the community of exiles, fearful of being arrested or of facing another type of reprisal.

The dictatorship found itself increasingly beleaguered. The Security Council entrusted one of its subcommittees to carry out a study to establish a set of recommendations for the UN to implement against the Spanish dictatorship. The subcommittee carried out the study between May and June of 1946, and concluded that the Spanish dictatorship was a fascist regime established thanks to the help it received from Hitler's Germany and Mussolini's Italy; it also concluded

54 Among other aspects, the international community bore witness to the image of the huge banner unfurled for Spanish prisoners upon their entry to the Mauthausen-Gusen concentration camp when it was liberated by the United States; it said: *Anti-Fascist Spaniards salute the liberating forces*. Bermejo and Checa, 2006.

55 Herrero Bernabé, 2012a, p. 194.

56 *Official State Gazette*, 21 December 1945.

that the Spanish dictatorship collaborated with Germany during the Second World War. In light of the report, the General Assembly of the UN dictated a resolution on 12 December 1946 which considered that Franco's government did not represent the people of Spain because the regime was imposed on them by force. Therefore, it recommended, among other things, the exclusion of the Spanish government from membership to international organisms established by, or connected to, the UN, and the exclusion of Spain from conferences or other activities undertaken by the UN or one of its associated bodies until Spain installed a new, acceptable government.[57]

This show of force from the international community reinforced the cause of the exiles, who still hoped that Franco's regime would be defeated. Within Spain, the resistance was localised to the armed struggles with the communist *maquis*, the guerrilla group that opposed the regime, which, around that time, was enjoying its greatest successes.

Once again, Franco's government was forced into making a move towards giving the appearance of being concerned about human rights. The Department of Justice published a Decree on 27 December 1946, which extended the Decree on pardons (9 October 1945) by six months, with the principal aim of facilitating the applications of the returning exiles. However, it continued to arouse minimal interest. The exiled community continued to harbour suspicions, as exemplified in Ramón Suárez Picallo's article of 28 February 1946, appropriately titled "In consideration of a false amnesty".[58] Suárez Picallo, who helped promulgate the Draft Statute of Galician Autonomy, pointed out that the aim of the decree was to replicate the latest agreement in the General Assembly of the UN, which roundly condemned Franco's totalitarian regime. For Suárez Picallo, the government sought the return of Spanish political exiles spread throughout the world to demonstrate "the generous magnanimity of our Leader". However, the Galician politician preferred to follow the line of the report from the General Assembly of the UN, and recalled that "in Francoist Spain, those who try to reorganise political groups, trade unions and religious and cultural bodies that in Spain have a secular history, are sent to prison, sentenced by their tribunals and often executed"; that is to say, Franco's government "sends to prison and kills its adversaries whose only *crime* is the simple fact that they are adversaries".

The call for the return of the exiles was, for Ramon Suárez Picallo, a way to "moderate, disarm, deny and correct" a universal belief about the regime that was guided by an extensive press campaign controlled by governmental censorship. The harsh reality was that exiles did not want to return while there remained a dictatorial regime that:

57 UN National Assembly, GA Res. 39(I), 59 plenary meeting, 12 December 1946, pp. 57–58.
58 Suárez Picallo, R. "En torno a una falsa amnistía", *La Hora*, Santiago de Chile, 28 February 1947. www.blogoteca.com/acsuarezpicallo/index.php?cat=11338&pag=1

> executed their families, seized their assets and dictated, through so-called *politically responsible* tribunals, inhumane sentences on the margins of the Law, founded on the accused's membership to parties, institutions and unions with 100 years of history and completely legal in Spain.
>
> Complaining about the attitude of those who don't believe in the amnesty that is on offer and refuse to return, the latest Spanish newspapers that have reached us express annoyance and confusion. [...]
>
> This is not an amnesty as such, but only a way to begin proceedings in the Supreme Council of Military Justice, whose mission and origin was not observed in any law or code in Spain prior to 1936.

As a way of confronting the propagandistic messages coming from Francoist Spain, Suárez Picallo illustrated the harsh reality with a letter from his mother, sent from Spain to her only son, who lived in Santiago de Chile, and from which he quoted the following paragraph:

> I long to see you, but I don't dare ask for your return, for here you would have to work in terrible conditions, adverse to your health. Those who have returned of late found work in the Big House that is in front of the church where your sister got married.

The "Big House" was, as Suárez Picallo explained, the public prison in a town in Andalusia where the few who had faith in the pardons, "magnanimously" granted by the government in Madrid to their political adversaries, ended up.

The regime decided to take a more credible step. The Ministry of Justice published a Decree on 17 January 1947 that enabled Spanish people resident outside the country to apply for pardons through Spanish embassies or consulates, which would then formally notify applicants whether their conduct in relation to the national insurgency carried a criminal sentence in Spain. In cases where this was so, the notification was required to indicate whether the charges were covered under the Decrees on general pardons from 9 October 1945 and 2 December 1946. The application was mediated through a duplicate of the statement, a copy of which was sent to the Supreme Council of Military Justice, which determined whether it was eligible for pardon. The notification of the agreement, properly authenticated, would be sent to the applicants, with one of the following possible results: (a) the events described were not considered of a criminal nature; (b) the events described were considered of a criminal nature, but were eligible for pardon; and (c) the crimes were not eligible for pardon. But the decree had a trap in it, because the agreement struck with the Supreme Council of Military Justice only related to events consigned to the statement of the applicant, and ignored any charges that could be levelled at the applicant once in Spain. Therefore, if these charges surfaced upon their return, applicants would then be incriminated, and could be detained and sent to prison, as in fact happened to some of the applicants.

The international front that was opposed to the regime soon changed its viewpoint due to the new international crisis, the Cold War, which aided the survival of the regime. Pragmatic politics took precedence over the theoretical condemnation of the dictatorship and the prosecution of crimes against humanity based on the parameters established in the recent Nuremberg trials.[59] Francoist Spain adeptly repositioned itself in this new political scenario, and Spain was to have an important strategic role in the Cold War. The anti-communist fervour of democratic Western political powers was led by the United States, which eventually advised against the effective implementation of measures against the Francoist dictatorship. In November 1947, the United States successfully opposed a renewed condemnation of the Francoist regime and the implementation of new sanctions put forward by the UN. The dictatorship cemented its position further in March 1948, when France reopened its borders to Spain. Following this, Franco made a decisive and consequential move when, on 7 April 1948, he decreed the end of the state of war in Spain, which had been in force since the coup of 1936.

This shift in attitude of the Allied powers alienated exiled political parties and organisations, which began to call for a political amnesty. Specifically, the Socialist Party and the monarchs of the opposition reached an agreement in August 1948, in San Juan de Luz (French Basque Country), wherein the conditions for a transition to democracy were established, highlighting the need for a broad amnesty for political crimes, as well as obstructing vengeful acts and retaliations for religious, social or political reasons.[60]

However, Franco's government did not go along with the idea of an amnesty, and instead continued to abide by the general pardon of 9 October 1945, whose period of validity was extended by six months by the Decree of 22 July 1948 for the benefit of exiles who returned to Spain and were covered by conditions set therein.

The return to Spain of exiles was, for the regime, the best way to project overseas a positive image of a seemingly normalised political situation. However, Franco's strategy was not altogether successful. From the 1950s onwards, what came to be called the community of "permanent" Republican exiles was made up of around 220,000 people, comprising soldiers who had fought in the war, politicians and civil servants directly committed to the republican cause, plus many intellectuals, teachers, scientists, artists, novelists and all sorts of people with different qualifications whose personal plight exemplified the dictatorship's lack of basic fundamental rights.[61] Any solution to the problem posed by the exiles could not be exclusive to an amnesty, as was embodied by the proposal for national reconciliation put forward by the Communist Party of Spain in its general meeting of 1956, in which it proposed a "true amnesty that would allow the return of

59 See Maogoto, 2004.
60 Juliá, 2003a, p. 154.
61 Balcells and Pérez Bowie, 2001.

exiles, without discrimination or harassment" and the "release of political prisoners" that, along with other measures, would pave the way "for an understanding and would create a common ground for a peaceful coexistence, giving Spanish people the chance to live free from fear of prosecutions and vengeance".[62]

5 Political pardons between 1964 and 1969

The number of prisoners continued to grow, as the political prisoners from the war and post-war were joined by enemies of the regime. Most notable among these were the *maquis* guerrilla group. A report from the Francoist service that had fought against the *maquis* between 1943 and 1950 relayed that the fight against the guerrilla group resulted in 2,036 fatalities on the *maquis* side, and 3,211 prisoners,[63] whom the regime put on trial in the war councils in accordance with the Military Justice Code.[64] With the *maquis* defeated, the 1950s saw the rise of new political enemies, mainly workers and university students, who by the end of the decade would be joined by the Basque pro-independence group ETA. The government strengthened its oppressive legal framework against political enemies and maintained military jurisdiction over crimes of military uprising, which subsumed crimes against the regime.[65] The Western international community, staunchly anti-communist, turned a blind eye to the constant transgressions against human rights perpetrated by the Francoist regime. Precisely for this reason, the regime's severity when dealing with its opponents was not a deterrent when it came to Spain ratifying the Geneva Conventions of 4 August 1952,[66] signing the Madrid Pact with the United States on 23 September 1953, or finally being admitted to the General Assembly of the UN on 14 December 1955.

The various pardons that were issued between the last years of the 1940s and the early years of the 1960s were not extended to political prisoners. A new regulation on amnesties and pardons was captured in the revised text of the 1963 Criminal Code[67] and served as a precursor to the pardon granted by the Office of the President on 1 April as part of the commemorations of "XXV years of peace".[68] It is not known whether the pardon was foreseen in governmental plans, or motivated by Franco's anger at an article published on 28 March 1964 in *Ecclesia*, the main journal of dissemination of the Spanish Church, which asked

62 Erice Sebares, 2013, pp. 8–9.
63 Suárez Fernández, 2011, p. 268.
64 Fraile, 2005.
65 García Rivas, 1990, p. 109.
66 *Official State Gazette*, 8 September 1952.
67 Wherein it was established that unspent sentences were quashed due to the amnesty and the pardon, specifying that the sentence and all its effects were quashed (article 112.3). Decree 691/1963, 28 March. *Official State Gazette*, no. 84, from 8 April 1963.
68 Decree 786/1964, from 1 April, in which a general pardon is granted as part of the commemoration "XXV years of Peace in Spain". *Official State Gazette*, no. 84, 7 April 1964, p. 4313.

for clemency and forgiveness to be added to the fanfare organised by the government. The governmental Decree dates from 1 April, but it was not published until 7 April. Between those dates a new article appeared in the same journal with the loaded title "Opportune moment for forgiveness", directly asking for "a measure of clemency and legal pardons for all those sentenced and for every crime they committed". The article in the *Ecclesia* issue of 11 April, which dealt with the same theme, failed to mention the pardons granted by the government under the recommendation of the Church.[69]

The Clandestine journal *Unity*, edited by the Barcelona Committee of the PSUC, published the article "The 1st of April Decree, there was no amnesty!",[70] explaining that the struggle for amnesty, which was steadily spreading throughout the country, had forced the government to issue a new pardon. Specifically, the article criticised Minister Manuel Fraga Iribarne, who, "with his usual cynicism", had tried to present this pardon to the public as if it were a *de facto* amnesty. The article carried out an analysis of the details of the pardon to demonstrate that it commuted one in six sentences, excluding sentences, in accordance with the Prison Regulations, for serious crimes. In this way, the anonymous author of the PSUC asked:

> who, if not the political prisoners commit *crimes* or *serious crimes*, as per the regulations, when they defend their freedom of conscience, their human dignity, with regards to their rights as political prisoners or show solidarity with a colleague unfairly sentenced? And how can this be considered an amnesty when it once again excludes the 60 prisoners whose death sentence has been commuted, locked up in the Burgos prison and sentenced many years ago, solely and exclusively for political crimes?

After relating examples from his personal experience, he concluded by resolving that a partial pardon, such as the one that Franco's government had just issued:

> is not the total amnesty that the people of Spain wish for and demand, backed up more and more by the broad sectors of international public opinion. Although it is a partial victory that must urge us on to spread out and intensify the fight for amnesty, until the return home of political prisoners, and the return of the exiles to the *Patria*, is achieved.

Complementary to this Law, the Decree of 10 November 1966 was issued to discharge political responsibility definitively.[71] Its preface explained that "with the

69 Aguilar, 2008, pp. 199–200.
70 "El decreto de indulto del 1° de Abril. ¡No hubo amnistía!", *Unidad*, año XIII, no. 2, 1 May 1968, pp. 4 and 6.
71 Decree 2824/1966, 10 November, on pardons for the abolishment of political responsibilities. *Official State Gazette*, no. 271, 12 November 1966, pp. 14218–14219.

consequences that brought with them legislation on political responsibility settled, it is nevertheless necessary to discharge said responsibility in cases that are still pending". To bring this into force, article 1 granted a "complete pardon for sanctions pending compliance of sentences derived from special legislation on political responsibility of any type and notwithstanding the authority or tribunal that imposed it". The second article established that the Commission for Discharge of Political Responsibilities would enforce this pardon up to the period ending on 31 December 1966, on which date it would be dissolved along with the bodies for which it was responsible. This Commission would be in charge of resolving any requests and incidents that could come up during the process of implementing the clemency being granted.

In truth, this pardon was more symbolic than practical given that in 1966, 26 years after the beginning of the Civil War, there were hardly any political prisoners left from the conflict. The majority of political prisoners were, at that time, people who had opposed the dictatorship during the 1940s, and especially during the 1950s and 1960s. In any case, the decree gave false hope to those who had been removed from their positions at work. As Paloma Aguilar[72] recalls, on 23 July 1968, a group of attorneys presented a proposal to the Francoist parliament to legislate the reintegration to public administration of civil servants "who had been removed for political reasons deriving from our Civil War". One of the attorneys, Juan Manuel Fanjul, said that the pardon of 1966, along with previous unofficial statements, "created the false image that this decision abated the discriminatory past that resulted from the national historical chapter of the 1936–1939 years". The proposal made by these attorneys consisted of clearing the way for civil servants who had been removed from their positions in the State Administration to apply for reintegration, and for those who were of retirement age to claim passive rights, and that these rights be extended to widows and beneficiaries of any person who had been removed from his position and who had subsequently died. The proposal even put forward measures for those who resided overseas to be able to present the application in the consulate closest to their residency and, "with the reintegration of the applicant approved, the applicant had to return to the destination assigned to them within a 3-month period, which was not extendable".[73]

The proposal was rejected by the government on 23 December 1968, arguing that it would require a significant increase in public spending.[74]

The Law of Political Responsibilities, one of the legal mechanisms through which the regime sustained its repression of the defeated, was abolished definitively by the Decree-Law of 31 March 1969.[75] This measure overturned all

72 Aguilar, 2008, p. 168.
73 Fanjul, 1970, pp. 35–36. See also Aguilar, 2008, pp. 168–169.
74 Aguilar, 2008, p. 169.
75 Decree-Law 10/1969, 31 March, which orders the prescription of all crimes committed before 1 April 1939. *Official State Gazette*, no. 78, 1 April 1969, p. 4704.

crimes committed before 1 April 1939, which, in a way, could be considered a precursor to the pardons for crimes committed before the end of the Civil War. The preface explained the motivation behind the regime's move towards this measure:

> The peaceful co-existence in Spain during the last 30 years has cemented the legitimacy of our Movement, which has given our generation three decades of peace, development and legal freedom hardly ever seen before in history.
>
> For this reason, and to celebrate the forthcoming 1st of April 1969, the 30 year anniversary of the final day of the War of Liberation, the time is ripe to expressly recognise the prescription of any possible legal responsibilities that resulted from that Conflict, the cessation and rendering obsolete of any legal consequences from what, at the time, was a conflict between brothers, today united as one in celebration of a more representative Spain and, now more than ever, ready to push the country forward towards its future greatness.

Article 1 of the Decree-Law mandated a statute of limitations for all crimes committed before 1 April 1939, and specified that this statute did not require a legal statement. Therefore, it would apply to all types of crimes, whoever the perpetrators, whatever the gravity of its consequences, without prejudice to its legal category or proposed sentences, and without taking into consideration the guidelines of the then-current Codes imposed on the permutation, interruption or resumption of said sentences. Article 2 established that no cases for crimes prior to the given date could be filed, and in those cases where no firm sentence had been handed down, a stay in proceedings would be declared and the file would be archived without the option of reopening it if the accused has been processed *in absentia*.

Minister Manuel Fraga went as far as claiming that the pardon of 1969 buried "once and for all the remains of the old divisions" and "brought to an end our last Civil War".[76] However, the problem that had arisen in Parliament in 1968 remained. Attorney Juan Manuel Fanjul once again put forward a proposal in April 1969, in which it was argued that, given the statute of limitations on all crimes committed during the Civil War, it rendered "legally obsolete any criminal consequences from what was on its day a conflict between brothers, united as one today in an affirmation of a common Spain". Therefore, it logically followed, according to Fanjul, that the reintegration to the Administration of public servants who had been "removed" from their positions for political reasons was a matter of urgency. The government responded in May, and while it was generally in agreement with the proposal, it claimed that there were economic and judicial considerations that prevented the reintegration of the public servants in question. Two months later, the government's answer led to Attorney Eduardo Tarragona arguing in Parliament that no such judicial considerations preventing

76 Aguilar, 2008, p. 172.

reintegration existed, and, in relation to the economic considerations, he requested concrete figures. In light of the government's lack of resolve on this matter, in October of the same year a third attorney, Francisco de Asís Gabriel Ponce, put forward two new texts, similar to the previous proposals, but which ended with the same result.[77] The government's inflexibility in this regard forced Spain to begin its transition years with the majority of its political prisoners pardoned, but without a resolution on the economic, labour and social consequences they were suffering.

6 The opposition's demands for amnesty and the inflexibility of the regime

The calls for general amnesty became more notorious and more publicised from the 1960s onwards. There were initiatives of great relevance, such as the 4th National Congress of Law, held in June 1970, where a petition for amnesty for political prisoners was approved by 195 to 187 votes, and where a petition for the abolition of the special courts for political crimes in the Public Order Tribunal[78] was approved unanimously. Months later, in December 1970, the Burgos trials against 16 members of ETA, tried under military jurisdiction, generated a wave of support for the concession of amnesties to political prisoners, in Spain as well as at the international level, where there were demonstrations in Europe and in South America against the Francoist dictatorship. Franco could not withstand this international pressure, and was thus forced to convene the Council of the Realm (29 December) and the Council of Ministers (30 December), bodies which unanimously agreed to commute death penalties to less severe sentences.

The calls for amnesties proliferated in the last five years of the dictatorship, especially in the Basque Country – members of ETA made up the largest proportion of political prisoners – but also in other regions where there were strongholds opposing the dictatorship. One of the mantras most often heard during those years, "Freedom, Amnesty and Statute of Autonomy", originated in the Catalan Assembly, established on 7 November 1971.[79] The general strikes of workers, especially during the intensified period between 1974 and 1975, included in their demands the concession of amnesties for political prisoners, the liquidation of the public order institutions and full democratic freedom. The calls for amnesty were also a feature of the clandestine association Democratic Justice, established in 1971, that brought together the few judges and district attorneys who opposed the regime. This association presented a report on October 1975 which expressed what it held to be urgent matters for the Spanish government. The first of these was a "blanket amnesty for so-called political crimes, which would pave the way for the reintegration into public

77 Aguilar, 2008, pp. 169–170.
78 Gómez Roda, 2004, p. 47.
79 This united Catalan anti-Franco platform, which owes its origins to the initiative of the Coordinator of Political Forces in Catalonia, gathered together the majority of political parties, unions and social institutions from Catalonia.

life of those who fought against the Francoist regime, and which would enable the return of political exiles to our *Patria* and the restitution of rights to those who were deprived of them for political reasons". Added to this, the report called on the government to observe the Universal Declaration of Human Rights, without which any amnesty would be worthless. To achieve this, there was a need to abolish "immediately laws that repressed, restricted or punished those who exercised their human rights".[80]

On the contrary, the government was unmoved by these demands. The new reform of the 1973 Criminal Code defined amnesty and pardon as reasons to expunge political responsibility (article 112), but the government was not willing to put it into practice, immersed as it was in the ever-growing armed attacks against the dictatorship. As well as ETA, other left-wing groups – among which it is worth mentioning FRAP[81] and MIL – joined the fight against the dictatorship. A member of MIL, the young anarchist Salvador Puig Antich, arrested in the autumn of 1973, was given a death sentence by the military tribunal for the homicide of a policeman during a shootout in Barcelona. The sentence generated a widespread social movement calling for pardons within Spain but also overseas, from where petitions were sent from various governments (the German Chancellor Willy Brandt played an important role in this respect), political parties, human rights organisations and even the Vatican. The petitions fell on deaf ears and the government proceeded to sanction the execution, carried out by garrotte, a macabre method.[82] The government adopted the same inflexible position when it ordered the execution by firing squad of three members of FRAP and two members of ETA on 27 September 1975. Of no use, this time, were the petitions for clemency that came from Pope Paul VI or the different continental governments, nor the gestures of solidarity such as Olof Palme, who personally led a campaign through the streets of Stockholm for the economic support of the families of the prisoners. The President of Mexico petitioned for Spain to be expelled from the UN. Franco, gravely ill, mustered enough strength to make his final speech, in which he defended the five death penalties and reiterated that the protests coming from within Spain were down to a left-wing masonic conspiracy.[83]

80 Democratic Justice Declaration, October 1975. Photographic reproduction from Díaz Sánchez, 2016, p. 169.
81 In October 1964, members of the newly establish Spanish Communist Party (m-1), a pioneering group of Spanish Maoists, proclaimed the need for a "people's war" against Franco that had to be undertaken by the Revolutionary Armed Forces. FRAP, officially established in Paris in November 1973, had as its main objective an insurrection to instate a Federal People's Republic.
82 Escribano, 2001.
83 Agencia de Prensa Española Popular, 2005. Amnistía Internacional España, 1995.

Chapter 2

The beginnings of the transition

1 Models of justice to avoid and models to follow

The death of Francisco Franco on 20 November 1975 led to the beginning of the transition process in Spain. Unlike previous transitions in Portugal and Greece, the transition in Spain would be led by the regime of the dictatorship, which had spent years getting ready for when the time came to replace Franco. The legacy of the dictatorship created a precarious context for politicians during the transition.[1] According to Jon Elster, the first challenge that the new political elites faced in the transition was "[having] to decide whether leaders of, collaborators with, or agents of the former regime should be brought to court or otherwise penalised, and if, and if so, how the victims of the regimes should be rehabilitated and compensated".[2] Paloma Aguilar took up this idea and applied it to the situation in Spain, highlighting that, after the death of Franco, there was no purge of the main civil and military institutions, no truth commission was created to investigate violations of human rights during the dictatorship,[3] and those guilty of murder, torture and illegal arrests during the same period were not prosecuted.[4] The result is that Spain emerged from the dictatorship but failed to free itself of its legacy.[5]

Spain followed in the footsteps of Italy, where the fascist regime was replaced by the democratic Republic. There a new leaf was turned over by granting impunity with two laws that amnestied crimes committed by the Mussolini regime. Issued by presidential decree on 22 July 1946, *Amnistía Togliatti* was especially important in this regard.[6] But there was no need to go back 30 years in time to the Italian model. Well-known

1 Barahona de Brito, González-Enríquez and Aguilar, 2001, p. 15.
2 Elster, 2008, p. 7.
3 One particular exception being the examination by the Commission of Historians in 1977 of the bombardment of Gernika (Bizkaia), which was supported by a collaboration between the governments of Germany and Spain that facilitated the archival sources to be consulted for the first time. Aguilar, 2001, p. 114.
4 Aguilar, 2001, p. 92.
5 Kritz, 1995.
6 On Italian amnesty, see Franzinelli, 2006. On Italian impunity, see Patrone, 2000, pp. 109–117. And for a comparative perspective on Italian and Spanish amnesties, see Mastromarino, 2016, pp. 155–159.

transition processes closer in time to the Spanish transition pointed in different directions, but these were ignored.

Above all else, the main aim of the Spanish regime was to shield itself against the possibility of being prosecuted, something which it could prevent only if it took control of the transition process and brought it to its conclusion with the concession of a blanket amnesty. Precedents set in other transitions worried officials within the dictatorship. There was a frustrated attempt to prosecute the Francoist regime under universal jurisdiction in 1974, the same year that Greece transitioned to democracy and, as part of its first transitional justice measures, prosecuted the members of the Colonel's regime who were responsible for violations of human rights. Added to this was the enormous social pressure that continued to call for a blanket amnesty for political prisoners and workers who had been removed from their posts for political reasons. This chapter will deal with these aspects, as they are crucial to understanding amnesty and pardons that were granted in Spain in the first phase of the transition.

1.1 The prosecution of the Francoist regime, instigated by the British Labour Movement (1974)

The British Labour Party, which had supported the anti-Francoist cause throughout the 1960s – mostly through the relationship it maintained with the exiled Spanish Socialist Workers' Party (PSOE) – increased its commitment to the Spanish cause in the 1970s. The Labour Party itself, as well as the TUC, followed very closely the case known as "Process 1001", also known as the "Carabanchel ten", in which ten members of the Workers' Commission union were charged with illegal association, of being controlled by the Communist Party and of intent to undermine the structures of the State. The trial took place in December 1973. Both the Labour Party and the TUC publicly condemned the violation of human rights and the Francoist suppression of political freedom and freedom to associate. It sought an official declaration of clemency from Franco's government after it was revealed that the members charged faced 12 to 20 years in prison. The Labour Movement in Britain led an international campaign that soon began to bear fruit. The Supreme Tribunal reduced the sentences in 1974, freeing four of the members and reducing the sentences of the remaining members to six years. Nevertheless, the Labour Party did not consider this outcome a triumph, interpreting the Spanish government's U-turn as a contrived way of projecting a more respectable image on the international stage.[7]

The Labour Party decided to go one step further. Harold Wilson, party leader and Prime Minister of the UK, decided to prosecute the Spanish dictatorship under universal jurisdiction. Among the 1.7 million documents published by Wikileaks in April, 2013, there was a document entitled "British Labour Party and TUC's Projected 'Trial' of Spanish Government", carried out by the US

7 Ortuño-Anaya, 1996, pp. 282–283.

embassy in the UK, dated 14 June 1974, and marked "confidential".[8] These "trials", aimed at raising awareness among the international community, were to be held in London between the months of October and December of that same year.[9] To set the process in motion, the British Labour Party would seek the support of the Spanish opposition to the regime, which they saw represented in the Labour organisations CCOO, UGT and USO, which would form part of a commission that would investigate the Spanish government's violation of human rights and would develop a file recording these crimes.[10] This plan was, in fact, an alternative solution to the possible amnesty for crimes of Francoism, something which calls into question the current consensus among historians that amnesty was a measure that was put forward by the forces in opposition to the regime – in some cases as far back as the 1940s and, in the case of the Communist Party, since 1956 – and which was consistently called for for the duration of the dictatorship and until the beginning of the transition.[11]

If the plan to prosecute crimes of Francoism had come to fruition, it would have been covered globally in the media and it would have brought about legal consequences for universal jurisdiction which are difficult to imagine, considering that between the Nuremberg trials on 1 October 1946 and the 1993 International Criminal Tribunal for the former Yugoslavia, there had been no International Criminal Court for human rights to shepherd in a new era of international law.

The Spanish Socialist Party was the real partner of the British Labour Movement, as the latter fundamentally distrusted communism. The Labour Party had committed its support to the socialist parties in Portugal and Spain to deter the

8 Wikileaks 1974MADRID03735b. https://www.wikileaks.org/plusd/cables/1974MADRID03735b.html (accessed on 26 April, 2016).

9 Specifically, the report points out that "Spanish clandestine Labor organizations are actively pursuing plans for participation in projected three-day Commission of inquiry into Spanish Government 'repression' and record on Human Rights. These groups now expect this oft-postponed international 'Trial' or tribunal sponsored by British Labor Party and TUC to be held in London between October and December."

10 Specifically, it says, "Three Spanish clandestine Labor organizations scheduled participate in projected British publicity 'Trial' of GOS are currently gathering material for this Tribunal. Socialist UGT expects play leading role but is somewhat */confidential page 02 Madrid 03735 170558Z/* suspicious British socialist hosts may give centre stage to communist worker commission rivals. UGT and catholic-oriented USO are doubtful British will invite participation other European socialists and believe Labor Party and TUC desire make London 'trial' a British socialist show. Other aspects are anti-American overtones may emerge during Tribunal's examination of role of multinational corporations in Spain, undercurrent of hostility and distrust by UGT and USO of communist dominated workers commissions, and added strain 'Trial' likely place on UK-gos relations." The report later adds: "Principal clandestine Labor groups committed paticipation in 'Trial' are communist-dominated workers commissions socialist UGT, and catholic-oriented USO. UGT and USO soueces have told EMB Labatt they are currently gathering material for use before London tribunal" (reproduced verbatim; all errors are in the original).

11 See Juliá, 1999, pp. 39 and 45–46.

Communist Party from getting a stronghold in nation States that were looking at transitions in the future.[12] All things considered, the CIA supported the Portuguese and the Spanish socialist parties during the first five years of the 1970s for the same reason.[13] On top of this, in the last years of the decade, the Spanish Socialist Party was going through a process of internal restructuring, which culminated in the Congress in Toulouse in 1972.[14] The British Labour Movement supported this renovation plan, and restated its support after Socialist International recognised the renovated PSOE as the true socialist party in Spain, at a time when the party, as well as the UGT, received funding from different foreign sources.[15]

By June 1974, when the United States carried out the confidential report, lawyers from the Spanish clandestine opposition group were already building a case, and were, at the time, committed to compiling evidence and preparing materials.[16] Chief amongst this group was the lawyer Pablo Castellano, renowned socialist and member of the UGT. According to the report, Castellano believed that the UGT should have led the process, given that the Labour Party and the other implicated organisations had bestowed upon the UGT this function. Castellano distrusted the Workers' Commissions because they wanted the trials to be a mere propagandistic exercise.[17]

12 As in Spain, the relationship between the Labour Party and the Portuguese Socialist Party, led by Mario Soares, was of great importance from 1969 onwards. See Soares, 1975.

13 Grimaldos, 2006.

14 The Congress of Toulouse split the PSOE into two divisions, the so-called "historic" division, led by Rodolfo Llopis and made up of exiles, and the "renovated" or interior division, led by Nicolás Redondo and Felipe González, and in which the lawyer Pablo Castellano held the office of International Relations for both the PSOE and UGT. Castellano also represented the PSOE in the Spanish Federal Council in the European Movement. Much has been written on the subject, but for special consideration, see Mateos, 1993.

15 Ortuño-Anaya, 1996, p. 283.

16 Specifically, the report stated that "Great care is being taken by Spanish opposition lawyers to get adequately authenticated evidence for tribunal from organizations, individuals, and institutions inside Spain".

17 Specifically, the report says that "Pablo Castellano, lawyer and leading figure of */confidential page 03 Madrid 03735 170558Z/* socialist UGT Trade Union (as well as of PSOE Socialist Party) told lavatt UGT expects play leading role and Labor Party and TUC organizers have assured him UGT will be granted such role. Nevertheless he expressed some distrust of Labor Party and TUC, whom he feels may seek play up role communist-dominated Workers Commissions, with whom TUC has been developing some ties during past two years, at UGT's expense. He is particularly hopeful avoiding any 'Carbanchel ten-type' situation whereby the Spanish Communist Party (PCE) would get all the glory and publicity for its activities in Workers Commissions and where democratic clandestine Labor groups, i.e. UGT and USO, would backstage treatment. He also hopes Commission of inquiry, despite its primary publicity purpose, will be conducted in serious and professional manner according to standards of British Law and Justice, and that it will not degenerate into mere propaganda carnival" (reproduced verbatim; all errors are in the original).

The British Labour Movement sought to focus the trials on three main areas. The first of these related to bringing criminal charges for the repression of unionised movements:

> Labor repression, with documentation on numerous members of UGT, USO, and Workers Commission awaiting Trial or already convicted (e.g. Communist Workers Commission leaders convicted in "Carabanchel ten" Trial last December).

The second area related to how political prisoners were treated and the repression of student movements, and the third area related to workers' rights in foreign multinationals and the implementation of international employment law. The Labour Movement planned the trials based on their profound knowledge of international rights, avoiding human rights violations during the Civil War and the post-war in order to focus on the dictatorship's repressions prior to the Nuremberg trials.

Towards the end, the report itself reflects on the foreseeable failure of the trials for a series of reasons that at the time seemed ominous, and which, along with other reasons, meant that the proposal of the Labour Party and Harold Wilson was not viable:

> UGT and USO sources half expected Tribunal be cancelled in wake British Elections and accession to power of Labor Party. However, they have been reassured on this point by British (reftel also confirms intention proceed with "Trial"). They also now confident principal British socialists organizers, such ans Jenny Little, Trade Union leaders Jack Jones and Will Paynter, and M.P. S. Ian Mikardo and Bob Edwards, Will Still actively participate. They somewhat skeptical however that Michael Foot, one of gos' strongest critics, will still participate in view his designation as Secretary of State in new British Government.
>
> Same sources also doubtful participation will be sought from other European socialists and Trade Unionists, aside from Spanish. They state British Labor Party and TUC have indicated other European socialist political, judicial, and Trade Union figures will eventually be invited participate, but they believe British are in fact reluctant invite prominent Foreing socialists. Reason for this is tnwer belief that British Labor Party and TUC, who after all are hosts, */confidential page 04 Madrid 03735 170558Z/* wish make Commission of inquiry a British Socialist show. UGT and USO believe, however, this British attitude is perhaps somewhat justifiable since alleged efforts proved unsuccessful early last year to get french Socialist Party and forcé ouviere, German Socialist Party and DGB, and Italians to host such "Trial" in their countries. Only British were eager to act as hosts.
>
> Comment: there no indication to date either GOS or Government-controlled Spanish Syndical Organization (SSO) concerned about forthcoming "Trial"

or have even focused on it. However, GOS and SSO will undoubtedly focus on problem as "Trial" approaches and when Commission of inquiry actually is held, and they can be expected vigorously protest it. Agree with amembassy London's assessment that Tribunal is bound place added strain on anglo-spanish relations.

Aspect of Tribunal agenda dealing with activities of Multinational Corporations in Spain likely to have anti-american overtones, since some of largest Multinational Corporations in Spain, for example Chrysler and ITT, are US firms. In addition, focus also likely be against giant american corporations such as Ford, which is entering Spain with major mew investment at this time, and General Motors, which is currently considering major investment in Spain.

Lastly, despite fact democratic Trade Union Organizations, i.e., UGT and USO, ar cooperating in this instance with totalitarian rivals, i.e., Communist-dominated Workers Commissions, competition between democratic groups and Workers Commissions likely continue as undercurrent throughout Tribunal and could very possibly break out into open perhaps even disrupting Commission of inquiry due to deeply rooted hostility and distrust between these organizations. [Reproduced verbatim; all errors are in the original.]

1.2 Purges in Portugal and trials in Greece

The Spanish transition to democracy was led by the Francoist regime, but had it been the result – as was the case in Greece and Portugal – of the emergence of an enlightened new regime, the resolutions in transitional justice would have been different – for instance, in the case of the purge of civil servants and employees of the dictatorial regime and the prosecutions of those responsible for the violation of human rights. The opposite was true, in fact, as the Francoist regime sought to avoid a repeat in Spain of what had happened in Greece and Portugal by maintaining stewardship of the transition process.[18] Instead, Spain opted for a blanket amnesty, which was incompatible with prosecuting those responsible for human rights violations.[19]

The transition process in Portugal is crucial to understanding the process in Spain because they are neighbouring countries and both suffered through very long dictatorships similar in length of time, but especially because the transition in Portugal took place during the last years of the Francoist regime (known as

18 There are many comparative studies that explore these three transitions, directly compare two, or even compare them with other transitional process. Especially relevant are the studies carried out by Poulantzas and Mercado, 1976; O'Donnell, Schmitter and Whitehead, 1986; Linz, 1996, pp. 21–45; Linz and Stepan, 1996; Huntington, 1991; De la Torre, 1989; Gunther, Diamandouros and Hans-Jürgen, 1995; Durán Muñoz, 2000; Durán Muñoz, 2009, pp. 157–178; Jiménez, 2009; Soto Carmona, 2009, pp. 7–30; and Huyse, 2013.

19 On the incompatibility of blanket amnesty with criminal trials, see Teitel, 2014.

tardofranquismo), when the dictatorship was devising a strategy to deal with the impending death of Franco.

Led by Antonio Oliveira Salazar, the Portuguese regime was, like the regime in Spain, characterised by its tough repression of the political enemy, a strategy that continued to be implemented from 1968 onwards with the dictator Marcelo Caetano, even if the regime found itself at a point in which it was becoming more liberal, as indeed happened in Spain. The last few years of the Portuguese dictatorship were marked by the Colonial Wars in Mozambique, Angola and Guinea Bissau. This conflict deepened the division between civilians and the military, which was further aggravated by the deteriorating economic crisis. Social protests were stamped out with tough repressions, and political dissidents filled the prisons in Portugal. This unsustainable situation came to a head with a military coup led by the leftist sector of the military on 25 April 1974. Civilians immediately sympathised with the insurgents, and so the coup turned into an all-out revolution which finally precipitated Caetano's surrender and the fall of the *Estado Novo* regime. The political prisoners in the Caixa prison were set free in the days that followed, and little by little the exiled leaders of the opposition parties returned to the country. The Colonial Wars ended and the old colonies began their respective independence processes in 1975.

The first two years of the Portuguese transition, characterised by the left-wing revolution, brought about profound changes to the social and economic make-up of the country, especially from March 1975 onwards, following the failed right-wing coup led by General Spínola, president of the Republic between April and September 1974. This first turbulent period of the transition ended with the celebration of the first free elections in April 1975, with the Socialist Party, led by Mario Soares, emerging as victors (38% of the votes), thus allowing PREC to march on.

From April 1974 onwards, there were widespread purges in revolutionary Portugal. Those affected included directors of the regime, high-ranking officers of the Portuguese Legion Party, civil servants from various ministries, members of the Republican National Guard, military police, university professors and civil servants in local administrations, among others. The so-called purge ended in 1975 with 20,000 affected by these "purge laws", which were designed to be an instrument for "revolutionary justice", a way of settling old scores. They were not carried out from a standpoint of retrospective justice, or as restitution for the violation of human rights;[20] they were carried out from a perspective of left-wing politics, which were still associated with the traditional socialist conceptualisation of human rights that undermines these rights in favour of social and economic rights.[21] The prosecutions of those responsible for the dictatorship lacked focus. Although there was a great demand from the public to see the former leaders of

20 Roht-Arriaza, 2014, pp. 109–138.

21 Costa Pinto, 1995. Costa Pinto, 2001, pp. 65–91. Costa Pinto, 2009, pp. 103–134. Encarnación, 2014, pp. 62–63.

Estado Novo on trial, they had left the country to take up exile in Brazil. Only members of the political police, the PIDE/DGS, the main enforcers of repression during the dictatorship, were prosecuted. The trials, based on a Constitutional Law of 25 July 1975, were brought to the military tribunal to process the criminal charges against the political police and high-ranking members of the government who were directly responsible for the repression.[22]

The Ongoing Revolutionary Process ended with the pronouncement of a moderate wing of the Portuguese Armed Forces as an interim government, supported by socialists and social democrats, on 25 November 1975, five days after the death of Francisco Franco. Thus, an inclusive and pluralist democracy was installed which approved the new progressive Constitution that had been adopted by the Constituent Assembly on 2 April 1976, and which came into force on the 25th of the same month. In it, article 161f bestows upon the Assembly of the Republic the capacity to grant a blanket amnesty and pardons. Despite this, none of the measures of clemency were applied to the criminals of the dictatorship during the next phase of the Portuguese transition. From that point onwards, the efforts for transitional justice instead focused on correcting the excesses of the previous revolutionary regime. Many civil servants were reintegrated and the return of exiles, who had fled fearing the radicalisation of the Revolution State, was facilitated. The purge laws were put to one side, and in their place solutions were offered for rehabilitation and dismissal for forced retirement. In this way, an intense policy for historical memory was begun, which handed out compensation to those that had opposed the dictatorship, and incorporated Salazar's personal file and the reports from the PIDE/DGS to the National Archive.

However, these new measures failed to put an end to the trials of those responsible of human rights violations during the dictatorship. In fact, article 309 of the Constitution exclusively dealt with the prosecution of agents and high-ranking officers of the PIDE/GDS by sustaining the validity of Law number 8/75, of 25 July,[23] but with the inclusion of new judicial determinations in relation to other articles contained within the Constitution.

In Greece,[24] the power vacuum in the Colonel's dictatorship after the failed coup in Cyprus and the Turkish occupation of half the island was filled by the conservative Konstantinos Karamanlís, who had been in exile. He returned on 23 July 1974 at the request of the States' Military Junta. With an interim government in place, the new Prime Minister re-established the Constitution of 1952, granted a blanket amnesty to the political victims of the dictatorship, freed political prisoners, facilitated the return of exiles, and legalised the Communist Party and other illegal organisations before the first elections. To pave the way towards

22 Ley n° 8/75, 25 July 1975. See Costa Pinto, 2009, pp. 140–141.

23 Article 309.1 keeps in force Law number 8/75, of 25 July with the modifications introduced by the Law number 16/75, of 23 December, and by Law number 18/75, of 26 December.

24 On the Greek transition, see Diamandouros, 1986, pp. 138–164; Alivizatos and Diamandouros, 1997, pp. 27–60; and Katsikas, 2014, pp. 259–279.

democracy, the new Prime Minister immediately called a general election in which his own centre-right party, New Democracy, garnered 54.7% of the votes (17 November 1974), thus electing Karamanlís as the first president of the Greek Third Republic. On 8 December 1974, the abolition of the monarchy was approved by referendum with 69.2% of the votes, a result which was taken into consideration by Francoism in Spain, which was in the process of putting in place a strategy in the coming transition for the figure of Juan Carlos de Borbón, married to Sofia from Greece, sister of the former King of Greece, Constantino. The following year, Greece ratified a new Constitution, which came into force on 11 June 1975. In it, article 47 legislated for blanket amnesty and pardons.[25] The regulation on pardons was similar to the analogous legislation in Spain. Pardons were reserved exclusively for political crimes and required a 3 to 5 majority vote in the Chamber of Deputies.[26]

However, and despite there being an adequate legal framework in place, the option of granting a blanket amnesty for crimes committed by the dictatorship was rejected from the very beginning. Unlike Spain in the succeeding years, there was a willingness to confront history and not forget it,[27] a stance which politicians of differing ideologies supported. The fact that from 1968 onwards Amnesty International continued to condemn the tortures and the human rights violation of the Colonel's regime strengthened their resolve to confront the past. The reports from Amnesty International on the torture in Greece served to expel Greece from the Council of Europe in 1968 for the violation of nine articles of the European Convention for the Protection of Human Rights and Fundamental Freedoms.[28]

Members of the Junta of the Colonel's regime and torturers were put on trial, something which the powers that be in charge of guiding Francoist Spain through the first phase of the transition needed to avoid at all costs. The first arrests occurred in January 1975, and by August of the same year, with the new constitution in place, charges were filed for high treason and insurrection against the

25 Greek Constitution, article 47: "1. The President of the Republic shall have the right, pursuant to a recommendation by the Minister of Justice and after consulting with a council composed in its majority of judges, to grant pardons, to commute or reduce sentences pronounced by the courts, and to revoke all consequences at law of sentences pronounced and served.

2. The President of the Republic shall have the right to grant a pardon to a Minister convicted as provisioned in article 86, only with the consent of Parliament.

3. Amnesty may be granted only for political crimes, by statute passed by the Plenum of the Parliament with a majority of three-fifths of the total number of members.

4. Amnesty for common crimes may not be granted even by law."

26 Spyropoulos and Fortsakis, 2009, pp. 93 and 113.

27 Besides the trials, and contrary to what would happen in Spain, an intense purge policy was developed to remove civil servants and collaborators of the dictatorship, especially those who had held higher offices. Around 100,000 people were purged.

28 Peters, 1987, pp. 216–218.

leader of the military regime, George Papadopoulos, as well as another 19 members of the Junta.[29] After the trials,[30] these men received long prison sentences. The three leaders of the coup, Colonels Papadopoulos and Makarezos and Brigadier General Pattakos, received death sentences which were later commuted to life sentences by the Karamanlis government. Those responsible for torturing and murdering the students who led the occupation of the Athens Polytechnic in November 1973 were also prosecuted. The Director of the Military Police, General Ioannidis, who committed those murders, was given seven life sentences. The trials were broadcasted live, adding to the social expectations amongst the Greek people. The Greek experience of prosecuting those responsible for human rights violations was recorded in an Amnesty International report, entitled *Torture in Greece: The First Torturer's Trial 1975*.[31] It is a comprehensive and detailed document that could have only been carried out in collaboration with the Greek government.

1.3 Blanket amnesty and pardons in France for the Algerian War

The Spanish Francoist regime kept a close eye on the various general amnesties and pardons the French government granted for the events that took place during the Algerian War, which, thanks to the Evian Accord of 18 March 1962, did not end in vain. The blanket amnesty and the pardons facilitated the independence of the North-African country and resulted in the expulsion of around a million European colonisers, mainly French, but also Spanish and Italian. The interests of the Francoist regime extended beyond the immediate Algerian post-war,[32] given that it offered refuge to members of the OAS, the French terrorist organisation, led by Raoul Salan, and which had originated from the 1961 coup d'état in Algeria. Spain also sheltered numerous *Pieds-Noir*, Algerian colonisers who went into exile after the declaration of independence and settled on the Levantine Coast.[33] The latter collaborated with the SECED in the dirty war against ETA.[34]

Article 34 of the French Constitution of 4 October 1958, the founding text of the Fifth French Republic, granted a blanket amnesty, provisioning a special law

29 From the beginning, the files on repression served as supporting evidence in these trials, as it was part of the body of evidence used to convict those responsible for human rights violations during the dictatorship. Political misuse by the future government and opposition parties destroyed these documents, which constituted a grave error for the future reconstruction of historical memory.
30 Deane, 1977. Roehrig, 2002. Katsikas, 2014, pp. 264–274.
31 Amnesty International, 1977.
32 See San Martín, 1983.
33 Fleites Marcos, 2009. Sempere Souvannavong, 2001, pp. 173–198. Aït Yahia, 2013.
34 The Basque pro-independence organisations were, in fact, influenced by the Algerian and Cuban revolutions when they put together their anti-imperialist thesis between 1963 and 1966 and when they prioritised an armed struggle in their three-pronged strategy for the independence of the Basque country, for the class struggle and for socialism.

for each case.[35] In this way, then, the Fifth French Republic facilitated the concession of amnesty for the crimes in Algeria.[36]

The blanket amnesty in Algeria originated in the Evian Accords, which dictated that a blanket amnesty would be immediately granted and prisoners would be set free. The day after these peace agreements came into force, no person could be subjected to judicial or policy measures, disciplinary sanctions or any type of discrimination before the day of the ceasefire.[37] Related to this premise, the Decree of 22 March 1962 granted amnesty for crimes carried out in the name of the Algerian insurgency.[38] The amnesty granted to the Algerian people covered crimes committed before 20 March 1962 relating to active participation in, or directly or indirectly supporting, the Algerian insurgency and other related crimes, as well as all crimes committed before 30 October 1954, which sought to overthrow the political regime in Algeria. This Ordinance also decreed the foundation of an amnesty commission, which would follow up on the process, settle lawsuits and differentiate between common crimes and crimes relating to the Algerian insurgency. This commission began to function immediately and was operative until 1 July 1962. Another Decree on 22 March 1962 granted amnesty for crimes committed before 20 March 1962, in the context of the preservation of public order against the Algerian insurrection.[39]

After Algeria declared its independence, the French Government published a law on 23 December 1964[40] to issue a blanket amnesty for all crimes committed in Algeria before 20 March 1962, in response to the excessive violations of human rights by the Algerian insurgency. The only condition was that these crimes could not be related to an organisation that attempted to subvert the authority of the State or that aimed to replace it with an illegal organisation. The Law also contemplated the possibility of the President granting an amnesty by decree for crimes and minor offences committed before 3 July 1962 in Algeria or related to the events in Algeria. Active members and Majors of insurgency groups, and those sentenced to 15 years or more of prison, could not avail of the amnesty.

35 Luchaire, Conac and Prétot, 2009.
36 On French amnesty for crimes in Algeria, see Gacon, 2002; Eftekhari, 2002–2003, pp. 413–474.
37 Evian Accords in *Journal Officiel de la République Française*, 15 April 1962, p. 3892.
38 Decree 62–327 and 62–328, 22 March 1962. *Journal Officiel de la République Française*, 23 March 1962, p. 3143. Its application became obligatory on French territory as per Order 62–427 of 14 April 1962. *Journal Officiel de la République Française*, 15 April 1962, p. 3892.
39 Decree 62–328, 22 March, 1962. *Journal Officiel de la République Française*, 23 March 1962, p. 3144. Its application on French territory was also obligatory as per Order 62–428 of 14 April 1962. *Journal Officiel de la République Française*, 15 April 1962, p. 3892.
40 Law 64–1269, 23 December, 1964. *Journal Officiel de la République Française*, 24 December 1964, p. 11499.

The policy of "forgetting" was driven forward by the Amnesty Law of 17 June 1966,[41] wherein article 3 extended the scope of the amnesty to cover "offences committed between the 1st of November, 1954, and the 3rd of July, 1962 in the context of administrative and judicial policy operations, manoeuvres to re-establish public order or the struggle against operations that sought to block State authority or to replace it with an illegal organisation", thus pre-empting any investigation into the massacres. Two years later, the Law of the 31 July 1968 granted a blanket amnesty for offences committed in relation to the events in Algeria by soldiers who had served in the country.[42] Finally, on 16 July 1974, Valéry Giscard d'Estaing issued one last amnesty for the events in Algeria,[43] granting a blanket amnesty for offences committed in the old French colony. He decreed the coming back of the militaries to their jobs, even if they got to automatically retire. It also upheld soldiers' orders of merit and decorations.

These amnesty laws were brought to their conclusions with the pardons granted by the president of the Republic. President Charles de Gaulle granted pardons to more than a thousand people, including members of the OAS.

Overall, French amnesty and pardons for events in Algeria focused on three types of crimes: those committed by pro-independence Algerians whom the French justice system could not prosecute on account of Algeria declaring its independence, the "offences committed within the frame of public order preservation" or "in response to the insurgency", and the so-called "subversion" acts committed by members of the OAS. As would happen in Spain with the Amnesty Law of 1977, every party in the conflict was viewed equally in terms of clemency. Added to this was the clause in the Evian Accords that facilitated the immediate liberation of fighters and political prisoners. The drafting of the legislation, on the other hand, concealed the true extent of the repression, as the regulation literature (as would happen in Spain) failed to mention, for instance, the systematic tortures and the mass executions carried out by the colonial French regime in Algeria, even though these actions were, in fact, amnestied.[44]

The amnesty and pardons granted by the French government influenced the grace measures in the Spanish transition. Miguel Herrero de Miñón confirmed that they were taken into consideration when the partial amnesty of 1976 was drafted, though the French example was not a determining factor.[45] But the influence of the French example could be felt further afield, even influencing Spain's strategy when it came to signing international treaties and agreements. The amnesties granted for the events in Algeria were the motivating factor

41 Law 66–396 of 17 June 1966. *Journal Officiel de la République Française*, 18 June 1966, p. 4915.
42 Law 68–697 of 31 July 1968. *Journal Officiel de la République Française*, 2 August 1968, p. 7521.
43 Law 74–643, of 16 July 1974. *Journal Officiel de la République Française*, 17 July 1974, p. 7443.
44 Branche, 2001. Lefranc, 2004, p. 15. Gacon, 2005, pp. 271–279.
45 Miguel Herrero de Miñón interview, 21 May 2016 (Herrero de Miñón, 2016).

behind France's refusal to sign the 9 December 1968 Convention[46] on the Non-Applicability of Statutory Limitations to War Crimes and Crimes against Humanity, and the European Convention on the Non-Applicability of Statutory Limitation to Crimes against Humanity and War Crimes, signed in Strasbourg by the European Council Member States on 25 January 1974. Following the example of the French, Spain also refused to sign these during its period of transition. To this day, with the 1977 Amnesty Law still in force, Spain refuses to sign.

1.4 The strategy in preparation for the Spanish transition rejects the possibility of prosecuting Francoism

The radical nature of Portugal in the two years after the Carnation Revolution motivated the Francoist government (as well as the Western powers, immersed in their particular Cold War conflicts against the Soviet front, but which guided the Spanish transition) to design a model that differed from the Portuguese one.

The British Labour Party continued to support the PSOE and the Portuguese Socialist Party, which was led by Mario Soares, through 1974 and 1975, with the aim, in the case of the latter, of ending the Portuguese revolution with a social-democratic alternative.[47] In the PSOE's case, support also came from the United States and Germany, which feared that the influence of the communist parties in the south of Europe could end the status quo between the Cold War blocs. The CIA and the BND, the German secret service, worked together with the Spanish SECED to avoid the possibility of the transition in Spain giving way to a Communist Party-led government. Communists would have to be excluded from future negotiations about the transition and the PSOE strengthened in order to weaken the Communist Party, which, at the time, had a large number of members among the working class thanks to years of well-organised clandestine efforts.[48]

With the stage set, the PSOE threw out the project for the prosecution of Franco's regime. The lawyer Pablo Castellano had, in fact, held meetings with the Spanish government (with Arias Navarro's consent) where issues relating to the future transition were discussed.[49] The resolutions passed in the Suresnes Congress (held in October 1974, the last congress the party held in exile) ignored any issues in relation to a possible prosecution of Francoism and those responsible

46 Adopted and opened for signature and accession by General Assembly resolution 2391 (XXIII), 26 November 1968. Entry into force on 11 November 1970, in accordance with article 8.

47 The fear of what was happening in Portugal forced the British Labour Party to regard the PSOE as the key party when it came to rebuilding democratic institutions after Francoism. Ortuño-Anaya, 2002.

48 Medina, 1996. Medina, 2004. Grimaldos, 2006. Díaz Fernández, 2006. Fernández Monzón-Altolaguirre and Mata, 2014.

49 Villar, 2016. These are issues that were not recorded by Castellano in his memoirs: Castellano, 1979, Castellano, 1994, and Castellano, 2001.

for human rights violations. Foreign support for the socialist party grew from March 1975 onwards, when the German SPD committed to strengthening the PSOE and the UGT so that they could compete with the Communist Party by giving logistical, financial (via the Friedrich Ebert Foundation) and political support.[50]

Contrary to how it was widely perceived, however, Spanish communism did not want to see itself reflected in the Portuguese model. The leader of the PCE, Santiago Carrillo, much like his counterparts in the communist parties in France and Italy, had distanced himself from the control the Soviet Union had over communism in Europe following the Soviet intervention in Czechoslovakia in 1968. Carrillo's vision, which was more independent, far removed from totalitarianism and would later become known as "Eurocommunism", clashed with the radical policies of Portuguese communism, which was led by Álvaro Cunhal.[51] In any case, the fear that the Francoist regime had of communism in Spain was logical; though it did not foresee prosecuting Francoism, it was the antithesis of what the political forces of the dictatorship envisioned for the future transition.[52]

2 Coronation of the King and the pardons that followed (27 November 1975)

With the death of Franco and with the transition process already in motion when Juan Carlos I was sworn in as King, a new self-perpetuating regime was installed to apply the policies developed by the first Francoist government after the death of Franco, led by Carlos Arias Navarro, and with Interior Minister Manuel Fraga as Vice-President of the government.

The appeals for a blanket amnesty for political prisoners were constant from political activist groups and clandestine syndicates around the Democratic Junta and the Democratic Convergence Platform, the unions, student and social movements, certain progressive Catholic sectors and peripheral national movements, among others. Added to this was the enormous pressure at the

50 Muñoz Sánchez, 2012.
51 Preston, 2013.
52 In the "National Reconciliation Manifesto" published in April, 1975, the PCE rejected the figure of Juan Carlos as it represented a continuation of the norm, and instead called for a democratic break-away. For its part, the Democratic Convergence Platform, created in June 1975, heavily influenced by the PCE and supported by the CCOO and other minor organisations and independents, announced itself with a programme that sought to replace the dictatorship. As Francisco Erice Sebares recalls, the programme was built on 12 points, amongst which were: amnesty and basic freedoms; the formation of a provisional government to establish these; the devolution of the assets of the Union to the labour movement; the political recognition of Catalan, Galician and Basque people, and the development of the regional communities; the separation of Church and State; a referendum on whether the future government would be founded as a monarchy or a Republic; and the integration of Spain into the European Community. Erice Sebares, 2013, pp. 27–28.

international level which demanded the liberation of political prisoners and the restoration of democratic freedoms. These, and other reasons, finally prevented Francoism from developing the minimal reforms they had proposed and forcing them instead to bring about more substantial reforms.

There was a need to begin the new era with a decisive move that would calm the unrest in the streets and that would project to the international community the regime's new liberal will. The government had planned the implementation of a fairly wide pardon following the death of Franco, granted in line with the State's Organic Law of 1967, which dictated that pardons would be the prerogative of the Head of State. Traditionally, the coronation of a new King is an opportune time for the concession of all types of pardons;[53] as such, the coronation of the new King was an appropriate moment for these clemency measures. The preamble of the 1975 Decree (25 November 1975[54]) explained that the pardon was a "statement of intent for the peaceful and solidary co-existence between Spaniards". The pardon in itself was considered "a tribute to the extraordinary figure of Generalísimo Franco", "artifice of the progressive development of the peace that Spain has enjoyed in the last four decades, during which it granted eleven general pardons and innumerable individual pardons".

The first article granted pardons for sentences and corrective measures – deprivation of freedom, pecuniary and driving licence embargo – that were imposed or could be imposed for crimes and offences under the Criminal Code, Military Justice Code and special criminal laws, committed before 12 November 1975.

This blanket pardon did not include clemency measures for political prisoners, and article 3 explicitly exempted from pardon "sentences imposed for terrorism and related activities, the dissemination of terrorist propaganda and for membership to associations, groups or organisations considered to be terrorist under the legislation". The result of this was that only 10% of the 750 prisoners were pardoned.[55]

The main beneficiaries, apart from common prisoners, were the thousands of people imprisoned for criminal conspiracy, thought-crimes, criminal syndicalism and disobeying press censorship, who were set free under the terms of the pardon. Some of these were well-known people, such as those implicated in the aforementioned 1001 process, which included charismatic figures such as Marcelino Camacho and Nicolas Sartorius. With this pardon, oriented towards unionism and labour movements, the government of Carlos Arias Navarro assumed that it had relieved itself of the pressure from the British Labour Movement and its plans to prosecute crimes of Francoism.[56]

The Decree of 25 November was developed thereafter through regulations that extended its application to other realms. Thus, the following day the pardon was

53 Herrero Bernabé, 2012b, pp. 687–709.

54 Decree 2940/1975, 25 November, for the concession of a general pardon in celebration of the coronation of His Majesty Juan Carlos de Borbón as King of Spain. *Official State Gazette*, no. 284, 26 November 1975. Correction of errors: *Official State Gazette*, no. 287, 29 November 1975, p. 24917.

55 Preston, 2003.

56 Pérez Amorós, 2009, p. 141.

extended (for "obvious reasons of equity") to those who had been convicted of breaching the 1964 Contraband Law (16 July 1964) before 22 November 1975.[57]

The pardon led to complaints from the groups that had not been included. The students who had staged protests and were subsequently punished by the regime, demanded to be on a par with the workers who had been granted pardons. To remedy this situation, an Order from 5 December 1975 overturned the sanctions imposed on students by Ministerial Order as per the Academic Discipline Regulations, for offences committed before 21 November of the same year.[58]

The previous pardons, in turn, highlighted that the administrative sanctions imposed at the time, in observance of the 1939 Law of Political Responsibilities (10 February 1939), were still in force, even though this Law, as seen in the previous chapter, had been abolished in 1969. The Decree of 5 December declared an *ex officio* revision of these sanctions, and later overturned them.[59]

The pardon had also failed to cover workers in local authorities. To remedy this, a Governmental Ministerial Order of 17 December[60] extended its application to disciplinary and pecuniary sanctions imposed by these authorities for offences committed before 22 November 1975.[61]

The pardon also failed to address a matter that was of some delicacy and of great political significance: the workers who had been penalised under the Decree of 27 February 1939 in the purge of civil servants and employees of public companies and corporations in the public service. It was a large group, given that it included companies which had a large workforce, such as RENFE, the national train service. Article 1 on administrative penalties, implemented in accordance with the Decree of 27 February 1939, declared an *ex officio* revision of these sanctions, and later overturned them.[62]

57 Order of 28 November, which extends to Contraband Jurisdiction the implementation of the pardon granted by Decree 2940/1975 of 25 November. *Official State Gazette*, no. 287, 29 November 1975, p. 24921.

58 Order of 5 December, 1975, which extends the beneficiaries of Decree 2940/1975, of 25 November, to the academic sector. *Official State Gazette*, no. 298, 12 November 1975, p. 25856.

59 Decree 3357/1975, of 5 December, which declared the sanction revised by virtue of their office and overturned the administrative sanctions implemented in accordance with 10 February 1939 Law of Political Responsibilities. *Official State Gazette*, no. 308, 24 December 1975, p. 26649.

60 Order of the 17 December 1975, which extended to local authorities the pardon by Decree 2940/1975, of 25 November 1975. *Official State Gazette*, no. 308, 24 November 1975, pp. 26650–26651.

61 Specifically, the Order gave local corporations authority to apply the pardon for disciplinary sanctions imposed on civil servants, for minor or serious offences, and to pecuniary sanctions for traffic violations, and violations of bylaws, police regulations and good governance; however, pecuniary sanctions for violations of local duties bylaws were exempted.

62 Decree 840/1976, of 18 March which extends the Decree of 5 December 1975 to civil servants from companies and corporations in the public service. *Official State Gazette*, no. 101, 27 April 1976, pp. 8230–8230.

The Attorney General of the realm believed that the number of people who benefitted from the royal pardons totalled 11,466 common prisoners and 733 political prisoners, of whom 688 were set free while the rest served reduced sentences.[63]

3 Public calls for a blanket amnesty for the enemies of the regime against a backdrop of law enforcement repression and the discourse of reconciliation

The pardon that accompanied the coronation of the King did not silence the public outcry, nor the dissenting voices of the beneficiaries, the trade unions and the workers, who had been removed from their posts for demanding their workers' rights. The pardon had not legalised the working-class trade unions nor established freedom of the press. But, above all, its application was limited because it did not overturn convictions, which is why the workers who continued to protest were detained by the police, if not imprisoned or fined, as happened to Marcelino Camacho, who was reincarcerated for being a member of an illegal trade union.

The people on the streets called for an amnesty that would wash away the past and reintegrate dismissed workers to their positions. In relation to political prisoners, as mentioned earlier, only a numbered few were pardoned. The majority of the political prisoners left behind were members of ETA, who were joined in prison by those convicted of belonging to various armed groups of the extreme left that had increased their activity during the months after the pardon was decreed. Almost immediately, a pro-amnesty campaign was born, driven by the Commission for Amnesty, which was founded in San Sebastian in 1976. The Commission, led by Miguel Castells, was made up of lawyers as well as other notable figures. It had legal status because it was established on the basis of the new Trade Unions Rights Act. Soon there would a proliferation of similar initiatives throughout the Basque Country, and, likewise, calls for amnesty spread throughout the Spanish state. COPEL joined the efforts of the Commission for Amnesty by calling for a blanket amnesty for social and labour prisoners.

The blanket amnesty for political prisoners and the repatriation of exiles, as well as the amnesty for unions, were the main thrust of the appeals coming from the Democratic Convergence, also known by its popular denomination, *Platajunta*. Founded on 26 March 1976, when the Democratic Junta of Spain and the Democratic Convergence Platform merged, it presented a united front against the dictatorship by bringing together the majority of the parties that opposed the regime. But its *raison d'être* went beyond its political party composite; as Santos Juliá accurately synthesises in the following quotation, the calls for amnesty gave way to a more stable movement during the first half of 1976:

63 Aguilar, 2008, p. 288.

> doctors' association and the national bar association, university presidents, judges and lawyers, city councils, neighbourhood associations and even the Spanish Episcopal Conference; there was no political party, unified body or trade union that had not included in its programmes the demand for a blanket amnesty as a first step towards democracy. The calls for amnesty were everywhere and it became a constant demand: unity, amnesty and Statute of Autonomy were the three mantras repeated thousands of times in the various protests staged until Carlos Arias stood down as the president of the government.[64]

As a case in point, the first months of 1976 were marked by numerous protests, lockdowns and petitions for the liberation of political prisoners and the return of exiles. These petitions were accompanied by appeals for a labour amnesty, two demands that were synthesised in a single demand for amnesty. The fall of the dictatorship gave way to a quasi-revolutionary atmosphere marked by protests and mass labour strikes,[65] in addition to the political and social protests, heavily reprimanded by the security forces,[66] which only served to intensify the calls for amnesty. However, the government refused to even consider it as an option, given that an amnesty would amount to a recognition of the illegality of the Francoist regime, which remained in power.[67]

The enormous tension of those years was reflected in the polls carried out by the Public Opinion Institute, which demonstrated that the Spanish public valued peace above justice, freedom or democracy,[68] a state of affairs that did not help in any way the proposals for a transitional justice defined by democratic parameters. The main clandestine opposition parties, the PSOE and the PCE,

64 Juliá, 2010.

65 The calculations show that between 1976 and 1978 the number of days lost due to the strikes rose to 13.2 million, with more than 5.7 million workers involved, or 60% of the active population at the time.

66 The repression by the armed forces was covered by law, as the governments of Arias and Suárez continued to enforce the Decree-Law 10/1975 of 26 August on the prevention of terrorism, in which articles 4 and 10 allowed the use of punitive measures against "groups or organisations that were communist, anarchist, separatist and others that extoled or used violence as an instrument for political or social action", whilst punishing their "implicitly or explicitly [justification] through said ideologies or violent actions". See Asúa Batarrita, 2002, p. 72. Police brutality led to 27 deaths (see Jiménez Villarejo and Doñate, 2012, pp. 241–244), which were added to by the dozens of deaths at the hand of terrorist groups of the extreme right (Casals, 1998). It is worth pointing out that the first phase of the transition, Francoism without Franco, was guided by members of the regime who kept the system of repression in place. The high-ranking officers of the police had not changed, nor would they until after the spring of 1977 when the regime's Political-Social Brigade was disbanded. At which point, the majority of its officers were redeployed to the various police forces of the State.

67 Ysàs, 2009, p. 35.

68 Aguilar, 1996, p. 349.

harnessed this sentiment and throughout 1976 expressed "the need for a national reconciliation" based on the liberation of political prisoners and the legalisation of the PCE, without proposing any major changes to political justice.[69] The nationalist parties in exile also put forward similar theses.[70]

The profound differences between the parties that were involved in the transition converged in their shared belief in a reconciliation[71] that was based on forgetting the past.[72]

Moreover, the act of reconciliation would safeguard against a repeat of the Civil War by forging a future that would guarantee the consolidation of democracy and the integration of Spain into Europe, ideas which had already been put on the table during the meeting, or "confabulation", between the moderate opposition to Franco, held in Munich between 5 and 8 June 1962.[73] The Church, which at the time was undergoing a profound renovation under the Second Vatican Council in an effort to highlight human rights issues, also subscribed to this idea. In Spain, this new direction was synthesised in a joint Assembly of bishops and priests in 1971, which culminated in a petition for forgiveness for not having been an instrument for reconciliation during the Civil War. Although the proposal obtained the majority of the vote, it was not approved because it did not reach the necessary votes.[74]

It is no surprise to find that after the royal pardons, one of the first measures put forward was aimed at finding a solution to the appeals from a group of Republican Army soldiers who had been wounded in the war. Their situation was recorded in Antonio Bravo-Tellado's book, published in 1976, which advocated for the wounded soldiers, widows and children of the Republican Army, as well as those who had been held captive, to be considered economically, socially and politically equal to the wounded from the Nationalist side. It was an act that reflected the doctrine stemming from the political discussions from 1971 and, more forcefully, since 1973.[75] In the spirit of reconciliation between the two sides of the conflict during the war, the Law of 11 March 1976, went some way towards improving the situation of the maimed soldiers on the Republican side[76] but it was not enough, and in the months that followed, Montserrat Tey Planas[77] and Eduardo Tarragona[78] appeared before Parliament and argued in favour of the regulation of the rights of widows of Republican soldiers.

69 Aguilar, 2001, pp. 100–101.
70 See, e.g. Rubio Caballero, 2014; Jimeno, 2015.
71 Aguilar, 2008, pp. 319–320.
72 See Helmick and Petersen, 2001; Humphrey, 2002.
73 Aguilar, 2008, pp. 34 and 177–187.
74 J. Tusell, 2005, p. 215.
75 Bravo-Tellado, 1976. See also Aguilar, 2008, pp. 166–167.
76 Law 5/1976, of 11 March, on Soldiers Wounded by the War for their Homeland. *Official State Gazette*, no. 63, 13 March 1976, pp. 5209–5215.
77 *Official Parliament Gazette*, no. 1497, 12 April 1976, pp. 36271–36272.
78 *Official Parliament Gazette*, no. 1525, 12 August 1976, pp. 36871–36872.

The Civil War victims on the Nationalist sides did not need transitional justice measures. Given that the Nationalists defeated the Republicans and went on to form a government, their victims were always institutionally and socially recognised. The widows and other cohorts of victims, including maimed soldiers and ex-Nationalist soldiers, were economically compensated through various decrees issued between 1938 and 1940 and were given pensions when they had no access to the labour market. As per the Decree of 12 March 1937, Public Administration was the preferred employer to reintegrate the ex-soldiers as civil servants in positions convened in three rounds: half of the vacancies were reserved first for those who had fought on the frontlines, second for those who had lost a family member fighting for the Nationalist side, and in the third and final round, the vacancy was opened to the public.[79] Furthermore, the Nationalist soldiers who were executed or killed in combat were nearly all identified and their remains were immediately exhumed and given a dignified burial. The Order of 1 May created a Central Registry for Disappearances with the aim of expediting the administration needed to localise and exhume the remains of the victims of the "Marxist hordes" who fought in the Civil War.[80] Victims of anti-Francoist terrorism after 1969 were treated in the same way. The families witnessed the memory of their lost family members honoured in tributes,[81] and were compensated with economic reparation even though there were no laws at the time regulating compensation packages for victims of terrorism.

The formula for reconciliation, based on forgetting the past, was reflected in the legislation and measures that followed, which avoided reflecting on the Francoist dictatorship and ignored the demands to recognise the Republican side and their democratic values.

4 Towards granting amnesty to crimes of Francoism

The formula for "national reconciliation" ultimately meant shelving the idea of prosecuting Francoism for human rights violations that had been planned in 1974 by the British Labour Party with the support of the PSOE and with the blessing of the trade unions, UGT, CCOO and USO. All the forces involved in the Labour plan now enthusiastically endorsed the idea of forgetting the past.

The amnesty for events during the dictatorship, and even dating back to the Civil War, was not proposed by politicians, nor by right or centre-right

79 S. Martín, "Génesis y estructura del *nuevo* Estado (1933–1945)", F. Fernández-Crehuet and D. J. García (eds), *Derecho, memoria histórica y dictaduras*, Granada: Comares, pp. 79–135.

80 Aguilar, 1996, p. 138.

81 The contrast can be seen between the grand State funeral that was granted to Carrero Blanco and the modest send-off that was given to José Pardines, buried in Malpica, where his funeral was held. It was not until years later that a tribute was held in his name in his local town, and a blue plaque with his name was placed in a street named after him.

organisations of the Francoist regime. According to Mercedes García Arán, the proposal, couched in the popular demonstrations in favour of the amnesty for those in favour of a democracy, was ignored because if the events were amnestied, then they would have been recognised as political crimes, meaning that the legality of the dictatorship would have been questioned and it would have recognised that it lacked validity as an instrument for legal security. But the political forces did not consider themselves subject to law, as a guarantee for civilians, given that officers liberally infringed against their own laws when they violated the fundamental rights enshrined in the Criminal Code of the dictatorship.[82] The first politician to put forward this idea was Jaime Ignacio del Burgo at a Social Democratic Party event in February, 1976. This politician, who became a member of the party in 1977, was a senator in the Navarre Constitutional Committee, having been elected, moreover, as Second Secretary to the Senate. In a speech he gave on 26 February 1976, in Pamplona, he maintained that this political initiative had to be democratic in nature:

> Democracy is coexistence, dialogue, mutual respect, participatory, elections, the right to vote. It is not violence, coercion, insults. In a climate of terror, of threats, of fear, it is not possible to conceive of a democracy [...] In order for democracy in Spain to be viable, it is important to once and for all heal the wounds of the civil war. I have enormous respect for anyone who acted in good faith, whether on one side or the other, in the fight for a better future. But in light of the atrocities that resulted from this fight between brothers, our hearts quiver. I only wish that this chapter of our history had never been written. An amnesty must be the final act of this great tragedy.[83]

Del Burgo himself highlights the reference to amnesty because "at the time it was a burning issue" and "a necessary sacrifice to forge a path forwards towards a democracy".[84]

In the same vein, Luis Saiz del Moral published a short book at the time, entitled *Amnesty for the Right Too*, wherein he claimed that a blanket amnesty would only be achieved when the left agreed to an amnesty for those responsible for repression, tortures and executions during Francoism. He put forward his idea as a solution that was not in the spirit of revenge, to achieve a stable and peaceful democracy that would leave behind the ghosts of the Civil War.[85]

The theory was put into practice, and on 8 September 1976, Adolfo Suárez met with high-ranking Army officers to put to them his proposals for government; among them, his proposal to avoid situations of revenge.[86] On the back of this meeting, plans to amnesty crimes of Francoism were drawn up.

82 García Arán, 2009, p. 190.
83 Reproduced in Del Burgo, 2015.
84 Jaime Ignacio del Burgo interview, 14 May 2016 (Del Burgo, 2016).
85 Saiz del Moral, 1976.
86 Aguilar, 2008, pp. 302–303.

5 The partial Amnesty Law of 30 July 1976

5.1 The 1976 amnesty

The government led by Carlos Arias Navarro was not only unable to bring about the necessary political reforms, but it had also become the main obstacle for change. Arias Navarro's resignation before the King on 1 July 1977 led to the presidency of Adolfo Suárez, who had, up until that moment, been the Minister Secretary General of the National Movement. Suárez was entrusted with leading the country towards a democracy through the political transition process; he, along with his peers, represented a generational changing of the guard, something which proved to be crucial because the people who took centre stage in the transition were not of the generation who had fought in the Civil War.[87]

The royal Decree-Law of 30 July 1976[88] came to be regarded as a symbol of change, which Adolfo Suárez wanted to be identified with in the eyes of the people in an effort to distance himself from the previous Arias Navarro government.[89] The Law was the result of years of social pressure. Regardless, as Louise Mallinder concluded after carrying out a comparative analysis of all the amnesties throughout the world, internal pressure is one of the main reasons behind the concession of political amnesty.[90]

Case in point, the preamble to the legal text amounted to a clear statement of intent, highlighting the "will to coexist of the towns and of the people that make up the indissoluble Spanish national community" and the need to "foster the reconciliation of all the members of the State". The aim was to achieve "total democratic normality" and to contribute to the fruition of an agreement to "forget any discriminatory legacy of the past to allow a fraternal coexistence between the people of Spain".

This partial amnesty was directed at concrete cases of people who had been imprisoned for political reasons, specifically those who had refused to serve in the military, those imprisoned for sedition and insurgency, and, in more general terms, those imprisoned for any crime committed in the name of the campaign against the dictatorship. But these prisoners, accused of personally or politically motivated crimes and offences, could not have made an attempt on the life of anyone or threatened the physical integrity of others. On the other hand, the First Additional Provision of this Law closed the door to any economic demands when it established that "there will not be any compensation or restitution for the criminal convictions, resolutions, administrative sanctions or penalties covered by the amnesty".

The progressive newspaper *El País* deemed the amnesty a generous measure, "the best possible solution, if not the most far-reaching", but "a real symbol of

87 Aguilar, 2008, pp. 34, 41.
88 Decree-Law 10/1976, 30 July, on Amnesty. *Official State Gazette*, no. 186, 4 August 1976, pp. 15097–15098.
89 For example, Ysàs, 2009, p. 36.
90 Mallinder, 2008b, p. 11.

how we have overcome the civil war".[91] Two hundred and eighty-seven prisoners were set free, most of them politicians. But around 250 members of ETA and other armed forces remained in prison. Miguel de Herrero Miñón, then Technical Secretary General of the Department of Justice, and in large part, the author of the Law, tells us that the Law:

> did not include the Basque political prisoners because they were reserved for a special amnesty that would be granted in symbolic act to be held Guernica. This project was developed during the summer of 1976, but like so many others, it could not be finalised, even though it had even been considered for the 1977 Amnesty Law under blood crimes.[92]

To avoid ambiguities, the State Attorney General issued a Circular Letter on 13 July 1976 to recall the guidelines for the application of the Royal Decree; specifically, neither that the explanatory memorandum nor article 1 considered as politically motivated crimes and offences, crimes "which are so atrocious that they cannot be forgotten". Furthermore, he differentiated "common crimes" and "political crimes". The existence or not of "political intentionality" would have to be determined by the courts in the event of ambiguous or subjective intentionality behind crime being considered for amnesty. He also pointed out that political intentionality would be presumed, unless the nature of the crimes contradicted the presumption, as well as crimes against the domestic and foreign safety of the State as per the Criminal Code.[93]

ETA continued to carry out terrorist attacks. It put forward its position in a statement issued on 6 October 1976, two days after it assassinated the president of the Gipuzkoa Provincial Council in San Sebastián, Juan María de Araluce, claiming that "not only has Suárez not granted a blanket amnesty, but he has worsened the conditions in prisons and has drowned in blood the public demonstrations defending this and other public demands".[94] The situation reached an impasse when the government decided against taking any further steps. On 10 December, the Minister for Justice, Landelino Lavilla, declared publicly that there had been no developments. He defended the scope of the 1976 amnesty and believed that it had been, generally speaking, correctly applied. He restated the limits of the amnesty for blood crimes, and claimed that he was not preparing any other decree-law on amnesty.

Among the prisoners who were freed under the 1976 amnesty were ex-soldiers who had been members of the clandestine association the UMD, an organisation which was founded in August 1974, to demand the elaboration of a constitution, the re-establishment for democratic freedoms and human rights, the fight against

91 *El País*, 31 July 1976. See Aguilar, 2008, p. 289; Juliá, 2008, p. 99.
92 Miguel Herrero de Miñón interview, 21 May 2016 (Herrero de Miñón, 2016).
93 Circular letter no. 3/1976, 13 July, on the application of DL 10/1976. Cited in Garcés, 2010, p. 261.
94 Cited in Portell Manso, 1977.

corruption, socioeconomic reforms to improve quality of life and, in relation to their profession, the reform of military justice and of the Military Service Law, and a profound restructuring of the three Spanish armies. In March 1976, nine members of the UMD were sentenced in a military court to 43 years in prison. Seven of the soldiers were also discharged from the military.[95]

The amnesty freed all nine prisoners, but their secondary sentences of military discharge were allowed to stand, meaning they could not rejoin the Army, as article 8 of the legal text established that those granted amnesty would be removed from their positions and their careers if the sentences carried with them a dismissal from work, military discharge or loss of place and rank. This was a point of concession the government had made to the military after a protracted and difficult negotiation, as Miguel Herrero de Miñón, then Technical Secretary General of the Ministry of Justice, and in large part the main instigator of this law, recalls in his memoirs. The opinion of the military was taken into account but, at the same time, it posed no objection to the negotiations with the opposition.[96]

Amnesty was applied legally at the behest of an interested party, except in cases which were already under way and or when sentences were close to being served in full – these cases were resolved *ex officio*.[97] Certain judges, remaining morally loyal to the regime, were reticent when it came to applying this law, often arriving at an excessively restrictive interpretation,[98] which, in turn, highlighted the inadequacy of the law.

There were prisoners who had been convicted of various charges and were granted amnesty for some but not all of the charges – Bixente Serrano Izko, for example. Serrano Izko was a member of ETA who had been in prison in Cartagena since 6 July 1976 for using false documentation in violation of articles 310 and 309 of the Criminal Code. Both charges were amnestied and erased from his criminal record, but he was informed that:

> the same Decree rejects granting amnesty for sentences imposed for terrorism and kidnapping as per article 294 bis b of the Military Justice Code; for illegal possession of firearms as per articles 254 and 255 of the Criminal Code; for assaulting a member of the Armed Forces as per article 308.3 of the Justice Military Code.[99]

The measure implemented by Suárez did not, on the other hand, align with the demands of anti-Francoists, who deemed the measure a false amnesty because the regime was still in force and prisoners who been set free under the amnesty could

95 Otero and Fortes, 1983. Gómez Rosa, 2013.
96 Herrero de Miñón, 1998, pp. 74–78.
97 Clavero, 2014, p. 108.
98 Aguilar, 2008, pp. 290–291. Pérez Amorós, 2009, p. 142.
99 Bixente Serrano Izko case file, appeal against the Decree of the judicial authority in relation to the rejection of Serrano Izko application for amnesty, Cartagena, 12 October 1976.

be arrested again and convicted of the same "crimes", such as belonging to a political association or a trade union, and for congregating and protesting. As P. Isàs said, in the face of this situation and with growing social indignation manifest in the public protests that called for a blanket amnesty, the government was forced to give orders to the police to exercise prudence when it came to using force – something which was not always observed by the police – and to be more tolerant in relation to the political groups that remained illegal, but at the same time maintaining the repressive pressure on the PCE and other left-wing parties.[100]

5.2 Granting amnesty to the trade union sector and full recognition of trade union rights

The problems that arose from the practical application of this partial amnesty law forced the government to issue the first of two additional regulations to extend the amnesty to the more problematic labour and trade union cases.

The Trade Union Organisation implemented the Agreement from 3 August 1976 in relation to the application of the amnesty in the trade union sector.[101] As indicated in the preamble, the Trade Union Organisation, "identifying with the spirit of harmony", cancelled the embargo on trade union rights which had originated from resolutions adopted by organisations affiliated to the trade unions that had benefitted from the amnesty. The measure affected all instances where trade unions had been incapacitated or discriminated against in relation to activities that had lost their original moral and legal standing. Under the first article, any resolution, sentence or instance resulting in the suppression or constraint of trade union rights was cancelled *ex officio* or at the request of an interested party. The third article specified that the effects of these restitutive regulations would not lead to compensation nor could they prejudice the rights acquired by a third party.

5.3 Granting amnesty to civil servants in purged local administrations

The second directive complementary to the 1976 amnesty was the Royal Decree of 1 October 1976, which regulated the special case of civil servants in local administrations, institutions which had been purged because of policies put forward by the Frente Popular and other local organisations which were sympathetic to the Nationalist cause.

The preamble specified that although the Decree-Law of 30 July did not expressly refer to civil servants in local governance, the law was applicable to their cases, "all the more where the regulation in force equates the local government of

100 Ysàs, 2009, p. 36.
101 Agreement with the Trade Union Organisation on the application of amnesty in the trade union sector and full recognition of trade union rights. *Official State Gazette*, no. 191, 10 August 1976, p. 15552.

said civil servants with the State Public Administration". Articles 2 and 3 clarified the regulations that were open to interpretation to avoid any possible ambiguities.[102]

This Royal Decree was developed through the National Ministerial Order of 6 July 1977.[103]

5.4 Granting amnesty to civil servants in the Catalan Generalitat

The Catalan Generalitat of the Second Republic was the first autonomous institution to be founded on 17 April 1931. President Macià formed a provisional Generalitat through decrees issued on 28 April 1931. The few years that the institution was active were enough to lay down its administrative foundations, employing many civil servants and regular employees, who received economic reparation as a result of the complementary measures to the amnesty.

The former Francoist deputy, Juan Antonio Samaranch Torelló, requested that the Royal pardon be extended to civil servants of the Catalan Generalitat.[104] His request was accepted and subsequently the National Ministerial Order of 6 July 1977 regulated the application process for the civil servants of the Generalitat who were eligible for amnesty.[105] The Royal Decree for the application of this amnesty was delayed until 2 May 1978.[106] The measure was finalised in the Order of 29 June 1978, which created the Inter-Departmental Commission for the concession of amnesty to civil servants of the Catalan Generalitat.[107] Economic reparation, however, was left to the Generalitat, who elaborated them through two decrees in 1978 and 1979, respectively.[108]

102 Royal Decree 2393/1976, 1 October, on the guidelines for the application of the amnesty to civil servants in local government. *Official State Gazette*, no. 256, 25 October, pp. 20918–20919.
103 National Ministerial Order, 6 July 1977, regulating the application of the Royal Decree 2393/1976 on Amnesty for the Civil Servants in Public Administration. *Official State Gazette*, no. 168, 15 July 1977, pp. 15907–15908.
104 *Official Parliament Gazette*, no. 1554, 8 February 1977, pp. 37565–37567.
105 National Ministerial Order, 6 July 1977, regulating applications for amnesty for civil servants in the Catalan Generalitat. *Official State Gazette*, no. 168, 15 July 1977, p. 15908.
106 Royal Decree 1081/1978, 2 May, on applications for amnesty for civil servants in the Catalan Generalitat. *Official State Gazette*, no. 126, 27 May 1978, p. 12279.
107 *Official State Gazette*, no. 156, 1 July 1978, p. 15671.
108 Decree of 14 November 1978, on passive rights of former directors of Generalitat in charge between 14 April 1931 and 10 February 1939 and members of the Catalan Parliament. *Official Catalan Generalitat Gazette*, 30 November, 1978. Decree of 12 March 1979, establishing regulation for the application and recognition of passive rights of directors of the Generalitat and former deputies in the Catalan Parliament. *Official Catalan Generalitat Gazette*, 2 April 1979.

5.5 Granting amnesty to the media

Article 10 of the Amnesty Law of 30 July 1976, indicated the need to develop additional measures to deal with the application of the amnesty in relation to the press and print media. This was realised in the Decree-Law of 18 October from the same year.[109] The first clause, in application of the amnesty law, annulled any restrictions on membership occasioned by crimes committed by the print and other media which had already been subject to the amnesty. In the same way, also annulled were the restrictions ordered by the Board/Panel of Professional Ethics. At the behest of the National Federation of Press Associations, the second clause, subject to membership in the latter organisation, made provisions for the inscription in the Official Council of Journalists of those accredited as such and those who had been excluded from the Council because of such issues, or those who had not been able to gain access to it due to the Francoist ministerial orders of 24 May 1939 and of 18 April 1940.

5.6 Granting amnesty to the auxiliary staff of purged courts and tribunals

A Royal Decree Law of 21 December 1978, regulated the situation in relation to the auxiliary staff in courts and tribunals which had been purged by the Francoist regime.[110] The coup d'état led to an extensive purge of the Department of Justice, removing the auxiliary staff of courts and tribunals who sympathised with the Republican cause, an especially significant cohort made up of forensic doctors, doormen and everything in between.[111]

6 Clemency measures after the elections of 15 July 1977

The Law of Political Reform, which came into effect on 5 January 1977, paved the way for the general election – which was to be held in July – and for the legalisation of the majority of the political parties in February of that same year.[112] The political agenda was, at all times, focused on the issue of amnesty.

The political community distrusted Suárez and King Juan Carlos I. The exiled PNV director, Manuel de Irujo, wrote the following in 1977:

109 Royal Decree 2716/1976, 18 October, in relation to the regulation of print and press media in the Royal Decree Law 10/1976, 30 July. *Official State Gazette*, no. 285. 27 November 1975, p. 23648.

110 Royal Decree-Law 44/1978, 21 December which regulates the situation of the staff of the courts who are removed from their roles for political reasons. *Boletín Oficial del Estado*, n° 306, de 23 de diciembre de 1978, pp. 29029–29030.

111 Lanero, 1996, pp. 220–221. Fernández-Crehuet, 2011, pp. 112–114. Jimeno, 2014, pp. 86–106.

112 Law 1/1977, 4 January, for Political Reform. *Official State Gazette*, no. 4, 5 January 1977, pp. 170–171.

> Spain is being led by a King and a Government that are the offspring of Franco, and the first thing they have done is deny their father. Who could trust this type of sheep? Suárez is a nice, understanding, ambitious and well intentioned man of the people. His program is mainly oriented at strengthening King Juan Carlos' throne. Everything else is marginal. On these margins are the opposition. And among these, us, represented by Julio Jáuregui and Juan Ajuriaguerra, the former representing the left, and that latter representing Christian Democracy. A few days ago, Juan Ajuriaguerra said to me, here in Paris, that we're going for a blanket amnesty.[113]

The partial amnesty of 1976 and its additional measures were not considered sufficient by the majority of the political class, which is why, on 11 January 1977, four representatives from the democratic opposition, Anton Cañellas (Centrists of Catalonia), Felipe González (PSOE), Julio de Jáuregui (PNV) and Joaquín Satrústegui (Liberal Alliance), demanded that the president grant a blanket amnesty for the Spanish general election.[114] According to Jáuregui's testimony, this amnesty had to overturn "all the politically motivated offences and crimes between the 18th of July, 1936, and the 15th of December, 1976", in order to forgive and forget "all the crimes and atrocities committed by both sides of the civil war, before, during and after the conflict and until today". This pardon and erasure from memory would be externalised in a grand solemn royal act in the name of peace and reconciliation, in what would become the "first honourable and glorious chapter of the beginning of the reign".[115]

The government, however, preferred to wait and grant the amnesty from the legislative body constituted after the election. In this way, the amnesty would enjoy a status of democratic legality, similar to the amnesty the French government granted in relation to events in Algeria. Incidentally, this is exactly what the specialist in this subject, Enrique Linde, proposed in his 1975 doctoral thesis which he read in Bologna in 1975 and was published the following year: amnesty is an instrument to facilitate political and social changes, but to be valid it has to be passed in Parliament.[116]

113 Cited in De Pablo Contreras, 2002, p. 174.

114 Juliá, 2008, p. 100. That same month, the clandestine association, Democratic Justice, made up of progressive lawyers and judges, called for, among other things, the abolition of the Decree-Law on terrorism and all other laws and precepts on the repression of democratic freedoms, a total amnesty for politically motivated crimes and sanctions for political infractions. Reproduced in Díaz Sánchez, 2016, pp. 210–311.

115 Julio de Jáuregui exemplified it with particular examples from enemy groups, maintaining that the amnesty would forgive and forget "those who killed president Companys and president Carrero; García Lorca and Muñoz Seca, Interior Ministers Salazar-Alonso and Zugazagoitia; the victims of Paracuellos and the dead in Badajoz; General Fanjul and Gernal Pita, and all who committed crimes and atrocities from both sides of the conflict". J. de Jáuregui, "La amnistía y la violencia", *El País*, 18 May 1977. See Juliá, 2008, p. 100.

116 Linde Paniagua, 1976a.

The winter and spring of 1977 was marked by high levels of violence, with numerous lethal attacks carried out by ETA, the kidnapping of soldier Emilio Villaescusa by the Maoist group GRAPO, and attacks from extreme right paramilitary groups, among which the most notable was the massacre of Atocha on 24 January 1977, when five communist lawyers from Madrid were murdered. The calls for amnesty were intensified, so much so that the first "Pro Amnesty Week" (from 26 February to 6 March) was organised, backed by the widespread support of the people, but strongly repressed by the police.

In practice, the lawyers representing political prisoners believed that either a pardon or a future amnesty would free those who had not been convicted of a blood crime. The lawyer Javier Añúa wrote a letter, dated 17 February 1977, to his client Bixente Serrano Izko, held in Cartagena on various charges stemming from his status as a member of ETA, informing him that "trials are being revised and pardons for specific issues are being granted to successful applications". It was a moment that they had to take advantage of, as the very freedom of Serrano Izko depended on it. Añúa also informed his client that Juan María Bandrés was exploring an alternative by negotiating with the minister in relation to granting an amnesty; he emphasised that:

> It is obvious that the first to be released are prisoners who were convicted of crime which did not endanger the lives of others; according to the data, at present there are 104 Basque prisoners and, in the words of the Government, 80 of them are going to be released step by step before the 10th of April. 24 prisoners will remain because the charges are of a more serious nature and their cases are therefore a more complicated political matter, but you are not included in this list.[117]

Three months from the general election, the government was forced to issue a pardon on 14 March 1977.[118] It was presented to the public as a mere technical adjustment intended to overcome the obstacles that had hindered the application of the partial amnesty from 30 July 1976. The omission of the exact phrase "in danger" from the 1976 legal text broadened the scope of the amnesty.[119] Its reach was truly extraordinary because, as José Enrique Sobremonte explained, it facilitated the liberation of the majority of the political prisoners.[120] According to statistics from the Attorney General of the Realm, up to 125 political prisoners

117 Bixente Serrano Izko, case file letter from Javier Añúa to Bixente Serrano Izko, Vitoria, 17 February 1977.

118 Royal Decree 388/1977, 14 March, on the General Pardon. *Official State Gazette*, no. 66, 18 March 1977, pp. 6301–6302. See also Order of 2 April 1977, which dictates the guidelines for the application of the pardon promulgated by the Royal Decree 288/1977, 14 March. *Official State Gazette*, no. 91, 16 April 1977.

119 Royal Decree-Law 19/1977, 14 March, on clemency measures. *Official State Gazette*, no. 65, 17 March 1977, pp. 6201–6202.

120 Sobremonte Martínez, 1980, p. 102.

were set free.[121] The Decree-Law avoided using the term "amnesty", preferring instead the euphemistic term "grace measures", which, as Bartolomé Clavero pointed out, amounted to mere forgiveness, an exercise in mercy which did not even recognise the crimes it amnestied because it did not consider them crimes as such.[122]

A few days later came the promulgation of the Decree-Law of 18 March to regulate the coming elections and established the D'Hondt electoral system, based on disproportionality, which favoured the UCD[123] and a UCD-PSOE bipartisanship.[124] A political basis was thus put in place to avoid radicalism in the next democratic phase of the transition. Following the consolidation of the D'Hondt system that made it impossible for the communist party to get to power, the party was legalised on 9 April, followed by the legalisation of the CCOO, UGT and USO trade unions on 28 April.

The Txiberta Summit took place two days later in Anglet, in the French Basque Country. The Summit was convened by the PNV politician Telesforo Monzón with the aim of creating a Basque nationalist political front. It was attended by representatives of every nationalist organisation in the Basque Country,[125] including the military faction of ETA. This faction demanded that the summit focus on its demands for amnesty because, without it, the elections of 15 June could not be deemed legitimate. A delegation representing the various groups was tasked with demanding amnesty and democratic freedoms from Adolfo Suárez at a meeting on 10 May. The President responded that, because of the pressure from the Army, he could not sanction the liberation of every political prisoner on the 24th of the month, the day the electoral campaign was set to

121 Aguilar, 2008, p. 291.
122 Clavero, 2014, p. 109.
123 The UCD was put together by Adolfo Suárez during the last pre-democracy government with the aim of attaining a parliamentary majority with only 35% of the votes, which is what the polls were predicting. See Urdánoz, 2014.
124 As Óscar Alzaga, UCD deputy, recognised years later, this was a system that was "totally original, and infinitely more original than it seemed at first glance, and fairly Machiavellian, It is original, because its method is based on the 1908 [sic, original reference: 1907] Law, and it is fairly Machiavellian because the current law is essentially a copy of the '77 Decree-Law, which, as per the official agreement between the pre-democratic government and the opposition, was developed by experts. I was fortunate enough to be one of these experts, and the bottom-line assignment was to find a way for the government to attain an absolute majority. Given that the opinion polls were predicting 36–37% of the votes for the UCD party, the aim was to find an electoral system in which 36–37% was enough for an absolute majority, and with a system that favoured rural areas, where there was more support for UCD in the electoral projections than in industrial areas, where the Socialist Party had more support [...] Thus the aim was to design the system so that the PSOE needed 39–40% of the votes for an absolute majority, rather than the 36–37% margin." Alzaga, 1989, pp. 127–128.
125 The following were in attendance: PNV, ANV, EKA, ESB, ESEI, EHAS, LAIA (bai), EIA, ETA-M, ETA-PM and a delegation of mayors.

begin. However, the president offered the group of delegates the possibility of "estrangement", an option which had been recommended by the lawyer Juan María Bandrés to the government,[126] using it as a bargaining chip in negotiations with ETA-PM and EIA. "Estrangement" consisted of freeing ETA prisoners on the condition that they remained outside the country. The first group of prisoners that would be freed would be the most popular, that is, the ones who had been prosecuted in the Burgos trials. The remaining prisoners would be freed after the general election.[127]

This meeting coincided with the second "Pro Amnesty Week", which had been scheduled to take place between 8 and 15 May 1977, by the various protest groups in Araba, Gipuzkoa, Biscay and Navarre, to demand amnesty for all the political prisoners. The protests, ruthlessly repressed by the forces of public order, ended with seven casualties and numerous injuries during the protests that spread throughout Madrid, Barcelona, Valladolid, Salamanca, Saragossa and Santiago de Compostela, where lockdowns took place. The harsh repressive measures of the police sparked a wide social and political response, aided by the coverage in the media, especially in stations with left-wing tendencies. From an institutional perspective, it is worth noting that the plenary meeting of the Pamplona city council agreed to officially condemn the protests.[128]

The government tried to placate the public's indignation with a pardon issued by the Council of Ministers on 20 May 1977, which sought to put into practice the strategy of "estrangement" in the case of those convicted of terrorism, the only alternative available to the Basque prisoners whose sentences were not covered by the amnesty decreed in July 1976, nor by its addendum in March 1977. Lawyers Miguel Castells, Juan María Bandrés and Ignacio Esnaola collected the 20 or so signatures of the ETA prisoners who accepted the terms and presented them to José Manuel Otero Novas, a trusted member of Adolfo Suárez's circle and future minister.[129] The kidnapping of businessman and ex-president of the Biscay's charter government, Javier Ybarra, did not stop the Council of Ministers from authorising "estrangement" on 20 May 1977, in the face of great resistance from the Army and even from some sections of the government.[130] The more reactionary sectors of Francoism – the so-called bunker – as well as ETA itself, interpreted the government's delay in issuing the "estrangement" amnesty as a sort of capitulation of the executive in the face the growing violence from the armed the group.[131] The kidnapping and eventual assassination of Ybarra on 22 July did not avoid the "estrangement" of 19 of the 32 ETA members who were still in prison, and who were relocated to Norway, Denmark, Austria and Belgium.[132]

126 Castro, 1998, pp. 145–148.
127 De Pablo, Mees and Rodríguez Ranz, 2001, pp. 342–343.
128 Jimeno, 2015, p. 333. Bueno Urritzelki, 2014–2015, pp. 88–96.
129 Otero Novas, 2015.
130 Castro, 1998, pp. 145–148. Oreja, 2011, pp. 170–171.
131 Preston, 2003, p. 431.
132 Letamendía, 1994, vol. 2, pp. 44–47.

The pardons granted to ETA prisoners and their subsequent relocation outside Spain caused a schism in the core of the organisation. EIA and ETA-PM believed that amnesty had been achieved. An EIA special Assembly on 29 May in Beasain (Gipuzkoa) decided to put forward its candidacy for the 15 July election, an extreme strategy which members from Navarre were not in favour of, and which was also heavily criticised by the ETA-M, which continued to demand an immediate blanket amnesty whilst it continued with its strategy of terrorist attacks.[133]

The electoral campaign began in a state of upheaval and uncertainty. During the campaign, the government granted a pardon on 27 May to military personnel to commemorate the Day of the Armed Forces. The pardon covered "sentences or fines handed or which could be handed to members of the Armed Forces for major and minor offences as defined by the Military Justice Code", although it excluded "military penalties" resulting from corrective measures or sanctions applied, or which could be applied, to governmental or administrative cases or when the sentence carried a dismissal from the corp. This blanket pardon covered members of the Armed Forces whose sentences resulted in a deprivation of freedom, imposed, or could be imposed in the military jurisdiction, if the sentence did not exceed two years. In cases where the prison sentence exceeded two years, it would be reduced to half the time, but never reduced under two years.[134] This measure was a nod to the Francoist core of the military, given that it justified this measure framing it within the "general policy of harmony which is being put into practice", pardoning "those who, as members of the Armed Forces, removed themselves from the line of action in which they belonged as a matter of circumstance" and excluded the members of the Military Democratic Union and those who served under the People's Republican Army.

This pardon was not the only clemency measure granted during the campaign. The Decree-Law 3357/75 and the Royal Decree-Law 10/76 had failed to include, in the teaching sector, some teachers who aspired to become national primary school teachers who had undertaken their studies under the 1931 professional plan, or who had participated in recruitment courses for the National Primary School Teachers body[135] and passed the selection process, but could not incorporate themselves to the body for political reasons. To ameliorate this situation, the Decree-Law of 2 June 1977 declared the integration of this cohort into the corps of national primary school teachers or to the teachers of General Basic Education body where appropriate or at the request of an interested party. The number of teachers who could return to serve under these bodies after nearly four decades of inactivity under the dictatorship was limited, given that, as established under article 2 of the regulation, the reintegration would come into

133 Onaindía, 2001. Uriarte, 2005. Fernández Soldevilla, 2010, pp. 55–96.
134 Royal Decree 1135/1977, 27 May, on the Pardon for the Armed Forces Personnel. *Official State Gazette*, n. 127, 28 May 1977, p. 11814.
135 Convened by decree on 14 March 1936.

effect from the day the Decree-Law was issued in the *Official State Gazette*, "unless the interested party was 70 years of age or older, or deceased, based on the date of birth or date of bereavement, if the party is deceased". However, article 3 granted a pension to retired or bereaved teachers affected by the pardon, if the time passed between 1 April 1939 and the day of retirement or death was equal to or longer than the minimum periods of service.[136]

During the month of transition between the general election (15 July), which Adolfo Suárez and UCD won,[137] and the beginning of the new constitutional legislation (13 July), the Interior Ministry issued two orders, both on 6 July, which were discussed above in relation to the application of the Royal Decree on the Amnesty of 1 October 1976 for civil servants in the Generalitat and local Administrations.

Another demonstration during this month of what would become the "policy of openness", related to the ETA prisoners who had been "estranged". These exiled prisoners secretly returned to the Basque Country, resurfacing in the Durango area of Biscay on 21 July 1977, to participate in a gathering for the March for Freedom on 28 August in Arazuri (Navarre). In the following weeks and months, the estranged members of ETA stayed in the Basque Country and clandestinely continued to participate in various political events. Only one of them, Xabier Larena, was arrested (on 29 July) and sent to the prison in Basauri (Biscay). The rest of the prisoners who had been "estranged" eventually legalised their situation in Spain thanks to the Amnesty Law of 15 October 1977.[138]

136 Royal Decree-Law 1555/1977, 2 June, on the integration to the General Basic Corp of the National Primary School Teachers corps for teachers qualified under the 1931 Professional Plan or the 1936 national primary school teacher trainer degree. *Official State Gazette*, no. 158, 4 July 1977, p. 14942.

137 UCD achieved 165 parliamentary seats, followed by PSOE (118), AP (16), PSC (15), PDC (11), PCE (12), PSUC (8), PNV (8), PSP-US (6), UCD-CD (2), CIC (2), EC-FED (1) y EE (1).

138 *El País*, *Egin*, 22 October 1977.

Chapter 3

The 1977 Amnesty Law and subsequent clemency measures

1 The draft law negotiations for the Amnesty Law

The Constituent Assembly convened for the first time on 13 July 1977, to elect the first President of Congress. Spain thus became a democracy. The political, institutional and social events that culminated in the passing of the Amnesty Law on 15 October 1977 are well known thanks to the work carried out at the time by José María Portell Manso,[1] Miguel Castells[2] and Aurelio Desdentado and Luis Enrique de la Villa,[3] in addition to the diachronic studies developed by Josep M. Colomer,[4] Paloma Aguilar,[5] Floren Aoiz,[6] Francisco Pérez Amorós,[7] Joaquín Leguina[8] and Santos Juliá,[9] to cite some of the more representative studies.

The day after the Assembly convened for the first time, the Communist Party put forward a Bill for a blanket amnesty, with the rationale that the results of the general election were a demonstration, according to the preamble of the Bill, of the Spanish people's will "to overcome once and for all the division of citizens into winners and losers of the Civil War". National reconciliation would be achieved through a blanket amnesty, which would not ignore the active and passive rights of maimed and disabled soldiers, nor their widows and legal heirs, irrespective of which side they had fought on. The Bill proposed the reinstatement of civil servants who had been purged or removed from work as a result of their loyalty to the Republican cause, with their full rights restored, and the reinstatement of the thousands of workers who had been removed from work for defending the trade union cause and for fighting for the rights of their colleagues,

1 Portell Manso, 1977.
2 Castells Arteche, 1978.
3 De la Villa and Desdentado Bonete, 1978, pp. 181–186.
4 Colomer, 1998.
5 Aguilar, 1995a. Aguilar, 1995b. Aguilar, 1996. Aguilar, 1997a. Aguilar, 1997b. Aguilar, 1999. Aguilar, 2008. Aguilar, 2012.
6 Aoiz, 2005.
7 Pérez Amorós, 2009.
8 Leguina, 2010.
9 Juliá, 2011, pp. 35–37.

for political amnesty and for an amnesty for crimes that affected women (adultery, abortion and the use of contraception).

New projects were put forward throughout the summer, all of them heavily anti-Francoist and calling for a blanket amnesty for workers, for political prisoners and for soldiers of the UMD. On 27 July, a group of Basque, Socialist and Progressive senators came together and presented a green paper in the Senate. After the summer, the Catalan and Basque minority in Congress presented a draft law (14 September); they considered that an amnesty was of the "utmost urgency", necessary "to pacify the people of Spain". This new era in Spain would begin by "putting to one side and forgetting all past grievances", a wilful amnesia that would be brought about by a "true amnesty for one and all".

On 20 September the Socialist Group proposed its Blanket Amnesty Bill. It did not insist on reconciliation as much, and instead focused on the demands of the public, who did not want to delay any further the concession of amnesty for "all acts considered as criminal offences under the current legislation or the previous legislation from the 18th of July, 1936, howsoever implemented with the political intention of establishing a democracy in Spain and restoring public freedom in all its towns [...] whichever the results". This Socialist Bill also included "adultery and related crimes".

Parallel to these processes, the trade unions also put forward their proposals for a future Amnesty Law;[10] most notable amongst these was the proposal of the CCOO, a trade union which had been recently legalised and had a solid foundation. The main aim of the amnesty, as indicated in its first article, was the reinstatement of workers dismissed for political reasons, for associating with a trade union, or for participating in collective disturbances of work. The objective of reinstating workers, however, conflicted with the interests of the powerful business community.[11]

None of the above-mentioned Bills struck a consensus among the opposition groups that were given to democratic values. A new Bill had to be drafted to seek this consensus. The Socialist, Communist, Basque-Catalan and mixed parliamentary groups appeared in the Congress of Deputies to propose a new Bill, drawn up on 1 October. Its preamble justified this measure, which had to be implemented immediately, as a reconciliation and a consolidation of a democratic State, a "true amnesty for one and all". The amnesty would not only cover political prisoners, but also "acts of a labour and unionised nature, considered as crimes under the current and abrogated legislations, although they were committed in the context of workers' individual or collective petitions, derived from labour relations, or in defence of their interests".

10 De la Villa and Desdentado Bonete, 1978, pp. 16 and 17. This study included annexes (pp. 165–216) which collect the legal texts of the various proposals (pp. 179–187).

11 Pérez Amorós, 2009, p. 145.

UCD presented its proposal for amnesty on 3 October, and it was characterised by two aspects: on the one hand, it deliberately omitted any reference to a labour amnesty, foreseeing that the matter would be predictably taken up by the opposition on the left and would thus provoke a negotiation.[12] On the other hand, it included granting the benefits of amnesty to "every crime and misdemeanour of a political nature committed before and up until the 15th of June, 1977"; point 4 therein also specified that the amnesty would be extended to the authorities, civil servants and public order agents who, in the persecution of crimes that would later be pardoned, may have been criminally liable or may have violated the rights of the people, as recognised by law.[13] The term "rights of the people" jars, as it seems a deliberate attempt to avoid using the term "human rights", which was widely used at the time and would later feature in the Amnesty Law.

We agree with Francisco Pérez Amorós that the main aim of this proposal was to create a political platform that would force a negotiation to strike a consensus for the future Amnesty Law, given that neither the opposition groups committed to democracy nor the government could make a unilateral proposal. In fact, the Amnesty Law ended up being one of the few laws that enjoyed a wide consensus, despite the exclusion of the AP, which was deemed crucial in relation to the consequences that a blanket amnesty would bring.[14] Strategising for future negotiations, the UCD agreeing to a labour amnesty forced the other groups to reciprocate and include Francoist crimes.[15]

A Commission was created on 3 October. It was made up of representatives from every parliamentary group except the AP, which chose not to participate. Its members included government representative Rafael Arias Salgado (UCD) and deputies Plácido Fernández Viagas and Pablo Castellano (PSOE), Pilar Brabo and Marcelino Camacho and Jaime Sartorius (PCE), Xabier Arzalluz and Mitxel Unzueta (Basque-Catalan minority, though both were PNV deputies) and Donato Fuejo (Mixed Group, though a deputy for the PSP-US). The Commission had to develop a proposal for consensus based on both texts, but negotiations were not minuted[16] and their content is known only through the information that was published in newspapers at the time and through the memoirs of the socialist deputy, Julio Busquets.[17] Finding a solution to the main political demand of the transition was an urgent matter because failure to find an agreement that satisfied

12 Pérez Amorós, 2009, p. 147.
13 Juliá, 2011, p. 37.
14 De la Villa and Desdentado Bonete, 1978, pp. 16–17.
15 Pérez Amorós, 2009, pp. 146–147.
16 Jaime Sartorius, youngest member of the Commission, minuted the first two meetings, but given that none of his colleagues agreed to sign them, he stopped recording the sessions. The original minutes and other notes on those meetings are filed in his own personal archive. J. Sartorius, "La Ley de Amnistía no ampara al franquismo", *El País*, 15 March 2010.
17 Busquets, 1999, pp. 247–248.

the parties involved could block the entire political process. It was an issue that was followed closely by the media, freed from the shackles of Francoist censorship. The legal solution to the public demands was in the hands of a few negotiators, as often happens with important legal matters during transitions from dictatorships to democracies.[18]

All parties agreed that the new amnesty had to overcome the limitations of the previous clemency measures, but there were important divergences when it came to extending it to the soldiers of the UMD, with regard to crimes that affected women, with regard to whether a labour amnesty should be included and, even, with regard to the scope of the political amnesty.

The Commission drafted a Bill on 7 October. The urgency of the matter meant that the text was somewhat improvised, and thus lacked a considered preliminary judicial analysis. It was presented that same day in the Congress of Deputies by the parliamentary groups UCD, Socialist MP, Communist, Basque-Catalan minority, Mixed and Catalan Socialists.[19] It included amnesty for political prisoners, labour amnesty and amnesty for Francoist crimes, but it excluded the UMD soldiers, the ex-soldiers of the Republican Army and adultery, cohabitation, abortion, contraception and crimes of homosexuality. There was no specific amnesty for common crimes either.

For the sake of consensus, the Bill did not have a preamble or justify its motivations, a complete democratic anomaly with laws of this nature. It was a wilful omission on the part of its authors, given that no group was completely satisfied by the agreement that was going to be passed. The preamble would have required a justification for the law, which would have given rise to numerous discrepancies and, ultimately, would have put the viability of the Draft Law at risk.[20]

The AP, which had been on the margins of the negotiations, rejected the legal text because it considered that it questioned the legitimacy of Francoism and amnestied terrorist crimes.[21] On the other extreme, ETA-M demonstrated its opposition to the Bill by assassinating the president of the Provincial Council of Biscay, Augusto Unzueta, and one of his bodyguards, on 8 October.

2 Parliamentary procedure to pass the Bill

The Bill agreed to by all parties was prepared for approval in Parliament, but before it could be sent it was necessary to pass provisional regulations for the Congress of Deputies, which did not happen until 13 October.[22] The urgency to pass this law motivated the full House to expedite the process, unanimously

18 Bermeo, 1992, p. 276.
19 Text in *Official Parliament Gazette*, no. 16, 11 October 1977, pp. 203–204.
20 Aguilar, 2008, p. 300. Pérez Amorós, 2009, p. 157.
21 Molinero, 2009, p. 47.
22 *Official State Gazette*, no. 256, 26 October 1977, pp. 23476–23486.

passing "regulations to process the Amnesty Bill". Because the process was such a hurried one, the second article established that corrections would have to be presented within "seven natural days" from the date of publication in the *Official Parliament Gazette*. The eagerness of the various political parties to pass the first law of the democracy was reflected in the fact that no corrections were made to the regulation or any of its articles, which is why it was immediately sent to a vote. The parliamentary debate was also defined by the swiftness of the interventions. The speakers avoided any controversial debating,[23] and barely added any judicial commentary. The process was in stark contrast to the dense and complex discussions that took place in future sessions where Bills were debated, and, of course, especially when debates on the constitution took place.

The Bill was debated and passed in Congress on 14 October. For those who participated in the debate – some abstained[24] – the idea of reconciliation and the need for a blanket amnesty was key in order to break away from Francoism and establish a new democratic order. Particularly noteworthy was Marcelino Camacho's speech, which explained the Communist Group's vote as "the result of a considered and coherent policy which was begun with the PC's policy for national reconciliation back in 1956".[25] Invoking one of the main demands of communism in Spain, he called for a labour amnesty, but also spoke of the need to "meet the Basque people halfway" in order to put an end to their conflict. For his part, Xabier Arzalluz, of the Basque-Catalan Group, rigorously defended the amnesty as the best solution to a difficult problem, agreeing that a wilful amnesia, a pact to forget the past, was "the only way that we could shake hands without rancour, and to listen to each other with respect", as was exemplified by Congress, "where people who suffered through prison sentences and exiles sit next to those who share the responsibility of the government's policies which brought about those prison sentences and those exiles". The deputy of the PNV believed "that the amnesty does not respond to politics, it responds to the need to find the best solution to a difficult problem". In much the same way, Josep María Triginer, spokesperson for the Catalan Socialist Group, believed that "the promulgation of the amnesty was the beginning of a new era of trust", in which political differences could be resolved in Parliament and formulas could be adopted to strengthen "understanding and solidarity between Spanish people". The same

23 *Diary of the Plenary Sessions in the Congress of Deputies*, Sesión Plenaria, n. 11, 14 October 1977. *Official Parliament Gazette*, no. 24, 14 October 1977.

24 Antonio Carro Martínez, AP deputy, argued that the amnesty they were debating on would not contribute to a national reconciliation, but to creating "social insecurity by institutionalising ignorance of the constitutional State and a profound erosion of authority".

25 He wanted to underline the magnanimity of the Communist Party when "it had been the communists, specifically, who had been so wounded, had suffered so much, had buried so many of their people along with their rancour. We are willing to drive forward through the path of freedom, the path of peace and progress."

spirit of harmony underlined Arias-Salgado's statement. The UCD representative said that the amnesty "was the ethical-political capital of the democracy".

The groups that supported the Bill believed it would put an end to terrorism. The Basque deputy of the PSOE, José María Benegas, called for calm from the Basque people and explained that it was a blanket amnesty for "all of the Basque people" because the measures extended to 6 October and therefore included ETA prisoners, who were in the Basque prisons of Basauri and Martutene, for crimes committed before 15 June. However, another Basque deputy, Francisco Letamendía, otherwise known as Ortzi, who abstained from the debate, did not agree. His position must be understood in the context of the internal circumstances of his party, the EE. While the majority sector, led by Mario Onaindía, was committed to driving the law forward,[26] the Congress deputy progressively distanced himself from his colleagues, and did not even enquire as to how they voted. Onaindía justified his abstention as serving the need to substitute "the heirs to the legacy of the dictatorship with others who can serve the devolved powers". A year later, Letamandía himself said that "the amnesty is not a humiliating forgiveness of people who are still considered criminals. On the contrary, it is the recognition of the rights of a people who had used whatever means were available to them to defend themselves from the attacks of the dictatorship."[27]

As mentioned previously, the debate on the law in Parliament was characterised by an almost complete lack of due judicial diligence, when, paradoxically, there were excellent jurists in Parliament and in the Senate. The only parliamentary spokespeople who critiqued the Law from a legal standpoint were Antonio Carro Martínez and Hipólito Gómez de las Roces. The former, an AP deputy, was a doctor at law and had been the last Minister for Justice of the Francoist government (between 3 January 1974 and 12 December 1975), during Arias Navarro's term; thus, he had been directly involved in drafting the pardons that were granted to commemorate the coronation of the King. Carro Martínez, in the spirit of the doctrine of the time – but without invoking it explicitly – stated that "dealing with the concept of an amnesty, which pardons ruthless crimes committed in cold blood, means that doubts are raised in relation to the legitimacy of those crimes, which could be socially intolerable and gravely pernicious". Poignantly, he said that amnesty is something "so extraordinary that some Western civilisation had not made use of them in centuries".

Hipólito Gómez de las Roces, of the Aragonese Centre Candidacy, had also been part of the Francoist regime. He was a barrister at law who belonged to the Juridical-Military Corp and was president of the Provincial Council of Saragossa between 29 March 1974 and 2 April 1977. He justified his abstention on grounds

26 Onaindía, 2004, p. 160.
27 Letamendía, 1978, p. 22. Along the same lines: Miguel Castells, *Iraultza*, no. 16, 4 November 1977.

of a lack of technical quality in the Draft Law,[28] and because the time limit for corrections had been eliminated.

3 Passing the Law

The Amnesty Law was passed on that same day, 14 October, by a majority of 296 in favour, 2 against, 18 abstentions (AL, Basque Country Left and Aragonese Centre Candidacy) and 1 void. The AP did not vote against in order to avoid being projected as obstructionists to democracy.[29] The vote was followed by a huge ovation and a prolonged applause, with the majority of the deputies on their feet.[30] The law was passed in the Senate with a majority of 195 votes in favour, 6 abstentions and no votes against.[31] Independent senator, Lluís María Xirinacs, of the parliamentary group Catalan Agreement of Progress, had stayed on his feet throughout the whole process to raise awareness of the importance of passing the amnesty. He finally sat down when the law was passed.[32]

Jaime Ignacio del Burgo, a senator for the UCD and then Second Secretary to the Upper House, recounts the emotional intensity of the vote in Parliament:

> It was an historic, exciting session that demonstrated the conciliatory and reconciliatory spirit that defined Spanish society at the time. There was a determined and sincere willingness to move on, to wipe the slate clean and start again. The speech of Socialist senator, José Prat, who had returned from exile after Franco's death, was striking. As secretary of the Committee I sat next to the vice-president of the Congress, Ramón Rubial, Biscay Senator and national president of PSOE, who had served time in jail and whose emotion was palpable.[33]

28 He stated, fairly reasonably, that "it was a legal text full of legal imprecisions. I only need to turn your attention to article no. 1 of this unstudied Draft Law. Simply, as I understand it, it lacks the fundamental requisites criminal law, and this is something that, as legislators, we cannot ignore."

29 Aguilar, 2008, p. 294, n. 120.

30 *Diary of the Sessions in the Congress of Deputies*, Plenary Session, n. 11, 14 October 1977. *Official Parliament Gazette*, no. 24, 14 October 1977.

31 *Diary of the Sessions in the Senate*, Plenary Session, no. 8, 14 October 1977. *Official Parliament Gazette*, no. 24, 14 October 1977.

32 In the first half of the 1960s, this activist had been imprisoned numerous times. He was a follower of Gandhi's pacifist theses, and amongst the protests for amnesty he participated in, the most noteworthy were the *Marxa de la Llibertat* (March for Freedom), and a set of protests and protest acts that began in Catalonia in the summer of 1976. Woking alone, he also protested for one year and nine months by standing for 12 hours in front of the Model Prison of Barcelona, something which he only stopped doing after the Amnesty Law of 1977 was passed. See Fernández Balbuena, 1978.

33 Jaime Ignacio del Burgo interview, 14 May 2016 (Del Burgo, 2016).

Many scholars claim that the political consensus behind the Amnesty Law strengthened its democratic value.[34] Yet the UN Special Rapporteur on Torture, Juan Méndez, has recently criticised the Spanish transitional model because, regardless of the overall majority that passed Law 46/1977, the law failed to recognise the victims of Francoist crimes, relegating them to a past that had to be forgotten while the crimes in question were granted impunity. The fact that the law makes no reference to human rights, or the fact that it was developed without the victims being involved, makes the law a falsely democratic one.[35]

The Amnesty Law 46/1977, of 15 October, came into force two days later when it was published in the *Official State Gazette*.[36]

4 Temporal limits of the law

The Amnesty Law did not specifically set a date for the beginning of the temporal scope of the law, which is in stark contrast to the level of precise detail regarding the date beyond which crimes could not be amnestied.

The authors of the law, under pressure from the political and social events of the times, focused on setting, in article 1, the most recent time limits in order to be able to extend the benefits of the amnesty to those that were still in prison for terrorist crimes. For this reason, and as was evinced by the speech given by deputy Benegas, those who had committed crimes between 15 December 1976 and 15 June 1977 were released from prison.

The lack of a concise start date was flagged in the first article with the explanation that it should be interpreted as "the moment in which the criminal activity in question was carried out". To frame it in such a way meant that many of the effects produced by the amnesty were *ex tunc*, that is, from the outset.[37] This temporal delimitation sought to include the Republican side because it had to take into account that the pardons granted by Francoism, although resulting in prisoners being set free, did not eliminate criminal records. This was finally achieved with the 1977 Amnesty Law. The measure was necessary so that the amnestied parties from the Republican side could have access to the other restitutive economic measures that would be implemented in the following months and years.

5 Applying the amnesty

Article 9 established how the Amnesty Law would be applied:

34 Cf. the work of Paloma Aguilar on the Amnesty Law referenced at the beginning of the chapter.
35 Méndez, 2013, p. 23.
36 Law 46/1977, 15 October, of Amnesty. *Official State Gazette*, no. 248, 17 October 1977, pp. 22765–22766.
37 Sobremonte Martínez, 1979, p. 329.

> The application of the amnesty, in each case, will be the exclusive responsibility of the corresponding Judges, Courts and Legal Authorities, who will make, in accordance with the procedural laws in force and as a matter of urgency, the pertinent decisions in observance of this law, whichever the stage of the process or the jurisdiction.
>
> The decision will be made within a time period of three months, without detriment to ulterior resources, with no suspensory effect.
>
> The amnesty will be applied *ex officio* or at the request of a party at a hearing. The act of applying for it will be public.

As Josep María Tamarit indicated, this meant that the extinction of criminal responsibilities would be decided on a case-by-case basis by a judge after beginning criminal proceedings. Three aspects would be necessary to reach a decision: the criminal act, the identity of its author or other people indirectly involved in the criminal act, and the political motivation behind it.[38]

This process was followed only in cases where the aim was to free those who, at the time, remained in prison. It was a complementary measure to article 10 of the law, which established that "the competent court would immediately sanction the release of those who remained in prison and were beneficiaries of the amnesty, and would withdraw the warrants for the arrest of those who were missing and declared in rebellion". This is confirmed by Miguel Castells,[39] lawyer of many political prisoners and one of the founding members of the pro-amnesty management group *Gestoras Pro Amnistía*. The procedure was carried out with haste and without due process, to the point that political prisoners who benefitted from the law (or the previous Amnesty Law) were not provided by the courts or the prison authorities with any legal document which certified their amnesty and their release from prison.[40] The thousands of amnestied politicians and civilians who were not in prison did not receive documentation to prove their court-ordered amnesty either,[41] which caused significant legal problems down the line, especially in the case of some amnestied workers.

6 Criminal amnesty for political crimes against Francoism

As per the first article of Law 46/1977, the amnesty was extended to criminal acts and offences that: (a) were motivated politically, whichever their consequences, and filed as crimes and offences that took place before 15 December 1976; (b) were crimes that took place between 15 December 1976 and 15 June 1977, and behind their political motivation was a motive to re-establish public liberties or to call for the autonomy of Spanish communities; and (c) were of the same nature and motivation

38 Tamarit Sumalla, 2012, p. 89.
39 Miguel Castells Arteche interview, 6 May 2016 (Castells Arteche, 2016).
40 Bixente Serrano Izko interview, 14 June 2016 (Serrano Izko, 2016).
41 Javier Urroz interview, 12 May 2016 (Urroz, 2016).

as described in point (b), and took place before and including 6 October 1977, and as long as they did not involve serious violent attacks against the life or integrity of people.

In article 2, the law also included: (a) acts of rebellion and sedition, as well as crimes and offences committed on the grounds of, or motivated by, these, and classified under the Military Justice Code; (b) refusal to serve for the Army as a conscientious objector on ethical or religious grounds; (c) obstruction of justice by refusing to reveal criminal activity of a political nature, witnessed while on professional service; and (d) acts of expression of opinion through the press or any other media.

The fourth article also granted amnesty to judicial disciplinary offences and politically motivated administrative or governmental infringements, excluding tax violations.

It is necessary to point out that the amnesty contained in article 2 a) for rebellion and sedition, as well as crimes and offences committed on the grounds of, or motivated by, these, as classified in the Military Justice Code, did not relate to "those who led the military insurgency against the Republic", as Josep María Tamarit contends.[42] The transition kept the Francoist legislature in force and did not restore the Republican legislature which had been derogated as a result of the 1936 coup d'état. The amnesty for rebellion referred to political prisoners who were sentenced in the military court under the Decree of the 21 of September, 1960, which equated acts of terrorism with military rebellion, whilst the amnesty for sedition referred to social prisoners sentenced for participating in hunger strikes that jeopardised the security of the State or caused a considerable disturbance to national production lines, according to the reform in the 1965 Criminal Code.

Francisco Bueno Arús[43] and Daniel Vallès[44] claim that the Amnesty Law interpreted political crimes subjectively, in terms of their purpose or the motivation behind the crime, instead of interpreting in terms of the nature of the law that was infringed. This meant that the parameters of the amnesty were wider than if they had adopted an objective interpretation, that is, a perspective that only took into account the crime committed, and thus, the particular political intention could cover a great variety of crimes.

The political amnesty, as mentioned above, had the support of every group except the AP, which, during the parliamentary debate, maintained that the law on amnesty "is not a panacea" for the terrorist attacks on Spanish democracy. The "only remedies that genuine and consolidated democracies use is a strict application of the law", that is to say that "a responsible democracy cannot continue to grant amnesties to those who are destroying it". When Antonio Carro spoke about granting amnesty for "ruthless crimes committed in cold blood", he

42 Tamarit Sumalla, 2012, p. 87.
43 Bueno Arús, 1977.
44 Vallès Muñío, 2004, p. 6.

was obviously referring to crimes committed by terrorist groups. Never did he apply the same criteria to evaluate his own actions or the actions of his political party, because, for the AP, the violations of human rights carried out by the Francoist regime were perfectly legal.[45] But there was one more twist of fate in his destiny. Carro, who had his unspent criminal responsibilities quashed by the Amnesty Law, was eventually charged by the Argentinian judge María Servini in 2014.[46]

Politicians from the left avoided talking about terrorism because they considered that the various anti-Francoism armed groups were fighting for freedom and democracy. The term was also avoided by Basque and Catalan nationalists. Xabier Arzalluz, during the parliamentary debate, went as far as saying that "it is not appropriate to talk about terrorism, because there was culpability on both sides", which carried the implied accusation that the Francoist regime was a terrorist State. The opposition to Francoism thus reconciled, in varying degrees and with different nuances, how ETA justified its own struggle. An example of this is the letter that prisoner Pedro Ignacio Beategui (also known as *Wilson*), wrote in relation to his hunger strike, calling for a blanket amnesty and the restoration of freedom for the Basque people. The letter is dated the end of the summer of 1977:

> What we understand as an amnesty is the cancellation of all court proceedings against us, and the restoration of all the guarantees and judicial rights we are entitled to. We are anti-Francoist fighters against fascism. This is not about us wanting a pardon or clemency. We want the right for freedom of an oppressed people to be recognised. A genuine, blanket amnesty for the Basque Country does not mean releasing political prisoners, it means changing the way politics are done, changing the structures of the system, and recognising human rights and the rights of our people. What we see nowadays, and it's something that doesn't make sense, is that, while political prisoners are being released, repression and imprisonments continue, and the police continue to act against the smallest demonstrations or manifestations where people are calling for their rights, their freedom. This is not a true amnesty. This is fascism with a mask on. While this situation is allowed to continue, the Basque Country will not be able to talk about peace, reconciliation or democracy.[47]

45 This is corroborated in his own legal research when he was a lecturer in the political law department in the University of Madrid (Carro Martínez, 1965, and Carro Martínez, 1975). This last work resulted from a conference he gave whilst he was Minister of Justice, during the commemoration of the 11th anniversary of the University's Centre for Advanced Studies in National Defence, on 4 February 1975.

46 He was charged along with ministers Licinio de la Fuente, Antonio Barrera, José María Sánchez-Ventura and Alfonso Osorio, all of whom faced life in prison.

47 Cited in Portell Manso, 1977.

This perspective views political amnesty in terms of an internal armed struggle. This would prove to be legally significant, given that, recently, article 6.5 of Protocol II, added to the 1949 Geneva Conventions on the protection of victims of international armed conflicts (8 July 1977), established that after the hostilities of an internal armed struggle ceased, "the authorities in power would try to grant the widest possible amnesty to the people who had participated in the conflict, or who were deprived of their freedom by being interned or imprisoned for reasons relating to the armed conflict".[48] This precept sought to foment acts of reconciliation that would contribute to re-establishing and normalising relationships in a divided nation.[49]

It is not uncommon to read that the political amnesty occasioned the release of numerous prisoners.[50] But the reality is that the majority of political prisoners had already been released. Only the 89 remaining prisoners who had been charged with terrorist activity were set free. These were: 53 members of GRAPO, 23 of ETA, 16 anarchists, 12 of FRAP, nine of the PCE (i) and four of the Catalonian Liberation Front.[51]

Article 1 I.b) – which fixed the aforementioned temporal scope between 13 December 1976 and 15 June 1977, "in the spirit of re-establishing public freedoms and in recognition of the autonomy of communities in Spain" – facilitated the release of the remaining prisoners.[52] It was, without doubt, a political decision that resulted from the agreement reached between those who redacted the Amnesty Law, which, as mentioned above, was opposed by the AP and a sector of the judicial doctrine of the time.[53] Nevertheless, with the passing of time, the Supreme Court began to understand article 1 I.b) in a way that contradicted its application of amnesty to pro-independence terrorism. The sentence passed in the Second Chamber of the Supreme Court on 30 December 1980 specified that when the Amnesty Law related to acts "motivated by the restitution of public freedom", it had to interpret:

> that such freedoms relate to human rights, to contributing to society by undertaking public duties, to pluralism and the multi-party system, to the freedom of political association and participation, to the freedom to unionise and to establishing a democratic regime based on the three traditional

48 Spain took 22 years to ratify it. Instruments for Ratifying Protocols I and II added to the Geneva Conventions of 12 August 1949, relating to the protection of victims of international and non-international armed conflicts, Geneva, 8 July 1977. *Official State Gazette*, no. 177, 26 July 1989, pp. 23828–23863.

49 Freeman, 2009, pp. 34–35.

50 For example, Gil Gil, 2009a, p. 57.

51 *El País*, 15 October 1977.

52 As happened with Francisco Aldanondo, *Ondarruxi*, member of ETA-PM, who had been arrested on 8 March 1977, in a police control exercise in Itsasu (French Basque Country), and who was the last of the 89 prisoners to be released from prison in December 1977.

53 Bueno Arús, 1977, pp. 6–7.

> powers and presided over by a representative Parliament [...] whose deputies or representatives are elected by a direct, universal and secret vote.[54]

The subsequent sentence on 28 November 1986, passed in the Second Chamber of the Supreme Court, established jurisprudence on the matter.[55] The sentence was passed in the trial of Carles Sastre i Benlliure, member of EPOCA, who was arrested in January 1985. On 28 October of that same year, he was found guilty in the National High Court and was sentenced to 48 years in prison for his involvement in the assassination of Catalan businessman Josep Bultó Marqués on 9 May 1977. The Supreme Court dismissed an appeal for annulment filed against the sentence passed in the National High Court on the grounds that Sastre's case was not covered by the Amnesty Law, which differentiated between pro-independence and pro-autonomy motives. The latter, which are covered under the Amnesty Law, do not threaten the integrity of the State, as reflected in the definitions of "autonomy" and "autonomous community" in the Spanish constitution.[56]

The release of prisoners in 1977 did not bring an end to terrorism. In the first instance, it was thought that this objective could be achieved, and the Gipuzkoa pro-amnesty management group even went as far as announcing that it was disbanding, a decision that was followed by the other management organisations.[57] But ETA-M, FRAP and GRAPO[58] decided to continue their armed struggle and intensified their activities. ETA tried to make a show of strength to offset the demobilisation of the people that resulted from the promulgation of the Amnesty Law, while at the same time it pressured the government with a war of attrition, with which it sought to achieve its objectives.[59] In such circumstances, politicians, jurists and journalists constantly invoked the Amnesty Law as an "end of story measure" (*punto y final*) to close the chapter of dictatorship in Spanish history.

The State enacted a new piece of anti-terrorism legislation that placed greater emphasis on distancing itself from the Francoist legislature. The so-called "Moncloa Pacts" in October 1977, agreements reached by the main political parties of the transition, laid the foundations for the "de-politicisation" of terrorism in future legal texts. Terrorism was reduced to mean merely "crimes committed by armed and organised groups", avoiding thus any suggestions of political persecution. This new criminal legislation on terrorism was inspired by the

54 Sentenced by the Supreme Court on 30 December 1980.
55 Sentence passed in the Supreme Court on 28 November 1986.
56 Sastre appealed the sentence passed in the Supreme Court in the Constitutional Court, but it was deemed inadmissible. Judicial resolution no. 417/1987 of the Constitutional Court, Section 4a, 1 April 1987.
57 *El País*, 11 December 1977. See Letamendía, 1994, vol. 2, pp. 64–65 and 74–75.
58 If, in the first few years of the transition, terrorist acts caused the relatively low number of less than 30 deaths a year (26 in 1975, 21 in 1976 and 28 in 1977), from 1978, this figure escalated to 85, reaching the maximum figure of 124 fatalities in 1980. To these figures we must also add the numerous kidnappings.
59 Sánchez-Cuenca Rodríguez and Aguilar Fernández, 2009.

contemporaneous European Convention on the Suppression of Terrorism (1977),[60] and set itself apart from Francoist tradition. As the years passed, the constant presence of terrorism during the 1980s paralleled the consolidation of democracy, which is why the majority of progressive Spanish people distanced themselves from identifying with ETA as a symbol for the fight against Franco.

This notwithstanding, repeat offenders with criminal records predating 6 October 1977 had their records quashed. In fact, judges were extremely careful not to take into consideration pre-amnesty crimes when dealing with recidivism, in observance of the Amnesty Law. Any previous crimes were no longer part of the defendant's criminal record, which is furnished by the Central Registry of Convicts and Fugitives at the beginning judicial inquiries The amnesty also had international repercussions, as evidenced by the French justice system and the case of Julen de Madariaga, one of the founding members of ETA, who had been convicted in the 1970 Burgos trials despite having been declared a fugitive. He was amnestied under Law 46/1977, and took refuge in Iparralde (French Basque Country), where he remained. He gained French citizenship in 1986, and on 27 May 1988 he was sentenced to four years in prison by the French justice system.[61] The district attorney did not bring up anything about his record before 1977 because he had been amnestied, and focused solely on the charges for which he was on trial.[62]

Terrorist acts were not the only crimes that were granted amnesty. There were others of great political significance that were not extensively covered by media, mainly those contained in article 2 b) (conscientious objectors for religious or ethical reasons), article 2 c) (obstruction of justice by refusing to reveal crimes of a political nature, witnessed while on professional service) and article 2 d) (expression of opinions through the press and any other media). There was really no need to include under the Amnesty Law these crimes, which were severely punished under the Francoist Criminal Code, as they were acts that were illegal under the new democratic code anyway because they were linked to the very essence of the democracy, especially in relation to freedom of speech and the expression of an opinion in public.[63] As José Antonio Martín Pallín states, it was "incidental or a legal oversight that had no precedents in any country where a democracy was established".[64]

60 Specifically, the laws originating from the convention were Law 56/1978, 4 December, in relation to special measures for terrorist crimes committed by armed groups (*Official State Gazette*, no. 293, 8 December 1978, p. 27785); Law 82/1978, 28 December, a modification to the Criminal Code in relation to terrorism (*Official State Gazette*, no. 11, 12 December 1979); the actual Spanish Constitution from the same year and the subsequent Law 11/1980, 1 December, on the envisaged circumstances contained in article 55.2 of the constitution (*Official State Gazette*, no. 289, 2 December 1980). See Asúa Batarrita, 2002, p. 72.

61 He was released on 14 August 1991, after serving three years in the Bois d'Arcy prison.

62 Bixente Serrano Izko interview, 14 June 2016 (Serrano Izko, 2016).

63 García Arán, 2009, pp. 188–189.

64 Martín Pallín, 2011, p. 62.

With regard to the amnesty for conscientious objectors on religious or ethical grounds, suffice it to say that it was directed at Jehovah's Witnesses, pacifists and libertarians who were rigorously prosecuted in military courts for refusing to do military service and given prison sentences.

7 Criminal amnesty for Francoist crimes

7.1 Amnesty for the violation of human rights by the dictatorship

Law 46/1977 failed to declare the illegality of Francoism, thus allowing the dictatorship to be forgotten, hidden behind the collective amnesia. "The amnesty became amnesia for the sake of governance, stability and peace",[65] as José Antonio Martín Pallín and Rafael Escudero said, summarising succinctly what happened with regard to the amnesty granted to the dictatorship for violation of human rights.

As mentioned previously, article 2e) granted amnesty to crimes and infringements that could have been committed by authorities, civil servants and public order agents when investigating or persecuting crimes covered under the law; and article 2f) to crimes committed by civil servants and public order agents for preventing people from exercising their personal rights. At the time the law was enacted, October 1977, these "personal rights" were ambiguous given that they had not been defined in any section of the Spanish constitution.

Beyond the stipulations contained in the law, Francoists who had violated human rights were also affected by another measure. Although the doctrine of the time moved quickly to establish that politically motivated acts – regardless of the result, and classified as crimes or infringements committed before 15 December 1976 – as per article 1b, would only be considered as such if they were crimes against the national security of the State, classified as such the moment the Amnesty Law was passed.[66] The subsequent legal application extended this conceptualisation to include Francoist crimes, which gave rise to the situation today, where the lack of legal precision in article 1b) meant that the amnesty was extended to both the groups that opposed the regime and the authorities and civil servants who were responsible for the crimes.[67]

Hundreds of Francoist repressors went unpunished, a situation that contrasted with the 89 political prisoners convicted of terrorist crimes who remained imprisoned until they were released under the Amnesty Law. It is difficult to estimate how many Francoists were amnestied, as it was only after charges were brought by Judge María Servini de Cubría that the process of identifying those responsible for human rights violations (and who were still alive) was initiated. The number

65 Martín Pallín and Escudero Alday, 2008, p. 10.
66 Bueno Arús, 1977, p. 6.
67 Vallès Muñío, 2004, p. 6.

continues to grow as new charges are added to the case. Obviously, the number was much higher in October 1977.

In relation to the amnestied public order forces, on top of going unpunished, their passive rights were recognised in observance of article 7e), even if these public bodies had been dissolved. In this regard, David Vallès gives the example of amnestied members of the public order force who had been suspended or convicted, for instance, for the unlawful killing of a protestor. With the amnesty, such public order enforcers would receive the salary that had been withheld while they were suspended from work, or their salary would be redeemed, equal to the duration of the sentence served.[68]

The very delicate political situation at the time, the weakened negotiating position of the opposition from the left, and the matters settled as part of the reconciliation discourse, meant that article 7e) could not be questioned by any of the parliamentary groups, not even by the PSOE, which years before had been the pillar of the project the British Labour Movement initiated to prosecute Francoist crimes. In 2002, amid criticism emanating from sectors of the left regarding the amnesty, the socialist leader, Felipe González, explained that the power relationships between the right and the left in 1977 made "any other situation impossible", because "they did not have enough strength or power to ask for justice, never mind explanations of the past".[69] As Josep Fontana said, it was a situation that was representative of the manner in which the transition was negotiated:

> the parties on the left abandoned their principles in exchange for an invitation to participate in the parliamentary game, which was led by the very people who had attacked it in 1936. They allowed amnesty for the crimes committed during the nearly four decades of the governmental dictatorship – never occurring to anyone to ask the opinion of the *victims of Francoist terrorism*, who had been systematically marginalised – and, worse than that, allowed those whose abuses had been forgiven to continue at the helm of the justice administration.[70]

According to Jaime Sartorius, the negotiations held by the parliamentary commission that prepared the Law did not bring up the matter of amnesty for Francoist crimes, and he himself, in 2010, seem to resist the idea that the overall tenor of the Law should make this reference, given that, in his opinion, it did not represent the will of those who drafted the legal text.[71] It may the case that article 2e) fell under the radar because it was not given a denomination and was only a part of a wider article.[72] The reality is that at no time during the parliamentary debate was the amnesty for Francoist crimes mentioned explicitly, although it was

68 Vallès Muñío, 2004, p. 9.
69 González Márquez and Cebrián, 2002, p. 26.
70 Fontana, 2012, p. 15.
71 J. Sartorius, "La Ley de Amnistía no ampara al franquismo", *El País*, 15 March 2010.
72 Clavero, 2014, p. 114.

implied in all the calls for forgetting the past and for reconciliation. Communist Marcelino Camacho, for example, stated that the communists saw the amnesty as "reparation for the injustices committed throughout the forty-year dictatorship", a "political and national policy, the only one of any consequence that can close the door on the Civil War and conflicts in the past". The speech of socialist José María Benegas was equally significant. He began by paying tribute to those who had died fighting against Francoism. He stated that "no democracy can be constructed while there are still prisoners, exiles and victims of the dictatorship that it is trying to replace". The new law would bury the "Civil War, the division between Spaniards and the responsibilities derived from those who had fought for freedom, who had opposed those who tried to silence the forces of reason with violence and authoritative power". The Basque nationalist Xabier Arzalluz went as far as calling for an amnesty "for one and all, and for all to forget", given that "both sides had blood on their hands".

The way this matter was dealt with, quietly and swiftly, was probably because it would have been shameful for the groups of the opposition to openly recognise it, especially at a time when it was important to highlight to the public what an achievement it had been to reach an agreement for the sought-after political and labour amnesties. For its part, the UCD could not publicly rejoice in a measure that granted amnesty to its own directors. Minister Rodolfo Martín Villa, for example, had been involved in recent crimes, such as the events in Vitoria on 3 March 1976, which ended with five workers murdered. But the silence had as much to do with the pressure to pass the Law quickly, which stemmed from the opposition's obsession with giving an immediate response to the political problem posed by the political prisoners. Thus, the mistake was made whereby the transition process was carried through without considering the violations of human rights in accordance with international law, failing to avoid granting impunity for these crimes, and without guaranteeing the recognition of victims' rights.[73] Impunity, as is well known, is an obstacle on the road to reconciliation.[74] Javier Chinchón rightly believes that the transition was marked by a "striking lack of legal coherence", given that, on one hand, Spain ratified an international treaty which obliged the nation to operate in a certain way, while, on the other hand, a law was passed which directly opposed the treaty.[75] The decision to avoid a legal discussion on the violation of human rights[76] was taken without consideration of the consequence this would have in the medium to long term.

Nowadays, commentators strongly criticise those who drafted the law, and in general, criticise the deputies and senators who supported it. Judge José Antonio Martín Pallín went as far as saying that they had demonstrated an "astonishing

73 Bonet Pérez and Alija Fernández, 2009, p. 13.
74 Martín Beristáin, 2000, pp. 21–22. Vinyes, 2011a. Skaar, 2012, pp. 54–103.
75 Chinchón Álvarez, 2008a, p. 348.
76 Chinchón Álvarez, 2013, pp. 181–182.

level of ignorance" of international law.[77] There were a few exceptions such as Pablo Castellano, who, as mentioned earlier, had been a key figure in the British Labour project to file a case against Francoism. The other deputies were anxious to pass the law, and made the mistake of not doing enough research. As far as the opposition to the regime was concerned, they were blinded by the idea of reconciliation, and were victims of their own political inexperience, which is why they felt that they were deceived on this and other occasions.[78]

At the same time, the other deputies and senators who voted in favour of the law, equally inexperienced in political arenas, were dealing with a huge workload coming from the various fronts that opened simultaneously, and therefore could not pay attention to the Amnesty Law, trusting instead in the competence of their colleagues in the Commission. Even Basque politicians, who had more interest than anyone else in passing the law, found themselves in this situation.[79]

With this impunity the deputies and senators tried to build a solid future for peaceful coexistence,[80] but their commitment to the institutional amnesia forewent any consideration of their ethical duty to historical memory, which had been a common concern of western civilisations after the Second World War, mainly thanks to the work of philosophers such as Primo Levi, Leonardo de Benedetti and Hannah Arendt in relation to the memory of crimes against humanity. The latter, a German philosopher of Jewish descent, explained that it was necessary to bring Nazi crimes against humanity to justice, even if the victims were willing to forgive and forget.[81] The survivors of the Nazi holocaust in Auschwitz used the slogan "never again" to appeal to the use of memory as a way of avoiding a repeat of this horrific part of history. In his book *If This is a Man*,[82] Jewish-Italian Primo Levi analysed the process of dehumanisation and the total deterioration of the human being in concentration camps, and also called for the recovery of historical memory as a way of avoiding a repeat of the attacks that the Jewish community of Europe had suffered, a universal responsibility which had to be taken on by all of humanity. Memory, he argued, is necessary in order to avoid making suffering invisible and to not dehumanise.[83]

Based on absolute erasure of the past – to use the terminology the Max-Planck Institute of Foreign and International Criminal Law applied to the Spanish case[84] – the perpetrators of human rights violations were given total legal

77 Martín Pallín, 2011, p. 62.
78 Xabier Arzalluz interview, 12 June 2012 (Arzalluz, 2012).
79 Gregorio Monreal interview, 10 April 2016 (Monreal, 2016).
80 Juliá, 2003b, pp. 16–17. Juliá, 2008, pp. 101–102.
81 Arendt, [1963] 1994.
82 Levi, [1947, 1958] 1987.
83 On the application of the theories of Primo Levi to the Spanish situation, see Jimeno, 1999, p. 32; Mate, 2003; Mate, 2008; Mate, 2011.
84 Sancinetti and Ferrante, 1999, p. 51.

immunity.[85] It was a "preventative amnesty" – according to Bartolomé Clavero – that left little room for official and non-official reviews of the past to reveal the truth.[86] The dead, the tortured and the imprisoned were all viewed equally under the umbrella of reconciliation.[87] But the transitional process in Spain had little in common with other processes that profusely used the term "reconciliation", such as the process in South Africa. The transitional process in Spain did not seek justice, the search for the truth or complete reparation.[88]

The amnesty granted to both sides of the conflict, the oppressed and the oppressors, was equal in every way, with the only difference that, as Alicia Gil points out, the latter had been previously persecuted and many were ex-prisoners – released thanks to a pardon – or still serving sentences, while the former were never prosecuted.[89] But the difference between both sides was far more transcendental. The perpetrators of tortures and other crimes were amnestied under an abstract rule that invoked "crimes that may have been committed". There was no need to confess to the crimes, and they were therefore relegated to the past in complete anonymity, something which led to an anomalous democratic situation with no precedent in the contemporaneous transitional processes in Greece and Portugal. On the contrary, the opposition to the regime was amnestied for *de facto* committed crimes.[90] This conflation of repressors and victims went a long way towards mitigating the amnesty's power as an institution for the normalisation of the public relationships which had suffered under the totalitarian regime.[91]

It was not a self-administered amnesty, as the law was the result of the consensus reached between the majority of the political forces resulting from the democratic elections,[92] but it is also true that impunity for the repressive authorities was introduced by the UCD, which in itself suggests a certain level of self-administration, especially in light of the then-recent human rights violations on the part of the State security under the command of ministers such as Adolfo Suárez or Rodolfo Martín Villa. As Mercedes García Arán says, the progressive sectors within the regime, united under the UCD, had misgivings and feared that the new situation could turn on them and they would eventually be held accountable for their crimes,[93] which is why the amnesty for the authorities and for their civil servants was a condition they were not prepared to compromise on.

85 Amnistía Internacional España, 2006. Muniesa, 2007. Chinchón Álvarez, 2007a. Chinchón Álvarez, 2008a. Chinchón Álvarez, 2012a.
86 Clavero, 2014, p. 113.
87 Vinyes, 2010, pp. 57–67.
88 Tamarit Sumalla, 2009, p. 131. Vicente, 2009, p. 169.
89 Gil Gil, 2009a, p. 53.
90 Martín Pallín, 2008a, p. 32.
91 Baylos Grau, 2008, p. 194.
92 Chinchón Álvarez, 2007a. Gil Gil, 2009a, p. 101.
93 García Arán, 2009, p. 191.

The senator by royal appointment, Alfonso Osorio, who had previously been second Vice-President in the Suárez government and, before that, Minister of Justice in the Arias Navarro government, stated in his memoirs in 1980 that the ultimate aim of the law was to grant amnesty to those who were in prison or were in exile for having opposed the National Movement.[94] He failed to mention anything about the amnesty for supporters of Francoism, even though they too had been granted amnesty. Currently, Osorio is one of many implicated in the Argentinian lawsuit against Francoism for violations of human rights.

The impunity for Francoist crimes meant that the 1977 Amnesty Law was seen as a *punto final*, the "end of the story". The term as such was not used at the time,[95] but it is used frequently nowadays.[96] In contrast to the opinions of some notorious transitional justice theorists, such as Jon Elster, who believe that Law 46/1977 was the "end of the story",[97] some Spanish historians maintain that this was not the aim of the legal text, which did not seek to grant impunity to perpetrators and collaborators of the dictatorship's repression.[98] The legitimacy of the term does not offer much grounds for debate, given that one of the "fathers" of the law, socialist José María Benegas, did not hesitate to describe it as such.[99] On the opposite side of the ideological spectrum, Jaime Ignacio del Burgo, UCD senator and current member of the People's Party (PP), holds a similar opinion. In his view, the Amnesty Law "was proposed as a way to end the story of the Civil War, an ending in the spirit of an authentic and true reconciliation. The amnesty was a way of wiping the slate clean for everybody. Nobody

94 Osorio García, 1980.

95 It is a well-known fact that the term *punto y final* ("end of story") with regard to amnesty originated from the controversial *Punto Final* Law 23.492, promulgated on 24 December 1986 by the Argentinian president, Raúl Alfonsín. It established the prescriptions of crimes of enforced disappearances committed during the military dictatorship in Argentina. This amnesty would be granted to those who were not called to give a statement during the first 60 days after the promulgation of the law. The Argentinian National Congress annulled the law in 2003, a measure which was ratified in the Supreme Court on 14 July 2005, on the grounds that the law was unconstitutional, and would therefore de derogated.

96 *Inter alia*, Sevillano Calero, 2003, p. 302; Vallès Muñío, 2004, p. 4; Escudero Alday, 2013a; Clavero, 2014; and Lacasta Zabalza, 2015, pp. 95–96.

97 Elster, 2004.

98 For example, Molinero, 2009, p. 51.

99 "We could not begin a new democratic era with trials outstanding from the previous era, with people in jail and thousands of people yet in political exile. As with everything else at the time, the law was a product of a pact for which the defeated in the civil war and those persecuted for forty years had to put their emotions to one side and make a show of political generosity in order to advance the democratic process. I say this because the Amnesty Law from October, 1977, was a law that represented an end point, which meant that nothing of what happened between the 18 of July, 1936, and the 15 of July, 1977, could be subject to a legal trial [...]. That is to say, we rejected a revision of the past and thus rejected bringing charges against the crimes committed during the forty years of the dictatorship." Benegas, 2007.

would be put on trial or convicted for criminal acts predating the concession of the amnesty".[100]

There was no debate on the impunity granted to Francoist crimes outside Parliament. Given that the topic was avoided in debates in the debates in Congress and the Senate, the newspaper reports of the following day did not mention anything about the impunity for the Francoist regime either; even the media linked to different left-wing ideologies and the various peripheral nationalist movements failed to mention it, and opted instead to highlight the amnesty for the opposition to the Francoist regime, framing it as a huge achievement. It is as if no journalists bothered to read the legal text, or, if any of them did, as if they were unable to identify the consequences it would bring. Their eyes would soon be opened. The indignation of people on the left began to be felt in the weeks that followed, when the media reported on the amnesty granted to well-known torturers, such as José Matute Fernández, member of the Social Investigation Brigade in the Canaries, who had been due to go on trial for murder. The same thing happened with a member of the ultra-right wing, Mariano Sánchez-Covisa. The indignation reached the level of a public scandal when the National High Court granted amnesty to the two people charged with the murder of the communist lawyers in Atocha, Madrid, even though the prosecution managed to get the case thrown out in January 1978.[101]

Within academic circles, the matter of the amnesty for Francoist crimes was not even discussed by the specialist in the area, Enrique Linde.[102] The first criticism of the amnesty for Francoist crimes did not, in fact, come from the field of legal studies. The prestigious sociologist and political scientist José Vidal-Beneyto, notorious anti-Francoist and author of some of the first essays criticising the transition, pointed out, on 15 November 1980, that:

> We all know that the democracy now in place was built upon the headstone under which our collective memory is buried. This reality has two interpretations. The first, in my view the least convincing, relates to the political parties and the break they made with their immediate past, which, for the PSOE, was crystallised with schism that was produced in the Suresnes conference where Rodolfo Llopis and his friends were replaced by the Basque-Andalusian group at the helm, and, for the PCE, is represented in the inability of their directors to offer a critical self-evaluation and a lack of transparency when it came to explaining the process that took them from Stalinism to Eurocommunism. The second interpretation relates to the historical pact of silence that the left-wing powers agreed with the government

100 Del Burgo, 2015, vol. 2, p. 39. In this case, Del Burgo uses the term "end point" to refer to all those amnestied, and not just those responsible for state repression during Francoism.

101 Aguilar, 2008, p. 302.

102 There are no mentions of the matter in any of his studies after 1977. Linde Paniagua, 1998. Linde Paniagua, 2000.

> on the 15 of July, 1977. It was the price they had to pay to be allowed to participate in the process of reform, in the process of the legalisation of their parties and of their social legitimacy in the new democracy. Without it, obviously, it was impossible to make the transition from Alcalá road to the Moncloa.
>
> Without structures for internal support, the history of the Spanish democratic resistance was at the mercy of the vicissitudes of some, to be robbed of it by others, and at the mercy of the ignorance and the indifference of the rest. And in this way, while some disillusioned bourgeoisie democrats that had participated in the struggle invoked, on more than one occasion and in this very newspaper, their political past as a beautiful, useless event and reduced its relevance to the mere nostalgic aura of their personal memories, Francoism forced itself into the legacy they fought against and appropriated it for themselves and for their ideological underpinnings; more than an enemy of the past, they were its executioner.[103]

Amongst jurists, criticisms were conspicuously absent. It is very significant, for example, that José Antonio Martín Pallín made no mention of the impunity granted to the Francoist criminals in an article relating to the right to clemency in 1992,[104] published long before the resurgence of historical memory and the subsequent debate on the Amnesty Law.

The reaction on the part of the victims could be classified in two ways: on the one hand, the more recent victims who, as mentioned above, did not realise the extent of the amnesty until their torturers began dodging the trials they had pending. These victims became indignant with these one-off events, but they never considered that the majority of these repressors, who had never been prosecuted, would have actually been convicted. The issue was, in practice, irrelevant in light of the amnesty as a way to end the story of the Civil War. And in any case, these victims still had a long road ahead, starting with their own economic reparation. For their part, the families of those who had been executed celebrated the fact that the amnesty reached back as far as the Civil War, but were at the same time resigned to accepting that the people who murdered their fathers and their grandfathers were also covered by the amnesty.[105] It was not the time to demonstrate their displeasure with this aspect of the amnesty. They had enough on their plate trying to overcome the enormous difficulties of identifying the bodies of their family members, exhuming their bodies and giving them a dignified burial, an endeavour which took place amidst the pressure exerted by the powers of repression who had inherited the legacy of the dictatorship, and threats from extreme right-wing groups.[106]

103 *El País*, 15 November 1980. Also, Vidal-Beneyto, 1981.
104 Martín Pallín, 1992, pp. 307–322.
105 Molinero, 2009, pp. 53–54.
106 Aguilar, 2008.

The victims felt abandoned as the political parties of the left adopted a stance based on amnesia and the discourse of reconciliation. This cohort considered taking legal action, even amidst the problems they were having registering those who had been executed in the registry.[107] Particularly poignant is the story that Josefina Campos tells. A leading figure in the localisation and exhumation of enforced disappearances of the Civil War, she recounts a conversation when the remains of a group of executed Republicans were found in San Adrián (Navarre) in 1980. A group of people, including Campos herself and the socialist leader Gabriel Urralburu, were contemplating the remains of the executed, arranged in coffins in the square in front of the city council, when Josefina Campos, overcome with the intensity and the emotion of the moment, said: "My God!, How could they kill so many people?", to which Urralburu answered, connecting the events to the Amnesty Law, that the matter had to be put to one side, "now we're an embarking on a new era, the past must remain in the past."[108] Although he did not, Urraburu could have finished his sentence with "end of story".

7.2 A law that turned its back on the international law in force in October 1977

As mentioned in the previous chapter, the British Labour Movement planned to bring charges against Francoism for crimes during the dictatorship, probably conscious of the doubts raised by universal jurisdiction in relation to prosecuting crimes against humanity that predated the end of the Second World War. The reality is that during those years there was a certain understanding that the crimes previous to 1945 had prescribed. Illustrious lawyer, journalist and Francoist writer Torcuato Luca de Tena did not hesitate in pointing out in 1976 that the massacre of Paracuellos del Jarama (November to December 1936), carried out by the Republican side, was unprosecutable, but not forgotten.[109] Obviously, the prescription of crimes applied to both sides.

The Hague Conventions of 1899 and 1907 – along with the Martens Clause – concerning the protection of civil persons in time of war gave way, after the new order was established following the Second World War, to the Geneva Conventions, ratified on 12 August 1949, which in turn led to the universal persecution of war crimes, although internal armed conflicts were not yet under the obligatory universal jurisdiction. Two decades later, in 1969, Francoist Spain ratified the 1948 Convention on the Prevention and Punishment of the Crime of Genocide.[110] Four years later, the UN General Assembly issued its first disposition against blanket amnesty, establishing that "States will not adopt legislative

107 Espinosa Maestre, 2013, p. 144.

108 Josefina Campos interview, 7 May 2016 (Campos, 2016).

109 T. Luca de Tena, "Un regalo para Carrillo" ("A Present for Carrillo"), *ABC*, 31 December 1976. See Juliá, 2011, pp. 20–21.

110 UN Convention on the Prevention and Punishment of the Crime of Genocide, UNGA Res 260 (III)A of 9 December 1948. In force: 12 January 1951.

measures, nor any other type of measures, which undermine their duty on the international stage in relation to the identification, arrest, extradition and punishment of those responsible for war crimes of crimes against humanity".[111]

In October 1977, in the context of a Spain that had just ratified the 1948 Universal Declaration of Human Rights – developed by the 1950 European Convention for the Protection of Human Rights and Fundamental Freedoms and the 1966 International Covenant on Civil and Political Rights – it did not make sense for the democratic Parliament to extend the amnesty to crimes of genocide and to crimes against humanity without making explicit reference to them in the Amnesty Law. As Josep María Tamarit points out, Parliament was trying to build a democratic State based on respecting rights and human rights, and therefore genocide and crimes against humanity could not be subsumed under "politically motivated crimes".[112] These crimes would not prescribe, nor would they be covered by the Amnesty Law, and could therefore be persecuted.[113]

On 20 and 21 October 2008,[114] the United Nations Human Rights Committee met with Spanish representatives and recommended the derogation of the Amnesty Law, as it was in violation of article 15.2 of the International Covenant on Political and Civil Rights signed in New York in December 1966, which was later ratified by Spain in April 1977.[115] This article establishes that the non-retrospective nature of criminal regulations cannot be applied to obstruct the trial or the conviction of a person for a crime or negligence that at the time of its occurrence was not considered a criminal offence according to the general principles recognised by the international community. These people could, in fact, be prosecuted and convicted, even if the crimes they committed were not considered as such under the national rule of law at the time. Every single crime against humanity was recognised by the general principles of law.

The International Covenant on Civil and Political Rights represented the doctrine of international law of the time, relative to the impunity of perpetrators of grievous violations of human rights. Their criminal responsibilities could not be extinguished, and article 2.3 obliged nation states to make available the necessary resources for the persecution of violations of rights, in much the same way as article 12 of the European Convention on Human Rights does. The international law community, from then on, considered that impunity infringed on the obligations of states to investigate human rights violations, as well as on their duty to

111 *Principles of international cooperation in the detection of persons guilty of war crimes and crimes against humanity*. Adopted by Resolution 3074 (XXVIII) of the UN General Assembly on 3 December 1973.

112 Tamarit Sumalla, 2012.

113 See also Bassiouni, 1992. Akhavan, 2012.

114 UN, Human Rights Committee, *Report of Spain*, CCPR/C/ESP/CO/5, para. 9.

115 Spanish instrument of ratification, 27 April 1977, *Official State Gazette*, no. 103, 30 April 1977, pp. 9337–9343. In force since 27 July 1977.

process and convict those responsible for human rights violations with proportional sentences, thus guaranteeing the victims access to justice.[116]

Spain's ratification of the Covenant bolstered article 1.1 of Law 1/1977, 4 January, on Political Reform, which established that "democracy in the Spanish State is based on the supremacy of the Law, an expression of the sovereign will of the people", with the exception of fundamental personal rights, which are "inviolable and are shared between all the institutions in Spain". The basic rights of the individual were established in the Covenant when Spain ratified it on 27 April.

The 1977 Amnesty Law ignored Spain's commitment on the international scene. Josep María Tamarit points out that the law would be compatible with the Covenant if it were interpreted in a more restrictive way. The Covenant imposes on States the duty to investigate violations of human rights and to offer its resources to the victims. Specifically, articles 2, 3 and 15.2 do not appropriately establish a duty on the State to carry out a criminal investigation of possible violations. But the Amnesty Law should be interpreted with the proviso that crimes committed by those in power are not included. The most serious crimes perpetrated or ordered by the authorities against civil society – excluding torture – could be considered implicitly excluded from the Amnesty Law, as they were not mentioned in the preamble or in the legal text of the law, nor were they mentioned in the decrees that preceded it.[117] This hypothetical possibility, however, became unviable in light of the sentence dictated by the Supreme Court in relation to the trial of Baltasar Garzón.

Furthermore, the impunity granted to the perpetrators of torture was surprising, given that, as seen in Greece, torture contravened international regulations, which considered it a crime against humanity. The way the Amnesty Law framed torture as a politically motivated crime was, as José Antonio Pallín stated, a legal abomination.[118]

A month and a half after the Amnesty Law was enacted, Spain joined the European Council (24 November 1977), which meant that it assumed the duty of defending the civil rights advocated by this organisation, created after the Second World War to safeguard democratic values throughout Europe.[119] On that same day, the Spanish Minister for Foreign Affairs signed in Strasbourg the European Convention on Human Rights.[120] Article 7.2 of this Convention stated that it "shall not prejudice the trial and punishment of any person for any act or omission which, at the time when it was committed, was a criminal offence according to the general principles of law recognised by civilised nations". Spain did not

116 Sáez Valcárcel, 2011, p. 64.
117 Tamarit Sumalla, 2012, pp. 86–87.
118 Martín Pallín, 2008a, p. 32.
119 Treaty of London, 5 May 1949.
120 European Convention for the Protection of Human Rights and Fundamental Freedoms, 1950, accorded in Rome on 4 November 1950, and amended with additional Protocols 3 and 5, on 6 May 1963 and 20 January 1966, respectively.

ratify the Convention, on the grounds of a few reservations that in no way affected the Amnesty Law, until 4 October 1979.[121]

Although the Amnesty Law ignored the international law of the time, it never considered rejecting international bodies. It was not the right moment to do so. The tensions created by the Cold War had forced both sides to turn a blind eye to the human rights violations being committed by the respective regimes, as had happened in the 1970s with human rights violations in Latin America, which were characterised by a complete lack of interest in implementing international law to establish transitional justice measures.[122]

8 Labour amnesty

8.1 Labour amnesty in Law 46/1977

Law 46/1977 amnestied workers who had been removed from their positions for participating in unionised movements, although it is worth pointing out here that the crimes committed by the civil servants of the Francoist regime (discussed above) implied a *de facto* labour amnesty. Not having been prosecuted or purged, these workers of the State security forces continued in their positions and, in some cases, were even promoted.

This section focuses on the labour amnesty for workers, one of the main social and political demands made during the final years of the regime and the first years of the transition. As was pointed out earlier, the UCD government, under pressure from the business community,[123] was reticent when it came to applying this measure, and thus chose to use it as bargaining chip during the parliamentary debate on the Bill.

The labour amnesty ordinance in the actual law lacked its own regulation, and was instead specified as part of articles 5 and 8, which led Francisco Pérez Amorós to wonder, rather perceptively, whether these precepts had been added or shoehorned into the legal text after it had been redacted.[124] At no point do these articles imply that the amnesty incriminated the State and the repressive measures it used, which the business community benefitted from, especially in relation to political dismissals of workers.[125]

Article 5 of the law amnestied labour related to infringements that were considered legitimate exercises of workers' rights, as recognised in the international regulations and conventions that were in force when the Amnesty Law was enacted. For its part, article 8 established that:

121 *Official State Gazette*, no. 243, 10 October 1979, pp. 23564–23570.
122 Barahona de Brito, González-Enríquez and Aguilar, 2001, p. 22.
123 Aguilar, 2001, pp. 105 and 107–110. Molinero, 2009, p. 48. Pérez Amorós, 2009, pp. 147–149.
124 Pérez Amorós, 2009, pp. 154–155.
125 Clavero, 2014, p. 115.

> The amnesty invalidates legal resolutions and governmental or administrative acts that resulted in dismissals, punishments, limitations or suspensions of active or passive rights of employees, derived from the acts contained in articles 1 and 5 of the present Law, and restores the full rights that the affected would have had at the time of the application of the same had those measures not been implemented, including pension contributions to Social Security and Labour Mutualism, which, upon workers joining the register, will become the responsibility of the State.

These articles addressed the situation of those who had suffered sanctions or punishments for defending democracy and their labour rights.[126] It was the second time in the transition that an amnesty was directed at workers. As discussed in the previous chapter, the Royal Decree-Law of 30 July 1976 foresaw the restitution of active and passive rights to the civil servants who had been dismissed or sanctioned for political or social reasons.

The scope of the 1977 Law was much greater as it included every type of worker, whether a civil servant or not. It has been estimated that around 60,000 people were covered by the amnesty, which, as Carme Molinero points out, is evidence of how the workers' movement triumphed over the dictatorship. However, it also demonstrates that the labour community had suffered the heaviest consequences for its opposition to the regime.[127] The labour and union amnesty, thus, was of a profound political significance, which is why it was included with the political amnesty in the same law.

One of the most curious aspects of this Amnesty Law was its mechanism: the legal resolution on dismissals, sanctions or privation of welfare rights for political and labour reasons. The private sector's repression of the workforce was thus brought into the legal framework, which, in turn, meant that the private sphere was made public.[128]

It is something that deputy Francisco Letamendía had called attention to during his intervention in the debate in Congress when he said, "the labour amnesty must also include cases that are left ambiguous within the Bill, the cases of people who had to go into exile or that were arrested and are in prisons for law enforcement reasons, and it should also include the soldiers that fought for democracy against Francoism".

8.2 Technical difficulties in the application of the law

From the outset, amnestied workers faced huge problems when it came to having their rights recognised, beginning with the technical difficulties that the Administration encountered when coping with the economic burden derived from the

126 The labour amnesty contained in the Law of 15 October 1977 has been studied extensively. Of these, the most notorious are José Manuel Sánchez-Cervera Senra (Sánchez-Cervera Senra, 1978, pp. 197–211), Luis Enrique de la Villa and Aurelio Desdentado (De la Villa and Desdentado Bonete, 1978), and, more recently, Francisco Pérez Amorós (Pérez Amorós, 2009, pp. 71–165).

127 Molinero, 2009, p. 47.

128 Baylos Grau, 2008, p. 194.

law.[129] The Prosecution Office of the Supreme Court had to publish a Circular letter on 20 October to provide lawyers with general guidelines for a uniform interpretation of Law 46/1977. The confusion generated by article 5 provoked the following clarification:

> The information in relation to labour could result in an infringement of the regulations corresponding to the various legal orders but, to the effects of the amnesty and this circular letter, only those which resulted in a disciplinary sanction for the worker will be considered.
>
> In accordance with the legal text of the Law, the application of the amnesty to such infringements of disciplinary regulations requires:
>
> - The existence of some type of disciplinary sanction.
> - A record of the infringement that motivated it.
> - That said infringement derive from workers exercising their rights as recognised by the international law of the time.
> - That the infringement be committed on any date, even if it was committed before the incorporation of international regulations to our internal rule of law, but always before the 6th of October of this year, which is the temporal limit established for the application of the amnesty.[130]

The Directorate General for State Litigation also had to publish a Circular letter on the interpretation of the Amnesty Law for the benefit of public prosecutors.[131] The Circular clarifies aspects such as issues relating to pension contributions to Social Security which had been suspended as a result of the dismissal of amnestied workers.

The biggest obstacle for the application of the Amnesty Law was that certain labour regulations from Francoist times and the transition period were still in force and incompatible with the freedom of trade unions. The labour relations model of October 1977 was not sufficiently democratic, which meant that the amnesty could not be applied to its full extent.[132] Although article 5 specified that the right to amnesty had to include the actions that were punished as result of people exercising their labour rights, as recognised in the "international regulations and conventions currently in force",[133] the confusing and incomplete labour legal system in Spain failed to facilitate the reinstatement of workers.[134] In fact, a

129 Sainz Moreno, 1978, pp. 361–371.
130 Circular Letter 1/1977, 20 October, Prosecution Office in the Supreme Court.
131 Circular letter 1/1978, 23 January, by the Directorate General for State Litigation, on the interpretation of Law 46/1977.
132 Pérez Amorós, 2009, p. 155.
133 These international regulations and conventions were identified by Sánchez-Cervera Senra, 1978, pp. 202–204.
134 Pérez Amorós, 2009, pp. 159–160.

sentence passed in the Madrid Labour Court on 2 January 1978 pointed out that the Amnesty Law could not be applied because it contradicted the Francoist fundamental laws which were still in force.[135]

The second biggest obstacle the labour amnesty faced related to its scope: it did not constitute a blanket amnesty. Although, as mentioned previously, the labour amnesty was of great political significance, it failed to take into account important groups that were affected by the political amnesty. It is something that deputy Francisco Letamendía had called attention to during his intervention in the debate in Congress when he said, "the labour amnesty must also include cases that are left ambiguous within the Bill, the cases of people who had to go into exile or that were arrested and are in prisons for law enforcement reasons, and it should also include the soldiers that fought for democracy against Francoism". These lacunae would be covered in time with complementary measures, and, in many cases, because of social pressure.

Furthermore, not every worker that was dismissed for participating in general strikes was amnestied. Only those who did not participate in illegal strikes were covered by the law, as per article 33j of the Royal Decree-Law on labour relations from 9 March 1977,[136] which considered active participation in an illegal strike, or in any other form of collective disturbance of work, grounds for a legitimate dismissal. Article 11 had established that a strike would be illegal under any of the following:

a When it is initiated or maintained for political reasons, or with any other aim extraneous to the professional interests of those affected.
b When it is based on solidarity or support, unless it directly impacts on the professional interest of those who promote or maintain it.
c When its objective is to alter, while it is still in force, an agreement reached through a Collective Agreement or established in a ruling.
d When its occurrence conflicts with the present Royal Decree-Law, or what is expressly agreed upon in the Collective Agreement on the solution of conflicts.

The workers who participated in strikes during the last few years of Francoism and during the first transition were also affected by article 7, whose first condition indicated that workers could "exercise their right to strike only by discontinuing their services and not occupying the premises of their place of work or any of its branches or offices"; workers were also affected by article 2, which established that "rotating strikes, carried out by workers who lend their services in strategic sectors with the aim of disrupting the production line, work-to-rule strikes and, in

135 Sentence passed in the Labour Court, no. 11 in Madrid, 2 January 1978. Partially transcribed in De la Villa and Desdentado Bonete, 1978, pp. 40–43. See also, Diéguez, 1978, pp. 131–143. Pérez Amorós, 2009, p. 160, n. 284.

136 Royal Decree-Law 17/1977 on labour relations, *Official State Gazette*, no. 58, 9 March 1977, pp. 5464–5470.

general, any form of collective disturbance in the work that differs from a strike, will be considered illegal or abusive".

These filters meant that workers who had participated in strikes that did not directly concern matter of professional interest could not avail of the labour amnesty. The root of the problem was that, at the time, it was difficult to determine political and labour grievances. From that moment on, a conveyor belt of cases passed through the Supreme Court (analysed by Vallès[137]) which determined on a case-by-case basis whether the labour amnesty could or could not be applied.

To sum up, not every case of the labour struggle could avail of the benefits of the amnesty. By applying the aforementioned articles 7, 11 and 33j of the Decree-Law, the Supreme Court excluded from the amnesty those who had been fired for participating in violent strikes or for occupying work premises, as well as cases in which labour disturbances were politically motivated.

Workers faced a third problem, which is that, frequently, penalties and dismissals for participating in labour movements were not formalised as such, thus concealing their real cause. They were processed simply as disciplinary action, which meant that they were outside the remit of the labour amnesty.[138] Added to this, application of the Amnesty Law was also blocked in corporate cases that had not been prosecuted legally, or in cases where dismissal was not formalised because a "conciliation" had been reached in the corresponding department of the Francoist Vertical Syndicate.[139]

If, after all of this, workers could in fact avail of the labour amnesty, they often found themselves up against one last problem: the intransigent attitude of business owners who were being forced to readmit workers; this issue is extensively studied by Francisco Pérez Amorós.[140] Business owners had to reinstate workers to the positions from which they were removed, and with the same conditions they had enjoyed prior to their dismissal. The amnesty had presupposed the annulment of the original prosecution, but disciplinary actions were also ceased, which is why workers could exercise their rights retroactively, as established in a sentence passed in the Constitutional Court on 25 November 1986.[141] By October 1977 there was still no legal framework for reinstatement; it was a time in which the entrepreneur did not forfeit any control of the business organisation to its employees or unions. A full recognition of union freedom and associated collective efforts, such as collective negotiations and workers' participation in the organisation of the business, had yet to be achieved. Added to this, of course, was the economic crisis of the time.[142] Part of the doctrine even went as far as considering the possibility of "the State assuming financially liability" for forcing business owners to reinstate amnestied workers.[143] However, as

137 Vallès Muñío, 2014.
138 Pérez Amorós, 2009, p. 159.
139 De la Villa and Desdentado Bonete, 1978, pp. 80–83.
140 Pérez Amorós, 2009, pp. 160–163.
141 Sentence passed in the Constitutional Court, no. 147, 25 November 1986, Plenary. *Official State Gazette*, no. 295, 10 December 1986.
142 Pérez Amorós, 2009, p. 161–162.
143 Zorrilla Ruiz, 1977, p. 124.

Francisco Pérez Amorós points out, this would have required an identical restorative solution for the worker who had lost his job and salary.[144]

Business owners were able to bear the brunt of the amnesty reinstatements thanks to, in large part, the flexibility allowed by the labour law of the time in relation to the employee workforce, leading to a notable increase in managers allowing contracts to run down without renewing them.

8.3 Establishing the regulations in article 8 in relation to Social Security (29 September 1978)

The labour amnesty also had a restorative effect, given that the State took into account previous sanctions that might have caused gaps in Social Security contributions, which would in turn lead to reduced social security benefits

It took almost a year to establish the regulations of article 8 of the Law 46/1977 in relation to Social Security, finally established by Royal Decree on 29 September 1978.[145] As Aurelio Desdentado and Luis Enrique de la Villa have pointed out,[146] this Royal Decree put serious limitations on the benefits derived from the amnesty in relation to Social Security. Since the promulgation of the Amnesty Law, the courts had been satisfactorily resolving issues in the application of the law in relation to Social Security. Generally, judges declared that the State Administrations had to pay the contributions corresponding to the period of time amnestied and, from the moment the sentence was passed, the beneficiary could solicit the recognition of the benefits from the management body, submitting any discrepancies that could arise from said recognition to the labour jurisdiction. The judicial bodies were, therefore, in charge of interpreting the scope of the amnesty.

This process changed with the Royal Decree of 29 September 1978. The interventions from judicial bodies were replaced with a simple application for benefits and by a new process to determine the contributions payable by the State, which began to be more partial when it came to recognising this right. The number of beneficiaries was significantly reduced[147] and benefits were also

144 Pérez Amorós, 2009, p. 162.

145 Royal Decree 2647/1978, 29 September, to establish the regulations for the application of article 8 of the Law 46/1977, 15 October, on Amnesties in relation to Social Security. *Official State Gazette*, no. 268, 9 November 1978, pp. 25635–25636.

146 A. Desdentado and L. E. De la Villa, "La destrucción de la amnistía laboral", *El País*, 19 November 1978.

147 It excluded from the Social Security benefits derived from the amnesty, among others, the following workers: (a) self-employed; (b) workers included in mutual funds in lieu of obligatory systems, which included companies of great importance, such as the Bank of Spain or the National Institute for Industry; (c) employees who were not legally recognised despite being dependent workers and included in the Social Security, as was the case of the staff employed by the administration, management and regular staff who lent their services to managing bodies, etc.; and (d) workers who were not affiliated at the time of the sanction, who had been prior to the implementation of the sanction.

cut.[148] Finally, the benefits of the amnesty were temporarily limited, as they only came into effect from the first day of the month after the application was submitted. This was clearly prejudicial to the interests of those who had been granted amnesty, given that the majority of workers could only submit this form after their application for amnesty.

9 Complementary regulations to the Amnesty Laws (1978–1982) for the reparation of the Republican side

The unique nature of the amnesty has been justified in relation to the extraordinary circumstances around the pacification and reconciliation of the people of Spain, so long as, from a transitional justice perspective, the needs for justice and reparation of the victims were not neglected.[149] But reparation is not exclusive to Spain. It is, in fact, a common mechanism in transitional processes as a way of compensating for a historical injustice committed against the victims.[150]

The application of the Amnesty Laws of 1976 and 1977 required copious complementary regulations, dictated through the succeeding years. From 1978 onwards, a series of Royal Decree-Laws and Orders were administered little by little; together they managed, as Javier Chinchón and Alicia Gil point out, to substitute the model based on forgetting completely the past, to a model based on forgetting the past but also rehabilitating the victims.[151] The process to approve these compensatory measures were delayed for too long, sometimes up until the first decades of the twenty-first century.

One of the main challenges facing the transition was the lack of equality when it came to compensating both sides of the conflict. On the one hand, the widows, orphans, maimed soldiers and ex-captives received favourable treatment from the Francoist side, benefitting from the welfare system, while, on the other, the maimed soldiers of the Republican Army, retired Republican soldiers and the widows and orphans of former Republican soldiers, could not avail of any social assistance. The same could be said with the analogous grievances that arose between those who had been appointed to positions that had been forcefully vacated as a result of the purges, and those who had been forcefully removed from said positions, many of whom had, in fact, been executed or exiled.[152] The amnesty strove for equality between all the parties involved in the conflict,[153] but this was impossible to achieve in practice, given the high number of victims and the unfeasibility of economically repairing suffering which was so traumatic and which extended so far back into the past. One cohort of victims was completely

148 It excluded contributions "corresponding to work-place accidents and occupational illnesses, healthcare, social assistance and social services".
149 Lascuráin, 2011, pp. 95–113. Tamarit Sumalla, 2012, p. 86.
150 Thompson, 2002. Elster, 2006.
151 Chinchón Álvarez, 2007a, p. 137. Gil Gil, 2011.
152 Aguilar, 2008, p. 102.
153 Pérez del Valle, 2001, p. 195.

forgotten about, the disappeared of the Civil War and post-war years, who were not mentioned in any of the various laws on reparation.[154] Enforced disappearances of children during Francoism and the transition – that is, the "stolen babies" that were sold or put up for illegal adoption[155] – were not mentioned either. It was a topic that was not openly discussed, with parents living through the ordeal in solitude at a time when it was unimaginable that their cause would be taken up by the people in a movement calling for its recognition.

The first reparation measures implemented by Suárez's government were profoundly symbolic of reconciliation, as the focus was on the side that lost the Civil War. The Order issued by the Department of Education and Science on 31 January 1978 validated in all its effects all baccalaureate studies carried out in Republican zones during the Civil War, as long as it could be demonstrated that these studies were "carried out and assessed in recognised official institutions and that proof was presented to professors and teachers employed in regular academic institutions".[156] It was a necessary measure for those who had been deprived of recognition of their academic achievements and therefore could not access the labour market corresponding to the baccalaureate level of qualifications and, in some cases, university level qualifications. The measure thus was a necessary intermediary step before further economic reparations could be made. In practice, the number of people who benefitted from this measure was not very high because those affected were 57 years old or older, and did not have many job prospects on which to base a career following the concession of the Order.

The Order was followed by a Royal Decree issued by the office of the Head of State on 6 March 1978,[157] restricted, as stipulated in article 1.1, to "officers, non-commission officers and troops who had taken up work or had registered as students in military academies", before 18 July 1936 and who, as "members of the armed forces or public order forces", had participated in the Civil War. The Republican soldiers who could not be reinstated to the armed forces in 1977 were given a pension; if the soldier in question was deceased, his widow and child or children were given the pension. The monthly contribution was calculated to include the years of service these soldiers could have given had they been able to continue with their military careers in normal circumstances. The measure did not contemplate any retroactive effects. This Royal Decree was especially controversial because it did not give sufficient reparation, leading to Senator Javier Paulino Pérez (PSOE), on 9 January 1980, to question whether the Amnesty Laws and

154 Escudero Alday, 2013d, pp. 141–161.

155 Vinyes, Armengou and Belis, 2003. Vinyes, 2006, pp. 53–71. Rodríguez Arias, 2008. López Ortega, 2014, pp. 319–340.

156 *Official State Gazette*, no. 40, 16 February 1978, p. 3768.

157 Royal Decree-Law 6/1978, 6 March, to regulate the situation of military personnel who participated in the Civil War. *Official State Gazette*, no. 56, 7 March 1978, p. 5384.

the Royal Decree-Law 6/1978[158] complied with the Constitution. The political pressure exerted on this matter led to the promulgation of a new law on 14 March 1980, which modified the Royal Decree-Law of 6 March 1978.[159] The new measure extended the economic benefits derived from the previous Decree-Law to those professionals who, "before the 18th of July, 1936, had reintegrated to a military force, or on this date were members of the public order forces, the security forces of the President of the Republic or were students in the Navy".

The measures for the concession of compensatory assistance for the victims of the Republican side took a lot longer. The parliamentary group Catalan Socialists, alarmed by the situation, presented a Bill on 16 November 1978 to expedite the administration of the amnesty for those who had participated in the Civil War. That same day the government issued a Royal Decree-Law[160] establishing pensions for the families of the soldiers who had died in battle during the Civil War, or who died as a result of injuries suffered during the conflict. In the spirit of equal treatment, the right to a pension was extended to the families of Republicans in regular units and voluntary militias who had been killed in battle or as a result of injuries sustained during the conflict. The measure was also extended to soldiers missing in action, as well as to the families of those who has suffered violent deaths or had been executed during the war, and also to those who died during those years from illnesses contracted in prisons. The measures were, all in all, extended to the victims of the harsh repression of the post-war, which had brought about thousands of casualties.

A crucial Royal Decree issued by the office of the Head of State on 21 December 1978[161] recognised the economic benefits of the maimed and injured soldiers of the Civil War who were integrated into the Maimed Soldiers Corp. The aim, as the preamble to the legal text pointed out, was to "overcome any remaining differences that still today could divide Spaniards as a consequence of the circumstance derived from the Spanish Civil War". The extension to the 1976 Decree sought to put an end to the differences between maimed soldiers from the National side, who had benefitted from numerous labour and economic privileges during the dictatorship, and the maimed soldiers from the Republican side who could now, without retroactive effects, avail of these assistances. The

158 The government's answer in *Official State Gazette of Parliament*, Senate, I, 63, 19 February 1980.
159 Law 10/1980, 14 March, on the modification to the Royal Decree-Law 6.1978, 6 March, which regulated the situation of military personnel who participated in the Civil War. *Official State Gazette*, no. 76, 28 March 1980.
160 Royal Decree-Law 35/1978, 16 November, for the concession of pensions to the families of the deceased as a consequence of the war (1938–1939). *Official State Gazette*, no. 276, 18 November 1978, pp. 26245–26246.
161 Royal Decree-Law 43/1978, 21 December, in recognition of the economic benefits to soldiers who were injured or maimed during the Spanish Civil War. *Official State Gazette*, no. 305, 22 December 1978, pp. 28932–28933.

Royal Decree-Law of 21 December 1978 was developed by the Orders of 9 January[162] and 11 June 1979.[163]

The reparative measures for Republican ex-soldiers nevertheless continued to be insufficient. On 6 July 1979, the senator of the Catalan Socialist Party, Francesc Ferrer i Gironés, looked into the applications for amnesty and the recognition of passive rights of armed soldiers on the Republican side,[164] an issue which was brought up again on 10 June 1980, in this case by Catalan socialist senator Josep Andréu i Abelló.[165] For his part, the above-mentioned senator Paulino Pérez, had raised the issue of the discrimination of soldiers loyal to the Republic in spite of the Amnesty Law. The question was not acknowledged, and was therefore never answered by the Minister for Defence in the information session during the Commission of 20 December 1979.

Progress was made in relation to reparation on 18 September 1979, when a law was promulgated to recognise pensions, pharmaceutical and medical assistance and social assistance for the following people: (a) widows and next of kin of soldiers killed in battle during the Civil War; (b) those who had been convicted, suffered violent attacks or had been imprisoned; and (c) those who had suffered an illness or an injury as a result of the Civil War, within a two-year period of the end of the conflict.[166] This law was heavily criticised for not recognising the right to a pension of the next of kin of soldiers killed by an unofficial execution, of soldiers who had been disappeared, or those killed in prisons or police stations as a result of the dictatorial repression. These shortcomings were not resolved until the 2007 Historical Memory Law, although economic reparation only took effect from 1 January 2008, as it was not retroactive.

The Law was elaborated through five complementary regulations: the Royal Decree of 16 November 1979,[167] the Resolution of the Directorate General of

162 Order by the Department of Finance, 9 January 1979, in observance of the Royal Decree-Law 43/1979, 21 December, in recognition of the economic benefits to soldiers who were injured or maimed during the Spanish Civil War. *Official State Gazette*, no. 12, 13 January 1979, p. 847.

163 Order from the Department of Internal Affairs, 24 February 1979, to regulate the procedure to follow in the files administered in observance of the Royal Decree-Law 43/1979, 21 December, in recognition of the economic benefits to soldiers who were injured or maimed during the Spanish Civil War. *Official State Gazette*, no. 51, 28 February 1979, pp. 5206–5209.

164 *Official State Gazette of Parliament*, Senate, I, 14, 6 July 1979. Government answer: *Official State Gazette of Parliament*, Senate, I, 24, 26 October 1979.

165 *Diary of Senate Sessions*, Plenary Session, no. 102, 29 April 1981.

166 Law 5/1979, 18 September, on the recognition of pensions, medical, pharmaceutical and social assistance for widows, children and other next of kin for Spaniards deceased as a result of the Civil War. *Official State Gazette*, no. 233, 28 September 1979, pp. 22605–22606.

167 Royal Decree 2635/1979, 16 November, for the application and compliance of the Law 5/1979, 18 September, on granting rights to the next of kin of soldiers killed as a result of the past Civil War. *Official State Gazette*, no. 277, 19 November 1979, pp. 26669–26670.

the Treasury on 27 November 1979,[168] the Resolution of the Directorate General of the Treasury on 18 September 1980,[169] the Royal Decree-Law of 20 September 1980,[170] and the Order issued by the Office of the Prime Minister on 27 January 1981.[171]

The pensions of maimed soldiers were regulated in the Law of 26 June 1980.[172] The aim behind the law was to foment more equality in the legal system applicable to the military, ex-soldiers and next of kin, regardless of which side soldiers had fought on. The Legal Memorandum exemplified the political will behind this and other reparation laws of the time when it outlined "the need to overcome the differences that divided the country during the past conflict, irrespective of the Army to which soldiers belonged", which therefore "obliged it to establish equal treatment". This law was elaborated through two complementary regulations, the first from 16 October 1980[173] and the second from 12 February 1982.[174] However, the inadequacy of this law motivated the issuing of the Law of 29 March 1982, which, this time, focused on maimed civilians, and which ostensibly improved the conditions of their pension and retribution system.[175] The Royal Decree that elaborated this law was delayed for a year, and was finally issued under the new socialist government.[176]

168 Resolution of the Directorate General, 27 November 1979, through which regulations are dictated for the compliance of Law 5/1979, 18 September, and the Royal Decree 2635/1979, 16 November, on pensions for next of kin of Spanish soldiers killed as a result of the Civil War. *Official State Gazette*, no. 284, 27 November 1979, pp. 27341–27342.

169 Resolution of the Directorate General, 18 September 1980, on the applications for pensions regulated in Law 5/1979, 18 September. *Official State Gazette*, no. 227, 20 September 1980, p. 21031.

170 Royal Decree-Law 8/1980, 20 September, on the overdue instalments payable on pensions derived from the Civil War. *Official State Gazette*, no. 236, 1 October 1980, pp. 21799–21800.

171 Order of the Prime Minister of the Government, 27 January 1981, on the regulation of pharmaceutical and medical assistance and social services, provisioned in article 3 of the Law 5/1979, 5 September. *Official State Gazette*, no. 24, 28 January 1981, pp. 1957–1958.

172 Law 35/1980, 26 June, on pensions of soldiers maimed in the Republican Zone. *Official State Gazette*, no. 165, 10 July 1980, pp. 15753–15756.

173 Resolution of the Directorate General of the Treasury, 16 October 1980, on the application for pensions for mutilation and next of kin, regulated by the Law 35/1980, of the 26 June, on pensions for maimed soldiers from the Republican Zone. *Official State Gazette*, no. 260, 29 October 1980, pp. 24089–24090.

174 Royal Decree 391/1982, 12 February, on the integration of maimed soldiers on the Republican Zone to the general Welfare System, to the full effect of social services and health care. *Official State Gazette*, no. 55, 5 March 1982, pp. 5805–5806.

175 Law 6/1982, 29 March, on pensions for maimed soldiers of the Civil War. *Official State Gazette*, no. 80, 3 April 1982, p. 8818.

176 Royal Decree 1071/1983, 16 March, by which the normative and regulations are approved for the elaboration of Law 6/1982, 29 March, which grants basic retribution to the maimed civilians of the war and their successors and assigns. *Official State Gazette*, no. 107, 5 May 1983, pp. 12521–12523.

Altogether, the pensions for Republican ex-soldiers were payed belatedly, which is why, during the first few years of the 1980s, new special measures were dictated to administer these overdue payments.[177]

Lastly, it is worthwhile noting that soldiers from the Republican side were not the only beneficiaries of reparation. The Royal Decree of 13 February 1979 recognised the years of service given by teachers who were members of the Basic General Education (EGB) from the 1931 Professional Plan and the 1936 members of the National Primary School Teachers body.[178]

10 The Amnesty Laws failed to include crimes of adultery, cohabitation, abortion and contraception

The authors of the law failed to answer the calls demanding amnesty for crimes of homosexuality and sexual offences committed by women. The latter were included, as mentioned above, in the Bills put forward by the communists and the socialists. The issue, however, fell by the wayside during the negotiations and were not part of the debate in Congress or the Senate, except for one tangential comment, made by the communist deputy Marcelino Camacho, on sexual offences committed by women. He pointed out that amnesty for these offences was provisioned in the Bill put forward by the PCE on 14 July, but during the debate the PCE decided to not raise the issue, preferring instead to wait and raise it at a future discussion.[179] Donato Fuejo, of the PSP-US, also touched on the topic when he said that he "could talk of adultery, cohabitation and other crimes that

177 Royal Decree-Law 8/1980, 26 September, on the instalments payable on overdue pensions derived from the Civil War (*Official State Gazette*, no. 236, 1 October 1980, pp. 21799–21800); Resolution of the 20 October 1980, from the Chair of the Congress of Deputies, on the publications of the Ratification Agreement of the Royal Decree-Law 8/1980, 26 September, on the instalments payable on overdue pensions derived from the Civil War (*Official State Gazette*, no. 256, 24 October 1980, p. 23705); Law 42/1981, 28 October, on the instalments payable on overdue pensions derived from the Civil War (*Official State Gazette*, no. 271, 12 November 1981, p. 26503).

178 Royal Decree 329/1979, 13 February, on the recognition of the years of service of members of the Body of Teachers of Basic General Education (EGB) from the 1931 Professional Plan and the 1936 members of the National Primary School Teachers body. *Official State Gazette*, no. 48, 24 February 1979, p. 4993.

179 Specifically, Marcelino Camacho pointed out in the Congress of Deputies on 14 October 1977, that "we also want to let the women of this country know that if the issue is not debated on today, if this law fails to include so-called 'women offences': adultery, etc., we want to remind them that the Communist Parliamentary Group put forward a bill on the 14th of July which we consider an urgent matter and which we, naturally, will debate. However, it is natural, my fellow deputies, that in the case of a working-class member, as is my case, if before I spoke of the honour and duty of defending here today, in the name of this minority, this blanket and general amnesty, explaining my vote in favour of the amnesty, when included within it is a labour amnesty, is a matter of honour multiplied by three."

revealed hypocrisy, discrepancies and even temerity", but in his view the time was not right.

The criminal reform of 1944 reinstated the articles relative to adultery and cohabitation, as well as crimes of passion, when it re-established special immunity from prosecution for the murder of a spouse for adultery, as recognised in article 428 in observance of the Criminal Code of 1848. A chilling murder of a wife and her lover at the hands of her husband in the late 1950s hastened the fundamental provisions of the 1961 Law, whose legal text, approved by Decree on 28 March 1963, decriminalised the murder of a spouse for adultery, although it allowed for the possibility of taking into consideration mitigating circumstances in relation to criminal responsibility, the type of adultery and cohabitation. Nevertheless, articles 449 and 450 of the Criminal Code made adultery punishable, but from a misogynistic perspective. This legal text only provisioned the punishment of women for adultery and, accordingly, their male lovers, but not adulterous husbands.[180]

In October 1976, a trial against a 21-year-old woman in the Saragossa Territorial Court of Appeal[181] prompted the ADMA to launch its first campaign to collect signatures, which were presented along with a letter of protest in the Department of Justice. This was the genesis of the important feminist movement that spread throughout the greater part of Spain calling for amnesty and decriminalisation through legal reforms.[182] These calls for justice, however, were ignored, and crimes of adultery, cohabitation, abortion and contraception were not included in the 1977 Amnesty Law.

It was not until the Law of 26 May 1978 that crimes of adultery and cohabitation were decriminalised, abrogating articles 449 and 452 of the Criminal Code, and article 84.7 of the Civil Code, which established that children would be considered illegitimate regardless of whether mothers attested to their legitimacy.[183] Adultery and cohabitation were decriminalised, but the convictions that predated the law were not amnestied, nor were they granted economic or moral reparation. The 2007 Historical Memory Law also failed to address this issue.

The progressive Republican legislation on abortion, the voluntary termination of pregnancy and the use of contraception were, to Francoism, crimes against the integrity of the race. The Francoist regime restored penalties for abortion, falling back on the 1848 Criminal Code. The Law of 24 January 1941, inspired in great part by the Italian Criminal Code,[184] modified the Spanish Criminal Code by increasing the severity of the penalties for abortion. This modified legislation established severe punishments for women who aborted and against those who

180 Rodríguez Gil, 1998, pp. 438–444.
181 The prosecution recommended five years in prison and a fine of 50,000 pesetas for this woman.
182 Especially noteworthy with regard to this topic are Moreno, 1977; Nash, 1986, pp. 223–238; Folguera, 1988; Larumbe, 2002; and Larumbe, 2004.
183 Law 22/1978, 26 May. *Official State Gazette*, no. 22, 30 May 1978 and 2 June 1978.
184 Gómez Llana, 1941, pp. 238–241.

carried out the abortion: article 416 mandated that those who suggested, sold, advertised, carried out or disseminated through any type of media a process that facilitated abortion or avoided procreation, would be arrested and fined between 5,000 and 10,000 pesetas. When it came to abortions, however, the sentence could be reduced if it was alleged that a single mother would bring great dishonour to the family.

Abortion became a central issue in the 1977 electoral campaign. The AP and the UCD were against the legalisation of abortion, considering it against the sanctity of life, while every progressive group called for its decriminalisation. However, these progressive parties forgot the electoral promise they made during the Amnesty Law negotiations, and the many feminist protests that took place at the time could not reverse the decision to exclude abortion under the amnesty.

The Law of 7 October 1978 finally modified the Criminal Code by reforming the legal texts of articles 343 and 416 to allow the sale and use of contraception. However, this did not mean that abortion was decriminalised. In fact, in 1980 a judge convicted a woman for an abortion she had carried out in London, giving the reason that there was an element of "extraterritoriality" to the crime. The regulation was not modified until the Organic Law of 5 July 1985, which only partially decriminalised abortion.[185] There were no accompanying complementary laws to the 1977 Amnesty Law for any of these measures, which would have extended the effects of the amnesty to women accused of abortion and those who had facilitated the voluntary termination of pregnancies. There was no public outcry in relation to this matter, as, frankly, only a few isolated cases resulted in prison sentences, the reason being that the majority of terminations were clandestine abortions.[186]

11 The Amnesty Laws did not include crimes of homosexuality

The dictatorship enacted an important piece of repressive legislation against homosexuals.[187] Articles 2 and 6 of the law on vagrancy of the Second Spanish Republic was modified on 15 July 1954 to include homosexuals, who would be "interned in special institutions and, with no exceptions, would be completely separated from the rest" (article 6.a).[188] On 5 August 1970, this legal text was replaced with the Law on Social Dangers and Rehabilitation.[189] Much like the

185 Organic Law 9/1985, 5 July, on the reform of articles 417 bis of the Criminal Code. *Official State Gazette*, no. 166, 12 July 1985, p. 22041. This law allowed decriminalised abortions in the following circumstances: when pregnancy was the result of rape, abortions could be carried out within the first 12 weeks of gestation; when there was serious risk to the mental or physical health of the mother, abortions could be carried out at any stage of the pregnancy; when the foetus suffered from a congenital disorder, abortions could be carried out within the first 22 weeks of gestation.

186 See Vinyes, 2004.

187 See Martín, 2009.

188 *Official State Gazette*, no. 198, 17 July 1954.

189 *Official State Gazette*, no. 187, 6 August 1970, pp. 12551–12557.

previous legislation, it did not penalise crimes, opting instead for different measures: on the one hand, it established that the "dangerous" individual would be interned and kept in custody in an official establishment or in appropriate employment, for no less than four months or longer than three years if the individual was interned and kept in custody, and for no less than the minimum length of time set in the judge's writ of review, and no longer than three years when internment in appropriate employment was imposed on the individual. Also, there was a provision made for internment in an establishment for re-education purposes, for no less than three months and no longer than three years. Lastly, individuals could be interned in a preservation establishment until they recovered or until the subject no longer posed a danger to society. The above notwithstanding, homosexuals would be interned in an establishment for re-education. Moreover, they were forbidden from taking residence in certain areas, as well as forbidden to visit certain places and public establishments.[190] Jordi M. Monferrer estimates that between the years 1970 and 1979 there could have been up 2,600 cases against homosexuality, of which 1,000 or so ended in convictions. The majority of these cases were against males.[191]

The doctrine of the time rebuffed the calls for amnesty for homosexual crimes by claiming that the law was not applicable to convictions of posing danger to society. This position was based on the arguments made by the criminal lawyer, Republican Mariano Ruiz-Funes, author of the 1933 Vagrancy Law, who said that "granting a collective clemency to those who pose a danger to society would be equal to ignoring the true nature of that danger. It would be as unusual as saying that someone who suffers an illness will be forgiven of their illness."[192] In this way, and as Jordi Monferrer pointed out, individuals who posed a "danger" were considered to have an illness, and therefore needed to be cured, not pardoned. The illness had to be contained and prevented from spreading, which is why it was necessary to isolate these people from society, re-educate them and reintegrate them once they were considered cured. They could not be, therefore, the subject of a pardon or amnesty, nor could they have their sentences reduced for good conduct or for work or be put on parole.[193]

The exclusion of homosexuals from the partial amnesty of 31 July 1976, based as it was on such questionable motives, prompted the first protests on this matter,

190 Soriano Gil, 2005.

191 He bases his calculation on the fiscal reports of the Supreme Court covering the years between 1970 and 1979, which record more than 58,000 case files and more than 21,000 convictions for posing a danger to society. This data is extrapolated from the data available on the trials on social danger held in Madrid between 1974 and 1975, where around 6% of cases related to crimes of homosexuality, and 5% ended in convictions, thus arriving at the estimation that between 1970 and 1979 there would have been around 3,600 cases relating to homosexual crimes, with 1,000 of these resulting in convictions without guarantees and crimes. Monferrer Tomàs, 2003, pp. 185–186.

192 Jorge Barreiro, 1976, p. 305.

193 Monferrer Tomàs, 2003, p. 186.

which became more notorious after the general election of 1977. On 26 June of that year, the first public manifestation was convened in Barcelona by the clandestine organisation, the FAGC. Around 4,000 people congregated to appeal for amnesty for those convicted for crimes of homosexuality and the derogation of the Law of Social Danger. The manifestation was violently dispersed by the riot police.[194]

The amnesty for crimes of homosexuality was not backed by politicians when the Bill for the Amnesty Law was discussed. The only exception was Lluís María Xirinacs, of the party Catalan Agreement for Progress, who pointed out the fact that homosexuals had been excluded from the law.[195]

It was not until the Law of 26 December 1978[196] that the references to homosexuality were removed from the Law on Social Danger and Rehabilitation. As happened with adultery, homosexuality was decriminalised, but those who had been previously convicted were not granted amnesty, nor were the later compensated with reparative measures. The 2007 Historical Memory Law did not address the issue either, and the victims had to wait for their economic compensation to be granted by Royal Decree on 17 April 2009.[197]

12 The 1977 Amnesty Law did not include members of the Military Democratic Union or ex-soldiers on the side of the Republican Army

As mentioned in the previous chapter, the 1976 amnesty freed nine members of the UMD, but the measure did not consider the possibility of reintegrating the seven soldiers who had been discharged from the Army. The UMD itself disbanded on 26 June 1977 after the general elections, believing that its existence did not make sense in the newly democratic State. The anti-Francoist political parties included the members of the UMD in the Bill they put forward, but the governing party, the UCD, was not willing to discuss the reintegration to work of the soldiers discharged from the Army. The Army had not been through any purge, so it was an institution that was still genuinely Francoist. The Lieutenant General Manuel Gutiérrez Mellado, vice-president of Defence Matters, met in his office with Rafael Arias-Salgado, minister of Parliamentary Relations, as well as other Lieutenant Generals, to discuss the issue. The Army closed ranks on any type of reintegration of democratic soldiers. It was Gutiérrez Mellado himself who

194 *El País*, 27 June 2002.

195 *Senate session records*, Plenary session, no. 8, 14 October 1977, p. 225.

196 Law 77/1978, 26 December, for the modification of the Law on Social Danger and Rehabilitation and its regulation. *Official State Gazette*, no. 10, 11 January 1979, pp. 658–659.

197 Royal Decree 710/2009, 17 April, for the elaboration of provisions of the Law 2/2008, 23 December, on the General Budget of the State for 2009 in relation to pensions for retired workers and particular social compensations. *Official State Gazette*, no. 105, 30 April 2009, pp. 37930–37942.

explained to Suárez that if the reintegration was forced upon the Army, he would have to tender his resignation.[198] He argued that reintegration would strengthen the sectors that were conspiring against the consolidation of democracy, which could lead to a coup d'état. Suárez did not hesitate and supported his minister; the opposition would have to concede in order to keep the political and trade union amnesties.

One of the discharged soldiers, Julio Busquets, Chief of Engineers, was elected as deputy in the general elections, which he had stood for as an independent in the Catalan Socialists candidacy. The exclusion of UMD soldiers from the law prompted Busquets to refuse to tow the party line and instead he voted against the Amnesty Law.[199]

The military jurisdiction capitalised on the exclusion of the progressive soldiers from the Amnesty Law when, on 27 December 1977, a war council convicted Captain José Ignacio Domínguez, member of the disbanded UMD, of conspiring to rebel. He had exiled himself after the war and was therefore the only UMD official who had not been imprisoned. He returned to Spain days after the promulgation of the 1977 Amnesty Law[200] under the false presumption that he had been pardoned. The most surprising thing about the process was that he was sentenced to seven years in prison. It is, as far as it is known, the only conviction after the Amnesty Law for an amnestied crime, a judicial anomaly that can only be explained as symbolic of the sentence that the military court had wanted to impose on Domínguez; that is, the prison sentence was merely symbolic and he did not serve any time because, in effect, the crime corresponding to the lawsuit 250/75, filed after the arrest of a chief and eight officials in July 1975, had already been amnestied. However, he suffered the penalties attached to the crime: he was discharged, and his professional responsibilities in public office and his right to vote were suspended for seven years.[201]

The situation with the UMD soldiers was not resolved until the Law of 24 December 1986. This matter will be discussed thoroughly in the following chapter.

The pressure from the Army also made it impossible to include members of the Republican Army under the amnesty; the Republican Army, despite being the legitimate Army of the democratic State, could not reintegrate into the Armed Forces. In this case, the people affected were relatively few. For decades after the conflict, there were not many professional Republican soldiers interested in going back to the Army. The few that still had some years left as active workers rededicated themselves to other professional work, and, if any felt a vocation and wanted to return to the Army, the essentially Francoist make-up of the Army was reason enough to not give the idea serious consideration.

198 Gómez Rosa, 2013, pp. 185 and 332.
199 Busquets, 1999.
200 Domínguez, 1977.
201 *El País*, 28 December 1977.

13 The Amnesty Law did not include common crimes

In 1971, prisons in Spain were at maximum capacity because of the large numbers of imprisoned common criminals. There was no considered, individualised study on a possible amnesty for cases which had clearly resulted in prison sentences because of trials that were not fit for purpose, a common occurrence during the dictatorship.[202] There were calls to remedy this situation from the public, especially after the Pardon of 14 March 1977, which not only established legal instruments for the liberation of every political prisoner, but also considered a possible reduction of sentences for every other conviction.[203] Donato Fuejo (PSP-US) was the only deputy that commented on the need to grant amnesty for common crimes. He pointed out that the Amnesty Law would only been complete if it included a pardon for common criminals, whom he considered political prisoners. He justified this claim by explaining that common criminals were "criminals during a time in history defined by laws that were shaped by a specific ideology, applied in a social context and a political era defined by Francoism". He was conscious of the fact that, in some cases, it would result in a revolving-door effect. Nevertheless, Fuejo believed that this amnesty would have to be accompanied by modifications to the criminal definitions in the Dangerousness and Social Rehabilitation Law of 1970 and a revision of the 1973 Criminal Code, to adapt them to the new democracy.

14 The Amnesty Law in the 1978 Constitution

14.1 Amnesty and pardon in the 1978 Constitution

The 1977 amnesty was the end of the story; a new leaf was immediately turned over. From that moment on, the focus turned to drafting the Constitution, which was approved by Parliament in the plenary sessions in the Congress of Deputies and the Senate on 31 October 1978. It was ratified by referendum on 6 December 1978, with 87.78% of the votes in favour, representing a turnout of 58.97% as per the population recorded in the census. The King sanctioned the Constitution in Parliament on 27 December, and it came into force two days later.[204] The legal text did not make a single mention of rehabilitation or reparation for the victims of Francoism. The Amnesty Law had cleared the way for the Constitution when it resolved the issue of grave violations against human rights by erasing the criminal legacy of the dictatorship and the first transition.[205]

Even though the Constitution abrogated the fundamental laws of the dictatorship, Francoist law was not completely removed from the legal system, as its effects extended to democratic times and, as the Constitutional Court established,

202 Clavero, 2014, p. 115.
203 *El País*, 12 March 1977.
204 *Official State Gazette*, no. 311, 29 December 1978.
205 Clavero, 2014, p. 103.

there was a pre-constitutional legal continuity when regulations could not be interpreted in accordance with the Constitution.[206] The amnesty laws of the transition, the amnesty the Nationalist side granted itself on 13 September 1936, as well as all the pardons, were adopted by the democratic legal order.

Unlike what had happened with the preparations for the Amnesty Law, where political interest and swiftness were imperative, the Constitution was subject to profound doctrinal reflections and weighty analysis from a comparative law perspective. The clemency measures, essentially arbitrary, had to be adequately positioned in the constitutional State and the law, anchored to the principle of legality and the limits demarcated by human rights.[207]

Amnesty was not expressly prohibited in the Constitution, but it was omitted, perhaps because its prohibition might have sparked a debate on the Law of 15 October 1977.[208] This indeterminacy, and the fact these grace measures would not have been discussed,[209] prompted a doctrinal debate. Fernando Sainz Moreno believed that the silence in 1978 was an implicit prohibition.[210] Enrique Linde, however, did not agree. He believed that amnesty, as a mechanism that implies the retroactive derogation (transitory or definitive) of the regulation of convictions, was compatible with the Constitution, given that the latter guaranteed the non-retroactive nature of sentences that were against, or restricted, individual rights (article 9.3).[211] The criminal lawyer Joan Huís Pérez Francesc did not believe that the omission was the same as a prohibition, given that new legislation regulating the amnesty could be passed in Parliament, such as the Law of Criminal Procedure and/or in the Criminal Code, which would facilitate its application in specific cases by competent judges, as long as it was convenient in terms of the public's interest in political intentionality. They base this idea on the fact that the omission did not stop the Spanish legal system from preserving the fiscal amnesty in accordance with article 10.f of the 1963 General Tax Law, modified by Law 58/2003, 17 December.[212]

Nevertheless, we agree with Carlos Jiménez Villarejo and Antonio Doñate[213] when they claim that the amnesty not being expressly prohibited in article 62 i) of the Constitution does not mean that one could be granted, even if a future law were to permit it. Article 62 i), for reasons of justice, prohibits general pardons. In Spain, pardons have always been less effective than amnesties, which leads us to

206 Constitutional Court Sentence 32/1981, 28 July, legal ruling 6. Constitutional Court Sentence 76/1986, 9 June, legal ruling 2.

207 Zúñiga Urbina, 1996, p. 378.

208 For this same reason, it was not prohibited in the Organic Law 10/1995, 23 November, of the Criminal Code. *Official State Gazette*, no. 281, 24 November 1995, pp. 33987–34058.

209 Linde Paniagua, 1979, pp. 55–56. Requejo Pagés, 2001, pp. 101–102.

210 Sainz Moreno, 1978, p. 161.

211 Linde Paniagua, 1979, p. 57.

212 Pérez Francesc, 2009, pp. 59, 66–67.

213 Jiménez Villarejo and Doñate, 2012, p. 273.

the conclusion that the Constitution prohibits amnesties. This fact is reaffirmed in the current Criminal Code. Passed in 1995, the new Code fails to include amnesty as a reason to expunge criminal liability (article 130), unlike in previous Criminal Codes.

Moreover, the Constitutional Court, with the sentence passed on 25 November 1985, clarified that amnesties were, at this time, "against the principles that inspired the new political order". It justified this declaration by stating that:

> It is an exceptional measure defined by the time when the new values it serves are being consolidated, its unifying aim does not cover up the fact that it is put into practice through a plurality of legal mechanisms that are unified precisely because of their common aim. In some cases – typically in relations where the State is involved as a public power – the application of the amnesty would lead to what the doctrine has called *retroactive derogation of the regulation*, removing the restrictions that the law and liberty suffered from, with all its consequences. It can be said, thus, that the law lives on retroactively. Nevertheless, the amnesty does not cease to be so because its effects are more limited, and this is especially true in relation to the relations under a private legal system, which, the majority of the time, tries to grant a series of rights in the present and the future.[214]

Pardons are the only clemency measure referenced in the Constitution. Article 62.i) maintains that the King has the authority to "exercise the right to clemency in accordance with the law, which will not authorise general pardons". For these, the King would need the support of the minister in charge, as per article 64. Thus, general pardons were eliminated.[215] The issues regarding the pardons from 25 November 1975 had to be resolved in regular court because the Constitutional Court considered that, once excluded from the Constitution, pardons were no longer under its jurisdiction, as mandated by the Sentence overseen by the lawyer Francisco Tomás y Valiente.[216]

Seeking to limit the arbitrary nature of possible pardons, article 102.3 of the Constitution indicated that the royal prerogative on clemency could not be applied to cases where members of the government carried criminal responsibility – which, it is worth pointing out, strengthened the Amnesty Law's

214 Constitutional Tribunal Sentence, no. 147, 25 November 1986, Plenary. *Official State Gazette*, no. 295, 10 December 1986.

215 Pérez del Valle, 2001, p. 192. Pérez Francesc, 2009, pp. 58–59. Years later, Law of 14 March 1988 modified the Law of 18 June 1870, removing the references to general pardons: Law 1/1988, 14 January, which modified the Law of 18 June 1870, establishing the regulations to exercise the right to clemency and pardons. *Official State Gazette*, no. 13, 15 January 1988, p. 1386.

216 Constitutional Court order, 32/1981 25 March, and Sentence issued by the Constitutional Court, 8/1981, 30 March. *Official State Gazette*, no. 89, 14 April 1981.

symbolism as the "end of the story" – and article 87.3 excluded the right to pardons from the people's legislative initiative.

14.2 An unconstitutional law?

The principles of the 1977 general amnesty did not sit well with the principles of equality and justice recorded in article 1.1 of the Constitution.

This inequality had already been pointed out by the lawyer Francisco Banús in 1977, when he stated that as long as the amnesty for political crimes of the opposition required a demonstrable political intentionality, while no such intentionality was required for political crimes committed by the forces of public order, then the amnesty would always have an element of inequality. Testament to this is that under this principle, personally motivated crimes could be pardoned by the amnesty.[217] Now that it was validated in the Constitution, for Blanca Lozano this inequality was an infringement of article 14 of the Constitution ("every Spanish person is equal under the law, without prejudice for reasons of birth, race, sex, religion, opinion or any other condition or personal or social circumstance"). Taking this into consideration, the Amnesty Law contradicts the Constitution.[218]

Carlos Jiménez Villarejo and Antonio Doñate went on to develop their arguments based on Law 46/1977 granting amnesty to "all politically motivated acts, whatever their consequences, defined as offences or infringements", and therefore obstructing an obligatory case-by-case review of the reasons for justice. The people affected were also deprived of the legal protection which was guaranteed in article 24 of the Constitution. Therefore, Jiménez Villarejo and Doñate conclude that the Amnesty Law was "inapplicable as it went against the 1978 Constitution; it was basically unconstitutional because it contradicted the principles of justice and equality that are guaranteed in article 1".[219]

On the other hand, we must also consider article 96.1 of the Constitution, which established that "Validly concluded international treaties, once officially published in Spain, shall form part of the internal legal order". As we have seen, the International Covenant on Civil and Political Rights was published in the *Official State Gazette* on 30 April 1977, and came into force on 27 July of the same year – that is, before the Amnesty Law. Article 2.3.a) of the Covenant stipulates that States must guarantee effective remedies for those who have suffered grave violations of human rights, even when the violation was committed by persons acting in an official capacity. Moreover, article 15.2 stipulates that "no one shall be held guilty of any criminal offence on account of any act or omission which did not constitute a criminal offence, under national or international law, at the time when it was committed. Nor shall a heavier penalty be imposed than the one that was applicable at the time when the criminal offence was committed."

217 Bueno Arús, 1977, p. 9. See, also, Vallès Muñío, 2004, p. 8.
218 Lozano Cutanda, 1991, p. 1039.
219 Jiménez Villarejo and Doñate, 2012, p. 274.

The Covenant, therefore, was in force before the Constitution in Spain, and, of course, before the Vienna Convention on the Law of Treaties, wherein article 28 establishes that "unless a different intention appears from the treaty or is otherwise established, its provisions do not bind a party in relation to any act or fact which took place or any situation which ceased to exist before the date of the entry into force of the treaty with respect to that party".[220]

The reality is that nobody has contemplated the possibility of Law 46/1977 being unconstitutional. The issue of non-constitutionality can be raised, either *ex officio* or by a third party, by judges and tribunals whenever they consider that a rule of law applicable to said process and on whose validity the decision which is to be made depends may constitute a contravention of the constitution.

Nor has any investigating judge opted to not apply the Amnesty Law on the grounds that it is unconstitutional.[221] The Constitutional Courts stated that the authority of ordinary jurisdiction could deem a pre-constitutional law inapplicable when "they consider that the law is inapplicable because it has been abolished on the grounds that it contradicts the Constitution; or, if in doubt, they can submit this issue to the Constitutional Courts by filing the issue as unconstitutional".[222]

If judges and lawyers, or any other party legally entitled to file an appeal on grounds of unconstitutionality as per article 192 of the Constitution, opted to not follow either of these channels, it is because they knew the matter would not be resolved after the legitimacy of the Amnesty Law was corroborated by Sentences 63/1983 and 147/10986 issued in the Constitutional Court, and because of the non-retroactive nature of the sentencing channels unfavourable to, or restrictive of, the individual rights of a person as per article 9.3 of the Constitution.[223] The law would be applied in the future, not to the past, according to the principle that was already guaranteed under article 2.2 of the Civil Code, which establishes that "law will not be retroactive, unless it was mandated otherwise". The non-retroactive principle established in article 9.3 of the Constitution prevents a derogation of the law because it could lead to criminal liability, which had been expunged by the Amnesty Law.

The Constitutional Court has given the non-retroactive principle a dogmatic robustness unparalleled in other democratic States that went through transitional

220 Vienna Convention on the Law of Treaties. UN: A/CONF.39/27 (1969). Entered into force 27 January 1980.

221 Jiménez Villarejo and Doñate, 2012, pp. 217 and 322. Escudero Alday, 2013a, pp. 58–59 and 198. Clavero, 2014, pp. 122–123.

222 Sentence in the Constitutional Court 4/1981, 2 February, legal basis 1.B). *Official State Gazette*, no. 47, 24 February 1981.

223 Article 9.3 of the Spanish Constitution specifically states: "the Constitution guarantees the principle of legality, the hierarchy of regulations, the publication of regulations, the non-retroactive nature of sentencing mechanisms unfavourable to, or restrictive of, individual rights, legal security, the responsibility and interdiction of the political powers."

processes.[224] The Constitutional Court has gone to great lengths to ensure this principle, even stating that – criminal laws that convict and restrict rights prohibited by the Constitution aside – legislators can draft laws with the retroactivity which they consider appropriate.[225] The "maximum retroactivity" of the Constitution is not admitted on the basis that it contravenes the principle of legal security safeguarded in article 9.3.[226] There are many examples of victims who are blocked by the impenetrable wall of justice, always for the same reason, epitomised in the following sentence issued in a case reviewing the death penalty handed down to José Humberto Baena Alonso:

> The Constitution does not have retroactive effects; therefore, it is not possible to apply it and prosecute acts which took place before it came into force [...]. It is also outside the jurisdiction of the Court to contrast the regulations, values and principles guaranteed under the 1978 Spanish Constitution with the conduct of the public forces, such as the dramatic execution of a death penalty, which belongs to the History of Spain prior to the moment the Constitution came into force. [...] The Sentence which is now being challenged imposed a death penalty which was executed before the Constitution came into effect. Its most immediate effect, the death of the convicted party, took place, tragically, during a period time that this Court has not power over.[227]

This doctrinal jurisprudence reached its epitome with the Sentence issued by the Supreme Court on 27 February 2012, which will be discussed thoroughly in Chapter 5. According to this Sentence, criminal investigations may not be initiated to investigate criminal actions during the Civil War and the dictatorship in the basis of the principle of legality and non-retroactive nature of detrimental criminal law as per article 9.3 of the Constitution. The supposedly non-retroactive classification of this criminal acts has been rightly described by Bartolomé Clavero as a covert amnesty.[228]

15 The covert amnesty for members of ETA Political-Military (7th Assembly) (1982)

The pro-amnesty management groups, which had reconvened following the impasse in the 1977 Amnesty Law, reissued the old discourse of blanket amnesty for all prisoners. The police renewed their persecution of members of ETA and

224 Constitutional Court Sentences, 27/1981, 20 July; 173/1996, 31 October; and 104/2000, 13 April.

225 Constitutional Court Sentence, 150/1992, 19 October.

226 Constitutional Court Sentences, 4/1981, 2 February; 9/1981, 31 March; 10/1981, 6 April; and 43/1982, 6 July.

227 Constitutional Court edict, 187/2004, 25 May 2004.

228 Clavero, 2014, p. 226.

GRAPO after these organisations continued to be active. The result was that some of their members were imprisoned.

In the Basque Country, the EE campaigned in favour of the 1979 Statute of Autonomy with the slogan *Estatutoarekin Presoak Kalera* (With the Statute, all prisoners must be freed). But there was a mutiny already between this section of ETA and those who had turned their backs on the Amnesty Law. The pro-amnesty management groups advocated voting against the Basque Statute, stating that:

> it is vital for us to denounce the demagogy of certain parties and particularly what EE are doing in relation to the Basque prisoners, wanting to deceive the people by saying that they will be set free once the Statute is approved. When the Statute refers to *legal administration*, it is expressly referencing what is established in the Constitution, which explicitly states that there can be no amnesty or general pardons.[229]

In any case, the participation of the EE coalition in the devolution process in the Basque Country prompted ETA to develop armed attacks to interfere with their political activity. But when ETA demonstrated that the preparation of the 1979 Statute of Autonomy for the Basque Country did not fulfil its political aspirations, it began a wave of terrorist attacks, believing that in this way it would strengthen its bargaining position when the time came to negotiate with the government. After a ceasefire that lasted almost a year, in 1982 ETA-PM convened in the 7th Assembly and approved its plan to continue with its armed struggle.

By then EE had distanced itself more and more from ETA's strategy of violence. A minority sector of the terrorist group, who had more of an affinity with EE, decided to leave the group under its previous guise, ETA-PM (7th Assembly). EE negotiated clemency measures with the Spanish government for these dissidents. It was, in effect, a covert amnesty that brought about the dissolution of ETA-PM (7th Assembly) on 30 September 1982, and the collective reintegration of its members.[230]

229 *Amnistia Osoa*, issue 1, October 1979.
230 Fernández Soldevilla, 2010.

Chapter 4

Amnesty during the post-transition years (1982–2007)

1 Development of international doctrine in relation to amnesty

The wilful amnesia of post-transition Spain contrasts with the international doctrine in relation to the fight against impunity and the need to reconstruct the truth around grave violations of human rights.[1] We will begin with a summary of the most significant and well-known events. The notorious Resolution no. 828 on enforced disappearances was issued on 26 September 1984 by the Parliamentary Assembly of the Council of Europe; it said that:

> Considering that such disappearances are a flagrant violation of a whole range of human rights recognised in the international instruments on the protection of human rights (Universal Declaration of Human Rights, International Covenant on Civil and Political Rights, European Convention on Human Rights), in particular the right to life, liberty and security of persons, the right not to be subjected to torture, freedom from arbitrary arrest or detention, and the right to a fair and public trial.[2]

In this resolution, point 13 a) rejected granting amnesty for enforced disappearances on the grounds that these are considered crimes against humanity.[3]

1 The bibliography on this topic is far too extensive to be reproduced here; however, it is important to note the following eminent studies, which are especially relevant: Bassiouni, 1992; Roht-Arriaza, 1995; Beigbeder, 2002; Freeman, 2009; and Freeman and Pensky, 2012. On how the international doctrine on human rights adapted to the situation in Spain, the following studies are particularly salient: Chinchón Álvarez, 2012a, and Pérez González, 2013.

2 United Nations, Parliamentary Assembly, Resolution no. 828 (1984) on enforced disappearances. Text adopted by the Assembly on 26 September 1984 (9th Sitting), para. 4.

3 The fact that sentence no. 101/2012, issued in the Criminal Chamber of the Criminal Court, which absolved Baltasar Garzón, wrongly stated that "the Spanish state has been recommended the derogation of the Amnesty Law" (Resolution 828, from 26 September 1984, Council of Europe general guideline 20 of the United Nations Human Rights Committee, of 10 March 1992), has led to mistakes in the numerous reports and studies that have reproduced these data – that no recommendation was

In light of this situation, international bodies began developing a conclusive doctrine on the suitability of amnesty for crimes against humanity, especially after the fall of the Berlin Wall (1989) and the Soviet Union gave way to a new world order and the globalisation of human rights. The first significant decision came from the UN Human Rights Committee, which, in 1992, redacted the general guideline 20 to observe article 7 of the International Covenant on Civil and Political Rights, which prohibits torture and other abuses. The Committee warned that some states granted amnesties for torture, but explained that:

> Amnesty is generally incompatible with states' obligation to investigate and to ensure that these occurrences no longer occur under their jurisdictions, and to guarantee that such atrocities are not committed in the future. The states cannot deprive the subjects of the law effective reparation, including compensation and the best possible rehabilitation.[4]

Not long after, the UN General Assembly approved the Declaration on the Protection of all Persons from Enforced Disappearance (18 December 1992). Article 19 therein ordered that those guilty, or allegedly guilty, of crimes of enforced disappearance cannot "benefit from a special amnesty law or any other analogous measure that could exempt them from criminal proceedings or sanctions".[5] On this basis, the UN Working Group on Enforced or Involuntary Disappearances explicitly recommended that governments observe the Declaration and comply with their obligation to facilitate research into amnesty laws and to break the vicious cycle of impunity.[6]

From that moment on, the validity of a blanket amnesty as a mechanism for the resolution of conflicts was questioned.[7] When El Salvador,[8] in the midst of a transitional process in which the UN played a crucial role, drafted an amnesty, international regulations were very much taken into consideration. The Law of National Reconciliation was passed by the Salvadoran legislation assembly on 23 January 1992.[9] The first article therein granted amnesty:

> to anyone who had participated directly, indirectly, or as an accomplice, in common crimes connected to these and common crimes committed by a

made to Spain – without questioning it, such as, Amnistía Internacional España, 2012, p. 22; and Chinchón Álvarez, 2012a, p. 115.

4 United Nations, Human Rights Committee, 7 April 1992. UN: CCPR/C/21/Rev.1/Add.3 (1992), para. 15.

5 United Nations, General Assembly, *Declaration on the Protection of All Persons from Enforced Disappearance*. 92nd plenary meeting, 18 December 1992. UN: A/RES/47/133.

6 United Nations, Commission of Human Rights, *Report of the Working Group on Enforced or Involuntary Disappearances*. 12 January 1998. UN: E/CN. 4/1998/43, para. 416.

7 See Ambos, 1997.

8 Hayner, 2010, pp. 102–104.

9 Legislation Decree no. 147, 23 January 1992, *Official Journal*, no. 14, issue 314, 23 January 1992.

> number of people no lower than 20, before the 1st of January, 1992, with the exception, in any case, of the common crime of kidnapping, as established in article 220 of the Criminal Code.

This was not the sole exception included in the legal text; article 6 excluded from the benefits of the amnesty those who, according to a future report from the Truth Commission, had participated in serious acts of violence after 1 January 1980. Nor would its benefits be extended to those convicted by jury for any of the crimes covered by the amnesty.

The detailed and exhaustive report published by the Truth Commission[10] cleared the way for the Legislative Assembly to pass the Law on Blanket Amnesty for the Consolidation of Peace on 20 March 1993. The first article therein granted:

> a blanket amnesty, absolute and unconditional to those who in any capacity had participated in political crimes, common crimes connected to these and common crimes committed by a group of more than 20 people before the 1st of January, nineteen ninety-two, irrespective of whether a sentence has been passed, or whether due process has been initiated for same. This clemency is extended to those who had participated directly, indirectly or as an accomplice, in the aforementioned criminal activities. The amnesty is extended to the people described in article 6 of the Law for National Reconciliation ....[11]

Around the same time, a blanket amnesty was also granted in South Africa, but it bore few similarities to the amnesty granted in Spain, which had been based on forgetting the past. The South African clemency measure was officially included in its 1993 Constitution, but it was finally regulated in the Promotion of National Unity and Reconciliation Act of 1995.[12] It was an "amnesty for the truth", directed at perpetrators who had violated human rights, but were willing to confess to their crimes. The process of transitional justice was also dependent on a truth commission.[13]

We must take into consideration that amnesty in El Salvador and South Africa was only granted when a confession was made to the corresponding truth and reconciliation commissions.

Amnesty in El Salvador and South Africa prompted a debate on whether amnesties were compatible with truth commissions.[14] The UN Commission on Human Rights of the Economic and Social Council contributed to the theory on the right to the truth and the illegitimacy of impunity. The final report, presented

10 *De la Locura a la Esperanza: la guerra de los Doce Años en El Salvador*, 15 March 1993.
11 Legislative Decree no. 486, 20 March 1993, *Official Journal*, no. 56, issue 318, 22 March 1993.
12 Promotion of National Unity and Reconciliation Act 34 of 1995.
13 Hayner, 2010, pp. 99–102. Sarkin, 2004.
14 Hayner, 2010, pp. 104–105.

by the UN Special Rapporteur, Louis Joinet, on 26 June 1997, highlighted the question of impunity for violations of human rights (civil and political). Joinet defined impunity as the "impossibility, de jure or de facto, of bringing the perpetrators of human rights violations to account – whether in criminal, civil, administrative or disciplinary proceedings – since they are not subject to any inquiry that might lead to their being accused, arrested tried, and, if found guilty, sentenced to appropriate penalties, and to making reparations to their victims". Joinet believed that in order to avoid impunity, states had to guarantee victims the right to justice and reparation. Principle no. 38 of his report highlighted the issue of amnesty, concluding that when an amnesty intends to "establish conditions conducive to a peace agreement or to foster national reconciliation", it recommended that, among other restrictions, "the perpetrators of serious crimes under international law and authors of mass or systematic violations, may not benefit from such measures unless the victims are provided with appropriate resources and obtain a just and effective decision".[15]

The principles found in the annex of Joinet's report were incorporated by the UN Commission on Human Rights of the Economic and Social Council in the Resolution of 18 April 1998, which adopted the principles for the protection of human rights and the campaign against impunity.[16]

Throughout the 1990s, international law became more preoccupied with the regulation of non-international armed conflicts, that is, civil wars. In 1995, the Appeals Chamber of the International Criminal Tribunal for the former Yugoslavia claimed that the Spanish Civil War was the origin of this new preoccupation:

> As early as the Spanish Civil War (1936–39), State practice revealed a tendency to disregard the distinction between international and internal wars and to apply certain general principles of humanitarian law, at least to those internal conflicts that constituted large-scale civil wars. The Spanish Civil War had elements of both an internal and an international armed conflict. Significantly, both the republican Government and third States refused to recognize the insurgents as belligerents. They nonetheless insisted that certain rules concerning international armed conflict applied. Among rules deemed applicable were the prohibition of the intentional bombing of civilians, the rule forbidding attacks on non-military objectives, and the rule regarding required precautions when attacking military objectives.[17]

15 United Nations, Sub-Commission on Prevention of Discrimination and Protection of Minorities, *Revised Final Report. Question of the Impunity of Perpetrators of Human Rights Violations (Civil and Political)*. UN: E/CN.4/Sub.2/1997/20/Rev1 (Final Report by Louis Joinet, 26 June 1997).

16 United Nations, *Commission of Human Rights, Considerations of reports submitted by states parties under article 40 of the International Covenant on Civil and Political Rights – Comments of the Human Rights Committee*. 18 April 1994. UN: CCPR/C/79/Add.32.

17 *Appeals Chamber of the International Criminal Tribunal for the former Yugoslavia, Prosecutor v. Tadic*, Case No. IT-94-1-AR72, Decision on the Defence Motion for Interlocutory Appeal on Jurisdiction, 2 October 1995, para. 100. See Schabas, 2002, p. 907.

On 16 October 1998, the National High Court judge Baltasar Garzón issued an arrest warrant for Augusto Pinochet under universal justice.[18] However, this turn of events prompted the doctrine of the time to question the apparent paradox that a Spanish judge could prosecute crimes committed by another dictatorship, ignoring the amnesty law in Chile, while the crimes committed by the Francoist regime in the judge's own country could not be prosecuted because of the Amnesty Law in force there.[19]

That same year, an extraordinary coordinated effort resulted in the Statute of Rome, which adopted new regulations on international crime and established the International Criminal Court. Spain ratified the Statute immediately, which came into force on 1 July 2002.[20] The preamble affirmed that the "most serious crimes of concern to the international community as a whole cannot go unpunished" and that "it is the duty of every State to exercise its criminal jurisdiction over those responsible for international crimes". Article 7.I.i) is particularly important in relation to Spain, as it defines enforced disappearance as a crime against humanity.

Around the same time there were some important changes to amnesties in Latin America.[21] In 1998, the IACHR criticised the Guatemalan 1996 Law on Reconciliation because "a state of impunity exists and continues to exist". It interpreted impunity as:

> the total lack of investigation, persecution, detention and sentencing of those responsible for the violations of human rights protected by the IACHR, when it is the duty of the State to deal with this situation through whatever legal mechanisms they have at their disposal, given that impunity enables repeat violations of human rights and perpetuates the defencelessness of the victims and their families.

Three years later, on 14 March 2001, the IACHR passed the notorious Barrios Altos (Peru) sentence, which stated:

> we cannot admit the provisions of amnesty, the provisions of prescription and limitations and the establishment of impunity, obstructing investigations and the sanctioning of those responsible for serious violations of human rights, such as torture, mass executions, extra-judicial or arbitrary and forced

18 This high-profile measure prompted other processes, in this case, national, such as in Chile and Argentina, as well as in Europe, specifically in Belgium, Denmark, Holland, Italy, France, Sweden and the UK. Roht-Arriaza, 2001, pp. 44–55.

19 Sancinetti and Ferrante, 1999, p. 15.

20 For the most relevant studies on this matter, see Triffterer, 1999; Politi and Nesi, 2001; Ambos, 2002; Ambos and Guerrero, 2003; Seibert-Fohr, 2003, pp. 553–590; Seibert-Fohr, 2009; and Schabas, 2010.

21 See the analysis carried out by Chinchón Álvarez, 2007a, pp. 323–472.

> disappearances, all of which are prohibited as they contravene unconditional rights recognised by the Universal Declaration of Human Rights.[22]

Moving on from America to Africa: in 1999, the UN Secretary General issued a clarifying addendum to the amnesty clause included as part of the Lomé Peace Accord in Sierra Leone. The amnesty guaranteed immunity and a pardon for those who participated in the armed conflict, but the clause specified that the measure could not be extended to cases of genocide, crimes against humanity, war crimes and other serious violations of human rights.[23] Lastly, moving on from Africa to return to Europe: the Amnesty Law promulgated by the Federal Republic of Yugoslavia on 26 February 2001 explicitly established that it could not be granted to those who had been convicted of crimes of terrorism or for crimes against humanity and against international law.[24]

To avoid situations of impunity, UN Resolution of 25 April 2003 warned States against adopting clemency measures that favoured those responsible for violations of human rights and international humanitarian law.[25] A year later, on 27 February 2004, the UN Secretary General recommended that the Human Rights Committee use an independent expert to review and update the principles of the fight against impunity.[26] The responsibility would fall on the shoulders of Diane Orentlicher, a matter which will be discussed later in this chapter.

The UN Secretary-General's report, *The rule of law and transitional justice in conflict and post-conflict societies* of 3 August 2004[27] stated that there was a "growing shift in the international community, away from a tolerance for impunity and amnesty and towards the creation of an international rule of law". Further on, the report stated that the UN Security Council "rejected any endorsement of amnesty for genocide, war crimes, or crimes against humanity, including those relating to ethnic, gender and sexually based international crimes, ensure that no such amnesty previously granted is a bar to prosecution before any United Nations created or assisted court".[28]

22 IACHR, *Case of Barrios Altos v. Peru*, Series C, No. 75, Judgment of 14 March 2001, para. 41. This judgment established precedent for future sentences which not only pointed out the legal inefficacy of self-administered amnesty, but also highlighted the fact that amnesty could not be granted for crimes against humanity. See, for example, IACHR, *Case of Almonacid Arellano v. Chile*, Series C, No. 154, Judgment of 26 September 2006.

23 Among the numerous studies on this matter, the following are especially relevant: O'Flaherty, 2004, pp. 30–62; Horovitz, 2006, pp. 43–69; and Schabas, 2006.

24 Amnesty Law, art. 2.

25 United Nations, Commission on Human Rights, Commission on Human Rights resolution 2003/72: Impunity. 25 April 2003. UN: E/CN.4/RES/2003/72.

26 United Nations, Commission on Human Rights, *Independent study on best practices, including recommendations, to assist states in strengthening their domestic capacity to combat all aspects of impunity*, by Diane Orentlicher. 27 February 2004. UN: E/CN.4/2004/88.

27 United Nations, Commission on Human Rights, *The rule of law and transitional justice in conflict and post-conflict societies*, 3 August 2004. UN: S/2004/616, para. 40.

28 United Nations, Commission on Human Rights, *The rule of law and transitional justice in conflict and post-conflict societies*, 3 August 2004. UN: S/2004/616, para. 64c).

That same year saw an event that was particularly important to comparative law. The UN declared invalid the amnesty in Sierra Leone, whose scope,[29] it must be said, was very similar to the amnesty granted in Spain. Specifically, the UN Appeals Chamber of the Special Tribunal for Sierra Leone declared in 2004 that the amnesty granted in 1994 was voided by international law, and declared it invalid because it contravened certain obligations established in treaties and conventions on the protection of humanity.[30]

By 2005, the international doctrine in relation to crimes against international law was established, based on the pillars of imprescriptibility, the impossibility of amnestying or pardoning a crime, universal persecution, not submitting to the principles of *res judicata* and the impossibility of invoking the non-retroactive principle of criminal law.[31] The international law, nevertheless, did not forbid granting limited amnesty to those convicted of minor crimes by the war crimes commission, as long as the amnesty was complemented with control measures, and that it was granted to facilitate the reinstatement of lasting peace.[32]

The international doctrine on amnesty was synthesised in the Report by the independent expert, Diane Orentlicher, to update the Set of principles to combat impunity. She presented the report to the UN Human Rights Commission on 8 February 2005.[33] The first principles established that:

> Impunity arises from a failure by States to meet their obligations to investigate violations; to take appropriate measures in respect of the perpetrators, particularly in the area of justice, by ensuring that those suspected of criminal responsibility are prosecuted, tried and duly punished; to provide victims with effective remedies and to ensure that they receive reparation for the injuries suffered; to ensure the inalienable right to know the truth about violations; and to take other necessary steps to prevent a recurrence of violations.

29 The ceasefire signed in Lomé (Togo) between the Sierra Leone government and the rebel army, the RUF, on 18 May 1999 was followed by a peace agreement, signed in the same city on 7 July 1999, which divided power between the RUF and the government. The latter had to concede to an unconditional reprieve of death sentences and pardon all the soldiers and collaborators in any related to their objectives in the armed conflict. The RUF had committed serious violations of human rights, even massacres of members of government.

30 *Prosecutor v. Morris Kallon, Brima Bazzy Kamara*, Case No. CESL-2004-15-PT, Case No. CESL-2004-16-PT, Decision on the challenge to Jurisdiction: Lomé Accord Amnesty, Decision of 13 March 2004 (SCSL-04-15-PT-060). Horovitz, 2006, pp. 43–69. Schabas, 2006.

31 Vicente, 2012, p. 158.

32 Naqvi, 2003, pp. 583–626.

33 United Nations, Commission on Human Rights, *Report of Diane Orentlicher, independent expert to update the Set of principles to combat impunity – Updated Set of principles for the protection and promotion of human rights through action to combat.* 8 February 2005. UN: E/CN.4/2005/102/Add.1.

Principle 2 establishes the inalienable collective right of the people to know the truth concerning heinous crimes and massive or systematic violations of human rights. Principle 3 establishes the duty to remember the history, and the State's duty to facilitate knowledge in order to avoid a collective extinction of memory. The next principle adds that victims and their families have the right to know the truth, and this individual right cannot prescribe. Therefore, principle 5 establishes the State's duty to give effect to the right to know in non-judicial processes that complement the role of the judiciary. Further on in the report, principle 19, on the State's duty with regard to the administration of justice, establishes that States must undertake prompt, thorough and impartial investigations of violations of human rights and humanitarian international law, and must also adopt appropriate measures in respect of the perpetrators, especially with regard to criminal justice, with the aim of prosecuting, trying and duly punishing them. Added to this, it states that:

> Although the decision to prosecute lies primarily within the competence of the State, victims, their families and heirs should be able to take initiative, on either an individual or a collective basis, particularly as *parties civiles* or as persons conducting private prosecutions in States whose law of criminal procedure recognizes these procedures. States should guarantee broad legal standing in the judicial process to any wronged party and to any person or non-governmental organization having a legitimate interest therein.

This principle on impunity is complemented by principle 24, which describes "Restrictions and other measures relating to amnesty":

> Even when intended to establish conditions conducive to a peace agreement or to foster national reconciliation, amnesty and other measures of clemency shall be kept within the following bounds: (a) The perpetrators of serious crimes under international law may not benefit from such measures until such time as the State has met the obligations to which principle 19 refers or the perpetrators have been prosecuted before a court with jurisdiction – whether international, internationalized or national – outside the State in question.

Lastly, it is worth highlighting principle 36, which established that "at a minimum, States should undertake the following measure: Public officials and employees who are personally responsible for gross violations of human rights, in particular those involved in military, security, police, intelligence and judicial sectors, shall not continue to serve in State institutions".

Two months later, on 20 April, the Office of the High Commissioner for Human Rights published the study *Right to the Truth*,[34] wherein article 60 clearly states that:

34 United Nations, Commission on Human Rights, *Right to the truth*, 20 April 2005. UN: E/CN.4/RES/2005/66.

> The right to the truth as a stand-alone right is a fundamental right of the individual and therefore should not be subject to limitations. Giving its inalienable nature and its close relationship with other non-derogable rights, such as the right not to be subjected to torture and ill-treatment, the right to the truth should be treated as a non-derogable right. Amnesties or similar measures and restrictions to the right to seek information must never be used to limit, deny or impair the right to the truth. The right to the truth is intimately linked with the States' obligation to fight and eradicate impunity.

Also in 2005, the UN General Assembly convened on 16 December to pass the resolution *Basic Principles and Guidelines on the Right to a Remedy and Reparation for Victims of Gross Violations of International Human Rights and Serious Violations of International Humanitarian Law.*[35] Among other aspects, it recognised the right of victims to access information concerning "violations and reparation mechanisms", which had to be reflected in the rule of law of every State, whose duty was to "develop procedures to allow groups of victims to present claims for reparation and to receive reparations, as appropriate".

With the international doctrine firmly set against blanket amnesty, in 2006 the IACHR delivered its judgment on the notorious case of *Almonacid Arellano et al. v. Chile*, which synthesised the arguments of international bodies and the doctrine of the time on the illegitimacy of blanket amnesty.[36] It is worthwhile fast-forwarding a few years to 2009 to remark also on the European Court of Human Rights decision to recognise as a general principle the incompatibility of blanket amnesty with the duty assumed by every State to investigate cases of torture.[37]

The theory was put into practice in new transitional justice scenarios, such as Kenya, where a Truth, Justice and Reconciliation Commission was created in 2008, around the same time as granting amnesty for gross violations of human rights was prohibited.

To all of the above, we must add the *International Convention for the Protection for All Persons from Enforced Disappearance* which was adopted by the UN General Assembly through the Resolution 61/177, 20 December 2006.[38] Article 13.1 established that "enforced disappearance shall not be regarded as a political offence or as an

35 https://documents-dds-ny.un.org/doc/UNDOC/GEN/N05/496/42/PDF/N0549642.pdf?OpenElement

36 IACHR, *Case of Almonacid Arellano et al. v. Chile, del Rosario Gómez Olivares and ors (on behalf of Almonacid Arellano) v. Chile*, Preliminary objections, merits, reparations and costs, IACHR Series C, No. 154, IHRL 1538 (IACHR 2006), 26 September 2006, paras 106–114.

37 Council of Europe, European Court of Human Rights, Fifth Section, no. 13113/03, 17 March 2009.

38 United Nations, International Convention for the Protection of All Persons from Enforced Disappearance. Adopted by the General Assembly at the Sixty-first Session, Resolution 61/177. 20 December 2006. UN: A/RES/61/177. Open to signature on 6 February 2007. Signed by Spain in September 2007 and ratified in September 2009.

offence connected with a political offence or as an offence inspired by political motives". There was no reference to amnesty in the document, but articles 8.2, 12 and 24 tacitly expressed the illegitimacy of granting amnesty for enforced disappearance.[39] As will be discussed later, Spanish judges do not take this Convention into consideration because of the above-mentioned argument regarding the non-retroactive nature of the amnesty granted in Spain, regardless of the international doctrine stance on non-retroactivity, amnesty or prescription. Non-retroactivity cannot be applied to enforced disappearances where a body has not been found, which is why the State must provide as many instruments as possible in the effort to localise the bodies, whether they were victims that fell during the Civil War or the post-war years, and to hand over the remains to the respective families. Spain ratified the Convention in 2009, which came into force in December 2010.

2 How a wilful amnesia developed in Spain

2.1 Amnesia during the Felipe González years

The PSOE's victory in the general elections held on 28 October 1982 marked the first of three successive Felipe González governments, covering a period of approximately 15 years (from 1 December 1982 to 4 May 1996). The tacit pact to forget the past was solidified after a failed coup d'état on 23 February 1981, which seemed to confirm that scratching the surface of the past resulted in a resurfacing of past tensions, creating an atmosphere of conflict similar to the years of the Second Spanish Republic before the Civil War broke out, threatening to destabilise the new democratic order.[40] The judgment passed in the Military Chamber of the Supreme Court against those responsible for the failed coup is a perfect example of the legal amnesia that took hold of the courts during those years. It described crimes of rebellion from a historically erudite perspective, alluding to various attempts to overthrow governments, but failing to specifically mention the coup d'état carried out by Franco and Mola in July 1936 against the Second Spanish Republic.[41]

Spain joined in the EEC on 1 January 1986, the year of the 50th anniversary of the Civil War. This serendipity gave Spain the chance to demonstrate the healthy state of the country in the eyes of Europe, but the PSOE chose instead to continue in line with the tradition instated by the transition, holding steadfastly to the principle of not invoking the past. The government did not stage any commemoration, with the pretext that the "Civil War was not worthy of commemoration", as it explained in a statement which limited itself to remembering and recognising those who fought for freedom, and expressing its "respect" for

39 Callejón, 2006, pp. 350–351. Chinchón Álvarez, 2008b, pp. 13–55. Ott, 2011.
40 Pinilla Martín, 2006, p. 538.
41 Supreme Court, Fifth Military Chamber, Sentence no. 791/1983, 22 April.

those who fought for a "different type of society".[42] The only measure remotely linked to the past was the Law of 8 January 1986, on the appropriation of seized trade union assets,[43] which only benefitted certain trade unions.

Despite the official contempt for historical memory, a new trend in academic historiography was taking hold, as articles on the repression during and after the Civil War and the post-war began to appear in newspapers, from both a general[44] and a regional[45] perspective that sought to conserve the memory of repression, as the first historian who investigated enforced disappearance, José María Jimeno, explained:

> History cannot cover up the terrible events suffered by one side. The unspeakable events for the victims and impossible to understand for the tormentors. The terrible events suffered by those who tried to keep alive the hope for freedom, peace, respect for human dignity and democracy, those who fought to build a society where all of the above were real, but saw their lives and ideals cut short. The terrible suffering of poor widows and orphans, scared, ridiculed, humiliated and forced to suffer the "peace" of the victors.[46]

In 1986 the Society for the Study of the Civil War and Francoism was created, and, with the help of the Castile-Leon Council, organised the conference on *History and Memory of the Civil War*, which was held in Salamanca. The event was a crucial one, and its proceedings are recorded in three weighty tomes.[47] The title of the conference was not looking to challenge the amnesia imposed by the transition, but was rather a historicist vindication of memory.[48]

42 *El País*, 19 July 1986. See Villagrasa Hernández and Alberola Suriñach, 2007, p. 7; Vinyes, 2011b, p. 267.

43 Law 4/1986, 8 January, on the appropriation of trade union assets. *Official State Gazette*, no. 12, 14 January 1986, pp. 1944–1946. This Law sanctioned the appropriation into the State assets of the patrimonial assets, rights and duties that had belonged to trade union organisations during the Second Republic and which had been taken away by the Francoist State. The use of these assets was handed over to labour trade unions and business associations. This Law was developed through the Royal Decree 1671/1986, 1 August, which approved the regulation of the Law on the appropriation of trade union assets (*Official State Gazette*, no. 189, 8 August 1986, pp. 28033–28036), which soon after had to be modified by the Royal Decree 2559/1986, 12 December (*Official State Gazette*, no. 304, 20 December 1986, pp. 41644–41645).

44 Biescas and Tuñón de *Lara*, 1982. Reig Tapia, 1984. Tuñón de Lara *et al.*, 1985. Fontana, 1986. Tusell, 1988.

45 Especially Hernández García, 1984. Solé i Sabaté, 1985. Moreno Gómez, 1985. Altaffaylla, 1986.

46 Jimeno Jurío, 1986, p. 19.

47 Aróstegui, 1988.

48 In the same vein but years before, Manuel Tuñón de Lara claimed that "these events and acts have to be forgotten as hindrances to the present and the future, and as political factors. However, they have to be studied and explained as history." Biescas and Tuñón de Lara, 1982.

The family members of those executed by the state were practically the only ones who assisted the commemorations that were held throughout the country. As far as can be ascertained, there was no call to abolish or modify the Amnesty Law in any of these events.

After the anniversary, the Catalan historian Eduardo Pons Prandes, an ex-Republican soldier who went into exile after the Civil War, denounced the impunity that the Amnesty Law granted to those responsible for the repression of the dictatorship (1987).[49] He was supported by the political scientist Josep María Colomer (1990).[50] However, these dissenting voices were in the minority in Spain, whereas in other post-transitional scenarios they were in the majority. For example, the Greek government of Constantino Mitsotakis, of New Democracy, proposed in 1990 to grant an amnesty to the members of the Colonel's Junta. The conservative, socialist and communist opposition to this proposal prompted Mitsotakis to drop the matter.

2.2 Amnesia during the José María Aznar years

The period covering José María Aznar's mandate, presiding over two governments (4 May 1996 to 16 April 2004), was characterised by a complete disregard for any issues that had anything to do with the victims of the Civil War or Francoism. Aznar, who in his youth had been a member of a Student Union Front supporting the Falange, was not willing to rectify the mistakes made prior to his government.

The PP government did not issue its first remedial measure until the Law of 15 December 1998, which reinstated the rights that had been revoked during the Civil War and its aftermath and appropriated assets, which had been seized by the state, to the democratic parties.[51] It was, according to Carlos Jiménez Villarejo and Antonio Doñate, a scandalous measure. Although the democratic parties benefitted from substantial compensation, there were no new measures for the benefit of those who had suffered at the hands of the dictatorship, nor any redress for those who had been unfairly tried by the Francoist courts.[52] Moreover, there was no normative measure to redress trespassing on family homes, looting or seizure of assets, properties and other personal effects of particular victims.

49 Pons Prandes, 1987. To not allow amnesia to be based on a lack of knowledge, he proposed carrying out "four or five hundred inquiry commissions at the regional level in order to investigate everything that happened between the 18th of July, 1936 and the 20th of November, 1975" (Pons Prandes, 1987, p. 314).

50 Colomer, 1990. See, also, Colomer, 1998.

51 Law 43/1998, 15 December, on the Restitution or Compensation to Political Parties of Revoked Rights and Seized Assets brought about after the application of the political responsibility legislation of the time between 1936 and 1939. *Official State Gazette*, no. 300, 16 December 1998, pp. 42087–42089. The Law was developed through the Royal Decree 610/1999, 16 April, which approved its Regulations (*Official State Gazette*, no. 92, Royal Decree 610/1999, 17 April, pp. 14482–14487).

52 Jiménez Villarejo and Doñate, 2012, p. 21.

However, there was an especially significant development for the victims when the General Archive of the Spanish Civil War was created in Salamanca on 12 March 1999,[53] based on the Spanish Civil War Section in the National Historical Archive. It was a project that had been three years in the making. Since the transition, no official institution had shown any interest in capitalising on the archives to reveal the truth, to redress and compensate the victims of grave violations of human rights and, where appropriate, to punish those responsible for repression. Speaking on this issue, Antonio González Quintana claimed that the lack of interest in primary sources of information reinforced the wilful amnesia that had been instated after the Amnesty Law.[54] The new archive in Salamanca opened the door to a new era, offering the victims of the war an opportunity to prove their victim status, and subsequently exercise their right to reparation.

The PP – the reincarnation of the defunct AP – added another element to the amnesia instated by the transition: it reinforced the democratic institutions with a kind of "new political consensus" for equality between those who had won and lost the war, deeming it unnecessary to recognise moral responsibilities to the recent past.[55] In any case, any legal liability continued to be extinguished under the Amnesty Law. However, the policy of complete amnesia was challenged by progressive organisations. The PP did not hold an overall majority in the Congress of Deputies. Thus, in September 1999, the PSOE presented in the Foreign Affairs Committee of the Chamber a motion lamenting and condemning the "military uprising against the legislation upheld by the political institutions of the Spanish Second Republic". The motion was passed by every group of the Chamber on 14 September 1999. Every group, that is, except the PP. It was the first explicit condemnation of the "fascist coup d'état against the legality of the Republic" in democratic times.[56] In a way, the spell of the unspoken rule of the democracy, to forget the past, was broken, given that every progressive politician

53 Royal Decree 426/1999, 12 March, for the creation of the General Archive of the Spanish Civil War. *Official State Gazette*, no. 62, 13 March 1999, pp. 10244–10246. Developed through the Resolution of 18 December 2001, of the undersecretary by which the Service Charter of the General Archive of the Spanish Civil War. *Official State Gazette*, no. 7, 8 January 2002, and the Order ECD/1555/2002, 17 June, which establishes the operation and capacities of the Learning Centre and Documentation of the Spanish Civil War. *Official State Gazette*, no. 151, 25 June 2002.

54 González Quintana, 2011, p. 95.

55 Sevillano Calero, 2003, p. 305.

56 The PP put forward a different motion that failed. It did not mention the military uprising and described the Civil War as a "fraternal dispute of a generation of Spaniards that sacrificed themselves in a supreme demonstration of folly and hatred". The PP spokesperson, José María Robles Fraga, without mentioning amnesty, appealed to forgetting the past, not without a certain cynicism, when he quoted the president of the Republic, Manuel Azaña, when he said that "after 40 years under the dictatorship", Spanish society had managed to keep looking forward and make "peace, mercy and forgiveness" a reality, values which the Republican Left leader had lost more than 60 years ago.

was against the policy of forgetting the past.[57] This notwithstanding, none of the interventions during the motion made explicit reference to the Amnesty Law.

On 5 April 2000, the beginning of the seventh legislature after the PP emerged victorious in the elections with an absolute majority was seen. However, the new political landscape did not deter the opposition from presenting various initiatives in the Congress of Deputies to discuss the amnesty of the transition. On 20 November 2000, the anniversary of Franco's death, the Congress of Deputies unanimously passed a new motion condemning the 1936 uprising.[58] However, the second paragraph of the motion described the 1977 Amnesty Law as a historical moment, fruit of the harmony which had put an end to hostilities between the two sides, and which deflected past tensions and alleviated the desire for revenge. And thus the 1977 Amnesty Law was endorsed by every progressive groups.

On 1 December 2003, the politicians of the opposition drove proceedings in the Chamber of Deputies to honour the victims of Francoism and the Civil War. The PSOE spokesperson, Jesús Caldera, made it clear that the tribute was a historical debt that had to be repaid in order to "avoid the country falling into the trap of amnesia and forgetting the past", and Felipe Alcaraz, of United Left, stated that forgetting the past was a huge mistake.[59] But none of the criticism mentioned the Amnesty Law, which was still regarded as sacred by left-wing groups. Later that year, the reform to the Criminal Code came into force, which reinforced the non-applicability of crimes against humanity and genocide (article 133.2), based on doctrine of the Statute of Rome. The regulation lacked retroactive effects.

By then there had been a profound change in civil society, leading to the first criticisms of the amnesty granted for Francoist crimes. The case of Pinochet and the change of tack of the progressive political parties in Spain were the sparks that ignited the rebirth of the movements for the recovery of historical memory in

57 The Socialist Deputy, Jesús Caldera, promoter of the initiative that was passed, said that the initiative was not born out of "rancour", but from the need to pass a declaration of "high emotional and symbolic value", given that "democracies cannot be built upon a foundation of forgetting the past". *El País*, 15 September 1999.

58 *Session Record of the Chamber of Deputies*, VII Legislature, Constitutional Commission, no. 625, 2002, pp. 20501–20524. Pinilla Martín, 2006, pp. 543–544. Aguilar and Ramírez Barat, 2014, p. 217. By way of restorative measures, it limited itself to stating, in the third paragraph, the duty of Spanish society to morally recognise the victims of the Civil War and of the dictatorship's repression. The motion stated that institutions would have to support initiatives for the corresponding moral recognition presented by the families of those affected, but with the condition that it could not reopen old wounds. It further stated that the government should develop a policy to recognise and to offer social and financial protection to those exiled by the war and those known as "children of the war". The government and opposition were still far from understanding the need to exercise post-transitional justice, but the symbolic gesture gave greater legitimacy to the demands of the families of the victims, and served as a new point of departure for further initiatives.

59 *El País*, 2 December 2003.

Spain, which were now driven by the grandchildren of the victims, many of whom had been born during the dictatorship, and were therefore not influenced by the consensus that had been struck by the 1977 Amnesty Law or bound to any pact to forget the past.[60] The initiatives that were developed at this time, unlike the ones that were initiated during the transition, no longer put their instigators at risk. The biggest reason for the reignited interest in recovering historical memory, above all, was the fact that enough time had passed, helping to clarify the atrocities in hindsight with the access to data that had, until then, remained hidden.[61] A new era was begun by the Association for the Recovery of Historical Memory, constituted in December 2000, under the imitative of Emilio Silva, grandson of an executed soldier. His first act was to launch the localisation and exhumation of the remains of various executed Republican soldiers who had been buried in mass graves, an example which was followed by various other groups.[62] This endeavour was further aided by the growing historiography on repression.[63]

2.3 Questioning amnesia during the José Luis Rodríguez Zapatero years

In April 2004, José Luis Rodríguez Zapatero, grandson of an executed Republican soldier, became Prime Minister of Spain. It seemed that the moment had come to begin a new post-transitional justice process that would reveal the truth of the past and would lead to the full reparation of victims of Francoism at a time when the victims and their families were driving the pro-memory movement forwards. From the very beginning of the eighth legislature, peripheral nationalist groups and the forces of the left had made the recovery of historical memory their main demand, rectifying in this way what they had been too afraid to address during turbulent times.[64] Thus began what Madeleine Davis appropriately called the break from the pact of forgetting.[65] Politicians were responding to the demands made by civil society, which were encapsulated by the numerous victims' associations and an infinite number of events throughout Spain. Undoubtedly, civil society, and not the politics, was the main driving force behind the Historical Memory Law with its constant demands of the political class for conclusive action on the recovery of historical memory relative to repression during

60 Encarnación, 2014, pp. 132–149.
61 Teitel, 2000, pp. 138–139.
62 Silva and Macías, 2003. Silva, 2006, pp. 571–580; Silva, 2011, pp. 69–75. Ferrándiz, 2006, pp. 529–548. Aróstegui and Gálvez, 2011.
63 Even before the archives were opened to the public, historians had begun taking a more in-depth look at repression during Francoist times, such as Santos Juliá (Juliá, 1999) and Julián Casanova (Casanova 2002), to which we must add the abundance of more localised research, such as the work carried out by Francisco Espinosa Maestre (Espinosa Maestre, 2003), on the Southeast of Spain.
64 Aguilar, 2008, p. 77.
65 Davis, 2005, pp. 858–880.

the Civil War and the dictatorship, as well as extending dignity to the victims who had been inhumanely treated.[66]

The issue of historical memory was a feature of the debate on the inauguration of Zapatero's term as Prime Minister. Joan Herrera i Torres, spokesperson for the ICV, laid down the foundations for how the debate on amnesty would be dealt with throughout the entire legislature when she said that "the compulsive attempts appealing to amnesia were nothing more than a Francoist legacy", and that "forgiving and forgetting" could not be confused.[67]

It was not possible to put an end to the amnesia and to revoke the impunity granted to Francoist crimes without the derogation of the 1977 Amnesty Law. The era of historical memory seemed propitious to bring about the end of the amnesty. As Paloma Aguilar said, the agreements reached during the transition to circumvent the past, although in the short term establishing what could or could not be done, need not last forever; once democracy is instated and the balance of power is re-established, legal obstacles can be bypassed in order to investigate the most grievous violations of human rights, as had, in fact, happened in Chile.[68] Just as Gregorio Monreal, who voted in favour of Law 46/1977, intimated when we interviewed him, what worked in the past does not necessarily work in the present, which is precisely why in the twenty-first century it did not make any sense to maintain the Law.[69] The derogation of the Law would have been justified from a legal standpoint, as it would have fallen in line with the international doctrine and its strong stance against amnesty. However, it was not in the State's interest to revoke the impunity granted to Francoists responsible for the violation of human rights, and therefore it continued to cultivate the Amnesty Law as a symbol of the foundations upon which democracy was built, as can be seen in the process prior to the Historical Memory Law.

On 1 June 2004, the plenary session in the Congress of Deputies passed a motion on the recognition of the victims of the Civil War and Francoism.[70] It urged the government, among other things, to undertake a study on the damages and losses brought about by the war and the subsequent repression during the years of the dictatorship, as well as an analysis of the rights of victims and the compensation they had been issued up to that date. It also sought a study of public and private archives, with the aim of organising them in order to get the most out of them, and to make them available so that the victims could have access to existing aid or new aid packages. New packages included the financial compensation for those who had been killed violently during the transition, which could be received once, as long as the event in question took place between 1 January 1968 and 6 October 1977, as per the temporal scope of the 1977

66 Vinyes, 2009. Martín Pallín and Escudero Alday, 2008, pp. 12 and 17. Escudero Alday, 2009, p. 35.
67 *Official Parliament Gazette*, Congress, no. 2, 15 April 2004, p. 73.
68 Aguilar, 2008, p. 286.
69 Gregorio Monreal interview, 10 April 2016 (Monreal, 2016).
70 *Official Parliament Gazette*, 8 June 2004.

Amnesty Law. It also called upon the government to draft a Bill supporting the victims.

An inter-departmental commission was created to comply with the petition from Congress. Its remit was to publish reports on the state of the victims of the Civil War and the dictatorship and on the conditions to access the public and private archives, as well as drafting a Bill for the regulation of appropriate measures to give recognition and moral satisfaction to the victims.[71] The first measures were concretised in the months that followed through various reparations, both symbolic and material, and with the creation of the Historical Memory Documentary Centre in Salamanca.[72]

The *General Report of the Inter-Departmental Commission on the Situation of Victims of the Civil War and Francoism*, published on 28 July 2006, defended the Amnesty Law, although it recognised that it forfeited the prosecution of Francoist repression.[73] The section entitled "Amnesty and pardon" began by stating that "the Amnesty Law 46/1977, 15th of October, was the most significant milestone in the reparation and restitution of personal liberties for those who had been deprived of them for political reasons linked to the war and the dictatorship".[74] After a careful review of the different measures of clemency granted during the transition, from the coronation of the King up until the 1977 Amnesty Law, the report put forward a "series of proposals for the recovery of memory for those who had been unlawfully convicted", in which the benevolent nature of the Amnesty Law was highlighted once again:

> In the context of the unjustified privation of personal liberties and of unlawful convictions, a lot of people had their personal liberties restored thanks to the Amnesty Law. This was, without any doubt, the main aim of the Law, product of a Spain that was taking its first unstable steps towards democracy, in a Spain that decided to look forward and conquer personal freedoms without looking back.

In the lines that followed the above, the commission recognised that perhaps this was why many of the groups from which it had sought opinions highlighted that "nothing has been done since a constitutional democracy was installed to officially recognise the injustice behind those convictions, and the convictions suffered by many more Spaniards who had already served their time to the full extent of the

71 Royal Decree 1891/2004, 10 September, for the creation of an Inter-Departmental Commission to analyse the situation of the victims of the Civil War and Francoism. *Official State Gazette*, no. 227, 20 September 2004, pp. 31523–31524. Correction of errors, *Official State Gazette*, no. 228, 21 September 2004. The pro-memory associations criticised the Commission for inviting FET-JONS to participate and contribute to the report. See Espinosa Maestre, 2013, p. 134.

72 Egido León, 2006, pp. 1–23. Aguilar and Ramírez Barat, 2014, pp. 218–219.

73 Comisión Interministerial, 2006, p. 30.

74 Comisión Interministerial, 2006, p. 27.

sentence and, for this reason, felt that the Amnesty Law was merely symbolic as it supported them only indirectly". The report, far from criticising Law 46/1977, recommended possible formulas for reparations, and raised the question of whether those formulas could, 30 years after the fact and "without opening the door to the past", acknowledge:

> the profound illicit nature of those convictions, recognising thus, publicly and personally, the civilians who so unfairly suffered from a deserved amnesty which was strictly civic. Time has vindicated the reasons for dealing with these situations, which today ought to reaffirm, through recognition of the past and Memory, our democratic convictions.[75]

The report was a clear indication of the government's intention to sustain the validity and continued enforcement of the 1977 Amnesty Law. Paradoxically, during the "Year of Historical Memory",[76] the year in which the European Council recommended that Spain grant reparations for the multiple violations of human rights during the Civil War and the dictatorship,[77] and the year in which the European Parliament officially condemned Francoism,[78] the policy of not questioning the Amnesty Law meant that the crimes of the dictatorship were erased from memory by a wilful legal amnesia of the past.

2.4 Reports and studies critical of amnesty that generated debates from a legal and historical perspective

Pro-memory associations began to adopt the international doctrine of the time, which was staunchly against blanket amnesty, but these associations did not limit themselves to merely studying the past; they also began to regard the recovery of memory as a matter of justice and made memory an indicator of human rights, therefore making it a legal matter. The challenge before them was daunting, especially given how the doctrine positioned itself with regard to the prescription and the non-retroactive nature of amnesties. To confront this position, the Spanish Association for International Human Rights was founded in 2004 to collaborate with existing societies and to condemn the impunity that was granted by the amnesty in Spain. The work of this association has been crucial. In a relatively short amount of time, it has contributed extensively with its own ideas

75 Comisión Interministerial, 2006, pp. 27–31.

76 The government proclaimed 2006 as the "Year of Historical Memory", after a tortuous process that was began towards the end of 2005. Law 24/2006, 7 July, on the proclamation of 2006 as the Year of Historical Memory. *Official State Gazette*, no 162, 8 July 2006.

77 Permanent Commission of the Parliamentary Assembly of the Council of Europe (PACE), Recommendation 1736(2006), 17 March 2006.

78 In the session of 4 July 2006, the majority of political groups in the European Parliament expressed their condemnation of Franco's regime. Aguilar, 2008, p. 216.

and collaborated with branches of the UN – for example, the Working Group on Enforced or Involuntary Disappearances of the Human Rights Council, the Human Rights Committee and the UN Committee Against Torture[79] – helping to raise awareness of the matter on the international scene.

The team led by Nizkor is another society which has made a valuable contribution from a legal studies perspective to the question of impunity. On 14 April, on the anniversary of the Second Republic, it published, together with 16 other associations,[80] a report entitled *The question of impunity in Spain and crimes under Franco.*[81]

The report published by Nizkor highlighted that crimes against humanity were not subject to statutory limitations, the accountability of the individuals who commit these crimes, whether or not a member of an institution of the State, the impossibility of granting territorial asylum or refuge to those responsible, or suspected as responsible, for crimes against humanity, and that these crimes could not be amnestied. It also pointed out the conditions for demonstrating responsibility are set by international law, irrespective of whether the internal laws of a State fail to impose a sentence for an act constitutive of a crime against humanity, which would not absolve the individual from responsibility under international law. Crimes against humanity, moreover, are subject to the principles of universal criminal jurisdiction.

According to the report, "the failure to respect the rights of the victims of the Francoist repression form part of the context of the impunity which still exists in Spain today". To support the arguments of the report, reference was made to the conclusions reached in Louise Joinet's report from 1997, which was discussed in the previous chapter. In any case, of the 18 measures that the authors of the report proposed as solutions to the problems of historical memory in Spain, none made reference to the 1977 Amnesty Law.

During the lengthy interstice between the presentation of the aforementioned petition in Congress and the 2006 report of the Inter-Departmental Commission, the Spanish section of Amnesty International weighed in on the matter, elaborating important reports that dealt with the matter of amnesty from a legal

79 Villán Durán, 2012, pp. 15–25.

80 Specifically, the other organisations involved were: the Association of Relatives and Friends of the 2nd Republic Victims of Reprisals by the Franco Regime; Gragero Group, Leon; Friends of the Fallen for Liberty (1939–1945); Historical Memory Murcia; Association for the Creation of an Archive of the Civil War; the International Brigades; the Children of the War, Resistance and the Spanish Exile; AGE; APDH (Argentina); Association for the Descendants of the Spanish Exile; the Manuel Azaña Association; Association of Valladolid for the Recovery of Historical Memory; Association of Salamanca for Memory and Justice; the Corporation for the Promotion and Defence of Rights of the People (Chile); Human Rights (California, USA); Forum for Memory; Republican Institute of Human Rights; Young People for Historical Memory "Amnesia"; and Serpaj Europe (Brussels, Belgium). Other organisations were added later.

81 Equipo Nizkor, 2004.

perspective. In December 2004 came the publication *Spain: End the double injustice: Victims of torture and ill-treatment without adequate or just reparation*,[82] which condemned the Spanish impunity for Francoist crimes and the democracy, an issue which it tackled again in 2007 with the report *Spain: Adding insult to injury: The effective impunity of police officers in cases of torture and other ill-treatment.*[83]

Amnesty International turned its attention to the Civil War and the post-war in 2005 when the ARMH asked for its support in the cause of enforced disappearances. Thereafter, Amnesty International published the report *Putting an end to silence and injustice: The pending debt with the victims of the Spanish Civil War and the Franco regime.*[84] It emphasised the idea that many of the crimes committed during the Civil War and the dictatorship contravened international law.[85] But, for the first time in Spain, a new avenue was opened up: article 7 of the Republican Constitution of 1931 declared the incorporation of universal regulations of international law, which linked the principles of the protection of human rights to Spain.[86] According to the democratic state of law prior to the coup d'état and the dictatorship, there were no grounds for amnesty. It is my personal opinion that, as things stand, this avenue does not offer any solutions, unless the constitution is modified, because, as seen in earlier chapters, it does not deny the legitimacy of the dictatorship, considering it a constitutional state, as demonstrated by the legal resolutions passed by the political and military courts against those that opposed Francoism, resolutions whose legality was corroborated by the Supreme Court, despite the lack of the required minimum procedural guarantees.

The Inter-Departmental Commission's general report and the preparation of the historical memory bill motivated Amnesty International to publish a new report, *Victims of the Civil War and Francoism: There is no justice.*[87] The study was particularly preoccupied with what was known of the draft Bill, which, if passed, would cancel and erase from memory the crimes against international law which took place during the transition. Furthermore:

> This interpretation aims to take crimes against international law committed throughout the 20th century (which are excluded from any possible benefits of impunity) and assimilate and include them as political crimes. The legislative proposal made by the Spanish government is equivalent to bringing an end to the cycle with this "end-of-story" law on crimes which under international law, cannot be covered by an amnesty. Two mechanisms of impunity in this bill are specifically oriented towards this "end-of-story", denying the right to the truth and justice.[88]

82 Amnistía Internacional España, 2004.
83 Amnistía Internacional España, 2007.
84 Amnistía Internacional España, 2005.
85 Amnistía Internacional España, 2005.
86 Amnistía Internacional España, 2005, p. 12.
87 Amnistía Internacional España, 2006.
88 Amnistía Internacional España, 2006, pp. 18–19.

As well as these reports from international and Spanish organisations, new academic studies began to emerge. International law Professors Margalida Capellá[89] and Javier Chinchón Álvarez[90] were pioneers in this research area. In their first publications, they put forward their main findings, which they would analyse more in depth in subsequent studies, making them the experts on this matter. In 2006, another internationalist, Antonio Remiro Brotóns, went as far as claiming that promulgation of the amnesty laws, "by offering impunity for crimes which were grave according to international law, is itself illegal, as it is not compatible with the law that makes its prosecution obligatory".[91]

The legal arguments were preceded by an intense debate in historiographic circles, which began in 2003, on whether the transition and subsequent democracy had willed erasure of the past.[92] The main contributors to this debate will suffice to summarise the positions of each side. Santos Juliá published a controversial article which closed ranks and staunchly defended the transition, rejecting the idea of an amnesiac society that was too afraid to face the past. The 1977 Amnesty Law, and its orientation towards looking ahead in the years following its promulgation, was, in practical terms, antithetical to amnesia, as the transition and consolidation of the democracy did not stop the emergence and dissemination of academic studies, memoirs, documentaries, exhibitions, symposia, newspaper articles, etc.[93] Juliá was countered by various historians, among whom Francisco Espinosa is the most prominent, author of various articles which he collected in his book *Contra el olvido* (*Against forgetting*).[94]

Both historians continued their dispute. Santos Juliá maintained his position that removing the past from the political debate did not imply amnesia when it came to investigating the repression of the Civil War and Francoism.[95] Espinosa, for his part, put forward his arguments in his book *Shoot the Messenger? Spanish Democracy and the Crimes of Francoism. From the Pact of Silence to the Trial of Baltasar Garzón*, published in 2013.[96] In his view, the pact made during the transition, extending throughout the 1980s and 1990s, prolonged the amnesia and the silence on Francoist repression, and it was exacerbated by the lack of sensibility towards historical memory demonstrated by the PP and PSOE governments, which prejudiced the establishment of a cultural democracy in Spain. In relation to the 1977 Amnesty Law, Espinosa distances himself from Juliá's views by claiming that the law is evidence enough that the right wing was in control of the transition process, allowing it to put in place measures that prevented prosecuting

89 Capellá i Roig, 2005a. Capellá i Roig, 2006.
90 Chinchón Álvarez, 2007a.
91 Remiro Brotóns, 2006, p. 500.
92 For a balanced historiographical account, see López Villaverde, 2014, pp. 263–283.
93 Juliá, 2003b, pp. 14–24.
94 Espinosa Maestre, 2006, to which he added a further article (Espinosa Maestre, 2007). See, also, Faber, 2007, pp. 165–190.
95 Juliá, 2008, p. 107.
96 Espinosa Maestre, 2013.

Francoism, or creating a truth commission to reveal the true extent of the repression, to which he added that there had been insufficient reparation.

My personal opinion is that Santos Juliá is mistaken when he, on the basis of a so-called freedom for historical research, denies that the 1977 Law encouraged erasure of the past. Article 2 of the Law 26/1977 put measures in place to avoid prosecuting Francoist crimes, as had happened in Greece and Portugal. Official institutions did not present any initiatives to reconstruct historical memory until many years later, nor did they put forward any mediating measures to facilitate research on Francoist repression. Although these were not issues strictly derived from the Amnesty Law, they were a direct result of the "pact to forget" agreed by politicians at the time.[97] The pioneers in the study and dissemination on the repression of 1936 and on the Francoist violation of human rights during the dictatorship and the transition were not subject to a "gag order" – to use Holmes'[98] expression, which would delight Juliá, no doubt – that stopped them from undertaking their studies and reconstructing the past. But it is also true that those studies were undertaken in very difficult circumstances, even under the threat of death at times, as happened to my own father, José María Jimeno Jurío.[99] The violent actions of extreme right groups against pro-memory magazines, such as *Punto y Hora de Euskal Herria* or *Interviú*,[100] which were the first to publish the history behind the 1936 repression, and against the exhumations that took place during the transition, are proof enough that Juliá's so-called freedom ignores the reality of the situation.

Historiography, as Batolomé Clavero points out, cannot be a substitute for justice, and especially not as an excuse to deny justice.[101] Research into the past, commendable and courageous as it was, could not fulfil the function of legal investigations. Judges could have ordered an investigation of archival sources which are still unavailable to researchers, they could have stopped the purging of this material in the interest of the truth, or they could have summoned witnesses to declare and imposed appropriate sentences. The Amnesty Law blocked all these possible measures in Spain's transitional justice, which was not the case in other transitional processes that took place around the same time. Historical research cannot be a substitute for a truth commission, inexistent in Spain, which would have analysed Francoist crimes.

2.5 The Congress of Deputies debate on Spain's wilful amnesia

The Amnesty International report *Spain: Putting an end to silence and injustice*[102] was brought to the Congress of Deputies by Gaspar Llamazares, United Left deputy,

97 See Sartorius and Alfaya, 1999.
98 Holmes, [1988] 1993.
99 Jimeno, 2006, pp. 18–19.
100 Ferrándiz and Aguilar, 2016, pp. 1–25.
101 Clavero, 2014, p. 276.
102 Amnistía Internacional España, 2008a.

on 8 August 2008, when he raised an issue in relation to the provisions put in place to deal with the recommendations made by Amnesty International vis-à-vis justice for the victims of the Civil War and Francoism. The government's answer was anchored to the discourse of amnesia and reconciliation,[103] and, we could add, to the implied legality of the Francoist State and its repressive laws and the concomitant illegality of the Republican constitutional State.

There were also two Bills on historical memory that were dismissed in the Congress of Deputies. The Bills, presented by the parliamentary groups Republican Left of Catalonia (ERC) and United Left-Initiative for Catalonian Greens (IU-ICV) on 21 November 2005, were dismissed in the Plenary of 21 February after the PSOE, the PP, the CiU and the Canary Islands Coalition voted against it. These were the first Bills that were directed at the victims of Francoism, but neither recommended the derogation of the Law 46/1977. The ERC proposal, entitled *Bill on historical memory, Republican and Anti-Fascist*,[104] at least criticised the impunity that was extended to Francoist crimes under the Amnesty Law in the preamble:

> In terms of the legal aspect, Spain is far from complying with the obligation placed on a constitutional state that observes the international doctrine. We refer to the jurisprudence that was established on the back of the Nuremberg trials, which described the crimes committed by Nazis as crimes against humanity. By extension, we include under this description the crimes committed by the Francoist regime, which will never prescribe.
>
> Neither the death of Franco on the 20th of November, 1975, nor the period of transition, brought about a genuine reconciliation after the period under the military dictatorship, which was described as change without breaking away.
>
> In Spain, the continued legal status of Francoism during the transition process leading to the 1978 constitution, impeded the creation of a truth and reconciliation commission that could prosecute those responsible for crimes against humanity during the Francoist regime. The Amnesty Law of the 15th of October, 1977, set democratic political prisoners free, but at the same time, it granted impunity to the politicians of the Francoist regime for the crimes they had committed [...].

The second additional provision of the Bill took up the matter of international criminal law in relation to the statutory limitations of crimes against humanity, and stated that the government should support claims made by citizens, entities or institutions regarding crimes against humanity during the Francoist regime.

103 Government's answer: *Official Parliament Gazette*, Congress of Deputies, no. D-298, 29 November 2005, p. 767.

104 *Official Parliament Gazette*, Congress of Deputies, series B, no. 219–1, 2 December 2005, pp. 1–9.

It was the first time that a Bill was presented in Parliament which, had it succeeded, would have opposed the Amnesty Law. The Bill put forward by the ERC was scrupulously based on the international law on crimes against humanity, and thus described Francoist crimes as crimes against humanity. The Bill gave a political form to the recommendations made in the report published by the pro-memory associations led by the Nizkor Group (2004) and in the Spanish section of Amnesty International (2004 and 2005).

The Bill promoting the recovery and development of Democratic Memory and Culture, put forward by IU-ICV,[105] was not as ambitious. It made no mention of the amnesty which had been granted to Francoist criminals or the impunity for crimes against humanity committed during the dictatorship, with the exception of the null convictions in the summary trials held by the War Councils and the revocation of full rights in all the resolutions dictated by courts with political responsibilities.

Both these Bills were debated at length on 21 February 2006.[106] Neither the parliamentary spokespeople, nor those in favour or against the Bill made any mention of the Amnesty Law. However, Joan Tardá i Coma (ERC) did point out that the socialist governments led by Felipe González imposed a "historic amnesty", which subsequent governments "led by *Caudillo* Aznar" reoriented in an exercise of "enthusiastic historical revisionism that sought to legitimise the coup d'état in the 1934 annals of history".

Manuel Atencia Robledo (PP) made a rigorous defence of the constitutional pact, which led to the "pact of reconciliation, harmony and freedom". He denied that Spain was amnesiac about its history, given that those who forged the constitutional pact "invoked the past in order to avoid making repeating the mistakes of the 20th century".

In contrast to the PP, Jordi Xuclà i Costa (CiU) recognised that the pact had instated a "collective and selective amnesia" during the transition, which could only be abated by the willingness to "set in motion" the Historical Memory Law; nevertheless, he agreed on the point of reconciliation.

The spokesperson for the socialist group, Ramón Jáuregui, also defended the transition. He maintained that the process was sustained "by a pact to forgive (I said forgive, not forget), for reconciliation and to install a new democracy on the basis of a political consensus". However, he did not offer any guarantees that the government and the socialist party would drive the law on historical memory, given that "wounds are healed by the truth and justice, not by concealment and amnesia".

In the view of Joan Herrera i Torres (IU-ICV), the problem was not forgiving but "the prior amnesia, whose consequences are still felt today, such as, for the

105 *Official Parliament Gazette*, Congress of Deputies, series B, no. 218–1, 2 December 2005, pp. 1–11.

106 *Sessions record of the Chamber of Deputies*, no. 152, Plenary session 141, Plenary and Permanent Council, 7th Legislature, 21 February 2006.

lack of public policy in this country for the due recovery of historical memory". He remarked on the "extraordinary anomaly of living in the European country that had the longest dictatorship, yet issued the fewest public policies on the recovery of memory", and furthermore, he said, "the amnesia has transformed itself in to a kind of indifference towards those dark years, and, worst of all, indifference towards the struggle of hundreds, thousands of people who fought for democracy in this Spain".

It is significant that every parliamentary spokesperson, irrespective of their position in relation to historical memory, avoided using the terms "pact of forgetting" or "pact of silence". Forgetting, amnesia and silence were words that carried a negative connotation for every group. Those in favour of perpetuating the myth around the transition used terms such as "constitutional pact" (PP) and "pact to forgive" (PSOE) instead. But neither of these terms is faithful to the reality of the Amnesty Law. The "constitutional pact" cannot be applied to "amnesia", given that the latter did not derive from the constitution, but from the Law 46/1977, which came before the constitution; while the "pact to forgive" was also false because those who have to forgive are the victims of Francoist crimes, who did not have any transitional justice mechanisms at their disposal to get justice and the truth, and who had to make do with piecemeal measures for partial or insufficient reparation adopted during the transition.

3 Restorative and reparative regulation for the Republican side, subsidiary of the Amnesty Laws (1983 to March 2007)

3.1 Restorative regulations for ex-Republican soldiers (1983–1985)

When the PSOE came to power in 1983, the families of the victims of the Civil War and the dictatorship had reason to hope once more, but they soon realised that the pact of forgetting did not extend beyond partial reparation. The absence of an official investigation into human rights violations meant that adequate economic and moral reparations for the victims and their rights could not be made. Moreover, the State did not initiate any public policies with a view to holding public acts calling for a State apology or to recognise the harm caused by the Francoist regime, tributes, or educational programmes on memory.[107] To add insult to injury, the democratic State that emerged from the transition continued to legitimise the dictatorship by not abrogating its legislation or overturning sentences passed during the regime, which concomitantly implied the illegality of the Second Spanish Republic.[108]

107 Escudero Alday, 2013b, pp. 200 and 204.

108 In 1982, the Constitutional Court denied that Republican regulation was legal or still valid. Constitutional Court sentence 28/1982, 26 May. *Official State Gazette*, no. 137, 9 June 1982.

The assumed illegality of the Second Spanish Republic was not a problem when it came to formulating, in theory, a balanced and fair system to distribute the 1977 Amnesty Law reparation to both the public servants of the Republican State and the civil servants of the preceding Francoist state; in practice, however, the preparation system was fraught with inequality. The Republican soldiers felt that they were treated unfairly regarding the amnesty reparations, which went against the principle of equality enshrined in the constitution.[109] The Constitutional Court dismissed an appeal by the Aviation Association of the Republic and other claimants on the grounds of unconstitutionality on 20 July 1983.

Through these years, new measures had to be adopted to deal with the groups of people who benefitted from a pardon or amnesty. The first measures of 1983 focused on developing preliminary legislation for the retributions and pensions extended to soldiers who had been maimed in the war,[110] and setting up provincial bodies to administer the Special Pensions File related to the Civil War.[111]

The Law of 22 October 1984[112] extended the scope of the Decree of 6 March 1978 in relation to Republican soldiers. Because this decree focused solely on professional soldiers, its scope excluded many civilian soldiers. The decree itself promised a solution to the problem that was not resolved by the Law of 15 October 1977. The preamble spoke of the "legal duty to recognise the service provided during the Civil War by such civilians". The new Law was extended to "those who did not belong to the Armed Forces before said war, but participated as rank members of the Republican Army, obtaining in these a job or a degree, similar to those who, during the war, integrated into armed corps or institutions". This recognition gave civilian soldiers the right to "use the honour bestowed and based on the condition and official rank as determined by the scope provisioned in this Law, as well as access to a pension and benefits derived from medical assistance for the civilians in question and their families". The Law was developed through the Royal Decree of 19 June 1985.[113]

The legal text highlighted the beginning of a problem. Those who had not been professional soldiers prior to the beginning of the war had to prove their military status during the conflict, a process that needed an investigation into

109 Constitutional Court sentence 63/1983, 20 July. *Official State Gazette*, no. 189, 9 August 1983. See Baylos Grau, 2008, pp. 189–190. Pérez Amorós, 2009, p. 157.

110 Royal Decree 1071/1983, 16 March, for the approval of the regulatory measures for the Process for the Law 6/1982, 29 March, whereby basic retribution is extended to the maimed soldiers of the Civil War and pensions for their next of kin. *Official State Gazette*, no. 107, 5 May 1983, pp. 12521–12523.

111 Order of 9 May 1983, to set up provincial competent bodies to administer the Special Pensions File derived from the Civil War. *Official State Gazette*, no. 123, 24 May 1983.

112 Law 37/1984, of 22 October, to uphold the rights and recognise the service provided of those who, during the Civil War, were part of the Armed Forces, Public Order Forces and the Police Corp of the Republic. *Official State Gazette*, no. 262, 1 November 1984, pp. 31689–31690.

113 Royal Decree 1033/1985, 19 June, to develop Law 37/1984, 22 October. *Official State Gazette*, no. 156, 1 July 1985, pp. 20544–20548.

documents which were stored in a file that was not particularly accessible, especially for those who needed to obtain information.

Although the Law was issued by a Socialist government, lawmakers resisted fully equating Republican soldiers to the Falangist soldiers, as can be seen in article 2, which automatically granted military retirement to Republican soldiers. The inequality in another two articles motivated three more appeals on the grounds on unconstitutionality.[114] The first two were summarily dismissed,[115] but the third culminated in a sentence, passed on 7 July 1987, which established that the temporal scope of the law prejudiced Republican soldiers depending on whether they had incorporated to the Republican Army before or after the beginning of the war, especially because there was no such caveat for civil servants. The sentence declared articles 1 and 4 to be partially unconstitutional, and equated the situation of civil servants with that of the soldiers;[116] however, civilian soldiers were not included in this soldier bracket.

3.2 Reparative regulation for workers in Catalan and Basque autonomous administrations

As discussed earlier, civil servants who worked in the Catalan Generalitat during the Republic were economically compensated during the transition; however, those who were not civil servants but worked in the same institution were not included in this reparative measure, and had to be compensated through the regional Law of 20 March 1984.[117]

The Basque Country was the second autonomous community to pass its Statute during the Second Spanish Republic and install administrative institutions, although the advancement of the Civil War in this territory prevented it from developing as many institutions as in Catalonia. The Law of 22 June 1983 sought to economically compensate all the workers in the Basque Country Autonomous Administration,[118] a measure which was completed in 1985[119] and 1986.[120]

114 See Chinchón Álvarez, 2007a, pp. 138 et seq. Baylos Grau, 2008, pp. 190–191.

115 Constitutional Court sentence 164/1987, 27 October, which dismisses the appeal on grounds of unconstitutionality 390/1986. Constitutional Court sentence 163/1987, 27 October, which dismisses the appeal on grounds of unconstitutionality 389/1986.

116 Constitutional Court sentence 116/1987, 7 July, which declares articles 1 and 4 of Law 37/1984 partially unconstitutional.

117 Law 8/1984, 20 March, on eventual staff, hired or temporary, in the Generalitat during the period prior to 1939. *Official Diary of the Catalan Generalitat*, 4 April 1984.

118 Law 11/1983, 22 June, on the labour and passive rights of the staff that lent their services to the Autonomous Administration in the Basque Country. *Official Basque Country Gazette*, 4 July 1983.

119 Law 8/1985, 23 October, to complement Law 11/1983, 22 June, on the labour and passive rights of the staff that lent their services to the Autonomous Administration in the Basque Country. *Official Basque Country Gazette*, no. 241, 25 November 1985.

120 Legislative Decree 1/1986, 13 May, passing the text merging labour and passive rights of the staff that lent their services to the Autonomous Administration in the Basque Country. *Official Basque Country Gazette*, 24 May 1986.

A sentence issued by the Constitutional Court rejected the Spanish government's appeal on grounds of unconstitutionality against the two laws passed by the Basque government in 1983 and 1985, on the labour and passive rights of people who worked in the Basque Country Autonomous Administration between 1936 and 1978. The constitutionality of the regulation backed up the autonomous communities' move to recognise the rights derived from judicial situations that emerged from the legality of the Autonomous Statutes of the Second Spanish Republic.[121]

There was one final measure, issued on 27 March 2002, which recognised and economically compensated the teaching staff in Basque schools opened during the Francoist period, and which had not been legally recognised.[122]

3.3 Rehabilitation of the professional soldiers excluded from the Amnesty Laws (1986)

The Law of 24 December 1986 to rehabilitate professional soldiers concluded the 50th anniversary of the Civil War.[123] The law meant that soldiers from the UMD had to be included in the amnesty. These soldiers, as discussed earlier, had been released from prison by the 1976 Amnesty Law, but they were not able to return to their jobs because the 1977 Amnesty Law did not abolish the penalty of discharge from the Army. The soldiers affected continued to demand their reintegration.

This law originates in the second socialist legislature, strengthened by its re-election with an overall majority and the successful referendum on Spain's continued membership of NATO. Nevertheless, the topic was still controversial. The Defence Council of the Chamber of Deputies had debated the Bill on 2 December 1986. Enrique Curiel, of United Left, advocated for an explicit mention to UMD soldiers in the preamble of the legal text, but the Socialist Group went against the proposal, and it was struck down. On the other hand, all the groups of the opposition wanted the benefits of the law to extend to those in the second lieutenant rank who had been separated or discharged for political reasons, thus enabling them to return to work in their respective ranks. Once more, however, the Socialist Group said that this was not possible, as the objective of the Bill was different and specific.[124]

121 Constitutional Court sentence, 76/1986, 9 June. *Official State Gazette*, no. 159, 9 June 1986. See Baylos Grau, 2008, p. 190.

122 Law 3/2002, 27 March, in relation to the recognition and compensation for the teaching staff in Basque schools prior to their legal normalisation. *Official Basque Country Gazette*, 10 April 2002. Developed through Decree 99/2003, 6 May. *Official Basque Country Gazette*, 9 May 2003.

123 Law 24/1986, 24 December, on the rehabilitation of professional soldiers. *Official State Gazette*, no. 312, 30 December 1986, pp. 42370–42371.

124 *El País*, 3 December 1986.

The Law recognised that the application of the amnesties established in the 1976 and 1977 Laws fostered inequality in relation to other public employees. The measure only affected 13 UMD soldiers, nine of whom were able to apply for re-integration to the Army with the rank that would have corresponded to their years of service had they remained active. All of the soldiers applied to go on temporary standby, which equated to retirement but with a full salary, as if they had been active all along. The other four were second lieutenants discharged from the Infantry Academy in 1973. In their case, rehabilitation allowed them to obtain the corresponding military rank that they would have been entitled to had they not been discharged, but they could not re-integrate in the Armed Forces, and thus went into active standby or retirement.[125]

These 13 soldiers were publicly recognised by the Council of Ministers in 2009.[126]

3.4 The regulation of aid for those who were deprived of liberties as a consequence of the acts observed in the Amnesty Law (1990–2005)

The more ambitious restorative policies initiated by the Socialist government focused on compensating political prisoners. The aim was to give compensation for time served in jail when the incarceration was due to crimes covered by the amnesty. The first measure was the Law of 8 June 1984, which recognised in retrospect time served as work experience, granting access to the social welfare system for those who benefitted from the amnesty.[127]

Nevertheless, the first initiative in democratic times for the economic compensation of those who served time for amnestied crimes was not until the State Budget of 1990.[128] Specifically, the 18th additional provision established

125 *El País*, 31 December 1986.

126 Order PRE/3279/2009, 4 December, for the publication of the Institutional Declaration recognising members of the Armed Forces during the transition to democracy, with special mention to the Military Democratic Union (UMD). *Official State Gazette*, no. 293, 5 December 2009, pp. 103550–103551.

127 Law 18/1984, 8 June, on the transmutation of years served as a consequence of amnestied crimes in prison as years of work experience for Social Welfare purposes. *Official State Gazette*, no. 140, 12 June 1984, p. 16936. Developed by the Order of 1 October 1984, to establish regulations for the application of the provisions in Law 18/1984, 8 June. *Official State Gazette*, no. 236, 2 October 1984, pp. 28558–28559.

128 Law 4/1990, 29 June, on the State Budget for 1990. *Official State Gazette*, no. 156, 30 June 1990, pp. 18669–18710. It was completed with Resolution no. 14 issued from the Revenue State Secretariat, which ordered the publication of the Council of Ministers Agreement establishing the Prior Auditing System regulating article 95 of the redrafted text for the General Budget Law in relation to compensation for those who were imprisoned as a consequence of acts covered under Law 46/1977, 15 October, on Amnesty, as well as pensioners (*Official State Gazette*, no. 303, 19 December 1990, pp. 37847–37848) and the Resolution of the 26 December 1990, issued from the Directorate General for Personal and Public Pensions, on the delegation of powers in relation to pensioners (*Official State Gazette*, no. 313, 31 December 1990).

that those who had served three or more years in prison would be eligible for aid; however, it added an important caveat: only those over the age of 65 (as of 31 December 1990) would be eligible; in the event that the person in question was deceased, the compensation would be transferred to a living spouse who was in receipt of a widow's pension. Compensation was fixed at one million pesetas (913.24 pesetas per day) for every three years of time served, and 200,000 pesetas (182.64 pesetas per day) for any additional periods of three years.

The Directorate-General for Staff Costs and Public Pensions of the Department of Finance and Spanish Revenue received some 120,000 applications before the deadline, of which 65,000 compensation packages were awarded, with 90% of these worth a million pesetas in total, and only the remaining 10% (that is, corresponding to those who had served six or more years in prison) received more than a million.[129]

The State Budget Law was the subject of a number of appeals on the grounds of unconstitutionality, given that it understood an element of discrimination towards anyone who had not reached the stipulated age. The sentence passed by the Constitutional Court of 3 December 1993[130] confirmed the constitutionality of this measure, fixing the requisite age at 64 as of 1990. The sentence explained that the claims of unconstitutionality were without foundation because of the criteria geared towards limiting public spending and restraining access to available resources. This explanation opened the door for Public Administrations to develop further discretionary allowances. As we will see in the section that follows, the Constitutional Court pointed out that, although it was "compensation" in name, some measures were not compensations per se, but allowances "graciously" granted by the legislator in relation to the amnesty legislation.[131]

Complementary to the Law was an exemption from tax on compensation payments in the 1991 Annual Tax Declaration.[132]

The Law was modified at different stages,[133] until the 2007 Historical Memory Law established new mechanisms for reparation. These modifications were insufficient nevertheless, and the application of the Law was deficient. Between 2004 and 2006, deputy Isabel López Aulestia, of United Left, presented various

129 Vallès Muñío, 2004, p. 21.

130 Spanish Constitutional Court, 361/1993, Judgment of 3 December 1993. *Official State Gazette*, no. 311, 29 December 1993, pp. 66–72.

131 Chinchón Álvarez, 2007b, pp. 142–143. Chinchón Álvarez, 2009c, p. 68. Chinchón Álvarez, 2012a, pp. 34–35. Baylos Grau, 2008, pp. 202–204.

132 Tenth additional disposition of the Law 18/1991, 6 June, regulating income tax. *Official State Gazette*, no. 136, 7 June 1991, pp. 18665–18691.

133 Law 31/1991, 30 December, on National State Budget for the year 1992. *Official State Gazette*, no. 313, 31 December 1991, pp. 41871–41916. Law 42/1994, 30 December, on fiscal, administrative and social measures. *Official State Gazette*, no. 313, 31 December 1994, pp. 39457–39504. Law 30/2005, 29 December, on National State Budgets for the year 2006. *Official State Gazette*, no. 312, 30 December 2005. Law 35/2006, 28 November, on income tax and partial modification of Laws on corporate tax, non-resident tax and estates. *Official State Gazette*, no. 285, 29 November 2006.

parliamentary questions regarding the review of unsuccessful applications for compensation and on the delayed resolutions for some applications. Both these issues related to the application of the above-mentioned additional disposition.[134]

The same deputy also presented a parliamentary question on 8 February 2008, in the governmental forecasts in relation to granting compensation to the autonomous communities which had granted economic aid in application of the 18th additional disposition in Law 4/1990. The question was asked *viva voce* in the Commission,[135] and was answered by the government on 13 April.[136]

Beyond the goodwill expressed by the Socialist government and the future Historical Memory Law which promised to be a solution for all these problems, the reality was that the autonomous communities were responsible for the bulk of the economic aid for those who had been imprisoned for political reasons during the regime. The communities which had issued regulations continued granting the aid they had established in previous years, while the communities which had not, issued their corresponding regulation measures.

3.5 Aid granted by autonomous communities to people imprisoned for political reasons during the Civil War and the dictatorship (March 1995–2007)

The regulation of the 1990 State aid packages to compensate the victims who spent three or more years in jail during the Civil War and the dictatorship was harshly criticised for establishing a minimum of three years in order to access compensation for time spent in prison. To resolve this situation, the majority of the autonomous communities developed further complementary regulations for those who had been excluded from compensation packages related to the Amnesty Law, whether they missed out because of their age or because they had spent fewer than three years in prison. The autonomous communities could issue these regulations under the guise of a social welfare package because, like the State aid packages, they were also aimed at social reintegration. This autonomous regulation created certain irregularities when it came to the political prisoners, as those in specific autonomous communities received more money than others. At the present time, only Galicia and Extremadura have failed to regulate this matter.

134 Question put forward on 2 November 2004; government answer in *Official Parliament Gazette*, I, no. 156, 24 January 2005. Question put forward on 8 February 2005 (*Official Parliament Gazette*, I, no. 203, 5 April 2005, question asked orally in the Commission); government answer in *Official Parliament Gazette*, I, no. 210 13 April 2005. Question put forward on 30 March 2005 (*Official Parliament Gazette*, I, no. 213, 15 April 2005, recanted). Question put forward on 8 September 2005 (dropped).

135 *Official Parliament Gazette*, I, no. 203, 5 April 2005.

136 *Official Parliament Gazette*, I, no. 210, 13 April 2005.

According to one of the foremost experts on the matter,[137] Daniel Vallès,[138] the compensation packages granted by the autonomous communities in observance of the Amnesty Law, share the following characteristics: (a) the recipients are individuals who had been deemed ineligible for State aid by the Spanish State; (b) the concessions are based on territoriality criteria, such as duration of residency, registered residency, etc.; (c) single lump-sum economic benefit is proportional to the duration of imprisonment and, in some cases, the age of the individual in question; and (d) clause of incompatibility with any other type of aid or compensation granted by a Public Administration for imprisonment after the Civil War and according to the stipulations of the Amnesty Law.

The following is a list, in chronological order, of the various autonomous regulations issued up until March 2004. Those issued after this date will be taken up in the next chapter.

Navarre was the first to regulate compensation when it issued the Regional Decree 75/1995, of 20 March, regulating the payment of compensations to those who were imprisoned as a consequence of acts covered under Law 46/1977, and who did not benefit from the 18th additional disposition in the 1990 Law on General State Budgets.[139]

Three years later, Madrid issued its first Decree regulating the payment of compensation for those who had been imprisoned as a consequence of acts covered under Law 46/1977, but could not avail of State-aid packages because they did not satisfy the age requirements stipulated in the State legislation.[140] The Decree was completed by the Ministry of the President Order granting the corresponding aid packages.[141] The sheer volume of applications received meant that the deadline for applications was extended,[142] and new technical and legal problems in practice motivated modifications to the Order.[143] These measures in

137 *Official Parliament Gazette*, I, no. 210, 13 April 2005, pp. 25–42.
138 Vallès Muñío, 2004, p. 26.
139 *Official Navarre Gazette*, no. 42, 3 April 1995.
140 Decree 39/1999, 11 March, regulating compensation aid packages for those who had been imprisoned as a consequence of acts covered under Law 46/1977, 15 October, on Amnesty, but could not avail of State aid because they did not satisfy the age requirements stipulated in the State Legislation. *Official Madrid Community Gazette*, no. 65, 18 March 1999.
141 Ministry of the Presidency Order 491/1999, 22 March, granting aid to those who were imprisoned for acts covered under the Law 46/1977, 15 October, on Amnesty, but could not avail of State aid because they did not satisfy the age requirements stipulated in the State Legislation. *Official Madrid Community Gazette*, no. 70, 24 March 1999.
142 Ministry of the Presidency Order 1134/1999, 22 June, extending the deadline for applications set in Order 491/1999, 22 March, on economic aid for those who had been imprisoned as a consequence of acts covered under Law 46/1977, 15 October, on Amnesty, but could not avail of State aid because they did not satisfy the age requirements stipulated in the State Legislation. *Official Madrid Community Gazette*, no. 148, 25 June 1999.
143 Ministry of the Presidency Order 1342/1999, 15 July, modifying Order 491/1999, 22 March, granting aid to those who were imprisoned for acts covered under the Law

Madrid were followed by the 1999 Asturias Decree on compensation for former prisoners and victims of political reprisals.[144]

The year 2000 saw a proliferation of these measures. Asturias[145] and Madrid[146] regulated their compensation payments once again, while Aragon[147] and Catalonia[148] issued their first measures. The following year, Catalonia would issue two further laws to extend the deadlines established in its first Decree.[149]

46/1977, 15 October, on Amnesty, but could not avail of State aid because they did not satisfy the age requirements stipulated in the State Legislation. *Official Madrid Community Gazette*, no. 173/1999, 23 July 1999. Resolution of 20 October 1999, of the General Technical Secretariat of the Ministry of the Presidency, formulating a proposal for a provisional resolution in relation to Ministry of the Presidency Order 491/1999, 22 March, granting aid to those who were imprisoned for acts covered under the Law 46/1977, 15 October, on Amnesty, but could not avail of State aid because they did not satisfy the age requirements stipulated in the State Legislation. *Official Madrid Community Gazette*, no. 253/1999, 25 October 1999.

144 Decree 22/1999, 29 April, on compensation for former prisoners and those who suffered political reprisals. *Official Gazette of the Principality of Asturias*, no. 109, 13 May 1999.

145 Decree 21/2000, 2 March, on compensation for former prisoners and those who suffered political reprisals. *Official Gazette of the Principality of Asturias*, 15 March 2000. Modified by the Decree 89/2000, 21 December. *Official Gazette of the Principality of Asturias*, no. 301, 30 December 2000.

146 Decree 47/2000, 23 March, regulating compensation for those who were imprisoned for at least a year as a consequence of acts covered under Law 46/1977, 15 October, on Amnesty. *Official Community of Madrid Gazette*, no. 80, 4 April 2000.

147 Decree 100/2000, 16 May, regulating compensation for those who had their liberties embargoed as a consequence of acts covered under the Law 46/1977, 15 October, on Amnesty, but could not avail of compensation packages established in the 18th additional disposition in the Law 4/1990, 29 June, on General State Budgets for the year 1990. *Official Aragon Gazette*, no. 63, 31 May 2000. Completed with the Order of 26 June 2000, issued by the Department of Economy, Taxation, and Employment, publishing the definitive annexes of the Decree 100/2000, 16 May, issued by the Government of Aragon regulating compensation for those who had their liberties embargoed as a consequence of acts covered under the Law 46/1977, 15 October, on Amnesty, but could not avail of compensation packages established in the 18th additional disposition in the Law 4/1990, 25 June, on General State Budgets for the year 1990. *Official Aragon Gazette*, no. 81, 10 July 2000.

148 Decree 288/2000, 31 August, establishing requisites to regulate compensation for persons included in the Law 46/1977, 15 October, on Amnesty, but were excluded from the benefits in the 18th additional disposition in the Law 4/1990, 29 June, on General State Budgets for the years 1990 and 1992. *Official Gazette of the Catalan Generalitat*, no. 3221, 7 September 2000.

149 Decree 145/2001, 29 May, to modify Decree 288/2000, 31 August, establishing requisites to regulate compensation for persons included in the Law 46/1977, 15 October, on Amnesty, but were excluded from the benefits in the 18th additional disposition in the Law 4/1990, 29 June, on General State Budgets for the years 1990 and 1992. *Official Gazette of the Catalan Generalitat*, no. 3403, 6 June 2001. Law 16/2001, 29 November, extending the deadline for resolutions after the administration and submission of applications, as per Decree 288/2000, 31 August. *Official Gazette of the Catalan Generalitat*, no. 3525, 30 November 2001.

Andalusia,[150] Castile and Leon[151] and the Balearic Islands[152] followed suit in 2001. Catalonia demonstrated its sensibilities with regard to this matter when it issued a new measure in 2002, extending the scope of those who could benefit from economic compensation.[153] Four more communities issued their respective regulations: Castile-La Mancha,[154] Cantabria,[155] Canaries[156] and the Basque Autonomous Community.[157] The latter measures had to be modified twice in 2003,[158] the same year in which Castile and Leon[159] and Andalusia[160] issued two

150 Decree 1/2001, 9 January, establishing compensation for former prisoners and those who suffered from political reprisals who were in prison for more than three years, as well as agreeing on an open call for those who were in prison for fewer than three years. *Official Gazette of the Andalusian Government*, no. 11, 27 January 2001.

151 Decree 171/2001, 14 June, regulating the basis for application and concession of economic aid to persons covered under the Law 46/1977, 17 October, on Amnesty, but were excluded from the benefits in the 18th additional disposition in the Law 4/1990, 29 June, on General State Budgets for the years 1990 and 1992. *Official Castile-Leon Gazette of the Andalusian Government*, 20 June 2001.

152 Ministry of the Presidency Order, 27 December 2001, on compensation for persons resident in the Balearic Islands whose liberty was embargoed as a consequence of acts covered under the Law 46/1977, 15 October, on Amnesty. BOIB 31-XII-2001.

153 Decree 330/2002, 3 December, regulating economic compensation for persons under 65 years of age as of the 31 December, 2000, whose liberties were embargoed and were included in Law 46/1977, 15 October, on Amnesty. *Official Gazette of the Catalan Generalitat*, no. 3777, 9 December 2002.

154 Decree 31/2002, 26 February, regulating compensation for those who were in prison for the acts covered under the Law 46/1977 but were excluded from the benefits in the 18th additional disposition in the Law 4/1990, 29 June, on General State Budgets for the years 1990 and 1992. *Official Gazette of Castile-La Mancha*, no. 28, 6 March 2002.

155 Decree 77/2002, 28 June, regulating aid for persons included in Law 46/1977, 15 October, on Amnesty. *Official Gazette of Cantabria*, 12 July 2002.

156 Law 9/2002, 21 October, on compensation for persons excluded from the benefits in the 18th additional disposition in the Law 4/1990, 29 June, on General State Budgets for the years 1990 and 1992. *Official Gazette of the Canaries*, no. 143, 5 November 2002. Modified by Law 6/2005, 2 December. *Official Gazette of the Canaries*, 5 December 2005.

157 Decree 330/2002, 3 December, regulating compensation for persons under 65 years of age as of 31 December 2000, whose liberties were embargoed and were included in the Law 46/1977, 15 October, on Amnesty. DOGC 9-XII-2002.

158 Decree 3/2003 14 January, modifying the Decree on compensation for those whose liberties were embargoed for acts covered under the Amnesty Law. *Official Basque Country Gazette*, no. 11, 17 January 2003. Decree 301/2003, 9 December, on a second modification to the Decree on compensation for those whose liberties were embargoed for acts covered under the Amnesty Law. *Official Basque Country Gazette*, no. 245, 16 December 2003.

159 Decree 115/2003, 2 October, regulating economic aid for persons included in Law 46/1977, 15 October, on Amnesty. *Official Castile-Leon Gazette*, no. 195, 8 October 2003. Correction of errors: *Official Castile-Leon Gazette*, no. 205, 22 October 2003.

160 Decree 333/2003, 2 December, on compensation for former prisoners and those who suffered from political reprisals for a period longer than three months but under three years. *Official Gazette of the Andalusian Government*, no. 236, 9 December 2003.

new measures, and La Rioja issued its own regulation on compensation for those affected by Law 46/1977.[161] In March, 2003, Castile-La Mancha issued further Decrees establishing the value of the compensation packages granted to former prisoners and those who suffered political reprisals, and who were in prison for fewer or more than three years, including the cases contemplated in the Amnesty Law.[162]

In 2004, the Basque Autonomous Community[163] and Castile and Leon[164] issued further modifications to their respective Decrees, regulating compensation for those who suffered from an embargo of liberties for acts covered under the Amnesty Law. Cantabria also issued its second round of compensation with the same aim.[165] Similarly, Madrid issues new fiscal measures in relation to economic compensation for former prisoners.[166] Murcia, which at the time had yet to issue a measure, finally issued a Decree on 23 July 2004, to compensate prisoners covered under the Amnesty Law but who did not benefit from the compensation packages approved by the Spanish government because they did not satisfy the stipulated age requirements, had not been in prison long enough or because they were residents in Murcia.[167]

In 2005, the communities that modified their regulations were La Rioja[168] and the Canaries.[169] Once again, Madrid issued further fiscal measures for those who

161 Ministry of Taxation and Finance Order, 12 February 2003, on compensation for those affected by the acts established in Law 46/1977, 15 October, on Amnesty, but could not avail of the State-aid packages. *Official Gazette of La Rioja*, 18 February, 2003.

162 Decree 9/2004, 3 February, establishing the value of compensation for former prisoners and those who suffered from political reprisals for a period longer than three months but under three years, included in Law 46/1077. *Official Castile-La Mancha Gazette*, no. 17, 6 February 2004.

163 Decree 75/2004, 4 May, on a third modification to the Decree on compensation for those whose liberties were embargoed for acts covered under the Amnesty Law. *Official Basque Country Gazette*, no. 84, 6 May 2004.

164 Decree 110/2004, 14 October, modifying Decree 115/2003, 2 October, regulating economic packages for persons included in the Law 46/1977, 15 October, on Amnesty. *Official Castile-Leon Gazette of the Andalusian Government*, no. 203, 20 October 2004.

165 Decree 44/2004, 20 May, on economic aid for persons included in the Law 46/1977, 15 October, on Amnesty. *Official Gazette of Cantabria*, 1 June 2004.

166 Law 2/2004, 31 May, on Fiscal and Administrative Measures. *Official Madrid Gazette*, no. 129, 1 June 2004; *Official State Gazette*, no. 162, 6 July 2004. Correction of errors: *Official Madrid Gazette*, no. 176, 26 July 2004.

167 Decree 81/2004, 23 July 2004, granting compensation to prisoners covered under the Amnesty Law who could not avail of the compensation packages approved by the State for not satisfying the age, period in prison, and residency requirements. *Official Murcia Gazette*, no. 186, 12 August 2004.

168 Ministry of Taxation and Finance Order of 13 February 2005, regulating compensation for those affected by the acts stipulated in the Law 46/1977, 15 October, on Amnesty, but were excluded from State compensation packages. *Official Gazette of La Rioja*, no. 23, 18 February 2006.

169 Law 6/2005, 2 December, modifying Law 9/2002, 21 October, on compensation for persons excluded from the benefits in the 18th additional disposition in the Law 4/1990, 29 June, on General State Budgets for the years 1990 and 1992. *Official Gazette of the Canaries*, no. 238, 5 December 2005; *Official State Gazette*, no. 307, 24 December 2005.

had suffered from an embargo of liberties because of crimes covered under the amnesty, and who did not benefit from State aid.[170] Valencia, which had yet to develop its regulation, issued a Decree on 23 December 2005, regulating compensation from prisoners covered by the amnesty, but who could not avail of the compensation packages approved by the Spanish government and who were omitted from the census approved by the Valencian Generalitat on 6 May 2005.[171]

The last modifications came in 2006. On 21 February, the Andalusian Council established by Decree the administration of lump-sum compensation packages for former prisoners and those who suffered from political reprisals and an embargo of liberties because of acts contemplated in the Amnesty Law, and who were not included in the compensations regulated in the Andalusian Decrees of 2001 and 2003.[172]

For its part, the Basque government issued another Decree on 14 February establishing further economic compensation for those whose liberties were embargoed for political reasons; crucially, it included those who had been interned in the Disciplinary Battalions of Worker-Soldiers.[173] The reason for this was the Sentence passed in the Constitutional Court on 4 July 2005, which established that those who served sentences in Disciplinary Battalions of Soldier-Workers would be treated in the same way as prisoners.[174]

170 Law 5/2004, 28 December, on Fiscal and Administrative Measures. *Official Madrid Gazette*, no. 310, 30 December 2004, *Official State Gazette*, no. 42, 18 February, 2005. Correction of errors: *Official Madrid Gazette*, no. 27, 2 February 2005.

171 Decree 210/2005, 23 December, issued by the Valencian Generalitat, regulating compensation for the prisoners covered under the Amnesty Law who did not avail of the compensation approved by the State and were included in the Census endorsed by the Valencian Generalitat on 6 May 2005. *Official Gazette of the Valencian Generalitat*, no. 5163, 27 December 2005.

172 Decree 35/2006, 21 February, on the payment of a lump-sum compensation to former prisoners and those who suffered from political reprisals, whose liberties were embargoed as a consequence of acts covered by Law 46/1977, 15 October, on Amnesty, and who availed of the compensation packages established in the Decrees 1/2001, 9 January, and 333/2003, 2 December. *Official Gazette of the Andalusia Council*, no. 50, 15 March 2006. Modified by Decree 397/2009, 22 December. *Official Gazette of the Andalusia Council*, 8 January 2010.

173 Decree 22/2006, 14 February, regulating economic compensation for persons whose liberties were embargoed, including those interned in the Disciplinary Battalions of Worker-Soldiers, with the same conditions and requirements as per Decree 280/2002, 19 November, on compensation for those whose liberties were embargoed for acts covered by the Amnesty Law, except in the procedural modifications foreseen in the present legislation. *Official Basque Country Gazette*, no. 34, 17 February 2006.

174 Constitutional Court Sentence 180/2005, 4 July. *Official State Gazette*, no. 186, 5 August 2005.

The Autonomous Community of La Rioja regulated the compensations it had established the year before[175] and Madrid issued further fiscal measures for former prisoners subsumed in the Amnesty Law stipulations.[176]

3.6 The last economic reparations (2005–2007)

The State-aid packages for the victims of the war were modified in 2005[177] and 2006,[178] years which saw the first noteworthy increase in the number of victims compensated for the Civil War and the dictatorship thanks to the Law of 18 March 2005 on the so-called "children of the war".[179] In other words, this law dealt with the case of children who had been sent to foreign countries in order to spare them the hardships of the war. This law, which was particularly complicated because of its international extension, was developed through the Ministry of Employment and Social Security Order of 24 June 2005[180] and through the General Secretariat for Immigration and Emigration Resolution of 4 July 2006.[181] On this matter, it is also worth noting the Law of 26 December 2007 on restitution or compensation to political parties for seized assets and revoked rights, as per the regulation on political responsibilities covering the period between 1936 and 1939.[182]

175 Ministry of Taxation and Employment, 13 February 2006, regulating compensation for those affected by the provisions in Law 46/1977, 15 October, on Amnesty, but excluded from the State-aid packages. *Official Gazette of La Rioja*, 18 February 2006.

176 Law 7/2005, 23 December, on Fiscal and Administrative Measures. *Official Madrid Community Gazette*, no. 311, 30 December 2005. *Official State Gazette*, no. 52, 2 March 2006.

177 Law 30/2005, 29 December, on the State Budget for 2006. *Official State Gazette*, no. 312, 30 December, 2005.

178 Law 35/2006, 28 November, on personal income tax and the partial modification of laws on corporation tax, on non-resident tax and on Estates. *Official State Gazette*, no. 285, 29 November 2006.

179 Law 3/2005, 18 March, on economic benefits for civilians of Spanish origin but repatriated to foreign countries when under the age of consent, as a consequence of the Civil War, and who lead lives mainly outside of the national territory. *Official State Gazette*, no. 68, 21 March 2005, pp. 9708–9709.

180 Order of the Ministry of Employment and Social Security 1967/2005, 24 June, to establish the parameters for the development and application of Law 3/2005, 18 March. *Official State Gazette*, no. 151, 25 June 2005, pp. 22468–22474.

181 General Secretariat for Immigration and Emigration Resolution, 4 July 2006, to establish the time limits within which birth certificates must be produced and income must be declared in order to benefit from old-age pensions and economic benefits for citizens of Spanish origin repatriated to foreign countries before the age of consent. *Official State Gazette*, no. 168, 15 July 2006, pp. 26779–26779.

182 Law 50/2007, 26 December, modified by Law 43/1998, 15 December, on restitution or compensation to political parties for seized assets and revoked rights, as per the regulation on political responsibilities covering the period between 1936 and 1939. *Official State Gazette*, no. 310, 27 December 2007, pp. 53284–53285.

4 Complementary regulation to the labour amnesty

The labour amnesty granted by the Law 46/1977 had been restricted by subsequent jurisprudence, which applied the principles of statutory limitations to labour matters. Numerous fired workers were excluded from the amnesty because they had not applied before the stipulated deadline. A resolution to this problem was sought with the Law of 9 January 1984, by adding a new article to the Amnesty Law, whereby the non-applicability of statutory limitations of labour actions was applied in recognition of the rights established in articles 5 and 8 of the Law of 15 October 1977.[183]

The sentence passed by the Constitutional Court on 25 November 1986 blocked the application of the Law of 9 January 1984 to the labour amnesty. The sentence claimed that the reintegration foreseen in the original Amnesty Law text, which set a two-year prescription, did not jeopardise legal security or the companies' freedom, nor the dignity of the matter tried. On the contrary, it believed that the 1984 Law did jeopardise legal security, given that the decision of businessmen to fire employees who held contrary political opinions was protected by a judicial order that was still in force at the time. In this way, then, the Constitutional Court endorsed the legality of Francoist suppression of union and labour rights and the right to a political opinion, and absolved the State of any responsibility for the violations of labour rights during the dictatorship.[184]

5 The Amnesty Laws fail to extinguish criminal records

The 1976 and 1977 Amnesty Laws extinguished criminal liabilities for those covered by the amnesty, which, in theory, should have also resulted in extinguishing their criminal records. Criminal records are documentary evidence that a person has been convicted of carrying out a crime. Every definitive prison sentence must be filed with the Central Registry of Convicts and Fugitives, which is part of the Ministry of Justice. The Registry holds the file of every individual who has a criminal record, recording their identity (name and surname, and their National Identity Card), family information, the crime which has been committed and the length of the sentence.

There was an established jurisprudence in the Constitutional Court[185] on the matter of extinguishing criminal records, such as the sentence passed on 14 December 1984, which established that "the amnesty extinguished punishment

183 Law 1/1984, 9 January, to add a new article to the Law 46/1977, 15 October. *Official State Gazette*, no. 10, 12 January 1984.

184 Constitutional Court sentence 147/1986, 25 November, *Official State Gazette*, no. 295, 10 December 1986. See Pérez Amorós, 2009, p. 163. Baylos Grau, 2008, pp. 194–195.

185 Constitutional Courts sentences, 122/1984, 76/1986 and 147/1986, among the most significant.

and criminal effects derived from the crime or misdemeanour in question";[186] or the sentence passed on 25 November 1986, which stated that

> The application of the amnesty implies what the doctrine has termed *retroactive derogation of regulations*, completely reversing the restrictions on rights and freedoms, along with all its consequences; thus, it can be said that rights are re-established retroactively.[187]

This notwithstanding, the files containing criminal records were not destroyed, and, worse still, the data contained in those files were transferred to a digital database that is used by the police. As a result, a number of people have been retained at airports because their names figured in the Ministry of Home Affairs database. It became a matter of controversy in 1984, when politician Enrique Curiel, then vice-secretary general of the PCE, was detained for 45 minutes in the police quarters of the Barajas airport after returning from an international trip. In 1989, some 100,000 files with the criminal records of anti-Francoist soldiers continued to exist in the archives of the Ministry of Home Affairs,[188] and continued to be taken into consideration during the following decade. There are many stories like the Enrique Curiel one. Javier Urroz, for example, an ex-union leader and one of the main figures of one of the most important labour strikes of the last few years of the dictatorship, returned home in 1997 from an international trip, and just as had happened to Curiel, the police at the Barajas airport asked him what he had done in the past. Urroz simply answered that he had "fought for democracy in Spain". The police then asked Urroz to follow them, which he refused to do, and was therefore detained for a few hours until the matter was resolved.[189]

The failure to destroy criminal records had more serious consequences for those who had been convicted of terrorism and had been released from prison without any documentary evidence to certify the amnesty, whether they had been amnestied under the 1976 or 1977 Law. Bixente Serrano Izko[190] of the Basque Country Left, for example, had been pardoned through the measure of 14 March 1977, which complemented the 1976 Amnesty Law. He was released from Cartagena (Murcia) prison on 5 April 1977. The prison authorities had limited themselves to communicating orally that he had been freed under the amnesty law. Not long after, problems began to emerge. When the police checked his identity card, they would take him to the police station, at times in a humiliating manner, locked in the boot of the police car. After some hours, they would release him without charge, and without giving him any document or justification. Finally, indignant at the situation, he

186 Constitutional Court sentence, 122/1984, 14 December. *Official State Gazette*, no. 10, 11 January 1985.
187 Constitutional Court sentence, 147/1986, 25 November. *Official State Gazette*, no. 295, 10 December 1986.
188 *El País*, 15 November 2004.
189 Javier Urroz interview, 19 May 2016 (Urroz, 2016).
190 Bixente Serrano Izko interview, 14 June 2016 (Serrano Izko, 2016).

resorted to employing the services of lawyer José Fermín Arraiza, who was also a member of the Basque Country Left. Together they filed a formal complaint with the First Instance Criminal Court. The judge issued an edict indicating that Serrano was not a "wanted man" and had freedom of mobility. Bixente Serrano carried the document with him wherever he went, producing it at police or civil guard control points, and never had a problem again.

The failure to extinguish criminal records and the lack of documentation certifying the amnesty has continued to cause problems even today. Bixente Serrano again serves as an example. When he was preparing the documentation for his retirement as a history teacher from a public secondary school, the National Social Security Treasury Office asked him on 23 February 2001 to produce evidence of his amnesty. It was issued by the Provincial Court in Madrid on 12 March 2013 after the Public Prosecutions office issued a positive report on the matter on 22 February of the same year. The certificate revealed that the amnesty was for a conviction which Serrano himself had no knowledge of, as he had been convicted of a different charge.

6 The Amnesty Laws do not allow reparation and rehabilitation through the legal system

6.1 The Amnesty Law as an argument rejecting the extraordinary appeal for review for the symbolic rehabilitation of Julián Grimau (1990)

The communist leader, Julián Grimau, was arrested on 7 November 1962 and subjected to horrific torture. The summary trial, held on 18 April 1963, went through without the minimum procedural guarantees. He was accused of "war crimes and continued military rebellion". When Grimau was handed a death sentence, the communists of the world mobilised with numerous demonstrations in the capitals of Europe and Latin America demanding he be pardoned. But these demands, and the numerous requests for clemency from the Pope and world leaders, were not enough; Grimau was executed on the morning of 20 April.[191]

In 1990, his widow, Ángela Martínez Lanzaco, requested the rehabilitation of her husband in the Military Chamber of the Supreme Court. Her request was supported by the State Attorney General, Javier Moscoso, who presented an appeal for review against the sentence passed in the 1963 summary trial. Her family lawyer also supported the prosecution. The appeal asked for the sentence to be voided based on the fact that none of the members that formed part of the war council had a degree in law. The legislation of the time stipulated that at least the presiding judge of the war council had to be a member of the bar. Manuel Fernández Martín, the presiding judge of the military court that tried Grimau, was

191 Carvajal Urquijo, 2003.

not.[192] If the sentence was voided, the State could be declared responsible and Grimau's widow would incur rights to compensation.

Despite the individual vote of the president of the chamber, José Jiménez Villarejo, in favour of reviewing the 1963 summary trial sentence, the votes of the other seven judges corroborated the legality of the sentence. The 1990 sentence pointed out that extraordinary appeals to review a case were reserved for cases where "new facts or new evidence which proves the innocence of the convicted individual" are presented.[193] The main reason why the sentence was not voided was given as the need to safeguard "legal security" and "respect the matter judged on". As the defence lawyer pointed out later, the Fifth Military Chamber of the Supreme Court handed out a second guilty verdict to Grimau.

The sentence concluded with this final note: "As for everything else, and to conclude, it is hardly worth mentioning that, fundamentally, the results that the appeal was looking for have been obtained and secured, with greater scope, by the amnesty laws." The cynicism in this assertion is surprising, especially given that rejecting the appeal meant that Grimau's widow could not receive any compensation from the State. But Ángela Martínez should be happy – is what the seven judges behind the legal resolution must have been thinking – given that the Amnesty Law had quashed Grimau's conviction for war crimes and continued military rebellion.

The sentence itself pointed out that a request may be presented in the Constitutional Court. This request was presented by Grimau's widow and the Attorney General of the State, claiming, once more, that the war council that convicted Grimau was not constituted in accordance with Francoist legislation, which required that at least one member of the war council be a member of the bar. They also believed that the Supreme Court had violated the fundamental rights of the communist leader's next of kin, as recognised in the Constitution. The writ was deemed inadmissible by the Constitutional Court in the edict of 18 July 1990, which, at least, did not deem it necessary to mention the Amnesty Laws.[194]

Grimau's rehabilitation was attempted through legal mechanisms. On 15 April 2002, the federal parliamentary group United Left attempted the rehabilitation in the Congress of Deputies, presenting a Bill *on the public and democratic rehabilitation of Julián Grimau*. Every parliamentary group was in favour except the PP, which had absolute majority in Congress, and therefore the Bill did not prosper. In the debate, two opposing, fundamental positions on the impunity of Francoist crimes

192 In fact, on 22 September 1966, Manuel Fernández Martín was convicted by the Supreme Council of Military Justice of usurpation of authority and illegitimate use of his military uniform. Amnistía Internacional España, 2005, p. 35.

193 Sentence passed in the Military Chamber of the Supreme Court 626/1990, 30 January, rejecting the appeal for review.

194 Constitutional Court edict 262/1990, 18 June, dismissing the reasons for an appeal to the resolution passed in the Supreme Court. See Jiménez Villarejo and Doñate, 2012, pp. 60–78.

were put forward. On one side, the United Left deputy, Luis Carlos Rejón, complained at length that the democracy had rehabilitated people such as Manuel Fraga,[195] "who, at the time, fought against freedom", and it therefore did not seem fair that in the same democracy "the executioners have been rehabilitated, while some victims have not". On the other side of the debate, the PP deputy, Manuel Atencia, invoked the discourse of idealised amnesia: "in Spain we reached a constitutional pact and a process for national reconciliation. If what is being attempted here is the revisionism of the political transition process, then this group cannot be in favour. It would be disrespectful to our history. 25 years after the first free elections, our political situation is in perfect harmony."[196]

6.2 The trial for the murder of Enrique Ruano circumvents the Amnesty Law (1996)

The Amnesty Law did not allow for charges to be brought for amnestied crimes with the pretext that these crimes were of a political nature. The next chapter will discuss examples of this, but there is, however, one exception: the trial of the individuals alleged to have tortured and murdered the student Enrique Ruano Casanova. The lawyer for the prosecution, Manuel Gómez Benítez, skilfully circumvented the Amnesty Law, arguing that the murder charge was not filed under political intentionality.

This case went through various judicial processes. Enrique Ruano, a student and member of the People's Liberation Front, was arrested in Madrid on 17 January 1969, by agents of the Political-Social Brigade. He was accused of disseminating Workers' Commission propaganda against the Francoist regime. Two days later, on 19 January, three Political-Social Brigade agents, Francisco Luis Colino Hernanz, Jesús Simón Cristóbal and Celso Galván Abascal, transferred Enrique Ruano to an apartment on the seventh floor of a building on General Mola street – today known as Príncipe de Vergara street. From there, Ruano was thrown from the balcony to a lower-level patio, and died upon impact. The official version of the event, widely distributed in the press of the time and sustained by the first trial of the accused, claimed that Ruano had committed suicide by throwing himself from the balcony after the agents took the handcuffs off him.[197] Seven lawyers, led by Gregorio Peces-Barba, requested an inquest in front of the judge on duty to investigate the event. Demonstrations took place throughout Spain, and on 24 January a state of emergency was declared throughout the country. The issue was put to rest with the Summary 6/1969 by the Fifth

195 Manuel Fraga, one of the founding members of the PP, was president of the Galician autonomous community, where the PP held an overall majority.

196 C. E. Cué, "La recuperación de la memoria antifranquista: Grimau, condenado de nuevo en 1990", *El País*, 20 September 2004.

197 Alleging suicide was common for the police when torture resulted in death. Ruano's family were not allowed to appoint a doctor to supervise the autopsy.

Investigating Judge, who closed the lawsuit after admitting suicide as the cause of death.

Once democracy had been established, the case was reopened in 1991 after the Provincial Court initially ruled that the statute of limitations had passed.[198] Lawyer Gómez Benítez set in motion a strategy, in agreement with Enrique Ruano's sister, Beatriz Ruano, which consisted of not recognising the political motivation behind the crime to obtain, as a compromise, a confession from the accused during the trial.[199] The defence for the police and the Attorney General's Office tried to have the case dismissed by arguing that the crime was covered by the 1977 Amnesty Law. However, the Provincial Court rejected their request, interpreting that, as the prosecution had argued, the law was only applicable to crimes committed and recognised as politically motivated crimes, parameters which had not been proved during the proceedings and required, therefore, further elaboration in an oral hearing.[200]

Ruano's family appealed to the Supreme Court, which ordered that the case be reopened.[201] The defence blindly followed the strategy of denying that the three policemen had murdered Ruano and that, moreover, their actions were politically motivated. They made the mistake of not putting forward the amnesty argument in either the oral hearing or in their closing argument. The district lawyer and the State Attorney also failed to put forward the amnesty argument, preferring instead to focus their argument on the suicide version of the event.[202] The Amnesty Law was only referenced in the final reports to cover up the inconsistencies in the statements made by the three policemen, arguing that the 1977 Amnesty Law was passed with the purpose of avoiding trials of this type.[203]

198 Provincial Court in Madrid edict, 7 May 1992, confirmed by edict from the same Court on 20 July 1992.

199 Gómez Benítez believed that, even if the police were found guilty, the sentence would be covered by the Amnesty Law, given that the crime occurred before 15 December 1976, and was committed by public servants and public order agents who were investigating a matter which was politically motivated, as were, no doubt, the ones that had motivated Enrique Ruano's arrest.

200 Provincial Court in Madrid edict, Second Section, 19 December 1995.

201 Supreme Court Sentence, 45/1994, 25 January.

202 Ruano's family argued that Enrique died from a gunshot wound after one of the agents shot him during the interrogation. It was only after he died that the agents threw him from the balcony. Their argument was based on the forensic evidence that demonstrated that unknown individuals sawed off the part of the collar bone that corresponded to an orifice consistent with a gunshot wound found in Enrique's body. Gómez Benítez, 2011, p. 282.

203 The lawyer for the defence pointed out that Ruano's arrest for his political actions at the hands of the Political-Social Brigade, "if a guilty verdict for murder was passed, which I would find terrible", would be covered by the Amnesty Law. For his part, the State lawyer requested that the Amnesty Law be applied, as ancillary to the absolution. The prosecution requested that the Amnesty Law be applied "in any case", because in 1969 "the murder of students and workers who opposed the regime was

The sentence dictated on 19 July 1996 ignored the Amnesty Law, given that it interpreted that the statute of limitations had not passed, but nevertheless absolved the three policemen based on the lack of definitive proof, thus justifying the actions of the Political-Social Brigade.[204]

7 The Amnesty Law does not allow investigation into enforced disappearances (end of the 1990s–2002)

Carlos Jiménez Villarejo and Antonio Doñate Martín put forward the following typology for enforced disappearances relating to the period after 17 July 1936. Their typology is based on the complaints filed before judges and lawyers after the 1978 Constitution came into force:[205]

1 Persons who were arrested at home or outside by an armed group wearing Falangist, *requeté* or Civil Guard uniforms, and who were never heard of again.
2 Persons who were arrested at home or outside by an armed group wearing Falangist, requeté or Civil Guard uniforms, taken into police custody and who, after a few days had passed, were never heard of again.
3 Persons who were arrested at home or outside by an armed group wearing Falangist, *requeté* or Civil Guard uniforms, who were held in a detention centre or prison and, without the intervention of a civil or military law authority, were taken out by the Civil Guard, or by a group of Falangist or *requeté* soldiers, from said detention centre, and were never heard of again
4 Persons who were arrested at home or outside by an armed group wearing Falangist, *requeté* or Civil Guard uniforms, remanded in civil or military custody, legally processed but before the trial could be held and the corresponding sentence passed, were taken out of the detention centre or prison and were never heard of again.

During the final years of the 1990s and the first five years of the new century, the investigating judges argued that the statute of limitations had passed on illegal arrests that resulted in enforced disappearances during the 1936 coup d'état, and that the Amnesty Law did not allow the prosecution of the alleged perpetrators. For this reason, the lawsuits were routinely archived without practicing due diligence and investigating the criminal acts.[206] The Attorney General's Office was responsible for these archives, and never intervened against the judicial decisions.

common practice", in which, "the Politico-Social Brigade played a large part". *El País*, 5 July 1996.

204 Jiménez Villarejo and Doñate, 2012, pp. 116–117.
205 Jiménez Villarejo and Doñate, 2012, pp. 182–183.
206 Chinchón Álvarez, 2012a, pp. 45–50.

No investigating judge initiated *ex officio* criminal proceedings for enforced disappearances in light of the new facts which were slowly revealed the media and by historians, thus contravening their obligation as per articles 262 and 269 of the Criminal Procedure Law. Carlos Jiménez Villarejo and Antonio Doñate believe that the ignorance demonstrated by the legal system on this issue can be explained by the sway Francoism still held among the judges and lawyers who were not purged during the transition, but it may also be explained by the wilful amnesia that was instilled in the country after the Amnesty Law. This meant that judges were not open to considering whether Francoist permanent crimes were prosecutable, and therefore did not act *ex officio* as new information was revealed in the works published by historians. There was also a lack of knowledge resulting from the absence of jurisprudence on the matter, as no new complaints relating to enforced disappearances were made in the two decades that followed the new Constitution. However, when the first complaints started to come in around the end of the 1990s, there was a general lack of interest on the part of the institutions in instructing judges and lawyers on the casuistry of enforced disappearances which are not within the statute of limitations and are outside the scope of the Amnesty Law. At the time, there were no academic studies on this matter to fill this lacuna.[207]

The Amnesty Law argument in relation to filing complaints about enforced disappearances was not formulated again after Spain ratified the International Criminal Court statute, in force since 1 July 2002, wherein article 7.I.i) defines enforced disappearances as a crime against humanity. This jurisprudence change of tack coincided with the growing number of applications for exhumation, which forced the dissemination among the investigative courts of due diligence guidelines on the matter of investigations into enforced disappearances during the Civil War and the dictatorship.[208]

8 The Amnesty Law allows bestowing a distinction to a Francoist torturer (2001)

The PP's political position regarding historical memory was reflected in its application of the Solidarity with the Victims of Terrorism Law, 8 October 1999.[209] Therein, article 2.1 indicates that:

207 Jiménez Villarejo and Doñate, 2012, pp. 194–196. See, also, Escudero Alday, 2009, pp. 51–52.

208 On the role of the investigative judge in observing due diligence in the investigations into enforced disappearances during the Civil War and the dictatorship, see Olivas Díaz, 2008, and Jiménez Villarejo and Doñate, 2012.

209 Law 32/1999, 8 October in solidarity with the victims of terrorism. *Official State Gazette*, no. 242, 9 October 1999, pp. 36050–36052. The law was the result – as its explanatory memorandum pointed out – of a unanimous vote between the parliamentary groups in the Senate, which "expressed the recognition and solidarity in order to honour the victims of terrorism with the respect that, no doubt, their

> The victims of acts of terrorism or crimes committed by one or a number of individuals associated with an armed group or faction, or who were acting with the aim of gravely disrupting peace and jeopardising the safety of citizens, will have the right to state compensation, a responsibility assumed by the state to issue the extraordinary payments of the corresponding economic compensation packages in line with civil responsibility and in accordance with the provisions of the present law.

The individual application of the law was not limited to the victims of specific armed groups, which therefore included extreme right terrorism against those who opposed the Francoist regime. The same could be said of article 3.1, which indicated that "victims of terrorist acts or crimes perpetrated by one or a number of individuals associated with an armed group or faction, or who were acting with the aim of gravely disrupting peace and jeopardising the safety of citizens" would also benefit from compensation packages.

The temporal scope for its application was established in article 2.2, which went beyond the time limits established in the Amnesty Law. Specifically, the article indicated that it would grant compensation for physical and psychophysical harm suffered by said victims as long as the events in question took place between 1 January 1968 and the day in which the Law came into force. The initial date was set to coincide with the first death as a consequence of ETA terrorist activity, which took place in 1968, which therefore meant that the scope of this measure included the victims of ETA throughout the dictatorship, some of whom included Francoist officials and known Francoist torturers. This is the manner in which the anomaly linking convictions for terrorism and the "recovery of democracy" came to be. The effects of this new regulation and the rights of the victims of the dictatorship were extended to the crimes covered by the 1977 amnesty. The Solidarity with the Victims of Terrorism Law democratised the Francoist officials and the torturers murdered by ETA, and did not consider those who were murdered by extreme right groups as victims of terrorism.[210]

In accordance with this law, the government led by José María Aznar issued a Royal Decree on 19 of January 2001 granting the Civil Merit Medal for the Public Recognition of the Victims of Terrorism. One of the men honoured was Melitón Manzanas González,[211] murdered by ETA on 2 August 1968.

Various political parties in opposition and many civil associations were staunchly against the measure. Amnesty International, for example, published a

sacrifice merits", with the aim of contributing to the effort of reaching "peace as a result of reconciliation and justice and so that the victims of terrorism receive, once more, the respect, admiration and affection in which and with which they are held by the rest of the country".

210 Baylos Grau, 2008, pp. 197–198.

211 Royal Decree 55/2001, 19 January, granting the Civil Merit Medal for the Public Recognition of Victims of Terrorism to the individuals herein cited. *Official State Gazette*, no. 18, 20 January 2001, pp. 2546–2546.

statement on 30 January which recalled how Manzanas had been "responsible for torturing hundreds of Basque people during the Francoist regime, and was a known collaborator with the Gestapo, which had helped to capture Jews trying to flee through the southern border of France during the Nazi Occupation". The statement considered that "bestowing a decoration to someone who had flagrantly ignored basic human rights and the right to not be tortured made a mockery of any system granting decorations".[212] The Basque nationalist parties and United Left also expressed their staunch rejection of the honour, as did various trade unions, such as CCOO, UGT and the Basque nationalist trade unions.[213] For its part, the Parliament of Navarre passed a resolution against the concession on 21 May 2001 expressly requesting that the Spanish government withdraw the honour.[214]

Some political parties (PNV, IU), trade unions (UGT, CCOO) and the Catalan Association for the Protection of Human Rights, presented an appeal to the Chamber of Administration of the Supreme Court against the concession of the decoration, all of which were rejected on the same grounds.[215] The Supreme Court believed that there was no room to withdraw the concession based on the preamble of the Law, "taking into consideration the recent history of our social reality and, fundamentally, the transition to a democratic regime, as well as the manner in which the transition was negotiated and the basic principles that inspired it", as well as "the recovery of democracy put forward a project for social harmony determined to overcome the old conflicts that shaped our history".[216] But the High Court went further, offering its own considerations of the transition:

> This statement aims to resolve the issue of whether the principle of reconciliation ought to be limited to those who survived the dictatorship, excluding thus, those who did not have the fortune of experiencing the recuperation of

212 Amnesty International Spain, "Spain: rewards for torturers cannot be tolerated", 29 January 2001. AI: EUR 41/005/2001/s.
213 *El País*, *Egin*, 20 January 2001.
214 *Official Navarre Parliament Gazette*, no. 58, 30 May 2001, p. 11.
215 See, for example, Supreme Court, Appeals 220/2001; 137/2002.
216 The Supreme Court believed that the Law on Solidarity with the Victims of Terrorism demonstrated "the legislators will to apply, specifically to the case of victims of terrorism, the fundamental principle which has overseen our transition process towards a democracy, which is none other than the reconciliation of Spaniards by overcoming old conflicts which, in their day, originated from a civil confrontation and which subsisted, even below the surface, throughout the previous regime. The idea of reconciliation and overcoming old conflicts has allowed the reintegration of all into a democratic system which includes everyone and only rejects those who, after the instatement of political freedom, use unjustified and unjustifiable violence to undermine peace and harmony among citizens. For this reason, the regulation does not delimit the recognition it bestows upon the victims of terrorism to those who were attacked during the democratic period, extending this recognition instead to all victims, regardless of when the terrorist act was carried out and of the socio-political context of the time."

> liberties, or, alternatively, whether the latter should reap the benefits of reconciliation and the effort to overcome the old conflicts which are referenced in the preamble of the Law (on Solidarity with the Victims of Terrorism). This statement removes all doubt. One of the fundamental pillars of our democracy, which has bestowed our Democracy with a stability which this country has hardly enjoyed before, was and continues to be precisely that which allowed the integration of those who assumed our democratic principles by forgetting their past trajectory from a political point of view. For this reason, we think it is illogical and contrary to the principles contemplated in the explanatory memorandum of this Law, to exclude from the idea of reconciliation those who died at the hands of terrorists and were deprived of the opportunity of abiding by our democratic values, on the basis that there is no evidence that they, had they survived the previous regime, would not have abided by the values of the political transition in the way that the majority of Spaniards did, regardless of their past political trajectory, as evidenced by the fact that important figures of the previous regime served the country in important ways in our Democracy, from which only those who continue to abide by terrorism are excluded. These reasons justify the generality of the terms in article 4 of Law 32/99, whose application is established in the resolution referenced here.

It is worthwhile noting that judge Margarita Robles Fernández voted against the decision of the other judges in relation to the award granted to Melitón Manzanas in appeal no. 137/2002 presented by the Catalan Association for the Protection of Human Rights in the Chamber of Administration. Her position went against the majority in the chamber, because she believed that, although the Amnesty Law did not set a time limit with regard to the concession of an honorary award provisioned therein, subordinate to the restoration of democracy in Spain, there could be no doubt that the legislator "was inspired by the spirit of awarding an honorary distinction, a public recognition of victims whose civic integrity and ethical characteristics are aligned with those of any democratic system". She interpreted that the Law 32/1999 only allowed "the concession of the honorary distinction provisioned therein, to individuals whose civic action were defined by democratic values in the recovery of democracy". Given that Melitón Manzanas did not satisfy the requirements provisioned in article 4 of the Law of administrative appeal presented by the procedural representation of the Catalan Association for the Protection of Human Rights, the Law would be upheld.[217]

217 The Explanatory Memorandum of the Law, for this lawyer, demonstrated that the legislator wanted to "reaffirm democratic values by rejecting outright any demonstration of violence against these values, which are precisely the types of aggressions which should be especially extolled when they are attacked by terrorists", that is, according to the legislator, those individuals who defended democratic values and suffered terrorist attacks. The Spanish Parliament, to sum up, sought the honorary

Melitón Manzanas's award could have led to more inappropriate concessions. For example, Admiral Luis Carrero Blanco, president of the Francoist government, would have also been eligible as he, too, was a victim of ETA. However, a PSOE initiative, with the support of the IU, CiU, PNV and EA, prevented such situations from arising again. The proposal, which was presented in the Chamber of Deputies on 21 of December 2002, sought to reform article 4 of the Solidarity with Victims of Terrorism Law. The new wording stipulated that "in no case can a concession be made to individuals whose personal and professional trajectory is marked with behaviour contrary to the values represented in the Constitution and the present law, as well as to the human rights recognised in international treaties",[218] slight changes to article 4.3 of Law 2.2003, 12 March, modified Law 32/1999, 8 October, in solidarity with the victims of terrorism.[219]

recognition of those victims who demonstrated the "civic merits and democratic values enshrined in our Constitution".

218 *El Mundo*, 22 November 2002.

219 *Official State Gazette*, no. 62, 13 March 2003, pp. 9763–9764.

Chapter 5

Amnesty after the Historical Memory Law (2007–2016)

1 The Historical Memory Law fails to abolish or modify the Amnesty Law (2007)

1.1 Historical Memory Law and post-transitional justice

On 28 July 2007, the cabinet passed a Bill on historical memory, and on that same day it was processed in the Congress of Deputies. It is worthwhile noting that this Bill sought to restrict access to the information held in public archives, which complicated the task of investigating crimes, the individuals who participated in those crimes and the subsequent legal process. Public archive staff were entrusted with safeguarding the documentary evidence. Complementary Amnesty Law legislation restated the impunity of those who had committed human rights violations by not allowing the victims access to justice and truth. Several human rights and pro-memory organisations criticised the measure severely. Amnesty International, for example, published the study *Victims of the Civil War and Francoism*, in which it stated that the measure was a new "end of story" which was manifestly against the principles of human rights and international law.[1]

The Bill was subjected to intense political negotiations which took place against the backdrop of increased pressure from civil society. During the parliamentary process in March 2007, the IU-ICV and the ERC presented two alternative Bills as full amendments. Neither of these alternatives called for the derogation or modification of the Amnesty Law, even though they did call for an end to amnesty. The PP also put forward an amendment, but it did not propose an alternative Bill. Other parliamentary groups put forward partial amendments.[2]

The Bill hit a stumbling block, but it was finally carried thanks to an agreement signed on 10 October 2007, by the Spanish government and the socialist parliamentary group IU-ICV. Various aspects of the text were modified, such as the

1 Amnistía Internacional España, 2006.

2 The alternatives put forward by the IU-ICV and the ERC, and the partial amendments are recorded in the *Official Parliament Gazette*, Congress of Deputies, 14 March 2007.

aforementioned measure, to conceal the identities of those responsible for human rights violations. The Congress of Deputies passed the Law on 31 October 2007, with the endorsement of every parliamentary group except the PP and the ERC.[3] The Senate passed the Bill on 10 December 2007[4] without modification. Its official name became Law 52/2007, 26 December, "which recognises and expands the rights, and establishes measures in favour of those who suffered persecution or violence during the Civil War and the dictatorship". Even though the new denomination avoided its original name, the doctrine continued to refer to it as the Historical Memory Law, although it has been said, with some justification, that its contents undermine the idea and that it would be more appropriate to call it the "Ahistorical Anti-Memory Law".[5]

The name that was given to the Law was nothing more than a declaration of intent, as the legal text within failed to fulfil the promise in its title. In lieu of a political consensus, the legal text was modified and the measures relative to the genuine reparation for the victims were neutralised to the point whereby the three requirements for transitional justice were not satisfied. As Margalida Capellà appropriately summed it up: "Neither truth nor justice, and reparation only in half measures."[6] The Law also failed to legislate for a truth commission that would guarantee the victims' right to truth. Instead of legislating for an official investigation into human rights violations, the Law cemented the rule of impunity.[7] It is a mistake to interpret this Law as the milestone that marked the beginning of a second transition[8] or a return to transitional justice,[9] as some scholars have suggested. The associations for the victims of the Civil War and the dictatorship unanimously rejected the new Law. Many lawyers criticised the law to greater and lesser degrees, among them, Javier Chinchón,[10] Rafael Escudero,[11] José Antonio Martín Pallín, Juan María Terradillos Basoco,[12] Coral Arangüena,[13] Carlos Jiménez Villarejo and

3 Most the articles were approved with 185 votes in favour and 137 against, although some were passed by the slim margin of ten votes. Specifically, the PPA voted in favour of seven provisions, the ones that it had endorsed in the Constitutional Commission, such as the "de-politicisation" of the Valle de los Caídos (Valley of the Fallen) and aid for the victims of the Civil War and Francoism.

4 *Official Parliament Gazette. Senate*, Series II, no. 133-g, 12 November 2007, p. 67.

5 Clavero, 2014, p. 177.

6 Capellà i Roig, 2009, p. 234.

7 Gil Gil, 2009a, p. 76.

8 Encarnación, 2014, pp. 158–186.

9 Golob, 2008, pp. 127–141.

10 Chinchón Álvarez, 2008b. Chinchón Álvarez, 2009c. Chinchón Álvarez, 2011. Chinchón Álvarez, 2012a.

11 Escudero Alday, 2009. Escudero Alday, 2013a. Escudero Alday, 2013c. Escudero Alday, 2014.

12 Terradillos Basoco, 2010.

13 Arangüena, 2010.

Antonio Doñate,[14] Tomás de Domingo,[15] Josep María Tamarit,[16] Marcos Criado de Diego,[17] Albert Noguera[18] and Bartolomé Clavero.[19]

It is well known that the development of the Law was problematic. It was promulgated during the final phases of the José Luis Rodríguez Zapatero government at a time when opinion polls were predicting that the next government would be led by the PP, as indeed happened. Added to this, the autonomous governments would be in the hands of the new government, and the new president, Mariano Rajoy, put in place numerous obstacles to the implementation of many of the regulations that the Law required, using the economic crisis as a pretext. Furthermore, the regulatory development of the Law was delayed for a long time, only to come into force with several limitations to the rights of the victims.[20]

1.2 Amnesty and the Historical Memory Law

The need to end the culture of amnesia and the transitional justice triumvirate of truth, justice and reparation was ever present in the negotiations for the Historical Memory Law in both Chambers. Every political group, except the PP, agreed that there was a pressing need to remember, rather than forget, the Civil War and the dictatorship.

However, there was no mention of a possible derogation or modification to the 1977 Amnesty Law during the negotiations. Even the ERC failed to propose a modification. The numerous amendments the ERC put forward in March 2007 were limited to the issue of amnesty and the modification of the preamble of the legal text, calling for it to be replaced with the preamble to the Bill the ERC itself proposed in December 2005 (discussed above). Although the ERC did not demand the derogation of the Amnesty Law during the debate, neither did it endorse the Historical Memory Law text which was agreed by the PSOE, IU-ICV, CiU and PNV, arguing that the Law did not put an end to the "Spanish system of impunity" installed during the transition.[21]

Law 52/2007 sidestepped any reference to the Amnesty Law, but once again argued that the "spirit of the Transition makes the constitutional model for coexistence meaningful". It was:

> the spirit of reconciliation and harmony, and of respect for pluralism and a peaceful defence of every idea. It guided the Transition, and bestowed upon

14 Jiménez Villarejo and Doñate, 2012.
15 De Domingo, 2012.
16 Tamarit Sumalla, 2013.
17 Criado de Diego, 2013.
18 Noguera Fernández, 2013a. Noguera Fernández, 2013b.
19 Clavero, 2014.
20 Martín Pallín and Escudero Alday, 2009, pp. 9–25.
21 *Official Parliament Gazette*. Congress, Series A, no. 99–24, 7 November 2007, pp. 197–205.

> us the 1978 Constitution which brought about the legal manifestation of the reconciliation among Spaniards in a social and democratic rule of law committed to integration.

The silence on legal amnesty and the omission of any reference to the obligation to comply with international law created a context conducive to maintaining impunity.[22] The Historical Memory Law, as mentioned previously, was ineffective even in name. The desire was there, but not the will: desire to recover historical memory, but unwillingness to repeal the Amnesty Law. Memory and amnesia are contradictory ideas, as are impunity and justice. The courts continued to find recourse in non-retroactivity and legal security as a way of observing amnesty,[23] and, nowadays, as complementary to "historical memory". A section of academia also staunchly defended the law.[24]

1.3 Economic compensation and reparation provisioned in the Amnesty Law

The Historical Memory Law widened the scope of the reparation measures that had been progressively implemented as per the 1977 Amnesty Law. The new measures were established at state level in the 18th additional provision applied to budgets for the fiscal years of 1990 and 1992, which increased allocations for most autonomous governments. Specifically, article 10 in Law 52/2007 allocated €150,000 to the benefactors of the victims killed between 1 January 1968 and 6 October 1977, for "defending and demanding freedom and democratic rights". The fourth additional provision extended this compensation to those who had been maimed in their struggle for the same cause. Property and rights to reparations were also provisioned in articles 5, 6, 7, 8, 9 and in the fifth additional provision.

The new, partial reparative measures have significantly improved the compensation and pension schemes for the victims of Francoism.[25] However, this does not hide the fact that administrative reparation is not the right mechanism to bring an end to collective amnesia. The mere recognition of the right to benefits and compensation for professional reasons (for example, civil servants, republican soldiers) or having appeared in court is not enough to motivate a profound debate on the dictatorship, nor is administrative procedure an appropriate platform for extensive social and political debates, given that rights are exercised on an individual basis.[26]

22 Greppi, 2008, p. 116.
23 Chinchón Álvarez, 2012a, pp. 97–130. Jiménez Villarejo and Doñate, 2012, pp. 74–85.
24 Most notably, Gil Gil, 2009a, and Fernández Liesa, 2014.
25 Baylos Grau, 2008, pp. 198–208. Camisón Yagüe, 2013, pp. 153–154.
26 Criado de Diego, 2013, p. 41.

On the other hand, reparation is not automatic as individuals applying for aid need to furnish the Public Administration office with documentary evidence of their status as victims and prove their right to the corresponding reparation. It is, indeed, curious that the victims themselves must act as historians in search for documentary evidence in the public archives, when it would be more appropriate for the State to carry out the census of the victims, especially taking into consideration that the perpetrator was the State itself.

Other criticisms of the reparative measures focus on the initial date to calculate compensation. The date was taken from article 2.2 of the Law of 8 October 1999, in solidarity with the victims of terrorism,[27] which states that compensation is reserved for victims who suffered physical or psychophysical damages when the events or facts that caused the damages occurred on or after 1 January 1968. This date, as discussed in the previous chapter, is based on the year ETA began to carry out terrorist attacks. Given that the Historical Memory Law used the same date, it excluded all of those who were killed or injured in the struggle for democratic freedoms before 1 January 1968. The number of victims that were thus excluded from the law was huge, including the *maquis*, guerrilla soldiers who fought against the dictatorship until the beginning of the 1950s. According to an official 1950 report carried out by Francoist officials responsible for the fight against the *maquis*, 2,036 guerrilla soldiers were killed and 3,211 were imprisoned between 1943 and 1950.[28]

The failure to bring the initial date back to 18 July 1936 meant that the families of victims of enforced disappearances could not benefit from reparation. According to the calculations of the foremost expert in this area, Francisco Espinosa, Francoist repression is responsible for the death of 130,199 victims, a figure which continues to rise as new investigations come to light. The figure is in stark contrast to the number of victims killed by the Republican side, 49,272,[29] which, as discussed later, were compensated in full. It is surprising that the Historical Memory Law did not take into consideration article 24 of the International Convention for the Protection of All Persons from Enforced Disappearance, which guarantees the right to effective reparation for the victims and their next of kin. The Law also failed to take into consideration Resolution 60/174 in the General Assembly of the United Nations, which established the "basic principles and guidelines in the right to a remedy and reparation for victims of gross violations of human rights and serious violations of international humanitarian law".[30]

Another aspect of Law 52/2007 which was heavily criticised is the confusion between compensation and pensions. Compensation aims to repair damages (the death of a person), but it is not granted if those killed did not have family

27 Law 32/1999, 8 October 1999, on Solidarity with the Victims of Francoism. *Official State Gazette*, no. 242, 9 October 1999, pp. 36050–36052.

28 Suárez Fernández, 2011, p. 268.

29 Espinosa Maestre, 2011, p. 44.

30 Escudero Alday, 2009, p. 51.

members who were economically dependent on them, which is a frequent occurrence, given the young ages of those who contributed to the struggle against Francoism.[31]

Further discrepancies arise when the Historical Memory Law is compared with the Law on Solidarity with the Victims of Terrorism. The former stipulates that to be eligible for compensation, the victim could not be in receipt of compensation exceeding the value established in the Historical Memory Law for the same damages from another reparative scheme. However, article 5 in the Law of solidarity with victims of terrorism allows its beneficiaries to complement its compensation with other economic aid packages. Furthermore, the Historical Memory Law does not include any reference to victims who suffered minor injuries, and yet the Solidarity Law allows for compensation for permanent (but not disabling) injuries, temporary incapacitation after a kidnapping and even material damages. The Solidarity Law also included health, psychological, educational, labour and social allowances, as well as wide institutional recognition in the spirit of historical memory, which the victims of Francoism and the first transition have not received.[32] In this way, then, there is a discrepancy in the way victims are treated in the Spanish legal system, contravening the principle of equality enshrined in the 1978 Constitution.[33]

The Historical Memory Law was finalised through the Royal Decree of 3 November 2008, which regulated the conditions and the procedures for the allocation of compensation as per article 10 and the fourth additional provision of the Law on victims who were killed or maimed between 1 January 1968 and 6 October 1977 in their struggle to defend democracy.[34] Article 2.1 of the Decree added an extra requirement which had not been originally established in Law 52/2007: the cause of compensation, or the beneficiaries of the same, must not have belonged or belong to armed groups. This article thus excluded members of ETA, FRAP and other left-wing armed groups which had fought against the dictatorship and whose crimes, in any case, were subject to the 1976 and 1977 amnesties.

Francoist criminals continued to view the Amnesty Law as sacrosanct, but not so those who had belonged to armed groups. As Rafael Escudero has said, the fact that the Historical Memory Law did not originally establish this measure, and was later added during the development phase, is a flagrant abuse of the government's regulatory power, one which restricted the rights of those who could have benefitted from the compensation established in Law 52/2007. Moreover,

31 Escudero Alday, 2009, pp. 46–47.

32 Baylos Grau, 2008, pp. 205–208. Escudero Alday, 2009, pp. 45–47. Escudero Alday, 2013b, pp. 206–211. Jiménez Villarejo and Doñate, 2012, pp. 110–115.

33 Escudero Alday, 2013b, p. 214.

34 Royal Decree 1803/2008, 3 November, regulating conditions and procedures for compensation guaranteed in Law 52/2007, 26 December, in favour of soldiers killed or maimed in the struggle to defend democracy. *Official State Gazette*, no. 276, 15 November 2008, pp. 45394–45401.

this retraction of compensation did not take into consideration degrees of involvement or the nature of crimes committed while affiliated to an armed group. On top of this, the measure gave rise to a paradox: the family members of the last victims executed by the dictatorship for belonging to ETA and FRAP could avail of the declaration of reparation and personal recognition, as guaranteed under the Historical Memory Law, for having been convicted by a war council without the minimum legal guarantees or a competent defence counsel as moral reparation, but were excluded from receiving economic reparation.[35] The measure discredited armed resistance against dictatorial regimes and violators of human rights, and punished the family members, who would have been entitled to compensation. In this way, compensation was denied to the families of the last five victims executed by the Francoist regime, including two members of ETA and three members of FRAP,[36] who, as mentioned in the first chapter, were executed on 27 September 1975 after a trial in a war council, without the minimum legal guarantees and with no legal defence.

Law 52/2007 was modified on two occasions with regard to economic reparation: first, by the Law of 23 December 2008 on the State Budget for the fiscal year 2009,[37] established through the fifth final provision, the modification of article 10.1 of the Historical Memory, setting 31 December 1977[38] as the date before which the death would have had to occur in order for it to be covered by the compensation provision.

The Royal Decree of 17 April 2009 was issued as a complement to Law 52/2007, "in relation to retired people and particular social compensations". It was an anodyne title referencing the procedural regulation to grant compensation to homosexuals who had been interned.[39] The injustice of the exclusion of homosexuals from the Amnesty Law was somewhat rectified, at least with regard to compensation; the crime, however, which was not subject to amnesty, remains in official records.

The second modification to Law 52/2007 was implemented through the sixth additional provision of the Law of 23 December 2009 on the State Budget for the fiscal year 2010,[40] which modified article 10.2 of the Historical Memory Law. The modification abolished the stipulation that beneficiaries needed to be economically dependent on the deceased to be eligible for compensation. In future, when the deceased left behind no spouse or children, the beneficiaries would be

35 Escudero Alday, 2009, pp. 47–49. Escudero Alday, 2013b, p. 209.
36 Escudero Alday, 2013b, p. 208.
37 *Official State Gazette*, no. 309, 24 December 2008, pp. 51773–51897.
38 The original date in Law 52/2007 was set to 6 October 1977.
39 Royal Decree 710/2009, 17 April, for the development of the provisions in Law 2/2008, 23 December, on State Budgets for 2009, in relation to pensions for retired workers and specific social reparations. *Official State Gazette*, no. 105, 30 April 2009, pp. 37930–37942.
40 Law 26/2009, 23 December, on State Budgets for the year 2010. *Official State Gazette*, no. 309, 24 December 2009, pp. 108804–109227.

the parents, then the grandchildren, brothers and sisters of the deceased, and if none of these survive, lastly, the children of a partner.

These compensation packages were established in the 2009 General State Budgets Law, which set 31 December 2013 as the deadline for applications. Towards the end of 2016, the socialist deputy, Antonio Hurtado, raised the issue before Parliament of the number of people who availed of compensation packages before 2009. The answer he received demonstrate the sad truth of the situation. The government only compensated 116 former social prisoners, convicted during Francoism on grounds of their sexual orientation. The total of these compensation packages comes to €624,000, an average of €5,300 per individual. As Hurtado pointed out, this was "a fraction" of the thousands of people persecuted by Francoism because of their sexuality. He further believed that this low estimate was due to the lack of information given to those who could have applied for compensation, lack of publicity and the meagre sum offered as compensation. The figure of 116 homosexuals who were compensated in Spain is in stark contrast with the 5,000 or so homosexuals who were compensated for the persecution they had suffered from the Nazis.[41]

The qualitative and quantitative improvements of economic reparation which came from the Historical Memory Law and its subsequent modifications avoided the need for complementary regulation at regional level, with two exceptions. The regional government of Andalusia issued the decree of 21 September 2010, establishing compensation for women whose dignity, privacy and integrity suffered because of the repression during the Francoist dictatorship. To date, it is the only regulation in the entire state which compensates on grounds of gender.[42]

For its part, the Basque Autonomous Community sought to remedy the issue of the initial date for eligibility for compensation, as well as the measure denying compensation to members of armed groups who had been granted amnesty, based on the principle that every victim of human rights violation deserves equal recognition, respect and protection from public authorities. The Decree of 12 June 2012[43] acknowledged the victims who suffered from politically motivated violence in Euskadi between 1960 and 1978, and the need to end the culture of amnesia that has obviated these victims. As well as economic reparation, other measures granted moral reparation.[44]

41 http://www.huffingtonpost.es/2017/01/03/homosexuales-franquismo_n_13935298.html (accessed on 11 January 2017).

42 Decree 372/2010, 21 September, by which compensation is granted to women whose dignity, privacy and integrity suffered because of the repression during the Francoist dictatorship. *Official Gazette of the Andalusian Regional Government*, 13 October 2010.

43 Decree of the Department of Justice and Public Administration 107/2012, 12 June, on the recognition and reparation of victims who suffered unfairly because of human rights violations between 1960 and 1978 in the context of political violence that took place in the Autonomous Community of the Basque Country. *Official Basque Country Gazette*, 19 June 2012.

44 See Escudero Alday, 2013b, pp. 211–213.

1.4 Enforced disappearances: exhumations

As has been mentioned throughout, enforced disappearances during the Civil War and the post-war were the only crimes not included in the Amnesty Law because the statute of limitations had passed. Irrespective of the time that has passed, crimes of enforced disappearances do not expire nor can they be amnestied due to their nature as permanent crimes. Regardless of the absence of the person presumed dead or the retroactive measure legislated in article 607bis of the current Criminal Code, enforced disappearances are considered a crime until the person returns alive – something impossible given the amount of time that has passed, or when a forensic scientist and a judge certify the death, hence the importance of localising, exhuming and identifying the remains.[45]

The Historical Memory Law did not legislate for the creation of a truth commission to investigate enforced disappearances. It merely focused on the practical aspects of localising and exhuming the remains,[46] thus allowing the perpetrators to remain hidden behind the collective amnesia. It has, nevertheless, proven to be a useful instrument in the consolidation of the exhumation initiatives begun by civil society, but, with some justification, the public administration has been criticised for unburdening itself of the responsibility of developing initiatives to localise the remains, carry out exhumations and identify the bodies. Instead, these initiatives have been delegated to the private sector. Public authorities do not lead the processes to localise and identify the victims, preferring instead to fund the associations that carry out this work,[47] which means that the exhumations are carried out without any legal supervision to oversee the identification of the remains and without carrying out the appropriate inquiries.

2 The 2007 Catalan Memorial Law in the face of the culture of amnesia instated after the transition (2007)

Unlike the Historical Memory Law, the Memorial Law passed by the Catalan government on 31 October 2007 on the initiative of the Catalan public institution *Memorial Democràtic*,[48] was a more substantial attempt to recover the forgotten collective heritage.

The Catalan *Memorial Democràtic* is a public institution in the Generalitat and was one of the main driving forces behind the government presided by the socialist leader, Pasqual Maragall. It was founded in 2005 with the aim of conserving, investigating, recovering and disseminating information about the events between the proclamation of the Second Spanish Republic and the first

45 Jiménez Villarejo and Doñate, 2012, p. 193.
46 See Parejo Alfonso, 2008, pp. 145–174.
47 Escudero Alday, 2009, pp. 49–50 and 52.
48 Law 13/2007, 31 October, on "Memorial Democrático". *Official Catalan Generalitat Diary*, no. 5006, 12 November 2007; *Official State Gazette*, no. 284, 27 November 2007, pp. 48487–48491.

democratically elected government after the transition (1931–1980). Through this institution, the Generalitat instates public policies geared towards recovering democratic memory as a tribute to all the victims who fought for democracy, the values on which it is founded, and as a way of preserving the memory of the struggle against Francoism.[49]

Although the Bill was presented in 2006, it was not approved in Parliament until the following legislature, on 24 October 2007. The Law of 31 October on Memorial Democràtic laid the foundations for the development of Catalan policies for the recovery of historical memory, after "a transition based on silence".[50] Its preamble served as a statement of intent: it wanted to put an end to the silence. It claims that the current democratic system has its roots in the Republican memory and the anti-Francoist movement, and with regard to the transition, it recalls that "it was developed under the leadership of institutions and political actors who were clearly linked to the dictatorship", although it did "allow to overcome the divisions created by the Civil War and the dictatorship". It says further that:

> this process also hides a dark secret, forgetting to preserve the memory of citizens and institutions of all types who, under the difficult conditions of a dictatorial regime which lasted 40 years, sacrificed themselves and their families in the struggle to recover the freedoms which the Francoist dictatorship had taken away. They gave up work, put their physical integrity in jeopardy, and even sacrificed their lives. Viewed in this way, one of the failures of the transition to democracy was the institutionalisation of amnesia and forgetting the democratic tradition and its leading figures, who, nevertheless, give meaning and a special value to the current political system and the rights and freedoms that our society enjoys today.

The Law envisages the *Memorial Democràtic* as an instrument for the development of public policies on behalf of the Generalitat for the "recovery of the memory of the victims of the Civil War and the people, organisations and institutions who fought against the political, social, cultural and national repression by an ignominious regime". It aims to achieve a "full rehabilitation of the people, organisations and institutions punished during the Civil War and Francoism so that the survivors, their family members and future generations get the recognition they justly deserve".

3 The issue of amnesia in the trials investigating Francoist crimes in the Garzón case (2008–2009)

The impunity occasioned by the Spanish Amnesty Law became notorious on the international stage when, in the autumn of 2008, Baltasar Garzón, the presiding

49 Guixé, 2008, pp. 217–228.
50 *Diary of Sessions in the Catalan Parliament*, Plenary Session, no. 23, 24 October 2007.

judge in the Investigating Court no. 5 of the National High Court, began his investigation into Francoist crimes, leading to a tortuous and complex legal process. The case against this judge, who shot to fame after he ordered the arrest of the dictator Augusto Pinochet, led to a renewed doctrinal debate on the Amnesty Law and impunity. The literature on this issue is extensive, but it is particularly important to note the reports carried out by Amnesty International,[51] and the studies carried out by Javier Chinchón,[52] Javier Chinchón and Lydia Vicente,[53] Javier Chinchón, Lydia Vicente and Alicia Moreno,[54] Margalida Capellá,[55] Carlos Villán Durán and Carmelo Faleh Pérez,[56] Amaya Olivas,[57] Luis Jimena Quesada,[58] Alicia Gil,[59] Josep María Tamarit,[60] Ramón Sáez Valcárcel,[61] Mónica Zapico,[62] Javier González Vega,[63] Antoni Pigrau,[64] Julio Fernández García,[65] Joan E. Garcés,[66] Hernando Valencia Villa,[67] José Antonio Martín Pallín,[68] Joxerramon Bengoetxea,[69] Úrsula Urdillo,[70] Carlos Jiménez Villarejo,[71] Carlos Jiménez Villarejo and Antonio Doñate,[72] Naomi Roht-Arriaza,[73] Tomás de Domingo,[74] Carlos Castresana,[75] Perfecto Andrés,[76] Araceli Manjón-Cabeza,[77]

51 Amnistía Internacional España, 2008a. Amnistía Internacional España, 2008b. Amnistía Internacional España, 2008c. Amnistía Internacional España, 2012.
52 Chinchón Álvarez, 2008a. Chinchón Álvarez, 2008b. Chinchón Álvarez, 2009b. Chinchón Álvarez, 2009c. Chinchón Álvarez, 2011. Chinchón Álvarez, 2012a. Chinchón Álvarez, 2012b. Chinchón Álvarez, 2013. Chinchón Álvarez, 2013–2014. Chinchón Álvarez, 2013–2014.
53 Chinchón Álvarez and Vicente Márquez, 2010.
54 Chinchón Álvarez, Vicente Márquez and Moreno, 2014.
55 Capellá i Roig, 2008. Capellá i Roig, 2009. Capellá i Roig, 2011.
56 Villán Durán and Faleh Pérez, 2008.
57 Olivas Díaz, 2008.
58 Jimena Quesada, 2008.
59 Gil Gil, 2009a. Gil Gil, 2009b. Gil Gil, 2009c. Gil Gil, 2010. Gil Gil, 2011. Gil Gil, 2012b.
60 Tamarit Sumalla, 2009. Tamarit Sumalla, 2011. Tamarit Sumalla, 2012. Tamarit Sumalla, 2013. Tamarit Sumalla, 2014.
61 Sáez Valcárcel, 2009. Sáez Valcárcel, 2010.
62 Zapico Barbeito, 2009. Zapico Barbeito, 2010. Zapico Barbeito, 2012.
63 González Vega, 2009.
64 Pigrau Solé, 2009.
65 Fernández García, 2009.
66 Garcés, 2010. Garcés, 2011.
67 Valencia Villa, 2010.
68 Martín Pallín, 2011.
69 Bengoetxea, 2011.
70 Urdillo, 2011–2012.
71 Jiménez Villarejo, 2010.
72 Jiménez Villarejo and Doñate, 2012.
73 Roht-Arriaza, 2012.
74 De Domingo, 2012.
75 Castresana, 2012.
76 Andrés Ibáñez, 2012.
77 Manjón-Cabeza Olmeda, 2012.

Carlos Villán Durán,[78] Rafael Escudero,[79] Francisco Espinosa,[80] Silvia Soriano,[81] Patricio Galella,[82] José Antonio García Sáez,[83] Bartolomé Clavero,[84] Carlos Fernández Liesa,[85] and Paloma Aguilar and Clara Ramírez-Barat.[86]

3.1 The issue of amnesty in the case before the Investigating Court no. 5 in the National High Court

Various human rights associations chose the symbolic date of 18 July 2007 (the anniversary of the coup d'état against the Second Spanish Republic) to file complaints in the National High Court requesting an investigation into Francoist crimes. Specifically, it focused on the massacres in Badajoz and Paracuellos, considering them acts of genocide. The National High Court rejected the complaints, claiming that "the crimes had prescribed, and, in any case, were subject to the 1977 Amnesty Law".

It was a view that was not shared by the investigating judge no. 5, Baltasar Garzón. A new lawsuit arrived on his desk, filed on 14 December 2006 by the Platform of Victims of Enforced Disappearances of Francoism. It called for a recognition of the victims' right to the truth and demanded legal protection in their quest to recover the truth with regard to 114,266 enforced disappearances between 17 July 1936 and December 1951. The list of names was accompanied by a special report by the foremost expert in this area, the historian Francisco Espinosa.[87]

The judge commissioned a report from the Ministry of Justice with regard to the capacity of the Investigating Court no. 5 of the National High Court to investigate crimes against humanity. The report came back on 29 January 2008 with a denial, considering that the court should no longer admit the lawsuits because, among other reasons, the events in question were covered by the 1977 Amnesty Law. The Attorney General argued that the crimes were common crimes as per the criteria of the time, and that statute limitations could not apply in this case.

Meanwhile, the Spanish Society for International Law on Human Rights, at the request of the associations of the families of the victims, put together a 52-page report on enforced disappearances in Spain during the Civil War and the

78 Villán Durán, 2012.
79 Escudero Alday, 2013c. Escudero Alday, 2014.
80 Espinosa Maestre, 2013.
81 Soriano Hernández, 2013.
82 Galella, 2013.
83 García Sáez, 2013.
84 Clavero, 2014.
85 Fernández Liesa, 2014.
86 Aguilar and Ramírez-Barat, 2014.
87 F. Espinosa Maestre, *Informe sobre la represión franquista. Estado de la cuestión.* http://salamancamemoriayjusticia.org/der/espinosanacional.pdf (accessed on 11 July 2016).

Francoist dictatorship. The thrust of the argument will be analysed in the discussion of Garzón's edicts.[88]

Garzón ignored the opinion of the Ministry of Justice Attorney General, and in August 2008 he initiated proceedings. The judge asserted his jurisdiction in the subsequent edict of the Central Investigating Court no. 5 of the High Court of 16 October 2008, to process the lawsuit regarding the alleged crimes of internment, indefinite in respect of length of time and whereabouts, in the context of crimes against humanity.[89] Thus, the trial 53/2008 initiated the first legal process in history against those responsible for the coup d'état and the repression of the Civil War and the post-war.[90]

The court order specified that crimes against humanity during the dictatorship could not be classified as political crimes, and were therefore not covered by the 1977 Amnesty Law. Even in cases where unlawful arrests were made for enforced disappearances, the crimes were of a permanent nature, and therefore not subject to the statute of limitations. This notwithstanding, an amnesty law which seeks to pardon crimes against humanity would be nullified by the law. Crimes against international law of interest to the Spanish legal system do not admit pardons or amnesty.

The District Attorney appealed the court order in the Criminal Chamber of the High Court on 20 October 2008, on the basis that the case was outside the jurisdiction of the High Court. It argued that the crimes investigated in the Central Magistrates' Court no. 5 had been granted amnesty because of their "political motivation", and defended the non-retroactive nature of criminal law and the prescription of the crimes.

Garzón had to issue a new court order on 18 November[91] agreeing to process the cases in the magistrates' courts of the communities where the identified mass graves were located. The new court order declared competent more than 50 territorial courts which, according to the Attorney General's office, is where the jurisdiction to investigate enforced disappearances abided. What is of interest to this study is that the new court order stated that the 1977 Amnesty Law was not applicable to the crimes being investigated in the proceedings. Specifically, as per the difference between internal and international law, it argued that crimes against humanity could not be pardoned and that the perpetrator could be charged under international law because such crimes were punishable at the

88 Spanish Association for International Law and Human Rights, 2008.

89 Court order issued in the Central Investigating Court no. 5 in the High Court during the Preliminary Hearing 399/2006, 16 October.

90 The court order stated that "the acts in question have never been criminally investigated in the Spanish legal system, which is why to date, impunity has been the standard". Court order issued in the Central Investigating Court no. 5 in the High Court during the Preliminary Hearing 399/2006, 16 October, first legal reasoning, para. 1.

91 Court Order by the Central Investigating Court no. 5 of the High Court, Summary 53/2008, 18 November.

international level irrespective of the national doctrine. He based his argument on the national and international doctrine, legislation and jurisdiction on amnesty and the statute of limitations, especially in relation to enforced disappearances (of adults and children) and unlawful arrests. He further argued that the Attorney General could not classify the crimes in question as mere political crimes without offering a detailed and exhaustive case-by-case analysis of what crimes fall under the politically motivated denomination in criminal law, highlighting the circumstances, acts and participation of those who benefitted from the amnesty. Only in this way could they be known and evaluated by the legal authorities which are ultimately responsible for this issue, as per article 9 of the Law 46/1977.

A new court order issued from the criminal chamber of the National High Court on 2 December 2008 declared that the National High Court did not have jurisdiction to investigate the crimes, and thus invalidated the legal process and every resolution and all the court orders issued between 16 October and 18 November.[92]

The victims of Francoism decided to take the alternative and go down the universal justice[93] route, which resulted in the lawsuit filed in the Argentinian legal system on 14 April (discussed below). Civilians expressed their indignation with Francoist impunity at a protest attended by 60,000 people in Madrid on 24 April. It had been organised by the newly formed Platform Against Francoist Crimes. Since then, this group meets in the Puerta de Sol in Madrid every Thursday, inspired by the mothers and grandmothers of the Plaza de Mayo in Argentina, carrying photographs of the disappeared. For their part, the former prisoners of Francoism met in the La Comuna association with the same objective: to demand an end to the impunity of Francoism crimes.[94]

3.2 *The issue of amnesty during the criminal proceedings against Garzón*

On 26 January 2009, the *Manos Limpias* trade union brought a case against Garzón for alleged contempt of court for having declared himself competent to investigate the claims filed in his Investigative Court into crimes committed during the Civil War and the dictatorship.[95] *Manos Limpias* argued that the claims related to enforced disappearances during Francoism "completely ignored the established process, the non-retroactive nature of criminal law, the 1977 Amnesty Law and its own proceedings and court orders, refusing to classify the Paracuellos massacre as genocide". The case was admitted in the Criminal Chamber of the Supreme Court on 26 May 2009.[96]

92 Court order from the Criminal Chamber of the High Court, Ordinary Procedure no. 53/08 in the Investigating Court no. 5, Case file no. 34/08, 2 December 2008.
93 Hellman Moreno, 2012, pp. 299–323.
94 Silva, 2011, p. 74.
95 The lawsuit filed by Manos Limpias was followed by case 3/20153/2009, commenced for the same crimes by the extreme right group Association for Civil Liberties and Identity, as part of the class action.
96 Court order from the Criminal Chamber of the Supreme 6801/2009, 26 May.

The judge who prepared the criminal process 200048/2009 against Baltasar Garzón was Luciano Varela, who had been the rapporteur of the Supreme Court resolution that agreed to forward to the General Council of the Judiciary the investigation into funds that Garzón received during a stay in New York. On 3 February, Varela rejected the stay of proceedings that Garzón requested because, *inter alia*, "any consideration of the context of crimes against humanity is insufficient reason to bring back the criminal accountability which has prescribed and was pardoned by the amnesty", and it is "manifestly against the law not to exclude the legal implications of the matters referred to in the Amnesty established in Law 46/1977, 15th of October". He maintained that crimes of Francoism were politically motivated, and that international law did not exclude recourse to an amnesty either, at least at the time the crimes were carried out.[97]

Garzón appealed the court order with a writ on 9 February, wherein he gave a comprehensive account of the debate on accountability of human rights, the validity and interpretation of the amnesty laws and the statutory limitations in cases of enforced disappearance.

Two months later, on 7 April 2010, the Criminal Chamber of the Supreme Court issued a new court order indicating grounds to charge Baltasar Garzón for alleged contempt of court. In relation to amnesty, the court order stated that:

> Without doubt, public debate and debates of a theoretical nature can help those responsible for signing off on the court order. Whoever achieves overall majority in parliament will have within their reach the opportunity to fulfil these legal needs by promoting and passing the appropriate modifications to the legislation. It is a responsibility that they must take ownership of, and not leave it to the criminal judge. The Legislative Authority could then abolish the 1977 Amnesty Law and redefine the retroactive limits of prescription. All that would be left, in any case, would be to establish whether it is unconstitutional.
>
> These are the guidelines and points of reference for the process we find ourselves in. It is the limit and the sole *raison d'être* for the autonomy of judges in a democratic society: the strict application of the law in force. It is a duty that will not always be compatible with the opinion, more or less homogenous, of influential judges.[98]

On 11 May 2010, the Criminal Chamber of the Supreme Court finally ordered the commencement of the trial against Garzón for alleged contempt of court[99] as per article 446.3 of the Criminal Code.[100] Garzón was, at the same time, being

97 Court order from the Criminal Chamber of the Supreme Court 4739/2010, 3 February.

98 Court order from the Criminal Chamber of the Supreme Court 3766/2010, 7 April.

99 Garzón had ordered wiretappings in the context of an investigation into corruption, known as the Gürtel case, involving various PP officials.

100 Court order from the Criminal Chamber of the Supreme Court 5560/2010, 11 May.

processed for subversion of justice in the Criminal Chamber of the Supreme Court and on 9 February 2012 was disqualified from the bar for 11 years, and was removed from his position indefinitely.[101] Two weeks later, after Garzón had been removed from the High Court and suspended, the sentence of 27 February 2012 was delivered for the criminal trial 20048/2009 with regard to the investigation of crimes of Francoism. Garzón was absolved of any wrongdoing – although the legal text read more like a conviction[102] – and established that Civil War crimes and crimes of Francoism could not be investigated in the Spanish court system.[103] Enforced disappearances could only be investigated by the Investigation Courts.

The Sentence stated that the statute of limitations had expired for the crimes in question and, in any case, they were subject to the Amnesty Law. Impunity in the case of Francoist criminals was, at the time, a reality which was the result of both the time that had passed and the demise of those responsible, and which was translated into legal impunity due to the doctrine of the Supreme Court.[104] It is not surprising therefore that Bartolomé Clavero describes it as an "End of Story Sentence".[105]

The Supreme Court had to counter Garzón and the abundant jurisprudence generated by opening the criminal case 20048/2009. The fifth legal clause of the Sentence rejected that the crimes put before the High Court had an international element to them, arguing that at the time when the 1977 Amnesty Law was passed, Francoist crimes could not be granted amnesty because there was no international mechanism in force in Spain before October 1977 which obliged Spain to prosecute the crimes, and because Francoist crimes were not considered criminal and were not beholden to statutory limitations in Spain's criminal law of the time. Like the Attorney General's Office, it believed that the crimes committed during the Civil War and Francoism were politically motivated, and thus applicable to Law 46/1077 and subject to the regulation on prescriptibility. Attempting to draw a line under the matter, it stated that:

> Once we have excluded the existence of a single correct solution in the theory and practice of the law, it is always necessary to find grounds to defend *any* position, regardless of how unusual it is. In the vigorous debate that has arisen simply because this process was initiated, we have thus read that some understand the 1977 Amnesty Law as a measure that only eliminated the criminal liability of those of a specific ideology, but not the criminal liability of their political adversaries [...]

101 Sentence from the Criminal Chamber of the Supreme Court, 79/2012, 9 February.
102 Clavero, 2014, pp. 148–149.
103 Sentence from the Criminal Chamber of the Supreme Court, 101/2012, 27 February.
104 Manjón-Cabeza Olmeda, 2012, p. 5.
105 Clavero, 2014, p. 153.

The remaining references to the amnesty in the Sentence were of a political nature. It seems as if the judges foresaw the stream of doctrinal criticisms that were to follow because they put forward an "official" interpretation of the Amnesty Law and defined the spirit of the transition: the Law was promulgated by the political forces in the period after the 1977 democratic elections and was confirmed on 19 July 2011 in the Congress of Deputies when a proposal to modify Law 46/1977 was rejected. The Amnesty Law was "a necessary and considered measure in the endeavour to dismantle the Francoist regime". The Amnesty Law was "a necessary pillar, irreplaceable and necessary, in the effort to overcome Francoism and everything that it brought with it", a necessary step towards "the peaceful installation of a new regime to avoid a violent solution and a return to hostilities". It concluded that "the *transition* represented the will of the people as articulated in the law", hence why no judge or court can question the legitimacy of the process. In any case, it reiterated that "it is a Law that is currently in force. Its derogation is an exclusively parliamentary matter."

The arguments espoused in the Sentence elevate a pre-constitutional law to the status of the Constitution and, in practice, a higher legal standing, because as Bartolomé Clavero said, a meta-normative culture has enveloped the Law, the pinnacle of which is this Sentence. Thus viewed, the Amnesty Law is above the constitutional recognition of international human rights.[106] As if it were the very Constitution endorsed in a referendum, Law 46/1977 became the manifestation of the will of the people of Spain.

The Sentence rebuked Garzón for having initiated an investigation into the history of crimes which had been granted amnesty, and closed the door on any future truth commission in the Spanish legal system:

> It is difficult to reach a verdict on the legal truth of the matter, in accordance with the formal and safeguarding demands of the criminal process, without suspects or accused, as these have passed away, or by investigating crimes which have prescribed or were granted amnesty. The process of legal investigation is not the same as an investigation carried out by an historian. Indeed, if the differences between memory and history are evident, so too are those which exist between the latter and those which result from a judicial investigation carried out with a different objective from that of the historian.
>
> The search for truth is as legitimate as it is necessary. It is the duty of the State to carry it through its various institutions with the cooperation of every profession and discipline, especially so in the case of historians. But it is not the duty of the instructing judge, whose function is established in the procedural law in terms of inquiries which are concretised during the course of the process and restricts his role in accordance with the regulations that govern the criminal process and criminal law. It is imperative that there both be a possible crime and a possible defendant who is still living.

106 Clavero, 2014, p. 144.

The instructing judge's methods of inquiry are completely different to the investigation process carried out by a historian. It is not good practice to mix historical truth with forensic truth, because history is general and open to interpretation. It is not subject to established deadlines, and typically requires a longer time-scale in order to carry out an objective analysis. Judicial decisions, on the other hand, are restricted in their scope to a single event, imposes consequences which must be enforced, is subject to an established processes and timescales, must follow due diligence, and is declared in accordance with its own guarantees and refers to the elimination of a criminal liability demanded by the charge.

3.3 The consolidation of the Supreme Court doctrine on amnesty

On 28 March 2012, a Court Order from the Criminal Chamber of the Supreme Court resolved the issue of competence put forward by the Investigating Court no. 3 of Granada and no. 2 of El Escorial, in relation to granting jurisdiction for the investigation of mass graves to the territorial courts where the remains of victims had been located, establishing that the territorial courts had the power to continue the processes initiated, and would have to resolve the cases of enforced disappearances "in accordance with the interpretation of the law".[107] This new court order reiterated the stance of the Supreme Court in relation to amnesty by pointing out that, regardless of circumstances, solutions had to adhere to the contents of Sentence 101/2012, that is, to the triumvirate of non-retroactivity, amnesty and prescription.

The legal means to prosecute crimes of the Civil War and Francoism were closed, and the doctrine established by the Supreme Court in relation to the Amnesty Law was followed by other Spanish courts when they had to process cases of enforced disappearances.[108] The Court Order issued by the Investigating Court no. 2 of Aranda de Duero (Castile and Leon) is interesting because it concluded that the crimes had been prescribed. The instructing judge must have had doubts, given that the case related to an enforced disappearance, which is why he pointed out that "even in the event that the statute of limitations does not apply to this crime, it is nevertheless subject to the Amnesty Law", wherein article 6 implied the elimination of criminal liability for the crime in question. It underscored this assertion by pointing out that in the case of unlawful arrests, even when prescription is not applicable because the crime is of a permanent nature, the Amnesty Law would eliminate criminal liability.[109]

107 Court Order from the Criminal Chamber of the Supreme Court 3009/2012, 28 March.

108 See Olivas Díaz, 2008, pp. 86–102; Jiménez Villarejo and Doñate, 2012; Sáez Valcárcel, 2013; Chinchón Álvarez, 2013, pp. 187–189; Chinchón, Vicente Márquez and Moreno, 2014.

109 Court Order from the Investigating Court no. 2 in Aranda del Duero, Preliminary Hearing no. 304/09, 8 February 2010, pp. 3–4. See Chinchón Álvarez, 2013, p. 188.

In practice, most of the instructing judges who hear cases on enforced disappearances resulting from the Civil War or the post-war, close the case immediately on the basis of the principle of prescription, as per the guidelines set by the Supreme Court in the Sentence 101/2012. If an appeal is filed, it is not admitted, and if it goes forward, the Provincial Court dismisses it. If it goes to the Supreme Court after the appeal, the Supreme Court dismisses it.[110] There are some exceptions, such as the case when a circuit judge in the Investigating Court no. 1 of Almazán (Soria) agreed to process a suit on enforced disappearances. In June 2015, the circuit judge petitioned the criminal investigation department to locate the whereabouts of the soldiers responsible for the murder of ten civilians in Barcones (Soria) on the morning of 14 August 1936, with the aim of shedding light on the events by obtaining the testimony of the accused – if they are alive and their identities are known. She also requested documentation on the repression that took place in the area from the Provincial Historical Archive of Soria and the Historical Memory Documentary Centre in Salamanca.[111] The mass grave was located mostly thanks to the Memory and Dignity Association and the testimony of a witness. The exhumation was carried out by the Aranzadi Science Society team, led by Francisco Etxeberria. Six bodies were recovered, the other four remain disappeared.[112]

In theory, there is another mechanism. Rosa Ana Alija and Elisenda Calvet consider that the right to search, identify and the right to have the remains of the disappeared handed over to the families are enshrined in article 24 of the International Convention for the Protection of All Persons from Enforced Disappearance, and therefore requests can be made directly to the Administration. If the Administration fails to observe these rights, recourse can be sought in contentious administrative mechanisms, such as an appeal against the authorities for derogation of duty, the appeal for protection from infringement on the rights of victims to moral integrity and patrimony liability because of the administration's dereliction of duty.[113] It is not known whether any victims have used this mechanism.

4 Keeping the Amnesty Law come hell or high water (2008–2016)

4.1 Petitions for the derogation of the Amnesty Law

The fact that the Amnesty Law was invoked by the Public Prosecution Office in the National High Court as an argument against carrying out a legal investigation

110 Chinchón Álvarez, 2012a, pp. 77–91, 97–98 and 129–130.
111 http://www.eldiario.es/sociedad/Soria-declarar-responsables-asesinato-franquista_0_400010743.html (accessed on 18 July 2016).
112 http://sorianoticias.com/noticia/2015-08-18-este-miercoles-declara-otra-descendiente-asesinados-barcones-26230 (accessed on 18 July 2016).
113 Alija and Calvet, 2013, pp. 101–120.

into Francoist crimes against humanity motivated 12 pro-memory associations to sign a declaration on 18 July 2008 to, *inter alia*, request the derogation of the law.[114]

A few months before this, the "Report (*Amicus curiae*) on the effective recourse and fair and adequate reparation that is the right of the victims of enforced disappearances, crimes against humanity and other violations of human rights perpetrated in Spain during the Civil War and dictatorship" also heavily criticised the Amnesty Law. It was signed in Geneva and Las Palmas of Gran Canaria on 30 April 2008 by Carlos Villán Durán and Carmelo Faleh Pérez on behalf of the AEDIDH. It stated that Law 46/1077 contravenes international law because it violated the human rights cited in international treaties and declarations, and it promotes impunity for those responsible for crimes against humanity. It also noted that if Spain were to tolerate the elimination of criminal liability, both at the level of the State and the level of the individual, assumed for crimes against humanity during the Civil War and dictatorship under the Amnesty Law, then it would be undermining the aims and objectives of the International Convention for the Protection of All Persons from Enforced Disappearance.[115]

The voices of dissent against the Amnesty Law were strengthened by the support of the UN Human Rights Committee,[116] an institution constituted of independent experts with the aim of supervising the States which have ratified the International Covenant on Civil and Political Rights. On 5 February 2008, Spain submitted the fifth periodic report in compliance with article 4 of the Covenant. The Committee raised a number of issues in the report, but none in relation to amnesty,[117] which is why Spain did not pronounce itself on the matter in its reply.[118] The report was examined by the Committee in the sessions of 20 and 21 October 2008. It recommended that Spain implement the necessary legislative measures to recognise the non-applicability of statutory limitations of crimes against humanity in the Spanish courts; to legislate for the constitution of a commission of independent experts to establish the historical truth on the violations of human rights perpetrated during the Civil War and the dictatorship; to allow the families to identify and exhume the remains of the victims and, when appropriate, to compensate them. The ninth recommendation suggested the derogation of the Amnesty Law on the grounds that it contravened article 15.2 in the International Covenant on Civil and Political Rights, ratified by Spain on 27

114 Silva, 2011, pp. 72–73.

115 http://www.reei.org/index.php/revista/num16/notas/derecho-recurso-efectivo-obtener-una-reparacion-justa-adecuada-corresponde-victimas-desapariciones-forzadas-crimenes-contra-humanidad-otras-violaciones-derechos-humanos-cometidas-espana-durante-guerra-civil-dictadura (accessed on 8 July 2016).

116 On this and subsequent reforms, see Chinchón Álvarez, Vicente Márquez and Moreno, 2014; and Clavero, 2014, pp. 188–189 and 195–241.

117 United Nations, Human Rights Committee, *List of issues to be taken up in connection with the consideration of the fifth periodic report of Spain.* 7 August 2008. UN: CCPR/C/ESP/Q/5.

118 UN: CCPR/C/ESP/Q/5/Add.1, 14 October 2008.

April 1977. The Committee expressed its unease regarding the Law, and reiterated that crimes against humanity could not be prescribed, and the amnesty for grave violations of human rights are incompatible with the Covenant.[119]

These final Observations, published on 5 January 2009, were met with an unusual answer from the government, issued on 13 January 2009, whereby it expressed regret that the Committee did not allow a response to a substantive issue which was going to be part of the final recommendations. It defended amnesty following the argument detailed in Sentence 101/2012 in the Criminal Chamber of the Supreme Court, and concluded that the 1977 Amnesty Law "was called for by the democratic opposition and was one of the first laws passed by consensus in the same Parliament that instated the 1978 Constitution". Moreover, "not only in Spain, but across the world, public opinion is aware of and defends the transition process in Spain, which was possible in part because of the Amnesty Law".[120] Apparently, the victims and the pro-memory associations are not considered part of Spanish society, nor does the UN count towards international public opinion. In the face of these assertions, Octavio Alberola and Fèlix Villagrasa quite rightly say that amnesia has served the purpose of re-elaborating the past and has integrated memory with history, converting historical institutional amnesia into collective amnesia.[121]

History repeated itself months later. In 2009, the fifth periodic report submitted by Spain had to be examined, in this case to comply with article 19 of the Convention against Torture and Other Cruel, Inhuman or Degrading Treatment or Punishment.[122] This time, the Committee did express its unease with regard to the Amnesty Law among the various issues it raised.[123] It said that, "bearing in mind the long-established *jus cogens* prohibition of torture, the prosecution of acts of torture should not be constrained by the principle of legality or the statute of limitations". For this reason, it put the following questions before Spain: Does the State consider that part of the 1977 Amnesty Law contradicts its obligations in conformity with article 5 with regard to the exercise of its jurisdiction over crimes of torture and with regard to the prosecution and extradition of those accused of torture? What is the policy of the State with regard to bringing charges in relation to acts of torture which are subject to the 1977 Amnesty Law?

119 United Nations, Human Rights Committee, *Concluding Observations Spain*, 5 January 2009. UN: CCPR/C/ESP/CO/5.

120 United Nations, Human Rights Committee, *Consideration of reports submitted by States parties under article 40 of the Covenant: International Covenant on Civil and Political Rights: Spain: addendum: Comments by the Government of Spain on the concluding observations of the Human Rights Committee*, 26 January 2009. UN: CCPR/C/ESP/CO/5/Add.1, para. 9.

121 Alberola and Villagrasa, 2008.

122 United Nations, Committee Against Torture, *Convention against Torture and Other Cruel, Inhuman or Degrading Treatment or Punishment*, 18 February 2009. UN: CAT/C/ESP/5.

123 United Nations, Committee Against Torture, *Convention against Torture and Other Cruel, Inhuman or Degrading Treatment or Punishment. List of issues to be considered during the examination of the fifth periodic report of Spain*, 24 July 2009. UN: CAT/C/ESP/Q/5.

The Spanish government issued a written reply on 22 September 2009[124] repeating the arguments it gave the Human Rights Committee with new additional arguments. Specifically, it expressed that the statute of limitations could not be applied to the acts constitutive of crimes against humanity or genocide without taking into consideration the possible application of Law 46/1977, given that, as per article 1c) of the Law, amnesty will not be granted in the case of acts "that entailed serious harm to the life or inviolability of persons". The government further stated that is up to the jurisdictional bodies to consider whether that cases before them are subject to the Amnesty Law or not. In an attempt to draw a line under the matter, it stated that there was no conflict between the Amnesty Law and the duties of the State enshrined in article 5 of the Convention against Torture because the latter text was signed by Spain on 10 December 1984 and came into force on 26 June 1987. The Amnesty Law, for its part, applies to acts that took place before the Convention was adopted. In any case, it reiterated that the recent Historical Memory Law included measures for the reparation of the victims of torture, and that prescription in the Amnesty Law was not applied to crimes of torture which would have "entailed serious harm to the life or inviolability of persons" between 15 June 1976 and 15 December 1977.

On 9 December, the Committee Against Torture issued its final Observations on the fifth periodic report submitted by Spain.[125] It explained that, although the Convention against Torture came into force on 26 June 1987 and the Amnesty Law was applicable to acts before the adoption of the Convention, and "bearing in mind the long-established *jus cogens* prohibition of torture, the prosecution of acts of torture should not be constrained by the principle of legality or the statute of limitations". Furthermore, it matter-of-factly reminded Spain of its responsibility vis-à-vis ensuring that the statute of limitations does not apply to torture and enforced disappearances, crimes which are not subject to amnesty. The Committee encouraged the State "to continue and increase its efforts to help the families of the victims in the search for missing persons, to identify and exhume the remains, when possible", and reiterated that, as per article 14 of the Convention, the State has an "obligation to provide reparation and the right to compensation to all victims of acts of torture".[126]

A week later, on 21 December, the UN Working Group on the Spanish Universal Periodic Examinations and the UN Working Group on Enforced or Involuntary Disappearances concurred with the same ideas, that there "have been no investigations [in Spain] into disappearances that took place during the Spanish Civil

124 United Nations, Committee Against Torture, *Reply to List of Issues*. 22 September 2009. UN: CAT/C/ESP/Q/5/Add.1.

125 United Nations, Committee Against Torture, *Consideration of reports submitted by States parties under article 19 of the Convention. Concluding observations of the Committee against Torture. Spain*. 9 December 2009. UN: CAT/C/ESP/CO/5.

126 United Nations, Committee Against Torture, *Consideration of reports submitted by States parties under article 19 of the Convention. Concluding observations of the Committee against Torture. Spain*. 9 December 2009. UN: CAT/C/ESP/CO/5, paras 21–22.

War and General Francisco Franco's regime even though, under the continuous crimes doctrine for disappearances that remain unresolved, they continue to be committed". The Working Group on Enforced or Involuntary Disappearances remarked on the 1977 Amnesty Law and how it declared that the statute of limitations had lapsed on the crimes committed during the Civil War and the dictatorship, including enforced disappearances, which apparently "closes the door to any investigation".[127] The government replied explaining the difference between amnesty, pardon and prescription.[128] It claimed that the Amnesty Law should not be confused with an "end of story" and reiterated that, as per article 9, "its application, in any case, is exclusively incumbent on the authority of the competent judges, courts and judicial authorities, who will on a case-by-case basis find resolutions in accordance with the procedural law in force". The Working Group on Enforced or Involuntary Disappearances added that "the investigations into enforced disappearances have been carried out at the behest of the interested parties and there was no resolution issued on the matter which was subject to the Amnesty Law".[129] For its part, the Working Group reminded Spain of its "obligation under the Declaration, to conduct thorough and impartial investigations "for as long as the fate of the victim of enforced disappearance remains unclarified (art. 13.6) and to ensure that statutes of limitations, where they exist, relating to acts of enforced disappearance are substantial and commensurate with the extreme seriousness of the offence (art. 17.3)".[130]

After the UN report, Human Rights Watch issued a statement stating that the Spanish authorities had an obligation to comply with the recommendations made by the UN with the objective of putting an end to the 1977 Amnesty Law, instead of focusing on a judge seeking to hold accountable those who violated human rights in the past.[131]

Months later, a report from the Working Group on Spain's universal periodic review on 13 September 2010 did not mention the Amnesty Law, but it did recommend that the country carry out extensive investigations, punish crimes of enforced disappearances and put in place mechanisms for reparation, regardless of when it is commissioned.[132]

The petitions for the derogation of the Amnesty Law continued to increase in the years that followed. On 10 February 2012, the representative of the Office of

127 United Nations, Human Rights Council, *Report of the Working Group on Enforced or Involuntary Disappearances*, 21 December 2009. UN: A/HRC/13/31, para. 482.

128 United Nations, Human Rights Council, *Report of the Working Group on Enforced or Involuntary Disappearances*, 21 December 2009. UN: A/HRC/13/31, para. 487.

129 United Nations, Human Rights Council, *Report of the Working Group on Enforced or Involuntary Disappearances*, 21 December 2009. UN: A/HRC/13/31, para. 488.

130 United Nations, Human Rights Council, *Report of the Working Group on Enforced or Involuntary Disappearances*, 21 December 2009. UN: A/HRC/13/31, para. 502.

131 https://www.hrw.org/news/2010/03/19/spain-end-amnesty-franco-era-atrocities (accessed on 8 July 2016).

132 United Nations, Human Rights Council, *Report of the Working Group on the Universal Periodic Review, Spain Addendum*, 13 September 2010. UN: A/HRC/15/6/Add.1.

the UN High Commissioner for Human Rights, Navanethem Pillay, formally requested the derogation of the Amnesty Law, arguing that it contravened the international regulation on human rights.

The UN Working Group on Involuntary or Enforced Disappearances also requested the derogation of the Amnesty Law during its visit between 23 and 30 September 2013. Jasminka Dzumhur and Ariel Dulitzky reviewed the main initiatives and policies implemented by Spain to address involuntary or enforced disappearances. Following the Declaration on the Protection of All Persons from Enforced Disappearance, it analysed the issues of justice, truth and reparation, as well as the memory of the victims of enforced disappearances. The preliminary Observations[133] issued upon the conclusion of its visit on 30 September 2013 stated that the UN Declaration on enforced disappearance demands:

> The Declaration requires that the State guarantee to victims of enforced disappearance an effective remedy that includes a thorough and impartial ex officio investigation with a view to identifying those allegedly responsible for the disappearance and imposing the appropriate penalties. However, the combination of a defective legal framework, a judiciary that does not interpret the law in light of international human rights law, prosecutors who have not conducted investigations and the existence of the Amnesty Act and, in particular, the courts' interpretation of the Act, have established a pattern of impunity for enforced disappearances committed during the Civil War and the dictatorship. No effective judicial investigation into any named individual is under way and no one has been convicted for the disappearances during the Civil War and the dictatorship.

Later in the document, it recalled that, in October 1977, Spain passed the Amnesty Law with an overall majority in Parliament, and the Spanish authorities and large sections of society considered it "a fundamental measure which enabled a peaceful transition from the dictatorship to rule of law". However, article 18 of the Declaration:

> categorically states that persons who have or are alleged to have committed offences of enforced disappearance shall not benefit from any special amnesty law or similar measures that might have the effect of exempting them from any criminal proceedings or sanction. An amnesty law and the interpretation of that law should not permit the State's obligation to investigate, try and punish those responsible for disappearances to lapse completely.

The criticism went further by pointing out that:

133 http://www.ohchr.org/SP/NewsEvents/Pages/DisplayNews.aspx?NewsID=13800&LangID=S

> the combination of a defective legal framework, a judiciary that does not interpret the law in light of international human rights law, prosecutors who have not conducted investigations and the existence of the Amnesty Act and, in particular, the courts' interpretation of the Act, have established a pattern of impunity for enforced disappearances committed during the Civil War and the dictatorship. No effective judicial investigation into any named individual is under way and no one has been convicted for the disappearances during the Civil War and the dictatorship.

For this reason, the Working Group insisted that "the necessary legislative or judicial measures [be] adopted to remove any legal impediments to such investigations in domestic law, notably the interpretation given to the Amnesty Act, as has been noted by other international bodies".

This report caused the Committee on Enforced Disappearances to criticise the limits on prescription and the Spanish amnesty, urging the State:

> to ensure that the term of limitation actually commences at the moment when the enforced disappearance ends, i.e., when the person is found alive, his or her remains are found or their identity restored. It also urges the State party to ensure that all disappearances are investigated thoroughly and impartially, regardless of the time that has elapsed since they took place and even if there has been no formal complaint; the necessary legislative or judicial measures are adopted to remove any legal impediments to such investigations in domestic l aw, notably the interpretation given to the Amnesty Act; suspected perpetrators are prosecuted and, if found guilty, punished in accordance with the seriousness of their actions; and victims receive adequate reparation that includes the means for their rehabilitation and takes account of gender issues.[134]

The last petition for the derogation of the law came from transitional justice expert, Pablo de Greiff, who is also the UN special rapporteur on the promotion of truth, justice, reparation and guarantees of non-recurrence.[135] He visited Spain at the beginning of February 2014. In the final Observations, he stated that Spain should find the means to cancel the effects of the Amnesty Law because, in practice, it functions as an "end of story" law in the sense that in "all cases brought before Spanish justice for serious crimes committed during the Civil War and the dictatorship, either no investigations are opened, or the cases are shelved without the judges even gaining knowledge of the facts". He also stated that in countries where amnesty laws have not been abolished, the courts have interpreted the law

134 United Nations, Committee on Enforced Disappearances, *Concluding observations on the report submitted by Spain under article 29, paragraph 1, of the Convention*. 12 December 2013. UN: CED/C/ESP/CO/1.

135 Most notably, De Greiff, 2007, pp. 523–544, and De Greiff, 2012, pp. 31–77.

in ways that do not "prevent the investigation and prosecution of persons suspected of human rights violations". In Spain, however, the Amnesty Law is invoked constantly to deny the victims access to justice.[136] He made the same statements in his final report of 22 July 2014,[137] in which he concluded that Spain bases its transitional justice on "restrictive interpretations of the Amnesty Act" which "not only deny access to justice but they also impede any sort of investigation". According to De Greiff, "There is nothing in the existing law that would expressly prevent the initiation of investigations" into crimes committed during the dictatorship. In relation to article 6 of the Law, which establishes that amnesty will generally result in the extinction of criminal responsibility arising from primary or accessory penalties that have either been handed down or may be handed down, the UN special rapporteur concluded that for the amnesty to take effect it has to be granted after the facts are established and the responsibilities and penalties have been decided within a legal framework carried out in the context of a judicial investigation. Spain has, in fact, dealt with the matter of enforced disappearances in exactly the opposite way, shielding itself behind the Amnesty Law to shelve all complaints without carrying out an investigation.

The Spanish government sent its reply to the UN General Assembly and the Human Rights Council, defending the 1977 Amnesty Law.[138] Once more, it underlined that "the social support and political consensus justified the adoption of the 1977 Amnesty Law, which is not an 'end of story' law passed by the dictatorship to amnesty itself, but a law adopted by every democratically elected parliamentary group, conscious of the important step they were taking and all its implications". The government stated that the public support for the Amnesty Law was a clear indication that it was in favour of granting amnesty for Francoist crimes – which is what the report was about, when the reality is that the public supported political amnesty to those who opposed Franco and the labour amnesty. To back up its claims, it added a verbose paragraph explaining that even during the dictatorship, the Communist Party – still illegal at the time – campaigned for both sides to be granted amnesty. The arguments that followed addressed legal issues to conclude, once again, that "judges are not doing anything other than applying the legal principles and non-retroactivity of criminal law, pillars of the rule of law".

136 *El País*, 3 February 2014.

137 United Nations, Human Rights Council, *Report of the Special Rapporteur on the promotion of truth, justice, reparation and guarantees of non-recurrence, Pablo de Greiff. Mission to Spain*, 22 July 2014. UN: A/HRC/27/56/Add.1.

138 United Nations, Human Rights Council, *Informe del Relator Especial sobre la promoción de la verdad, la justicia, la reparación y las garantías de no repetición, Pablo de Greiff. Misión a España: Comentarios del Estado al informe del Relator Especial.* 17 September 2014. UN: A/HRC/27/56/Add.3.

4.2 Spain's failure to sign the Convention on the Non-Applicability of Statutory Limitations to War Crimes and Crimes Against Humanity

Gaspar Llamazares, Member of Parliament for the United Left, raised with the government the issue of diverse organisations and non-governmental organisations such as Amnesty International voicing their preoccupation with regard to the delay and shelving of cases on enforced disappearances and crimes against international law committed by Spain between 1936 and 1977. This matter attracted more attention after the Criminal Chamber of the Supreme Court declared regional courts competent in detriment of the National High Court. In his Exchange with the Executive, Llamazares asked for the reasons behind Spain's failure to sign the Convention on the Non-Applicability of Statutory Limitations to War Crimes and Crimes Against Humanity, which had been in force since December 2010.

The government formulated its reply on 15 April 2013:[139] the signing and ratification of the UN Convention on War Crimes was a commitment made by the previous legislature in the context of the 2008 National Plan for Human Rights; however, a legal analysis revealed doubts about the Convention. Specifically, it determined that certain measures were contrary to the principle of the non-retroactive nature of criminal law, and, for this reason, the government did not make provisions for signing the Convention, at least at that time. In its reply, the government repeated the arguments it had given the UN relating to the Amnesty Law, recalling that the measure had been adopted by democratic forces, in the context of "a transition from a dictatorship to a democracy", and that it had been "an instrumental measure for the reconciliation of the people of Spain". It rejected the claim that it was a "self-amnesty or unilateral amnesty articulated by the dictatorial forces", based on the fact that the Law was passed in Parliament almost immediately after the general election. The government also pointed out that the Constitutional Court endorsed the Law.

The government had to admit that the UN Committee that oversees the enforcement of the International Covenant on Civil and Political Rights (ratified by Spain in 1977) had furnished Spain with a set of observations on the derogation of the Amnesty Law, but added that these were "recommendations, not a notice of non-compliance", and that the derogation of the Amnesty Law can only be brought about in Parliament.

In any case, to return to the original question, the government pointed out that the International Convention for the Protection of All Persons from Enforced Disappearance applied to acts after the Convention came into force, that is, from December 2010, and therefore cannot be applied to crimes of Francoism. In the same vein, it recalled that the duty to prosecute crimes against humanity, as per the International Covenant on Civil and Political Rights, ratified by Spain in

139 *Público*, 15 April 2013.

1977, as well as the Statute of Rome, ratified in 2000, is only applicable to *a posteriori* crimes, therefore also excluding crimes of Francoism.

4.3 The Law on Victims of Terrorism and amnesty (2011)

A new law pertaining to victims of terrorism was prepared during the latter stages of the José Luis Rodríguez Zapatero government's term in office. As had happened in 1999, the debate centred on the initial date to be set for the time limit. If the date was brought back to the time when ETA began carrying out terrorist attacks, then known criminals who had been granted amnesty for human rights violations would be included.

The legal text prepared by the government set the date of the 1999 law back to 1 January 1960, just as the Association for Victims of Terrorism had demanded. The amendments presented by the ERC at the end of May 2011 were ignored. These amendments proposed that the new law should be applied to those affected by deeds perpetrated after 6 October 1977, the day of the passing of the law of amnesty. The ERC also proposed the inclusion of a clause that would allow members of armed groups to benefit from the Historical Memory Law and that the government should compile a list of victims who had suffered political violence during the transition so that they could also benefit from the Law on Victims of Terrorist Attacks. In accordance with its proposals, the ERC advocated the addition of "victims of political violence" to the beneficiaries of the law, and not just victims of terrorism. It underlined its proposals by remarking on the importance that the future law be based on "memory, dignity and justice" to keep alive the memory of the "involuntary sacrifice" that the victims had made for society.

Finally, on 13 July 2011, the Congress of Deputies passed the Law on Victims of Terrorism with only one vote against (Progress and Democracy Union). The Law expressly excluded terrorist acts that were carried out by the State, the police forces and extreme right groups. The Bill, after it was unanimously approved in the Senate, became Law 29/2011, of 22 September, for the Recognition and Comprehensive Protection of Victims of Terrorism.[140] Article 7 sets the date of commencement as 1 January 1960.

Various pro-memory groups complained about the exclusion of victims of the Francoist dictatorship. The UN Working Group on Involuntary or Enforced Disappearances criticised the law from a comparative perspective, citing its own report of 2 July 2014, which "gives more rights to the victims of the Historical Memory Law, thus creating a distinction between victims".[141]

140 *Official State Gazette*, no. 229, 23 September 2011, pp. 100.566–100.592.

141 United Nations, Human Rights Council, *Report of the Working Group on Enforced or Involuntary Disappearances. Addendum. Mission to Spain*, 2 July 2014. UN: A/HRC/27/49/Add.1.

4.4 The Bill for the amendment of the Amnesty Law presented by the BNG (2011)

In July 2011, the BNG, as part of the Mixed Group in Parliament, proposed a Bill for the modification of Law 46/1977, 15 October, on Amnesty. It made the proposal at a strategic time, given that the opinion polls predicted that the PSOE, immersed in the complicated negotiation of the economic crisis, would be ousted from government, and the PP would be elected.

The text merely proposed adding the following article to the existing Amnesty Law:

> Firstly, the directives in this law shall not apply to crimes of genocide or crimes against humanity, which will be subject to international law on such matters.
>
> Secondly, with regards to the definition of genocide and crimes against humanity, its universal application, and considering its imprescriptible status, it will conform to international law relating to human rights and crimes against humanity.
>
> Thirdly, the present article can be retroactively applied to administrative or judicial resolutions in relation to its remit, enabling the review or re-initiation to protect its remit.

The Bill was debated in the Chamber of Deputies on 19 July 2011. It was rejected by 320 votes (PSOE, PP, CiU, UPyD, Canary Coalition and the Union of Navarrese People) to 8 (ERC, IU-ICV, BNG and the socialist María Antonia Trujillo). A total of six PNV deputies and two from the PP abstained; the last two due to an error. The Amnesty Law was widely endorsed by a huge parliamentary majority, with the debate reflecting where each parliamentary group stood on the matter of amnesty.[142]

Defending the Bill, the BNG deputy, Francisco Jorquera, insisted on the importance of overcoming the collective amnesia and revisiting the perspective of the transition as idyllic, the result of "operations guided by those in high office with the aim of creating a false collective memory", but which have resulted in a model of impunity. It maintained the 1977 Amnesty Law was passed to grant amnesty to those who fought "for freedom, democracy and the right of the people and the nations that make up the Spanish State", only to be undermined to the point where its interpretation serves as an excuse to defend the unwillingness to prosecute crimes and violations of fundamental rights, protected by the Francoist regime. This interpretation added that:

> It does not apply international regulation on human rights to the crimes against humanity protected by the Francoist regime, which contradicts the

142 *Parliament. Diary of Sessions in the Congress of Deputies. Plenary and Permanent Delegation*, no. 264, IX Legislature, 19 July 2011, pp. 11–19.

> established doctrine that advocates for the universal application of international regulation on human rights and crimes against humanity, its imprescriptible nature and the exclusion of these type of crimes from the principle of non-retroactivity of the regulation.

Following this, it listed the relevant international regulations against blanket amnesty and the non-retroactivity of criminal regulation in cases of crimes against humanity. It also reiterated the recommendations of various UN bodies to abolish the Amnesty Law. He backed up his argument by citing article 10 of the Spanish Constitution, which establishes that the regulation on fundamental rights and freedoms recognised therein are interpreted in conformity with the Universal Declaration of Human Rights and the international treaties and covenants ratified by Spain. In relation to the model of amnesia installed during the transition based on the interpretation of the Amnesty Law as an "end of story" law, he compared the situation in Spain with Latin American countries where similar "end of story" laws were abolished. Jorquera gave the example of Argentina, which had recently convicted seven people for crimes which had been committed during the dictatorship, whereas, in Spain, Garzón was suspended and was forced to "sit on the bench, at the service of Francoist organizations, for attempting to investigate crimes of Francoism".

He concluded his intervention by stating that the Bill did not want to "reopen all wounds", but to help heal them once and for all, because "you cannot heal wounds with impunity and by forgetting about them. You can only heal them with the truth, with reparation for the victims and by delivering justice."

Joan Ridau, of the Left-Catalan Green Party Group, criticised heavily the impunity that resulted from the 1977 Amnesty Law. He endorsed its derogation, arguing that it would enable investigations into the "atrocious crimes", and would "deliver some justice for past abuses, something which has, by the way, stopped a judge from investigating war crimes and crimes committed during the dictatorship basically because this law exonerates politically motivated crimes committed after 1936". With regard to the official line on the transition, he recalled that for his parliamentary group it was not:

> in terms of historical memory, a democratic milestone nor an ideal model for which we should feel pride. The transition meant that, not only did Francoists disguise themselves as democrats, or that the dictator's widow received a State pension until the day she died, but also that murderers had their criminal responsibility eliminated and did not have to renege on their loyalty to Franco. The Amnesty Law was an attempt to erase the dividing line between winners and losers, a line drawn in blood and fire by the victims of the 18th of July, paying the price of being forgotten about, to bury the memory of thousands of victims of Francoism.

The PNV decided to abstain. It contextualised the Amnesty Law in its historical moment and concurred with the BNG proposal in relation to the need to end impunity. It justified its vote arguing that the principle of non-retroactivity of the criminal law contravened article 9.3 of the Constitution. This argument was repeated by the various groups that voted against the Bill, adding the common justifications that the Amnesty Law was an instrument for reconciliation and consolidation of democracy.

4.5 The Bill presented by Unidos Podemos (United We Can) to modify the Amnesty Law (2016)

The twelfth Spanish legislature began on 19 July 2016, led by the PP with an overall majority in Congress, but without absolute majority in government. The inauguration of President Mariano Rajoy did not take place until 29 October, mostly because of the debate that engulfed the PSOE, which had to choose between supporting a PP-led government, or to lead a socialist government with the support of the progressive forces in Parliament. The debate caused a rift within the PSOE, but, in the end, it opted to support the PP. It was the first time since the instatement of the democracy that a government was formed because the main force in opposition abstained from the investiture vote.

It was not long before the controversial 1977 Amnesty Law was raised in Congress. The *Unidos Podemos-En Comú* party presented a Bill to modify the Amnesty Law with a significant new element. Conscious of the fact that proposing the derogation of the law would never achieve the consensus it needed because of how Congress was structured, *Unidos Podemos* proposed reducing, instead of abolishing, the effects of the laws.[143] Specifically, the proposal entailed adding a new article declaring that the amnesty is not applicable to crimes of "torture, enforced disappearances, genocide and crimes against humanity" committed during the Civil War and the Francoist dictatorship.

It was a new orientation that avoided questioning the achievements of the Amnesty Law in the context of the transition, focusing instead on the current situation. The Bill proposed by *Unidos Podemos* argued that the modification sought to correct the 1977 Laws, "an instrument contrary to human rights", just as the Human Rights Committee had claimed in 2009. In this way, crimes against humanities could be investigated in the Spanish legal system.

The *Unidos Podemos* deputy, Eduardo Santos, argued that although the Amnesty Law can be understood in terms of the political climate that approved it, "laws must nevertheless adequately address current social realities", and in current times, it does not make sense to maintain the Amnesty Law. By proposing to limits its effects, the Bill sought to clarify that the Amnesty Law "does not include

143 *Público*, 20 December 2016, news article and interview with deputy Eduardo Santos. The statements in this section are derived from this interview and another interview we conducted with Eduardo Santos on 12 January 2017.

crimes against humanity, torture or enforced disappearances that were committed during the dictatorship".

The ERC and *Compromís* supported the Bill, arguing in favour of the non-application of statutory limitations to crimes of Francoism, as well as the need to bring impunity to an end.

The PP rejected the Bill, arguing that "voting in favour of the derogation of the Amnesty Law contravenes the Constitution, given that acknowledgment of the facts is one thing, but allowing criminal responsibility to surface is another". The PP once again argued that Francoist crimes had prescribed. The socialists also rejected the Bill, even though the PSOE had recently collaborated with the progressive forces in various city councils and autonomous communities, supporting initiatives and motions in favour of investigating crimes of Francoism, both in Spain and in Argentina. The socialists based their vote against the Bill on the jurisprudence established in the Supreme Court in 2012, arguing that even if the law is "derogated", it would still be impossible to prosecute Francoist crimes as crimes against humanity. Their stance in this regard did not stop the PSOE from criticising the PP for not "implementing and developing" the Historical Memory Law. The *Ciudadanos* (Citizens) party did not support the Bill either, arguing that Spain should invest in "clearing the path towards peace", by "closing old wounds"; *Ciudadanos* praised the transition, and stated that "we don't want to revise the past. We are proud of those on both sides of the conflict who overcame the disunion of the country. We are not willing to reopen wounds."

The PP brought into focus a new element during the debate on the Bill: the age of the alleged criminals. In an interview conducted by Alejandro Torrús for the newspaper *Público*, Eduardo Santos argued that age was not an obstacle as, 70 years after the end of the Second World War, 90-year-old Nazis are still being prosecuted. Criminal punishment does not automatically mean a prison sentence, given that the Criminal Code guarantees certain fundamental legal rights, such as the principle of need of punishment, and the principle of humanity. Criminal responsibility must be established; "without it there is no memory, and without memory there is no history", Santos concluded.[144]

The defence of the Amnesty Law is rooted in the fact that solutions presented by politicians are not allowed to prosper. The PP, PSOE and *Ciudadanos* representatives constantly claim that it was impossible to abolish the Amnesty Law, when, paradoxically, the novelty of the *Unidos Podemos* proposal consisted in maintaining the law, but including a new article. Deputy Eduardo Santos has his own take on this situation, predicated on those against the modification of the law, anchored to the past, and those in favour of looking towards the future:

> The 1977 Amnesty Law is associated with the Transition as a foundational element of the democracy. The parties involved in the development of the State since 1975, logically, are involved because of a generational ideology,

144 *Público*, 20 December 2016, interview with deputy Eduardo Santos.

which is why they clearly identify with it and are against abolishing it. What we have tried to explain today (Tuesday) is that we do not question what happened in 1977. What we are saying is that the Amnesty Law is still in force and its effects continue today. In 2015, the UN Human Rights Committee told us that we needed to consider the possibility of abolishing the Amnesty Law because it can impede the application of human rights in Spain, as per the Constitution and international covenants signed by Spain.

We are not talking of the past. The majority of the parties that voted against are speaking of the past, and not the present. We are talking about the present and the generations that work and live in Spain today, who did not vote on the Amnesty Law, not the Constitution, and are entitled to a Spanish State that deals with the legacy of human rights with complete neutrality. And if there is a law in force today that does not allow the State to assume its responsibility, it should be modified.[145]

5 The Amnesty Law in the European Court of Human Rights

Spain, as a member State of the European Convention for the Protection of Human Rights and Fundamental Freedoms, has accepted the jurisdiction of the European Court of Human Rights, hence the relevance of its jurisprudence. The demands made in relation to the repression of Civil War and the Francoist dictatorship are based on the most relevant sentences passed in trials on human rights issues in this court, especially those regarding enforced disappearances. The sentence passed on 18 September 2009 in the case of *Varnava et al. v. Turkey* is one of the most invoked. The case relates to the disappearance of nine men in 1974. The case is of interest to Spain because of how it is conceptualised and how it dealt with cases regarding disappearances as continuous crimes, as evidenced in the case of Dorado Luque against Spain, which will be discussed below. The Sentence against Turkey states that "the fact that no more than 34 years have passed without reliable news of the disappeared persons constitutes a strong circumstantial proof that the latter have died during this time, such does not warrant a dereliction of the procedural duty to investigate".[146]

The victims of Francoism have tried to abolish the Amnesty Law by appealing to this Court in Strasbourg when the Spanish courts have rejected their requests for truth, justice and reparation. The victims lodged a suit against Spain for failing to comply with the European Convention on Human Rights, which was ratified by Spain on 4 October 1979. The response issued by the Court was not

145 *Público*, 20 December 2016, interview with deputy Eduardo Santos.

146 European Court of Human Rights, Case Nos 16064–66/90 and 16068–73/90, *Varnava et al. v. Turkey*, judgment date 18 September 2009. See Gil Gil, 2012b, pp. 14, 17, 20–22; McEvoy, Anthony and Mallinder, 2014, p. 26; Chinchón Álvarez, Vicente Márquez and Moreno, 2014, pp. 83–85.

very satisfactory for the victims, given that the lawsuits were deemed inadmissible in most cases based solely on technicalities, and without in-depth investigations taking place. These rejections seem to indicate the Court has no desire to shed light on Spain's Francoist past. Below we discuss the two most interesting cases in relation to our object of study.

The case brought by Baena Alonso against Spain was deemed inadmissible by the Court in September 2005.[147] Xosé Humberto Baena Alonso was executed on 27 September 1975 after a war council which lacked the minimum legal guarantees for a fair defence. The family were not successful in reversing the death penalty in the Spanish courts, and therefore attempted to reverse it in the European Court of Human Rights. The case was deemed inadmissible because the crime took place before the European Convention on Human Rights came into force in Spain and because the charges did not constitute State interference into the rights guaranteed by the Convention. Although the Amnesty Law was not mentioned, the Court's decision, in practice, was impacted by the degree of impunity in the Law.

The case brought by Antonio Gutiérrez Dorado and Carmen Gutiérrez Dorado against Spain was deemed inadmissible on 27 March 2012.[148] The decision was based on the fact that too much time had lapsed before the case was brought to the courts. In the case of the enforced disappearances, because of their imprescriptible condition, the court could not apply the temporal criterion it had used in the Baena case. Instead, it established the obligations of States to carry out effective investigations even if the crimes in question predate the entry into force of the European Convention on Human Rights. The Sentence acknowledged the "difficulties involved in bringing cases to domestic courts, even in post-Franco Spain, in view of the 1977 Amnesty Law", which explains why "in the years that followed there were no official investigations in relation to the circumstances surrounding enforced disappearances". This guarded statement resonates with the Court's general coldness towards this matter; in fact, this was the only mention of legal prescription and amnesty as instruments with which the State shields itself against its duty to investigate enforced disappearances.

6 Sidestepping the Amnesty Law under universal jurisdiction

As Antonio Brotóns has said, if "a criminal can only be prosecuted by a judge whose jurisdiction is established solely by universal jurisdiction, then, frankly, we are in a terrible situation"[149] – to which we must also add that all mechanisms of

147 European Court of Human Rights, *Baena Alonso v. Spain*, judgment date 22 September 2005.

148 European Court of Human Rights, Case No. 30141/09, *Gutiérrez Dorado and Dorado Ortiz v Spain*, judgment date 27 March 2012, para. 39. See Chinchón Álvarez, 2012a, pp. 14–15, 48–49, 61, 119 and 130–137; Gil Gil, 2012b, pp. 1–29; Clavero, 2014, pp. 127–128; Mallinder, Moffett, McEvoy and Anthony, 2015, pp. 26–27.

149 Remiro Brotóns, 2006, p. 501.

national law had failed. The delay in the Garzón case and the court's refusal to answer the victims of Francoism motivated the ARMH to seek recourse in universal jurisdiction. The ARMH brought a case on 14 April to the National Criminal Court no. 1 in Argentina, which admitted the case in accordance with article 118 of its Constitution, contemplated in article 5 of the Law 26.200 of 13 December 2006 (Law on the Implementation of the Statute of Rome), which came into force on 5 January 2007 and establishes that Federal Courts with criminal jurisdiction can hear cases on crimes cited in the Statute as well as the Law 26.200. Over 30 years after the Labour Party in Britain had contemplated the possibility of bringing charges against Spain, the victims of the dictatorship began a similar course of action, uncertain, at the time of writing, of the outcome.

As charges can be brought under universal jurisdiction, the Amnesty Law is not an obstacle to the prosecution of crimes which have prescribed in the investigating country, as happened, albeit in reverse, with the warrant of arrest for Augusto Pinochet or the renowned sentences which convicted Adolfo Scilingo, both issued by the National High Court,[150] and by the Supreme Court in response to a cassation appeal.[151] The prosecution is carried out as per the jurisdiction of the country where the investigation is held, which is why it cannot answer to conditions imposed in a different jurisdiction. If the crimes prosecuted can be classified as international crimes as per the international law in force at the time, the prosecution in another State does not undermine the sovereignty of the country that granted amnesty in the first instance.[152]

The suit filed on 14 April 2010[153] stated that the Spanish 1977 Amnesty Law "was not in any way applicable to crimes against humanity, which are not mentioned explicitly or implicitly, given that article 15.2 of the International Covenant on Civil and Political Rights has been in force in Spain since the 27th of July, 1977". It also claimed that, considering the fact that the law restricted its scope to "politically motivated crimes", the amnesty *ipso jure* excludes genocide and crimes against humanity, which, unlike in Spain until 15 October 1977, are not classified as politically motivated crimes by international law, especially in the case of kidnappings, in and outside Spain, of children of Republican families handed over to Francoist families, enforced disappearances, arrests, etc.

The lawsuit explained that it applied the principle of universal jurisdiction because Spain was conducting a legal investigation into the matter, and the Amnesty Law, a domestic law, is not applicable to the jurisdictions governing legal bodies in other countries, as, for example, Argentina. The suit also added that "the same Spanish courts highlighted this possibility when it exercised its

150 Sentence in the High Court, 19 April 2005. See Capellá i Roig, 2005b; Gil Gil, 2005, pp. 7–16.
151 Sentence in the Supreme Court 798/2007, 1 October. See Gil Gil, 2009b, pp. 391–410; Fernández-Pachecho, 2008, pp. 101–117.
152 Gil Gil, 2009a, pp. 113–114.
153 Text of the complaint http://www.elclarin.cl/images/pdf/argentinaquerella.pdf (accessed on 8 July 2016).

jurisdiction in relation to similar crimes in Latin America when, finding justification in impunity laws, the courts in our countries could not, or would not, exercise their jurisdiction on same".

Judge María Servini de Cubría instructed the lawsuit against the Spanish dictatorship for genocide and crimes against humanity between 16 July 1936 and 15 June 1977. The handling of this case to date is well known.[154] A detailed account can be found, *inter alia*, on the CEAQUA (a support group for the victims) website.[155] To date, around 7,000 are involved in the complaints.

In relation to the Amnesty Law, it is important to note that, on 14 October 2010, an International Inquiry Committee of the Argentinian National Criminal Court no. 1, petitioned information on the existence, nature and state of proceedings of an investigation related to the existence of a systematic plan, generalised and deliberate, to eliminate the cohort of Spanish civilians who were in favour of representative government, and another aimed at disappearing under-age children and their identities, between 17 July 1936 and 15 June 1977.[156]

To comply with the Inquiry Committee, the State Prosecution Office issued a report on 6 July 2010,[157] stating that the charges in the lawsuit were being investigated in Spain in proceedings carried out by the Central Investigating Court no. 5 of the National High Court. As we have seen, by that time Garzón had to recuse himself and leave the case to the regional courts, which had jurisdiction over the territories where the mass graves were located. Furthermore, the report added that the Investigating Court, after carrying out the appropriate investigations, had agreed to close the case ordering the elimination of criminal liability on the grounds of the death of the suspects or because the statutory deadlines had lapsed for the prosecution of unlawful arrests, homicide and murder for which the same proceedings were initiated. The Public Prosecution Office had no record of any case being closed or shelved due to the application of the 1977 Amnesty Law, or any other clemency measure or pardon. It added to this assertion the list of proceedings opened and closed in Investigating Courts in the territories where the remains of enforced disappearances had been located.

The Amnesty Law resurfaced in the 2013 Argentinian lawsuit. Judge Servini ordered the arrest and the remanding in custody of four Francoist officials suspected of violations, a petition which was rejected by the National High Court because the crimes in question were subject to the 1977 Amnesty Law. A year later, Judge Servini ordered the arrest of 20 alleged criminals, and received the same answer. The Treaty of Extradition and Judicial Assistance in Criminal

154 Especially the work of Chinchón Álvarez, 2011, Messuti, 2012, Messuti, 2013a, and Messuti, 2013b.
155 http://www.ceaqua.org/ (accessed on 10 July 2016).
156 http://www.elclarin.cl/images/pdf/Exhorto%20Servini%20de%20Cubria.pdf (accessed on 10 July 2016).
157 http://www.elclarin.cl/images/pdf/ARGENTINARespuestadeEspa exhorto14102010607201l.pdf (accessed on 10 July 2016).

Matters was signed by Spain and Argentina in 1987, but Spain hides behind the Extradition Treaty, which prohibits surrendering perpetrators "after the elimination of criminal liability in accordance with legislation in the State from which the petition is made". The Amnesty Law eliminated this criminal responsibility. The Spanish government continues to argue that Spain has jurisdiction to process the accused, that the crimes for which they are accused were not considered so at the time they were committed, and that, moreover, the statute of limitations had lapsed.[158]

In the face of the decision taken by the Spanish Council of Ministers not to extradite the 17 Spanish citizens accused (including various ex-ministers) by Argentinian justice for grave violations of human rights committed during the Francoist regime, the UN group of experts on human rights warned, on 27 March 2015, that the Spanish government was obliged to extradite those responsible for grave violations of human rights if there are no measures to guarantee access to justice and if the right to the truth is not observed in the Spanish legal system.[159] They underscored that "the Spanish state cannot hide behind the principles of prescription and elimination of criminal responsibility to avoid extraditing or processing those responsible for grave violations of human rights", and reiterated that "crimes against humanity and crimes of torture are not prescribed", and therefore the state has the obligation to investigate and punish those responsible.

With this avenue closed, Judge Servini petitioned to visit Spain to hear the statements of 19 high-standing ex-security officials during the dictatorship, including the 17 people who were the subject of the application for extradition. However, in October 2016, the Public Prosecution Office, a governmental body, requested a stay in the declaration of the accused who were at the time before the Spanish courts to determine if the crimes committed come under the category of crimes against humanity. The Public Prosecution Office sent a petition to the various courts asking them not to comply with Judge Servini's request for judicial assistance because the "statute of limitations had clearly lapsed" on the acts she was attempting to investigate, and were therefore subject to Spanish, not Argentinian, jurisdiction. It argued that the acts were covered by the 1977 Amnesty Law, which was the result of "a clear and palpable demand of the political forces against Francoism", and something "invaluable in the operation to dismantle Francoist power". The Amnesty Law, according to the prosecution, was not "a measure passed by the winners, those in power, to amnesty their own crimes"; it

158 *Público*, 10 October 2015.

159 This was a joint statement by Ariel Dulitzky, president of the Working Group on involuntary and enforced disappearances; Christof Heyns, Special Rapporteur on extrajudicial summary or arbitrary executions; Juan E. Méndez, Special Rapporteur on torture and other cruel, inhuman or degrading treatment or punishment; and Pablo de Greiff, Special Rapporteur on the promotion of truth, justice, reparation and guarantees of non-repetition. http://www.ohchr.org/SP/NewsEvents/Pages/DisplayNews.aspx?NewsID=15765&LangID=S (accessed on 10 August 2016).

demanded a sacrifice of all the political parties involved in the transition. To sum up, for the prosecution, the Constitution did not abolish this regulation which was a "product of the will of the Spanish people, as articulated in the Law", as an "essential pillar in the struggle against Francoism".

A Mexican suit would soon be added to the Argentine case. In January 2016, various families of Francoist victims of enforced disappearances, with the endorsement of Amnesty International, the CMDPDH and the FIDH, filed a suit in the Mexican Public Prosecution Office to investigate the cases that the Spanish courts dismissed. The same organisations requested the next Spanish government – the elections had been held on 20 December 2015 – to guarantee that the Amnesty Law would not impede an investigation of crimes against international law committed during the Civil War and the dictatorship. It also called on the future government, as a matter of urgency, to adopt measures to guarantee that the statute of limitations not apply to crimes against international law and to expedite the ratification of the Convention on the Non-Applicability of Statutory Limitations to War Crimes and Crimes Against Humanity.[160]

7 Attempts to create a truth commission

As we have signalled throughout this book, Spanish transition and post-transition justice failed to create a truth commission, contrary to what in the previous decades had become common practice in transitional processes throughout the world.[161] Truth commissions have proven to be an extraordinary solution to the problems caused by impunity laws,[162] as well as being the primary instrument for the collection of evidence that is subsequently produced in criminal trials against those responsible for the violation of human rights.[163] But their objective does not have to be strictly limited to given trials, as light can be shed on past events, clearing the path towards reconciliation.[164]

The Catalan Democratic Memorial was partly set up to fill this void. Although it is not a truth commission as such, a lot of its operations are like those carried out by mechanisms for truth, reparation and rehabilitation after grave violations of human rights.

The Catalan Democratic Memorial was followed by a Basque initiative which originated in a petition presented in the Basque Parliament by various pro-memory associations. On 28 November 2008, the Basque Parliament passed a law for the creation of a truth commission. It was the first to be founded in Spain. The Human Rights Department of the Basque government, led by the criminal

160 https://www.es.amnesty.org/en-que-estamos/noticias/noticia/articulo/amnistia-internacional-presenta-en-mexico-una-querella-por-los-crimenes-del-franquismo-y-la-guerr/ (accessed on 9 July 2016).

161 See Hayner, 2010.

162 Guembe, 2005. Wlasik, 2010.

163 Osiel, 1997.

164 Clavero, 2014, pp. 164–165.

lawyer, Jon Mirena Landa, elaborated, after the corresponding legal analysis and consultations with various pro-memory groups, "Principles for the creation of a truth commission in the Basque Country", which synthesised the requests in the proposals it had received.[165] The most detailed proposal came from Lau Haizetara Gogoan, who in later years, taking into consideration opinions from other organisations, would continue to develop ideas on how a truth commission would function in the Basque Country. The conclusions reached were published in a book edited in 2011.[166] The proposal of the Basque Country was not successful; it should now be one of the objectives of the new executive formed after the 2016 parliamentary elections.

One of the main recommendation the UN Human Rights Committee made to Spain in 2003 was to "plan for the creation of a commission of independent experts that would re-establish the truth about the history of human rights violations committed during the Civil War and the dictatorship".[167] The Spanish government ignored the recommendation,[168] and, contrary to what had happened in the transitions from dictatorships to democracy in Latin America, rejected initiatives to put together institutional mechanisms that would investigate the true dimensions of the human rights violations that occurred in Spain.[169] Among other consequences, the victims themselves would have to prove their status as victims – as per the Amnesty Law, because there is no official list of victims; this makes the reparation process that much more difficult.[170]

There would be a long wait before – in the fashion of the Argentine lawsuit – various attempts (all of them unsuccessful) to create a truth commission in Spain. Once again, the Amnesty Law blocked an attempt to pursue the truth about the grave violations of human rights in Spain. In April 2012, Baltasar Garzón publicly requested the creation of a truth commission in a speech he gave at the commemoration of the 81st anniversary of the proclamation of the Second Republic.[171] The following May, various victims of the Civil War and Francoism and pro-memory associations came together in the Truth Commission Platform, which, to date, is made up of around 50 organisations linked to the recovery of historical memory, the trade unions CCOO and UGT, and the political parties IU, PCE and Equo.[172]

165 Dirección de Derechos Humanos del Gobierno Vasco, 2009.
166 Garmendia Amutxastegi and Lau Haizetara Gogoan, 2011.
167 United Nations, Human Rights Committee, *Considerations of reports submitted by states parties under article 40 of the Covenant. Concluding observations of the Human Rights Committee. Spain*, 5 January 2009. UN: CCPR/C/ESP/CO/5, para. 9.(c).
168 United Nations, Human Rights Committee, *Considerations of reports submitted by states parties under article 40 of the Covenant. Concluding observations of the Human Rights Committee. Spain. Addendum. Comments by the Government of Spain on the concluding observations of the Human Rights Committee*, 8 January 2009. UN: CCPR/C/ESP/CO/5. Add.1.
169 Comparative analysis in Aguilar, 2013, pp. 245–266.
170 Escudero Alday, 2013b, p. 205.
171 Aguilar and Ramírez-Barat, 2014, p. 212.
172 https://comisionverdadfranquismo.com/campana-comision-de-la-verdad/ (accessed on 20 July 2016).

Once again, the victims, congregated in grassroots movements, were the driving force behind Spain's transition justice. This platform made contact with every group in Parliament to promote the proposal of a parliamentary initiative that would compel the government to create a truth commission. On 21 November 2013, the progressive groups[173] put forward a Bill on the creation of a truth commission for debate during the Plenary Session in Parliament.[174] It justified the urgency with which it presented the Bill on the recommendations made by the UN Working Group on Enforced or Involuntary Disappearances in relation to the advancing age of the families and witnesses who were the last to see the victims alive before they disappeared during the Civil War or the dictatorship. It proposed the creation of a truth commission composed of independent experts, committed to carrying out "a comprehensive analysis of the enforced disappearances during the Civil War and the dictatorship", along with the proposals and compliance with the recommendations to public authorities. The PP's overall majority in Parliament prevented the Bill from being passed.

The need for a truth commission was once again called for during the "Conference on Universal Justice and Historical Memory: With Impunity there is no Democracy. To judge the crimes of the Francoist dictatorship", held at the European Parliament on 21 and 22 September 2015. Various victims, historical memory activists and judge María Servini attended and gave their testimonies

The latest initiative has been instigated by Baltasar Garzón, who, in March 2016, presented in the Chamber of Deputies a proposal on the platform Change.org for the creation of a truth commission to investigate Francoist crimes, with the aim of putting an end to impunity, to shed light on the more than 130,000 enforced disappearances, and to "treat with dignity the victims of Francoism so that their families can ascertain what happened". The petition requests signatures on the basis that "forgetting is never the solution".[175] As of 10 July 2016, 105,556 people have signed the petition. The petition may get some traction in Parliament, where the progressive parties are in the majority, after the next general election, which will be held on 26 July 2016. If a truth commission in Spain is not a possibility, then the next step would be to promote the creation of truth commissions in autonomous communities. I believe that this official channel, although restricted to specific territories, would be more effective than a truth commission solely motivated by civil society.[176]

173 Socialist Parliamentary Group; Parliamentary Group Plural Left (Izquierda Unida, Iniciativa per Catalunya Verds-Esquerra Unida i Alternativa, Chunta Aragonesista), and Basque Parliamentary Group (PNV).

174 *Official Parliament Gazette*, Congress of Deputies, X Legislature, Series D General, no. 367, 29 November 2013, pp. 15–16.

175 https://www.change.org/p/congreso-de-los-diputados-queremos-una-comisi%C3%B3n-de-la-verdad-sobre-los-cr%C3%ADmenes-del-franquismo?sourcelocation=searchindex&algorithm=curatedtrending&gridposition=1 (accessed on 10 July 2016).

176 See Pérez González, 2013.

The Spanish Commission for Truth, or the commissions of truth of the autonomous communities, will have to be undertaken with extreme attention to detail and with full consideration of the Argentine legal suit, so that there is no interference between both sets of proceedings, as has happened between trials and truth commissions in other settings of transitional justice.[177]

Any truth commission, whether for all of Spain or restricted to specific autonomous communities, would need to develop a powerful methodology. It must also avoid overlaps with the lawsuit filed in Argentina, which other transitional justices have warned against in relation to keeping trials and truth commissions mutually exclusive.

177 Schabas and Darcy, 2004.

Conclusion

As we have seen, the long and complex transition process in Spain was set in motion on 20 February 1975, when Franco, who had been in power for almost four decades, died. He was replaced as Head of State by King Juan Carlos I, who granted a momentous pardon to mark his coronation, followed by a succession of complementary measures in the years of transition that followed, culminating when amnesty was granted, first in 1976, just before the democracy was installed, and then again in 1977, issued by the courts formed after the first general elections. The pardons were granted in the first phase of the transition, when Carlos Arias Navarro was president of a government which represented continuity with Francoism after the death of Franco, and which failed to make any significant progress towards a future democracy. The Francoist powers guiding the transition opted to grant pardons because these did not extinguish criminal records. They regarded full or blanket amnesty as a vindication of those who opposed the regime and believed it would end the dictatorship and instate a new democratic state. The difference between the solutions offered by amnesty and pardons can be appreciated in the appeals made by an anti-Francoist group made up of clandestine judges, lawyers and public prosecutors. In the final years of Francoism, they criticised pardons as an arbitrary measure,[1] but in the same breath called for a "blanket amnesty for politically motivated crimes and infractions and sanctions imposed for political or labour reasons".[2]

Both Spanish amnesties, largely inspired by the Algerian-French precedent and, to a lesser degree, by the Greek and Portuguese amnesties, were issued during Adolfo Suárez's tenure, in the reformist phase of the transition, with the aim of reconciling the people of Spain. Most of the public demands were satisfied with the Law of 15 October 1977, granting a blanket amnesty to those who opposed the regime – even those who had committed murder, as well as workers who had been dismissed for participating in labour strikes. Prisons were emptied of political prisoners and exiled Spaniards could return to their country.

1 Martín Pallín, 2016, p. 11.
2 Justicia Democrática, 1978, pp. 310–311.

But the amnesty was also extended to members of the fascist regime responsible for grave violations of human rights during the dictatorship and the transition. Not only did the State fail to condemn the dictatorship, it condoned it.[3] Spain has had to carry the burden of having amnestied Francoist crimes for the last four decades, unable to make any headway regarding its human rights duties, continuing instead to ignore the matter.

After the promulgation of the Constitution and the corresponding institutions were founded, the political forces that guided the transitional process to democracy propagated the myth that the Spanish transition had been exemplary, a veritable paradigm of peaceful transitions. The widespread consensus reached between the old dictatorial forces and the majority in opposition regarding the need to forget the past was heralded as its greatest virtue, achieving the reconciliation of a divided country. This discourse, epitomised by the words of Nicolás Sartorius and de Alberto Sabio, framed the Amnesty Law as "the first victory of all the people in Spain".[4] The benefits of the law were soon accepted by historiographers and the legal and political doctrines – the law was even praised by specialists on the international scene.[5]

It is, frankly, difficult to find an exemplary transitional process,[6] but in no way can the Spanish transition be described in such terms. The years that followed began to cast a shadow on the apologetic literature of the Spanish transition. For one, the international doctrine on amnesty continued to evolve, and in the 1980s established the idea that impunity did not contribute to preventing crimes. No conduct considered a crime against humanity could be completely amnestied, which is exactly what happened in Spain in 1977. The rights of victims to the truth, justice and reparation, the triumvirate of transitional justice, were cemented as legal principles in international doctrine. Of these three, Spain only partially complied with one, reparation, through the measures which were issued during the transition and continued to be adopted incrementally during the post-transition period.

The international doctrine has condemned the impunity that resulted from the 1977 amnesty, as it infringes on Spain's duty to comply with international law and to investigate crimes against humanity. Spain continues to ignore its obligations by refusing to process, prosecute and sentence those responsible for human rights violations and by blocking victims' access to justice, reparation and truth. Even when various UN organisations, such as the Human Rights Committee or the Committee Against Torture, have expressly asked Spain to abolish the Amnesty Law and to take appropriate transition justice action, Spain has arrogantly refused to comply. The government's answer is always the same: the

3 Clavero, 2014, p. 244.
4 Sartorius and Sabio, 1977, p. 304.
5 As in, for example, the section dedicated to Spain in the work of O'Donnell, Schmitter and Whitehead, 1986.
6 Carothers, 2002, pp. 5–21. McAuliffe, 2011, pp. 32–44.

Spanish transition was "exemplary", the fruit of a consensus which achieved the reconciliation of its people.

The controversy between the UN and the Spanish government seems destined to continue. Amnesty, prescription and prohibition on retroactivity were once again questioned by the doctrine against granting amnesty for violations of human rights in the *Rule-of-law instruments for post-conflict states: amnesties* report, published by the Office of the United Nations High Commissioner for Human Rights (2009):

> Amnesties are now regulated by a substantial body of international law that sets limits on their permissible scope. Most importantly, amnesties that prevent the prosecution of individuals who may be legally responsible for war crimes, genocide, crimes against humanity and other gross violations of human rights are inconsistent with States' obligations under various sources of international law as well as with United Nations policy. In addition, amnesties may not restrict the right of victims of violations of human rights or of war crimes to an effective remedy and reparations; nor may they impede either victims' or societies' right to know the truth about such violations.
>
> The United Nations policy of opposing amnesties for war crimes, crimes against humanity, genocide or gross violations of human rights, including in the context of peace negotiations, represents an important evolution, grounded in long experience. Amnesties that exempt from criminal sanction those responsible for atrocious crimes in the hope of securing peace have often failed to achieve their aim and have instead emboldened their beneficiaries to commit further crimes. Conversely, peace agreements have been reached without amnesty provisions in some situations where amnesty had been said to be a necessary condition of peace and where many had feared that indictments would prolong the conflict.
>
> These experiences call into question the commonplace assumption that a choice must be made between peace and justice. The United Nations has recognized that, when properly pursued, justice can help ensure a just and sustainable peace. By opposing amnesties that establish impunity for atrocious crimes, United Nations policy seeks to safeguard a space for justice even when conditions for prosecutions are not yet adequately established.[7]

Every transition leads to an uncertain democracy,[8] which can then be consolidated and transformed into a democracy built upon solid values if the appropriate transition justice mechanisms are implemented.[9] The Amnesty Law was successful in ensuring a peaceful transition, but it was detrimental to the process

7 Office of the United Nations High Commissioner for Human Rights, 2009, p. V.
8 On the use of this terminology, see O'Donnell, Schmitter and Whitehead, 1986.
9 Skaar, Gianella Malca and Eide, 2012. Skaar, Gianella Malca and Eide, 2015.

of establishing a democracy.[10] A transition and post-transition such as the one in Spain, led "from above", produces a weak democracy, or a stable but limited democracy, as Marcus Buck describes it, quoted by Vincent Navarro,[11] or, as Rafael Escudero[12] describes it, an imperfect democracy.

The fact that criminal responsibility was extinguished for authorities and civil servants of the dictatorship is indicative of the quality of democracy in the newly democratic state, especially in light of the fact that members of the Francoist regime went on to become democratic, which led to the unique and exceptional situation in Spain where being democratic did not necessarily mean being anti-fascist.[13] The impunity for crimes against humanities, the abandonment of the victims and the complete lack of pro-memory policies are at the root of a weak democracy in Spain.[14] A democratic system that protects fundamental rights should not ignore its responsibility towards the reality and the abuses of the dictatorship it replaces. Yet, this is exactly what happened in Spain. A new democracy was instated, turning its back on the past with new pacts and agreements between the democratic opposition, weak and in disarray, and those who held office during the dictatorship, who continued to guide the transition process.[15]

Germany, Greece and Portugal prosecuted crimes against humanity, and in doing so, showed Spain the way, but Spain refused to follow in their footsteps. Fortunately, the attempts to export the Spanish transition model to Latin America failed. Argentina, Chile, Uruguay, Guatemala, El Salvador and other countries set up truth commissions. Even Cambodia had a truth commission, setting an example for what Spain should have done because, as Amnesty International reported, Spain is second from the bottom in the list of enforced disappearances whose bodies have not been recovered or identified; only the bloody Pol-Pot regime is worse.[16] In light of this unflattering comparison, in October 2013 the Association of Judges for Democracy pleaded with the Spanish government, remarking on the "need to establish a programmatic administration plan, systematic and financed with public funds to facilitate the localisation and exhumation of all those victims who were murdered as a result of the 1936 coup d'état and the subsequent repression during Franco's regime".[17]

Spain has shielded itself behind amnesty, prescription and the ban on retroactive effects, and continues to neglect its duty to investigate, prosecute and sentence members of Francoism responsible for crimes against humanity. The victims continue to be denied the truth, justice and full reparation.

10 Aguilar, 2001, pp. 92–118.
11 Buck, 1998, pp. 1630–1634.
12 Escudero Alday, 2013d, pp. 141–161.
13 Escudero Alday, 2011, p. 9.
14 Escudero Alday, Campelo, Pérez González and Silva, 2013.
15 Sáez Valcárcel, 2013, pp. 92–93.
16 Amnistía Internacional España, 2008a. Amnistía Internacional España, 2008b.
17 *El País*, 9 October 2013.

When impunity is granted for State crimes, that is, crimes committed by those in power, it becomes an "indicator of a failed rule of law, a culture of unfit legislation and of a high level of injustice in society", as Ramón Sáez Valcárcel has said. We agree with this judge that granting impunity for State crimes corrupts the courts in charge of subjecting public and private institutions to the rule of law, and, finally, society itself.[18] That said, the security forces and the administrations of justice were already corrupted, or, better said, were allowed to remain corrupted, in a transition model that failed to carry out any purges. Politicians responsible for repression, policemen responsible for torture and judges and lawyers responsible for political trials became democratic without ever showing any signs of remorse or guilt. In fact, it is likely that they did not feel any remorse, protected as they were by a culture of impunity.[19] Just as Antonio Remiro Brotóns has pointed out, "the will, capacity and independence of judges is seriously compromised when criminals are part of the hierarchies of the legal establishment and the state delegations of power or when, during a transitional process towards democracy, those guiding the process attempt to replace justice with a mere statement of historical truth, granting amnesty to those responsible".[20]

Francoist lawyers and judges continued in their offices after democracy had been established, an indication of how it was going to do justice,[21] evident in jurisprudence practice, denying the rights of the victims of Francoism and raising serious doubts on the concept of legal independence.[22] The first time the Spanish legal system investigated crimes against humanity during the Civil War and the first years of the dictatorship was in response to a lawsuit filed by the victims, families and pro-memory associations on 14 December 2006 in the National High Court. As had happened in Latin America,[23] in the midst of an uninterested political establishment, it was left to Spanish civil society to call for the derogation of the Amnesty Law and to put an end to impunity. Judge Baltasar Garzón set in motion the investigation into 114,226 reported forced disappearances, as well as other crimes, between 17 July 1936 and December 1951. He implemented international doctrine and declared that amnesty cannot absolve those responsible for crimes against humanity, genocide or war. The investigation, however, was cut short with the legal consolidation of the impunity granted to Francoist politicians.

Garzón, the judge who acted in the lawsuit against individuals who had potentially committed serious human rights violations during the Civil War and the dictatorship, was charged with subverting the courts. He was absolved of this crime, but the sentence passed in the Supreme Court in February 2012 established jurisprudence to block judges from investigating crimes against humanity

18 Sáez Valcárcel, 2011, pp. 63 and 68.
19 Jiménez Villarejo and Doñate, 2012, p. 277.
20 Remiro Brotóns, 2006, p. 500.
21 Jiménez Villarejo and Doñate, 2012. Jimeno, 2014, pp. 102–106.
22 On legal independence during transitions, see Dyzenhaus, 2003, pp. 345–364.
23 Collins, 2012, pp. 399–423.

committed by Francoism, based on the Amnesty Law, the prescription of crimes, that crimes were not considered as such when they were committed, that the perpetrators had perished or by arguing that the criteria to identify crimes against humanity could not be applied to that era. The victims were denied access to effective recourse in the Spanish legal system, and impunity was extended to crimes after 1951, and even to the first phase of the transition, on the strength of the Amnesty Law.

The Amnesty Law obstructs any civil society initiative seeking the truth, or justice after four decades of grave violations of human rights following the 1936 coup d'état against the Second Republic.[24] Prescription and non-retroactivity block any attempt to prosecute those responsible for Francoist crimes, but they also obstruct victims from exercising their right to justice. We agree with Javier Chinchón when he says that the Spanish State does not believe it is bound by international duty to investigate the thousands of violations of human rights, instead believing that it only needs to investigate human rights violations committed in the 1980s and thereafter, after democracy had been established.[25]

The efforts to shed light on enforced disappearances during the early years of Francoism have also gone through some difficulties. The victims and their families continue to be denied legal protection – the outstanding cases are not being investigated in judicial headquarters. More than 30,000 people remain disappeared, another 100,000 were extra-officially executed and remain buried in unknown locations, with little prospect of a dignified burial. The case of the stolen babies who have yet to be identified is even more dramatic, as there is no public policy to deal with the matter, when, in fact, it is a problem that could be easily exempted from the Amnesty Law, given the difficulty of ascribing a political motive to the crime.[26]

After the Spanish legal system proved to be a dead-end, the victims sought recourse in the European Court of Human Rights, only to suffer a huge setback when the first case filed by a victim of Francoism was dismissed in 2012. The lawsuit, alleging the enforced disappearance of socialist deputy Luis Dorado Luque at the hands of the armed forces on 18 July 1936, filed by his daughter and grandson, was dismissed on the grounds that the statute of limitations had passed. But the Court admitted to being aware of the difficulties of filing such cases in the Spanish courts, even after the end of the Francoist regime, because of the 1977 Amnesty Law.

These "from below" initiatives were not matched with corresponding "from above" initiatives.[27] The victims, united together in the various pro-memory associations, continued condemning impunity and demanding that their rights as victims be respected. Universal jurisdiction was their last hope, but the lawsuit

24 Valencia Villa, 2012, p. 185.
25 Chinchón Álvarez, 2013, p. 191.
26 Tamarit Sumalla, 2014, p. 64.
27 McEvoy, 2007, pp. 411–440. McEvoy, 2008, pp. 15–47.

filed in Argentina has been blocked by the Amnesty Law. In this case, Spain, taking refuge under the triumvirate of non-retroactivity, amnesty and the statute of limitations, refuses to comply with Judge Servini's requests for extradition. Despite Spain's attempts to derail the Argentinian legal system, the lawsuit could be successful if a sentence is passed in favour of the retroactive application of the international law regulations on human rights to cases of grave violations committed during the Francoist dictatorship and the early years of the transition, which would blow Spain's sacred Amnesty Law wide open.

Most of the individuals responsible for these crimes have passed away, even those who participated in the transition, such as Manuel Fraga, who died on 15 January 2012 without ever being prosecuted for his crucial role in the events in Montejurra and Vitoria. The few who do remain and could be prosecuted for violating human rights during the dictatorship and the transition have been named in the Argentinian lawsuit; some of whom are notorious Francoist figures, such as ex-ministers Rodolfo Martín Villa, Fernando Suárez González and José Utrera Pacheco (otherwise known as "Billy the kid"), or judges, such as Rafael Gómez Chaparro, of the Public Order Court. These individuals continue to be protected in Spain by the impunity granted under the Amnesty Law, but are bound to remain in the country for fear of suffering the same fate as Pinochet.

Because of the reform enacted by the Organic Law of 13 March 2014 relative to universal jurisdiction, the conditions leading to the arrest warrant for Pinochet, which resulted from a lawsuit filed by Attorney General Miguel Miravet, could not be repeated in Spain; nor could cases be brought to Spain under universal jurisdiction, such as the notorious case of the Argentine ex-soldier, Adolfo Scilingo. In order to avoid mandatory reports, expert opinions and expert counsel, the ratification of the law was expedited with a single vote by the PP, which was able to drive forward the reform because it had an overall majority. Spain's economic interests in China were the motivation for this reform, whose aim ultimately was to block an arrest warrant for ex-Chinese leaders, Jiang Zemin, Hu Jintao and Li Peng, for their role in Tibet.

Spain should abolish or modify the 1977 Amnesty Law. This is what various UN organisations have repeatedly requested and recommended since 2008. But simply abolishing the law would not resolve the problems that continue to hamper the efforts to prosecute Francoist crimes. Even if it is abolished or modified, the authorities can still invoke the non-retroactive nature of criminal regulations in article 9.3 of the Spanish Constitution, as well as prescription. In light of this, Alicia Gil points out that, even if the law is abolished, the amnesty would have already taken effect, which means that criminal responsibilities extinguished while the amnesty was in force could not be brought up again. There could be a declaration of invalidity, something for which there is no protocol, or a new retroactive restrictive interpretation of how the law is applied. Either way, these regulations could not be retroactively applied to crimes covered by the amnesty without undermining the principle of legal certainty guaranteed in the Spanish Constitution. The problem of prescription would also remain; a new interpretation of this matter is needed, one that would allow the argument that the time during which the Amnesty Law was in force, a time in which prosecutions were not allowed, does not count towards the time constraints for prescription.[28]

As things stand, it does not seem as if the Parliament that was formed after the 2016 elections is going to abolish or modify of the Amnesty Law (the last attempt to modify the Amnesty Law, on 20 December 2016, did not prosper), but neither does it seem as if there is going to be any pressure on the Spanish government to ratify the UN Convention on the Non-Applicability of the Statute of Limitations to War Crimes and Crimes Against Humanity. It is unlikely that Spain – traditionally reticent to call referenda – would allow its citizens to vote on the matter, as in fact happened in Uruguay. An amendment to the Constitution seems equally improbable, even though the Constitution, as we have seen here, has not proved a useful tool in the creation of an equal and democratic society.[29] Any amendment to the Spanish Magna Carta would have to comply with the requirements of international law, which would then ensure the effective application of these regulations on the non-applicability of the statute of limitations to crimes against humanity. Only in this way could the criminal responsibility extinguished by the Amnesty Law be brought up again. But any future constitution would have to go further, for the sake of the health of its democracy. It should declare the Francoist regime illegitimate and illegal, concomitantly annulling its legislation, sentences or administrative decisions regarding events which are considered criminal under international law.

Since the turn of the century there has been a proliferation of memorial acts and tributes for the victims of Francoist repression; every year there are more exhumations, and historians continue to make considerable headway in their investigations. Yet legal impunity remains a reality. But "from below" initiatives are, little by little, re-establishing the truth. This should in no way be considered as a substitute for the remaining mechanism of transitional justice that is still open to Spain: a truth commission. A truth commission would have to be an official body created by the government to investigate, document and disseminate the violations of human rights perpetrated during the years of Francoism. Truth commissions have proven useful in different conflicts in shedding light on the dictatorial regimes throughout the world which have caused enforced disappearances or have suppressed information regarding policies for the persecution of its political opposition.[30] A truth commission for Francoist crimes could be developed through a specific law, or a law that modifies the Historical Memory Law. If the progressive parties, the PSOE included, are consistent with what they have been promising, it will very likely happen. The creation of a truth commission, made up of independent experts, would have to officially restore the truth

28 Gil Gil, 2009a, p. 112.
29 Escudero Alday, 2013a, p. 302.
30 Teitel, 2000, 2003. Ferrara, 2014.

regarding the violations of human rights that occurred in Spain between July 1936 and October 1977, and put together a set of recommendations which the authorities would commit to implementing. I agree with Josep María Tamarit when he says that, given that so much time has passed and the volume of cases that need to be looked at, this truth commission could not be created in the image of other truth commissions that operated in contexts immediately after a conflict. A Spanish truth commission would have to be unique, it would have to begin its work based on the facts we already know, and it should have a certain extra-judicial dispensation so that it could carry out its own investigation, such as the authority to open mass graves and identify the remains.[31] If a truth commission to serve the needs of the entire nation is not possible for political reasons, individual commissions would have to be created in regions where the autonomous parliament is sensitive to the victims of Francoism.

If there is a lack of political will regarding this matter and no truth commission is created, not even at a regional level, the only viable option left would be transformative justice, that is to say, a justice that seeks to resolve conflicts and foster relationships through a commission of experts from various disciplines who exhaustively analyse the conflict and its history, and then fix a set of conclusions in a programme that the institutions of the country are committed to implementing, especially through the legal institutions, in order to install a culture of peace.[32]

As Ramón Sáez Valcárcel would say, this is not about putting history up on trial or even rewriting history. We have shed light on those abhorrent crimes, systematic and on a mass scale that offend all of humanity, affect the victims, and are not beholden to a statute of limitations. In other words, crimes which question the identity of a civilised society.[33] The Spanish democracy will only be credible when the non-applicability of the statute of limitations, the amnesty and the prescription of Francoist crimes are replaced with the truth, justice and full reparation. Only then will we be able to speak of true Spanish transition, even if it does come at this late stage.

31 Tamarit Sumalla, 2014, pp. 64–65.
32 Gready and Robins, 2014, pp. 339–361.
33 Sáez Valcárcel, 2009, pp. 93–95.

Bibliography

Agencia de Prensa Española Popular ([1976] 2005) *27 de septiembre de 1975. Cinco héroes del pueblo*, Madrid: Tiempo de Cerezas (3rd edn).

Aguado Renedo, C. (2001) *Problemas constitucionales del ejercicio de la potestad de gracia*, Madrid: Civitas.

Aguilar, P. (1995a) *La memoria histórica de la guerra civil española (1936–1939). Un proceso de aprendizaje político*, Madrid: Centro de Estudios Avanzados en Ciencias Sociales.

Aguilar, P. (1995b) "La amnistía y la memoria histórica de la guerra civil en la transición", J. Tusell (ed.), *Historia de la transición y consolidación democrática en España (1975–1986)*, Madrid: Universidad Nacional de Educación a Distancia, vol. 1, pp. 3–13.

Aguilar, P. (1996) *Memoria y olvido de la Guerra Civil española*, Madrid: Alianza. Translated by M. Oakley, *Memory and Amnesia: The Role of the Spanish Civil War in the Transition to Democracy*, New York: Berghahn Books, 2002.

Aguilar, P. (1997a) "La amnesia y la memoria: las movilizaciones por la amnistía en la transición a la democracia", M. Pérez Ledesma and R. Cruz Martínez (eds), *Cultura y movilización en la España contemporánea*, Madrid: Alianza, pp. 327–357.

Aguilar, P. (1997b) "Collective Memory of the Spanish Civil War: The Case of the Political Amnesty in the Spanish Transition to Democracy", *Democratization*, 4(4), pp. 88–109.

Aguilar, P. (1999) "Memoria histórica y legados institucionales en los procesos de cambio político", *Revista Internacional de Filosofía Política*, 14, pp. 31–46.

Aguilar, P. (2001) "Justice, Politics and Memory in the Spanish Transition", A. Barahona de Brito, C. González-Enríquez and P. Aguilar (eds), *The Politics of Memory. Transitional Justice in Democratizing Societies*, Oxford: Oxford University Press, pp. 92–118.

Aguilar, P. (2008) *Políticas de la memoria y memorias de la política*, Madrid: Alianza.

Aguilar, P. (2012) "The Spanish Amnesty Law of 1977 in Comparative Perspective: From a Law for Democracy to a Law for Impunity", L. Payne and F. Lessa (eds), *Amnesty in the Age of Human Rights Accountability. Comparative and international perspectives*, Cambridge: Cambridge University Press, pp. 315–335.

Aguilar, P. (2013) "Judiciary Involvement in Authoritarian Repression and Transitional Justice: The Spanish Case in Comparative Perspective", *The International Journal of Transitional Justice*, 7(2), pp. 245–266.

Aguilar, P., Bacells, L., Cebolla, H. (2011) "Determinants of Attitudes towards Transitional Justice: An Empirical Analysis of the Spanish Case", *Comparative Political Studies*, 44(10), pp. 1397–1430.

Aguilar, P. and Hite, K. (2010), "Memoria histórica y legados autoritarios en procesos de cambio político. España y Chile en perspectiva comparada", C. Macón and S. Rotemberg (eds), *Mapas de la transición. La política después del terror en Alemania, Chile, España, Guatemala, Sudáfrica y Uruguay*, Buenos Aires: Ladosur, pp. 119–168.

Aguilar, P. and Ramírez-Barat, C. (2014) "Amnesty and reparations without truth or justice in Spain", N. Wouters (ed.), *Transitional Justice and Memory in Europe (1945–2013)*, Cambridge: Intersentia, pp. 199–257.

Aït Yahia, K. (2013) "España y el golpe de estado contra De Gaulle", *Cahiers de Civilisation espagnole contemporaine*, p. 10. https://ccec.revues.org/4412

Akhavan, P. (2012) *Reducing Genocide to Law. Definition, Meaning, and the Ultimate Crime*, Cambridge: Cambridge University Press.

Alberola, O. and Villagrasa, F. (2008) *Miedo a la memoria. Historia de la Ley de reconciliación y concordia*, Barcelona: Flor del Viento.

Alija, R. A. and Calvet, E. (2013) "La exigibilidad en España de los derechos de la víctimas de desapariciones forzadas por vía contencioso-administrativa como alternativa a la vía penal", R. Escudero Alday and C. Pérez González (eds) *Desapariciones forzadas, represión política y crímenes del franquismo*, Madrid: Trotta, pp. 101–120.

Alivizatos, N. C. and Diamandouros, N. P. (1997) "Politics and the Judiciary in the Greek Transition to Democracy", J. McAdams (ed.), *Transitional Justice and the Rule of Law in New Democracies*, Notre Dame and London: University of Notre Dame, pp. 27–60.

Altaffaylla (1986) *Navarra 1936. De la Esperanza al Terror*, Tafalla: Altaffaylla.

Alzaga, O. (1989) "I rapporti tra Capo dello Stato, Governo e Parlamento", G. Rolla (ed.) *Il X anniversario della Constituzione spagnola: bilancio, problemi, prospettive*, Siena: Centro Stampa della Facoltà di Scienze Economiche i Bancarie, pp. 69–82.

Ambos, K. (1997) *Impunidad y Derecho penal internacional. Un estudio empírico dogmático sobre Colombia, Bolivia, Perú, Chile y Argentina*, Bogotá: Konrad Adenauer; Instituto Max Plank, Comisión Andina de Juristas, CIEDLA.

Ambos, K. (ed.) (2002) *La nueva justicia penal supranacional. Desarrollos post-Roma*, Valencia: Tirant lo Blanch.

Ambos, K. and Guerrero, O. (2003) *El Estatuto de Roma de la Corte Penal Internacional*, Bogotá: Universidad Externado de Colombia.

Ambos, K., Malarino, E. and Elsner, G. (2009) *Justicia de Transición. Informes de América Latina, Alemania, Italia y España*, Berlin: Georg-August-Universität-Göttingen; Montevideo: Fundación Konrad Adenauer Stiftung.

Amnesty International (1977) *Torture in Greece. The First Torturer's Trial 1975*, London: Amnesty International Publications; Villiers Publications.

Amnistía Internacional España (ed.) (1995) *La pena de muerte y su abolición en España*, Madrid: Los Libros de la Catarata.

Amnistía Internacional España (ed.) (2004) *España: Acabar con la doble injusticia: Víctimas de tortura y malos tratos sin reparación justa y adecuada*, Madrid: Amnistía Internacional.

Amnistía Internacional España (ed.) (2005) *España: Poner fin al silencio y a la injusticia. La deuda pendiente con las víctimas de la Guerra Civil española y del régimen franquista*, Madrid: Amnistía Internacional.

Amnistía Internacional España (ed.) (2006) *Víctimas de la guerra civil y el franquismo: no hay derecho. Preocupaciones sobre el Proyecto de Ley sobre "Derechos de las víctimas de la guerra civil y del franquismo"*, Madrid: Amnistía Internacional.

Amnistía Internacional España (ed.) (2007) *España: Sal en la Herida: La Impunidad Efectiva de Agentes de Policía en casos de tortura y otros malos tratos*, Madrid: Amnistía Internacional. AI: EUR 41/006/2007.

Amnistía Internacional España (ed.) (2008a) *España: ejercer la jurisdicción universal para acabar con la impunidad*, Madrid: Amnistía Internacional.

Amnistía Internacional España (ed.) (2008b) *Víctimas de la guerra civil y el franquismo: no hay derecho*, Madrid: Amnistía Internacional.

Amnistía Internacional España (ed.) (2008c) *España: la obligación de investigar los crímenes del pasado y garantizar los derechos de las víctimas de desaparición forzada durante la Guerra Civil y el franquismo. Informe de la sección española*, Madrid: Amnistía Internacional.

Amnistía Internacional España (ed.) (2012) *Casos cerrados, heridas abiertas. El desamparo de las víctimas de la guerra civil y el franquismo en España*, Madrid: Amnistía Internacional.

Andrés Ibáñez, P. (2012) "Casos Garzón: Necesario distinguir", *Isonomía. Revista de Teoría y Filosofía del Derecho*, 37, pp. 169–200.

Aoiz, F. (2005) *El jarrón roto. La transición en Navarra, una cuestión de Estado*, Tafalla: Txalaparta.

Arendt, H. ([1963] 1994) *Eichmann in Jerusalem: a report on the banality of evil*, New York: Penguin Books.

Arangüena, C. (2010) "La Ley de Memoria Histórica y sus limitaciones: una visión desde la óptica del derecho procesal", J. M. Tamarit (ed.), *Justicia de transición, justicia penal internacional y justicia universal*, Barcelona: Atelier, pp. 119–142.

Arasa, D. (2005) *Los españoles de Stalin*, Barcelona: Belacqva.

Aróstegui, J. (ed.) (1988) *Historia y memoria de la guerra civil*, Valladolid: Junta de Castilla y León, 2 vols.

Aróstegui, J. and Gálvez, S. (2011) *Generaciones y memoria de la represión franquista. Un balance de los movimientos por la memoria*, València: Universitat de València.

Asociación Española para el Derecho Internacional de los Derechos Humanos (2008) *Informe sobre el derecho a un recurso efectivo y a obtener una reparación justa y adecuada que corresponde a las víctimas de desapariciones forzadas, crímenes contra la humanidad y otras violaciones de los derechos humanos cometidas en España durante la guerra civil y la dictadura*, Ginebra and Las Palmas de Gran Canaria, 30 de abril de 2008. http://www2.ohchr.org/english/bodies/hrc/docs/ngos/AEDIDH.pdf

Asúa Batarrita, A. (2002) "Concepto jurídico de terrorismo y elementos subjetivos de finalidad. Fines políticos últimos y fines de terror instrumental", J. I. Echano Basaldúa (ed.), *Estudios jurídicos en Memoria de José María Lidón*, Bilbao: Deusto, pp. 41–85.

Azpitarte, M. (2008) *Cambiar el pasado*, Madrid: Tecnos.

Balcells, J. M. and Pérez Bowie, J. A. (eds) (2001) *El exilio cultural de la Guerra Civil (1936–1939)*, Salamanca: Universidad de Salamanca.

Barahona de Brito, A., González-Enríquez, C. and Aguilar, P. (2001) "Introduction", A. Barahona de Brito, C. González-Enríquez and P. Aguilar (eds), *The Politics of Memory. Transitional Justice in Democratizing Societies*, Oxford: Oxford University Press, pp. 1–39.

Bassiouni, M. C. (1992) *Crimes against humanity in international law*, Boston and London: Martinus Nijhoff Publishers.

Baylos Grau, A. P. (2008) "Derechos económicos e indemnizaciones derivados de la memoria histórica", J. A. Martín Pallín and R. Escudero Alday (eds), *Derecho y Memoria Histórica*, Madrid: Trotta, pp. 185–208.

Beigbeder, Y. (2002) *Judging criminal leaders. The slow erosion of impunity*, The Hague and London: Kluwer Law International.

Bell, C. (2009) "Transitional Justice. Interdisciplinarity and the State of the Field or Non-Field", *International Journal of Transitional Justice*, 3, pp. 5–27.

Benavides Vanegas, F. S. (2011) *Justicia en épocas de transición. Conceptos, modelos, debates, experiencias*, Barcelona: Institut Català Internacional per la Pau.

Benegas, J. M. (2007) "La amnistía de 1977", *El Siglo*, p. 761, 5 November 2007. http://www.elsiglodeuropa.es/siglo/historico/2007/761/761benegas.html

Bengoetxea, Joxerramon (2011) "Seven Theses on Spanish Justice to understand the Prosecution of Judge Garzón", *Oñati Socio-Legal Series*, 1(9). http://papers.ssrn.com/sol3/papers.cfm?abstractid=1986790

Bermejo, B. and Checa, S. (2006) *Libro Memorial. Españoles deportados a los campos nazis (1940–1945)*, Madrid: Ministerio de Cultura.

Bermeo, N. (1992) "Democracy and the Lessons of Dictatorship", *Comparative Politics*, 24(3), pp. 273–291.

Biescas, J. A. and Tuñón de Lara, M. (1982) *España bajo la dictadura franquista (1939–1975)*, Barcelona: Labor.

Bonet Pérez, J. and Alija Fernández, R. (2009) *Impunidad, derechos humanos y justicia transicional*, Bilbao: Universidad de Deusto.

Branche, R. (2001) *La Torture et l'armée pendant la guerre d'Algérie, 1954–1962*, Paris: Gallimard.

Bravo-Tellado, A. (1976) *Los mutilados del Ejército de la República*, Madrid: Gráficas Clarcilla.

Buck, M. (1998) "The Exemplary Transition from Authoritarianism, Some Notes on the Legacy of Undemocratic Decision-making in Spain", S. U. Larsen (ed.), *Modern Europe After Fascism. 1943–1980s*, Boulder, CO: Social Science, pp. 1630–1634.

Bueno Arús, F. (1977) "Una nota sobre la Ley de Amnistía", *Boletín de Información del Ministerio de Justicia*, 1113, 15 November 1977.

Bueno Urritzelki, M. (2014–2015) "La lucha proamnistía en las provincias vasco-navarras en la transición española", *Gerónimo de Uztariz*, 30–31, pp. 83–100.

Busquets, J. (1999) *Militares y demócratas. Memorias de un fundador de la UMD y diputado socialista*, Barcelona: Plaza & Janés.

Callejón, C. (2006) "Une immense lacune du Droit International comblée avec le nouvel instrument des Nations Unies pour la Protection de Toutes les Personnes contre les Disparitions Forcées", *Revue Trimestrelle des Droits de L'Hommes*, 17(66), pp. 337–358.

Camisón Yagüe, J. A. (2013) "Ley de Memoria Histórica: luces y sombras a propósito de las medidas de reparación", M. Criado de Diego (ed.), *El itinerario de la memoria. Derecho, historia y justicia en la recuperación de la memoria histórica en España. Vol. 1. El derecho y la memoria*, Madrid: Sequitur, pp. 127–160.

Capellá i Roig, M. (2005a) *La tipificación internacional de los crímenes contra la humanidad*, Valencia: Tirant lo Blanch.

Capellá i Roig, M. (2005b) "Los crímenes contra la humanidad en el caso Scilingo", *Revista Electrónica de Estudios Internacionales*, 10.

Capellá i Roig, M. (2006) "Las desapariciones forzadas en España durante la Guerra Civil: crímenes y violaciones del Derecho Internacional sin castigo ni reparación", J. Soroeta Liceras (ed.), *Cursos de Derechos Humanos de Donostia-San Sebastián*, Bilbao: Universidad del País Vasco/Euskal Herriko Unibertsitatea, vol. 6, pp. 265–302.

Capellá i Roig, M. (2008) "La recuperación de la memoria histórica desde la perspectiva jurídica e internacional", *Entelequia*, 7, pp. 273–279.

Capellá i Roig, M. (2009) "Represión política y derecho internacional: una perspectiva comparada (1936–2006)", M. Capellá i Roig and D. Ginard i Féron (eds), *Represión política, justicia y reparación. La memoria histórica en perspectiva jurídica, 1936–2008*, Palma de Mallorca: Documenta Balear, pp. 161–254.

Capellá i Roig, M. (2011) "Crímenes contra la humanidad", R. Escudero Alday (ed.), *Diccionario de memoria histórica: conceptos contra el olvido*, Madrid: Los Libros de la Catarata, pp. 112–117.

Capellá i Roig, M. and Ginard i Féron, D. (eds) (2009) *Represión política, justicia y reparación. La memoria histórica en perspectiva jurídica, 1936–2008*, Palma de Mallorca: Documenta Balear.

Carothers, T. (2002) "The end of the Transition Paradigm?", *Journal of Democracy*, 13(1), pp. 5–21.

Carrillo, M. (2006) "El marco legal de la represión en la dictadura franquista durante el período 1939–1959", F. Gómez Isa (ed.), *El derecho a la memoria*, Donostia/San Sebastián: Diputación Foral de Gipuzkoa; Universidad de Deusto, pp. 501–528.

Carro Martínez, A. (1965) *Derecho político*, Madrid: Universidad de Madrid (3rd edn).

Carro Martínez, A. (1975) *El Estado y las Fuerzas Armadas*, Madrid: Presidencia del Gobierno.

Carvajal Urquijo, P. (2003) *Julián Grimau: el último muerto de la guerra civil*, Madrid: Aguilar.

Casals, X. (1998) *La tentación neofascista en España*, Barcelona: Plaza & Janés.

Casanova, J. (ed.) (2002) *Matar, morir, sobrevivir. La violencia en la dictadura de Franco*, Barcelona: Crítica.

Castellano, P. (1979) *Sobre el partido obrero*, Barcelona: Iniciativas Editoriales-El Viejo Topo.

Castellano, P. (1994) *Yo sí me acuerdo: apuntes e historias*, Madrid: Temas de Hoy.

Castellano, P. (2001) *Por Dios, por la Patria y el Rey: una visión crítica de la transición española*, Madrid: Temas de Hoy.

Castells Arteche, M. (1978) *El mejor defensor, el pueblo*, San Sebastián: Ediciones Vascas.

Castresana, C. (2012) "El Estado español y las víctimas del franquismo, frente al derecho internacional", *Jueces para la Democracia*, 75, pp. 17–26.

Castro, R. (1998) *Juan María Bandrés. Memorias para la paz*, Majadahonda: Hijos de Muley-Rubio.

Chinchón Álvarez, J. (2007a) *Derecho Internacional y transiciones a la democracia y la paz. Hacia un modelo para el castigo de los crímenes pasados a través de la experiencia iberoamericana*, Madrid: Ediciones Parthenón.

Chinchón Álvarez, J. (2007b) "El viaje a ninguna parte: Memoria, leyes, historia y olvido sobre la guerra civil y el pasado autoritario en España. Un examen desde el derecho internacional", *Revista del Instituto Interamericano de Derechos Humanos*, 45, pp. 119–233.

Chinchón Álvarez, J. (2008a) "Transición española y justicia transicional: ¿qué papel juega el ordenamiento jurídico internacional en un proceso de transición? A propósito de la coherencia, buena fe y otros principios de derecho internacional postergados en la transición política de España", *Entelequia*, 7, pp. 331–354.

Chinchón Álvarez, J. (2008b) "La Convención Internacional para la protección de todas las personas contra las desapariciones forzadas: nunca es tarde si la dicha es ¿buena?: examen general y perspectivas en España tras la aprobación de la Ley de Memoria Histórica", *Foro. Revista de Ciencias Jurídicas y Sociales*, 7, pp. 13–55.

Chinchón Álvarez, J. (2008c) "Examen del Auto del Juzgado de Instrucción N°. 5 de la Audiencia Nacional por el que se acepta la competencia para investigar los crímenes contra la humanidad cometidos en la Guerra Civil y el franquismo", *La Ley: Revista Jurídica Española de Doctrina, Jurisprudencia y Bibliografía*, 5, pp. 1388–1397.

Chinchón Álvarez, J. (2009a) "Formulando las preguntas correctas sobre los problemas de cumplimiento de las obligaciones de investigar, juzgar, sancionar y reparar los crímenes pasados", J. Almqvist and C. Espósito (eds), *Justicia transicional en Iberoamérica*, Madrid: Centro de Estudios Políticos y Constitucionales, pp. 255–289.

Chinchón Álvarez, J. (2009b) "La actuación de la Audiencia Nacional en la investigación y juicio de los crímenes contra la humanidad cometidos en la Guerra Civil y el franquismo: Del Auto de 16 de octubre a la decisión del Pleno de la Sala de lo Penal de 2 de diciembre de 2008", *La Ley: Revista Jurídica Española de Doctrina, Jurisprudencia y Bibliografía*, 1, pp. 1415–1424.

Chinchón Álvarez, J. (2009c) "Justicia transicional: Memoria Histórica, y responsabilidad internacional del Estado: Un análisis general a propósito del cumplimiento de ciertas obligaciones internacionales en juego después de más de tres décadas del inicio formal de la transición política española", *Revista de Derecho de Extremadura*, 4, pp. 49–74.

Chinchón Álvarez, J. (2011) "The challenges posed to the recent investigation of crimes committed during the Spanish Civil War and Francoism", J. Almqvist and J. Espósito (eds), *The Role of Courts in Transitional Justice Voices from Latin America and Spain*, New York: Routledge, pp. 343–367.

Chinchón Álvarez, J. (2012a) *El tratamiento judicial de los crímenes de la Guerra Civil y el franquismo en España. Una visión de conjunto desde el Derecho internacional*, Bilbao: Universidad de Deusto.

Chinchón Álvarez, J. (2012b) "El concepto de impunidad a la luz del Derecho internacional: Una aproximación sistémica desde el Derecho internacional penal y el Derecho internacional de los derechos humanos", *Revista electrónica de estudios internacionales*, 24, pp. 1–31.

Chinchón Álvarez, J. (2013) "La obligación internacional del estado de investigar las violaciones a los derechos humanos ocurridas en el pasado", M. Criado de Diego (ed.), *El itinerario de la memoria. Derecho, historia y justicia en la recuperación de la memoria histórica en España. Vol. 1. El derecho y la memoria*, Madrid: Sequitur, pp. 161–192.

Chinchón Álvarez, J. (2013–2014) "The reform(s) of universal jurisdiction in Spain. For whom the bells tolls?", *Spanish Yearbook of International Law*, 18, pp. 231–237.

Chinchón Álvarez, J. and Vicente Márquez, L. (2010) "La investigación de los crímenes cometidos en la guerra civil y el franquismo como delito de prevaricación. Análisis crítico del Auto del Tribunal Supremo de 3 de febrero de 2010 desde la perspectiva del Derecho internacional", *Revista electrónica de estudios internacionales*, 19, pp. 1–43.

Chinchón Álvarez, J., Vicente Márquez, L. and Moreno, A. (2014) "La posición del Tribunal Supremo respecto a la aplicación del derecho internacional a los crímenes del pasado en España: Un análisis jurídico tras los informes del Grupo de Trabajo sobre Desapariciones Forzadas, el Comité contra la Desaparición Forzada y el Relator Especial sobre Justicia Transicional de las Naciones Unidas", *Anuario Iberoamericano de Derecho Internacional Penal*, 2, pp. 66–101.

Clavero, B. (2014) *España, 1974. La amnesia constituyente*, Madrid: Marcial Pons.

Colomer, J. M. (1990) *El arte de la manipulación política*, Barcelona: Anagrama.

Colomer, J. (1998) *La transición a la democracia, el modelo español*, Barcelona: Anagrama.

Collins, C. (2012) "The End of Impunity? Late Justice and Post-transitional Prosecutions in Latin America", N. Palmer, P. Clark and D. Granville (eds), *Critical Perspectives in Transitional Justice*, Cambridge: Intersentia, pp. 399–423.

Comisión Interministerial (2006) *Informe general de la Comisión Interministerial para el estudio de la situación de las víctimas de la Guerra civil y del Franquismo*, Madrid: Gobierno de España. http://www.memoriahistorica.gob.es/es-es/LaLey/Paginas/TrabajosPrevios.aspx

Contreras Casado, M. and Cebrián Zazurca, E. (2014) "La ley para la reforma política: la memoria de la Guerra Civil en los inicios de la transición", G. Pasamar Alzuría (ed.), *Ha estallado la memoria: las huellas de la Guerra Civil en la transición a la democracia*, Madrid: Biblioteca Nueva, pp. 81–118.

Costa Pinto, A. (1995) *Salazar's Dictatorship and European Fascism Problems of Interpretation*, New York: SSM-Columbia University Press.

Costa Pinto, A. (2001) "Settling Accounts with the Past in a Troubled Transition to Democracy: The Portuguese Case", A. Barahona de Brito, C. González-Enríquez and P. Aguilar (eds), *The Politics of Memory. Transitional Justice in Democratizing Societies*, Oxford: Oxford University Press, pp. 65–91.

Costa Pinto, A. (2009) "El ajuste de cuentas con el pasado en una turbulenta transición a la democracia", S. Baby, O. Compagnon and E. González Calleja (eds), *Violencia y transiciones políticas a finales del siglo XX. Europa del Sur-América Latina*, Madrid: Casa de Velázquez, pp. 103–134.

Criado de Diego, M. (2013) "Derecho y memoria. La memoria histórica como valor y como conflicto", M. Criado de Diego (ed.), *El itinerario de la memoria. Derecho, historia y justicia en la recuperación de la memoria histórica en España. Vol. 1. El derecho y la memoria*, Madrid: Sequitur, pp. 11–47.

Davis, M. (2005) "Is Spain Recovering its Memory? Breaking the Pacto del Olvido", *Human Rights Quarterly*, 27(3) pp. 858–880.

De Domingo, T. (2012) *Justicia transicional, memoria histórica y crisis nacional*, Cizur Menor: Civitas; Thomson Reuters.

De Greiff, P. (2007) "Vetting and Transitional Justice", A. Mayer-Rieckh and P. de Greiff (eds), *Vetting as Prevention: Vetting Public Employees in Transitional Societies*, New York: Social Science Research Council, pp. 523–544.

De Greiff, P. (2012) "Theorizing Transitional Justice", M. S. Williams, R. Nagy and J. Elser (eds), *Transitional Justice*, New York: New York University Press, pp. 31–77.

De la Torre, H. (ed.) (1989) *Portugal y España en el cambio político (1958–1978)*, Mérida: Universidad Nacional de Educación a Distancia, Centro Regional de Extremadura.

De la Villa, L. E. and Desdentado Bonete, A. (1978) *La amnistía laboral: una crítica política y jurídica*, Madrid: Ediciones De la Torre.

De Pablo, S., Mees, L. and Rodríguez Ranz, J. A. (2001) *El Péndulo Patriótico. Historia del Partido Nacionalista Vasco, II, 1936–1979*, Barcelona: Crítica.

De Pablo Contreras, S. (2002) "Manuel de Irujo. Un nacionalista vasco en la Transición democrática (1975–1981)", *Vasconia*, 32, pp. 169–184.

Deane, P. (1977) *I Should Have Died*, New York: Atheneum.

Del Burgo, J. I. (1976a) *Los Fueros del futuro. Ideas para la reforma foral*, Pamplona: Self-Publishing, pp. 77–79.

Del Burgo, J. (1976b) "Los principios forales y la realidad navarra", *Navarra hoy, ante su futuro*, Pamplona: Ediciones y Libros.

Del Burgo, J. (2015) *La epopeya de la foralidad vasca y navarra. Principio y fin de la cuestión foral*, Bilbao: Fundación Popular de Estudios Vascos, 2 vols.

Diamandouros, N. P. (1986) "Regime change and the prospects for democracy in Greece, 1974–1983", G. O'Donnell and P. Schmitter (eds), *Transitions from Authoritarian Rule.*

Tentative conclusions about uncertain democracies, Baltimore: John Hopkins University Press, pp. 138–164.
Díaz Fernández, A. M. (2006) *Los servicios de inteligencia españoles. Desde la guerra civil hasta el 11-M. Historia de una transición*, Madrid: Alianza.
Díaz Sánchez, P. (ed.) (2016) *Los jueces contra el franquismo: Justicia Democrática*, Madrid: Maia Ediciones.
Diéguez, G. (1978) "Ante una importante sentencia sobre amnistía laboral", *Revista de Política Social*, 118, pp. 131–143.
Dirección de Derechos Humanos del Gobierno Vasco (2009), *Bases para la puesta en marcha de una Comisión de la Verdad en Euskadi*, Vitoria-Gasteiz: Gobierno Vasco.
Domínguez, J. I. (1977) *Cuando yo era un exiliado*, Madrid: Cambio, p. 16.
Durán Muñoz, R. (2000) *Contención y trasgresión. Las movilizaciones sociales y el Estado en las transiciones española y portuguesa*, Madrid: Centro de Estudios Políticos y Constitucionales.
Durán Muñoz, R. (2009) "Fortaleza del Estado y acción colectiva en el cambio de régimen: España y Portugal en perspectiva comparada", S. Baby, O. Compagnon and E. González Calleja (eds), *Violencia y transiciones políticas a finales del siglo XX. Europa del Sur-América Latina*, Madrid: Casa de Velázquez, pp. 157–178.
Dyzenhaus, D. (2003) "Judicial Independence, Transitional Justice and the Rule of Law", *Otago Law Review*, 10(3), pp. 345–364.
Eftekhari, S. (2002–2003) "France and the Algerian War: From a Policy of Forgetting to a Framework for Accountability", *Columbia Human Rights Law Review*, 34, pp. 413–474.
Egido León, A. (2006) "La historia y la gestión de la memoria. Apuntes para un balance", *Hispania Nova. Revista de Historia Contemporánea*, 6, pp. 1–23.
Elster, J. (2004) *Closing the Books: Transitional Justice in Historical Perspective*, New York: Cambridge University Press.
Elster, J. (ed.) (2006) *Retribution and Reparation in the Transition to Democracy*, New York: Cambridge University Press.
Elster, J. (2008) "Coming to Terms with the Past. A Framework for the Study of Justice in the Transition to Democracy", *Archives Europeénes de Sociologie*, 39(1), pp. 7–48.
Encarnación, O. G. (2014) *Democracy without Justice in Spain. The Politics of Forgetting*, Philadelphia: University of Pennsylvania Press.
Equipo Nizkor (2004) *The question of impunity in Spain and crimes under Franco*, Madrid: Equipo Nizkor. http://www.derechos.org/nizkor/espana/doc/impuspa.html
Erice Sebares, F. (2013) *Evolución histórica del PCE (II). De la reconciliación nacional a la crisis de la transición*, Madrid: Partido Comunista de España.
Escribano, F. (2001) *Cuenta atrás. La historia de Salvador Puig Antich*, Barcelona: Península.
Escudero Alday, R. (2009) "La sombra del franquismo es alargada: el fracaso de la llamada Ley de Memoria histórica", F. Fernández-Crehuet López and D. J. García López (eds), *Derecho, memoria histórica y dictaduras*, Granada: Comares, pp. 33–60.
Escudero Alday, R. (2011) "Conceptos contra el olvido: una guía para no perder la memoria", R. Escudero Alday (ed.), *Diccionario de memoria histórica: conceptos contra el olvido*, Madrid: Los Libros de la Catarata, pp. 7–14.
Escudero Alday, R. (2013a) *Modelos de democracia en España. 1931–1978*, Madrid: Península.
Escudero Alday, R. (2013b) "Los derechos de las víctimas de la transición", M. Criado de Diego (ed.), *El itinerario de la memoria. Derecho, historia y justicia en la recuperación de la memoria histórica en España. Vol. 1. El derecho y la memoria*, Madrid: Sequitur, pp. 193–214.
Escudero Alday, R. (2013c) "Jaque a la transición: análisis del proceso de recuperación de la memoria histórica", *Anuario de Filosofía del Derecho*, 29, pp. 319–340.

Escudero Alday, R. (2013d) "Los desaparecidos en España: víctimas de la represión franquista, símbolo de la transición y síntoma de una democracia imperfecta", R. Escudero Alday and C. Pérez González (eds) *Desapariciones forzadas, represión política y crímenes del franquismo*, Madrid: Trotta, pp. 141–161.

Escudero Alday, R. (2014) "Road to Impunity: The Absence of Transitional Justice Programs in Spain", *Human Rights Quarterly*, 36(1), pp. 123–146.

Escudero Alday, R., Campelo, P., Pérez González, C. and Silva, E. (2013) *Qué hacemos para reparar a las víctimas, hacer justicia, acabar con la impunidad y por la construcción de la memoria histórica*, Madrid: Akal.

Espinosa Maestre, F. (2003) *La columna de la muerte. El avance del ejército franquista de Sevilla a Badajoz*, Barcelona: Crítica.

Espinosa Maestre, F. (2006) *Contra el olvido. Historia y memoria de la guerra civil*, Madrid: Crítica.

Espinosa Maestre, F. (2007) "De saturaciones y olvidos. Reflexiones en torno a un pasado que no puede pasar", *Hispania Nova. Revista Electrónica de Historia Contemporánea*, 7, pp. 416–440.

Espinosa Maestre, F. (2011) "Represión", R. Escudero Alday (ed.), *Diccionario de memoria histórica: conceptos contra el olvido*, Madrid: Los Libros de la Catarata, pp. 39–45.

Espinosa Maestre, F. (2013) *Shoot the Messenger? Spanish Democracy and the Crimes of Francoism. From the Pact of Silence to the Trial of Baltasar Garzón*, Sussex: Sussex Academic Press.

Faber, S. (2007) "The Debate about Spain's Past and the Crisis of Academic Legitimacy: The Case of Santos Juliá", *The Colorado Review of Spanish Studies*, 5, pp. 165–190.

Fanjul, J. M. (1970) *Dos años de procurador en Cortes por las familias de Madrid*, Madrid: Artes Gráficas.

Fernández Balbuena, S. (1978) *Xirinacs*, Barcelona: San Román Yribas.

Fernández-Crehuet, F. (2011) *Jueces bajo el franquismo. Once historias (y una nota sobre la depuración de los funcionarios judiciales)*, Granada: Comares.

Fernández García, J. (2009) "Juicio a la memoria: los crímenes de la guerra civil y la dictadura franquista", *De los delitos y de las penas hoy: la nueva reforma del Código Penal*, Salamanca: Ratio Legis, pp. 95–125.

Fernández Liesa, C. (2014) *La Guerra Civil española y el ordenamiento jurídico internacional*, Madrid: Civitas.

Fernández Monzón-Altolaguirre, M. and Mata, S. (2014) *El sueño de la transición. Los militares y los servicios de inteligencia que la hicieron posible*, Madrid: La Esfera de los Libros.

Fernández-Pachecho, C. (2008) "La jurisprudencia española en aplicación del principio de jurisdicción universal: el caso de la represión en Argentina", *Jueces para la Democracia*, 61, pp. 101–117.

Fernández Soldevilla, G. (2010) "Agur a las armas. EIA, Euskadiko Ezkerra y la disolución de ETA político-militar (1976–1985)", *Sancho el Sabio*, 33, pp. 55–96.

Ferrándiz, F. (2006) "Exhumaciones y políticas de la memoria en la España contemporánea", F. Gómez Isa (ed.), *El derecho a la memoria*, Bilbao: Diputación Foral de Gipuzkoa; Universidad de Deusto, pp. 529–548.

Ferrándiz, F. and Aguilar, P. (2016) "Memory, Media and Spectacle: Interviú's Portraval of Civil War Exhumations in the Early Years of Spanish Democracy", *Journal of Spanish Cultural Studies*, 17(1), pp. 1–25.

Ferrara, A. (2014) *Assessing the long-term impact of truth commissions: the Chilean truth and reconciliation commission in historical perspective*, New York: Routledge.

Ferré Olivé, J. C. (ed.) (2006) *El Derecho Penal de la posguerra*, Valencia: Tirant lo Blanch.

Fleites Marcos, A. (2009) "Un acercamiento engañoso: las relaciones políticas hispano-francesas entre 1958 y 1970", *Cahiers de Civilisation espagnole contemporaine*, p. 4. https://ccec.revues.org/2738

Folguera, P. (ed.) (1988) *El feminismo en España: Dos siglos de Historia*, Madrid: Fundación Pablo Iglesias; Siglo XXI.

Fontana, J. (1986) *España bajo el franquismo*, Barcelona: Crítica.

Fontana, J. (2012) "Prólogo", C. Jiménez Villarejo and A. Doñate Martín, *Jueces, pero parciales. La pervivencia del franquismo en el poder judicial*, Barcelona: Pasado & Presente, pp. 13–16.

Fraile, A. (2005) "Maquis y justicia militar en España (1944–1945). Imagen personal y memoria colectiva". https://tel.archives-ouvertes.fr/tel-00192814

Franzinelli, M. (2006) *L'amnistia Togliatti. 22 giugno 1946 colpo di spugna sui crimini fascisti*, Milano: Mondadori.

Freeman, M. (2009) *Necessary Evils. Amnesties and the Search for Justice*, Cambridge: Cambridge University Press.

Freeman, M. and Pensky, M. (2012) "The Amnesty controversy in International Law", F. Lessa and L. A. Payne (eds), *Amnesty in the Age of Human Rights Accountability: Comparative and international perspectives*, Cambridge: Cambridge University Press, pp. 42–65.

Gacon, S. (2002) *L'Amnistie: De la commune à la guerre d'Algérie*, Paris: Seuil.

Gacon, S. (2005) "Les amnisties de la Guerre d'Algérie (1962–1982)", *Revue Histoire de la Justice*, 16, pp. 271–279.

Galella, P. (2013) "La obligación de investigar las desapariciones forzadas y su aplicación a los crímenes del franquismo en España", *Anuario Mexicano de Derecho Internacional*, 14, pp. 77–116.

Garcés, J. E. (2010) "La acusación particular y los crímenes de lesa humanidad", *Cuadernos Penales José María Lidón*, 7, pp. 253–281.

Garcés, J. (2011) "La Ley española 46/1977, de Amnistía, más citada que leída, no tiene por objeto actos de naturaleza genocida y lesa humanidad", *Escrits. Revista d'informació i debat*, 30, pp. 19–29.

García Arán, M. (2009) "Repercusiones penales de la ley de amnistía de 1977", M. J. Espuny Tomás and O. Paz Torres (eds), *30 años de la ley de amnistía (1977–2007)*, Madrid: Universidad Autónoma de Barcelona; Dykinson, pp. 187–191.

García Mahamut, R. (2004) *El indulto, un análisis jurídico-constitucional*, Madrid: Marcial Pons.

García Rivas, N. (1990) *La rebelión militar en derecho penal*, Albacete: Universidad de Castilla La Mancha.

García Sáez, J. A. (2013) "Memoria histórica y aplicación retroactiva de las de la sanción penal. Algunos fundamentos desde el pacifismo jurídico de Hans Kelsen", *Eunomía. Revista de Cultura de la Legalidad*, 4, pp. 139–153.

Garmendia Amutxastegi, G. and Lau Haizetara Gogoan (2011) *Euskal Herriko Egiaren Batzordea. Verdad, Justicia y Reparación, con las garantías de no repetición*, Donostia: Lau Haizetara Gogoan.

Gete-Alonso y Calera, M. C. (2009) "El derecho de asociación y la amnistía", M. J. Espuny Tomás and O. Paz Torres (eds), *30 años de la ley de amnistía (1977–2007)*, Madrid: Universidad Autónoma de Barcelona; Dykinson, pp. 193–210.

Gil Gil, A. (2005) "La sentencia de la Audiencia Nacional en el caso Scilingo", *Jueces para la Democracia*, 53, pp. 7–16.

Gil Gil, A. (2009a) *La Justicia en la transición en España. De la amnistía a la memoria histórica*, Barcelona: Atelier.

Gil Gil, A. (2009b) "Principio de legalidad y crímenes internacionales. Luces y sombras en la sentencia del Tribunal Supremo en el caso Scilingo", A. R. Cuerda Riezu and F. Jiménez García (eds), *Nuevos desafíos del derecho penal internacional: terrorismo, crímenes internacionales y derechos fundamentales*, Madrid: Tecnos, pp. 391–410.

Gil Gil, A. (2009c) "España", K. Ambos, E. Malarino and G. Elsner (eds), *Justicia de Transición. Informes de América Latina, Alemania, Italia y España*, Berlin: Georg-August-Universität-Göttingen; Montevideo: Fundación Konrad Adenauer Stiftung, pp. 471–501.

Gil Gil, A. (2010) "¿Es posible todavía la persecución de los crímenes de la guerra civil y el franquismo?", M. Requena y Díez de Revenga (ed.), *Luces y sombras de la seguridad internacional en los albores del siglo XXI*, Madrid: Instituto Universitario General Gutiérrez Mellado, vol. 1, pp. 225–244.

Gil Gil, A. (2011) "Spain as an example of total oblivion with partial rehabilitation", J. Almqvist and C. Espósito (eds), *The Role of Courts in Transitional Justice Voices from Latin America and Spain*, New York: Routledge, pp. 103–131.

Gil Gil, A. (2012a) "Breve comparación de los mecanismos de superación del pasado adoptados en las transiciones brasileña y española", S. Alda Mejías and H. L. Saint-Pierre (eds), *Gobernabilidad y democracia. Defensa y transiciones de Brasil y España*, Santiago de Chile: RIL, pp. 77–108.

Gil Gil, A. (2012b) "Los crímenes de la guerra civil española. ¿Responsabilidad del Estado Español por infracción del Convenio Europeo de Derechos Humanos?: Análisis de la decisión del TEDH de 27 de marzo de 2012, caso Gutiérrez Dorado y Dorado Ortiz contra España", *InDret*, 4, pp. 1–29.

Gill, G. (2004) *The Dynamics of Democratization: Elites, Civil Society, and the Transition Process*, New York: Cambridge University Press.

Golob, S. (2008) "Volver: The Return of/to Transitional Justice Politics in Spain", *Journal of Spanish Cultural Studies*, 9(2), pp. 127–141.

Gómez Benítez, J. M. (2011) "El caso Ruano: memoria histórica e historia de una infamia", A. M. Domínguez Rama (ed.), *Enrique Ruano: memoria viva de la impunidad del franquismo*, Madrid: Editorial Complutense.

Gómez Bravo, G. (2007) *La redención de penas: la formación del sistema penitenciario franquista. La formación del sistema penitenciario franquista, 1936–1950*, Madrid: Los libros de la Catarata.

Gómez Bravo, G. and Marco, J. (2011) *La obra del miedo*, Barcelona: Península.

Gómez Isa, F. (ed.) (2006) *El derecho a la memoria*, Bilbao: Diputación Foral de Gipuzkoa.

Gómez Isa, F. (2012) "Retos de la justicia transicional en contextos no transicionales: el caso español", S. Ripol Carulla and C. Villán Durán (eds), *Justicia de transición: el caso de España*, Barcelona: Institut Catalá Internacional per la Pau, pp. 172–184.

Gómez Llana, J. (1941) "El aborto provocado y la Ley de 24 de enero de 1941", *Revista General de Legislación y Jurisprudencia*, 4, pp. 238–241.

Gómez Roda, J. A. (2004) *Comisiones obreras y la represión franquista*, Valencia: Universitat de Valencia.

Gómez Rosa, F. (2013) *UMD. Los militares olvidados por la Democracia*, Madrid: Vive Libro.

González, M. (2009) "Local Histories: A Methodology for Understanding. Community Perspectives on Transitional Justice", H. van der Merwe, V. Baxter and A. R. Chapman, *Assesing the impact of transitional justice. Challenges for empirical research*, Washington: United States Institute for Peace, pp. 295–312.

González Márquez, F. and Cebrián, J. L. (2002) *El futuro ya no es lo que era*, Madrid: Punto de Lectura.

González Quintana, A. (2011) "Archivos", R. Escudero Alday (ed.), *Diccionario de memoria histórica: conceptos contra el olvido*, Madrid: Los Libros de la Catarata, pp. 94–100.

González Vega, J. (2009) "Memoria histórica vs. impunidad: las obligaciones impuestas por el Derecho internacional", *Memoria histórica, ¿se puede juzgar la historia*, Madrid: Fundación Antonio Carretero, pp. 67–84.

Gormally, B. and McEvoy, K. (1995), *Release and Reintegration of Politically Motivated Prisoners in Northern Ireland: a Comparative Study of South Africa, Israel/Palestine, Italy, Spain, the Republic of Ireland and Northern Ireland*, Belfast: Northern Ireland Association for the Care and Resettlement of Offenders.

Gready, P. and Robins, S. (2014) "From Transitional to Transformative Justice: A New Agenda for Practice", *International Journal of Transitional Justice*, 8(3), pp. 339–361.

Greppi, A. (2008) "Los límites de la memoria y las limitaciones de la ley. Antifascismo y equidistancia", J. A. Martín Pallín and R. Escudero Alday (eds), *Derecho y Memoria Histórica*, Madrid: Trotta, pp. 105–125.

Grimaldos, A. (2006) *La CIA en España. Espionaje, intrigas y política al servicio de Washington*, Barcelona: Debate.

Guembe, M. J. (2005) "La reapertura de los juicios por los crímenes de la dictadura militar Argentina", *Sur. Revista Internacional de Derechos Humanos*, 2(3). http://www.scielo.br/scielo.php?pid=S1806-64452005000200008&script=sci_arttext&tlng=es

Guixé, J. (2008) "El memorial democrático y los lugares de la memoria La recuperación del patrimonio memorial en Catalunya", *Entelequia*, 7, pp. 217–228.

Gunther, R., Diamandouros, P. N. and Hans-Jürgen, P. (eds) (1995) *The Politics of Democratic Consolidation. Southern Europe in Comparative Perspective*, Baltimore and London: The Johns Hopkins University Press.

Hayner, P. (2010) *Unspeakable Truths: Transitional Justice and the Challenge of Truth Commissions*, New York: Routledge, 2nd edn.

Helmick, R. S. J. and Petersen, R. (2001) *Forgiveness and Reconciliation*, London: Templeton Foundation Press.

Hellman Moreno, J. (2012) "El vilipendiado principio de justicia universal en España", G. I. Anitua *et al.* (eds), *Derecho penal internacional y memoria histórica: desafíos del pasado y retos del futuro*, Buenos Aires: Fabián J. Di Plácido, pp. 299–323.

Hernández García, A. (1984) *La represión en La Rioja durante la guerra civil*, Logroño: Ingrabel, 3 vols.

Herrero Bernabé, I. (2012a) *El derecho de gracia: indultos*, Doctoral Thesis directed by M. I. Serrano Maíllo and A. Serrano Maíllo, Madrid: Universidad Nacional de Educación a Distancia, Facultad de Derecho.

Herrero Bernabé, I. (2012b) "Antecedentes históricos del indulto", *Revista de Derecho UNED*, 10, pp. 687–709.

Herrero de Miñón, M. (1998) *Memoria de estío*, Madrid: Temas de Hoy.

Holmes, S. ([1988] 1993) "Gags Rules or the Politics of Omission", J. Elster and R. Slagstad (eds), *Constitutionalism and Democracy*, New York: Maison des Sciences Press, pp. 195–240.

Horovitz, S. (2006) "Transitional criminal justice in Sierra Leone", N. Roht-Arriaza and J. Mariezcurrena (eds), *Transitional Justice in the Twenty-First Century: Beyond Truth Versus Justice*, New York: Cambridge University Press, pp. 43–69.

Humphrey, M. (2002) *The politics of atrocity and reconciliation: from terror to trauma*, London: Routledge.

Huntington, S. (1991) *The Third Wave: Democratization in the Late Twentieth Century*, Norman: University of Oklahoma Press.

Huyse, L. (2013) *Transitional Justice after War and Dictatorship, Learning from European Experiences (1945–2000)*, Brussels: Centre for Historical Research and Documentation on War and Contemporary Society, CEGES-SOMA.

Jimena Quesada, L. (2008) *Dignidad humana y justicia universal en España*, Cizur Menor: Thomson Reuters Aranzadi.

Jiménez, J. C. (2009) *España y Portugal en Transición. Los caminos a la democracia en la Península Ibérica*, Madrid: Sílex.

Jiménez de Asúa, L. (1932) *Proceso histórico de la Constitución de la República española*, Madrid: Reus.

Jiménez Villarejo, C. (2007) "La destrucción del orden republicano (apuntes jurídicos)", *Hispania Nova. Revista de Historia Contemporánea*, 7, pp. 1–31.

Jiménez Villarejo, C. (ed.) (2010) *La solidaridad con el Juez Garzón*, Córdoba (Argentina): El Páramo.

Jiménez Villarejo, C. and Doñate, A. (2012) *Jueces pero parciales. La pervivencia del franquismo en el poder judicial*, Madrid: Pasado & Presente.

Jimeno, R. (1999) "La memoria de los derrotados", *Gerónimo de Uztariz*, 14–15, pp. 19–38.

Jimeno, R. (2006) "Notas a la edición de 2006", José María Jimeno Jurío, *La Guerra Civil en Navarra (1936–1939)*, Pamplona: Pamiela; Udalbide: Euskara Kultur Elkargoa, pp. 17–30.

Jimeno, R. (2014) "La represión y depuración en la Administración de Justicia: Navarra, 1936–1945. Una primera aproximación", *Jueces para la Democracia*, 79, pp. 86–106.

Jimeno, R. (2015) *Miguel Javier Urmeneta (1915–1988). Segunda República, Franquismo y Transición*, Pamplona: Pamiela.

Jimeno Jurío, J. M. (1986) "Prólogo", *Navarra 1936. De la Esperanza al Terror*, Tafalla: Altaffaylla, pp. 19–22.

Jorge Barreiro, A. (1976) *Las medidas de seguridad en el Derecho español. Un estudio de la Ley de Peligrosidad y Rehabilitación Social de 1970, y de la doctrina de la sala de Apelación de Peligrosidad*, Madrid: Civitas.

Juliá, S. (ed.) (1999) *Víctimas de la guerra civil*, Madrid: Temas de Hoy.

Juliá, S. (2003a) "Política y Sociedad", S. Juliá, J. S. García Delgado, J. C. Jiménez and J. P. Fusi (eds), *La España del Siglo XX*, Madrid: Marcial Pons.

Juliá, S. (2003b) "Echar al olvido. Memoria y amnistía en la transición", *Claves de Razón Práctica*, 129, pp. 14–24.

Juliá, S. (2008) "Presencia de la guerra y combate por la amnistía en la transición a la democracia", J. G. Beramendi, M. J. Baz Vicente and M. Pérez Ledesma (eds), *Identidades y memoria imaginada*, Valencia: Universidad de Valencia, pp. 85–108.

Juliá, S. (2010) "Las dos amnistías de la transición", Blog, Tendencias 21. España Siglo XXI, 25 April 2010. http://www.tendencias21.net/espana/Las-dos-amnistias-de-la-transiciona13.html

Juliá, S. (2011) *Elogio de historia en tiempo de memoria*, Madrid: Marcial Pons.

Justicia Democrática (1978) *Los jueces contra la dictadura. Justicia y política en el franquismo*, Madrid: Túcar.

Katsikas, S. (2014) "Transitional Justice after the collapse of dictatorship in Greece (1974–1200)", N. Wouters (ed.), *Transitional justice and memory in Europe (1945–2013)*, Cambridge: Intersentia, pp. 259–287.

Kritz, N. J. (1995) *Transitional Justice: How Emerging Democracies Reckon with Former Regimes, Volume I: General Considerations: General Considerations v. 1*, Washington: United States Institute of Peace Press.

Lacasta Zabalza, J. I. (2015) *La memoria histórica*, Arre: Pamiela.

Lanero, M. (1996) *Una milicia de la justicia (1936-1945)*, Madrid: Centro de Estudios Constitucionales.

Larumbe, M. A. (2002) *Una inmensa minoría. Influencia y feminismo en la Transición*, Zaragoza: Prensas Universitarias de Zaragoza.

Larumbe, M. (2004) *Las que dijeron no. Palabra y acción del feminismo en la Transición*, Zaragoza: Prensas Universitarias de Zaragoza.

Lascuráin, J. A. (2011) "Los límites de la amnistía", *Doctrina penal*, 28, pp. 95–113.

Lefranc, S. (2004) *Políticas de perdón*, Madrid: Cátedra.

Leguina, J. (2010) *El duelo y la revancha. Los itinerarios del franquismo sobrevenido*, Madrid: La Esfera de los Libros.

Letamendía, F. (1978) *Denuncia en el Parlamento*, San Sebastián: Txertoa.

Letamendía, F. (1994) *Historia del nacionalismo vasco y de ETA*, San Sebastián: R & B, 3 vols.

Levi, P. ([1947, 1958] 1987) *If This Is a Man The Truce*, translated by S. Woolf, with an introduction by P. Bailey, London: Abacus, Sphere Books.

Linde Paniagua, E. (1976a) *Amnistía e indulto en España*, Madrid: Túcar.

Linde Paniagua, E. (1976b) "La clemencia en Italia: Amnistía e Indulto", *Revista de Administración Pública*, 79, pp. 457–486.

Linde Paniagua, E. (1979) "Amnistía e indulto en la Constitución española de 1978", *Revista de Derecho Político*, 2, pp. 55–69.

Linde Paniagua, E. (1998) "La Clemencia (Amnistía e Indulto) a la luz de la Jurisprudencia de los Tribunales Supremo y Constitucional y del Código Penal de 1995", *Boletín del Ministerio de Justicia*, 1823, pp. 1413–1428.

Linde Paniagua, E. (2000) "El indulto como acto de administración de Justicia y su judicialización. Problemas, límites y consecuencias", *Teoría y Realidad Constitucional*, 5, pp. 161–175.

Linz, J. J. (1996) "La transición española en perspectiva comparada", J. Tusell, and A. Soto (eds), *Historia de la transición 1975–1986*, Madrid: Alianza Editorial, pp. 21–45.

Linz, J. J. and Stepan, A. (1996) *Problems of Democratic Transition and Consolidation: Southern Europe, South America, and Post-Communist Europe*, Baltimore: Johns Hopkins University Press.

Llorca Ortega, J. (1997) *La Ley de indulto (Comentarios, jurisprudencia, formularios y notas para su reforma)*, Valencia: Tirant lo Blanch (2nd edn).

López Aguilar, J. F. (1996) "Una reflexión a propósito del control parlamentario del ejercicio del derecho de gracia", *Revista de las Cortes Generales*, 37, pp. 329–342.

López Ortega, J. J. (2014) "Las desapariciones forzadas en España a la luz de la Convención de las Naciones Unidas", M. Casado González and J. J. López Ortega (eds), *Desapariciones forzadas de niños en Europa y Latinoamérica. Del convenio de la ONU a las búsquedas a través del ADN*, Barcelona: Universidad de Barcelona, pp. 319–340.

López Villaverde, A. L. (2014) "La cultura de la memoria. Nuevo balance bibliográfico", *Studia historica. Historia contemporánea*, 32, pp. 263–283.

Lozano Cutanda, B. (1991) "El indulto y la amnistía ante la Constitución", S. Martín-Retortillo Baquer (ed.), *Estudios sobre la Constitución española: Homenaje al profesor Eduardo García de Enterría*, Madrid: Civitas, vol. 2, pp. 1027–1051.

Luchaire, F., Conac, G. and Prétot, X. (eds) (2009) *La Constitution de la République française: Analyses et commentaires*, Paris: Economica (3rd edn).

Lundy, P. and McGregor, M. (2008) "The Role of Comunity in Participatory Transitional Justice", K. McEvoy, and L. McGregor (eds), *Transitional Justice From Below: Grassroots Activism and the Struggle for Change*, Oxford: Hart Publishing, pp. 99–120.

McAuliffe, P. (2011) "Transitional Justice's expanding Empire; Reasserting the value of the paradigmatic Transition", *Journal of Conflictology*, 2(2), pp. 32–44.

McConnachie, K. and Morison, J. (2008) "Constitution-making, Transition and the Reconstitution of Society", K. McEvoy and L. McGregor (eds), *Transitional Justice from Below: Grassroots Activism and the Struggle for Change*, Oxford: Hart Publishing, pp. 75–98.

McEvoy, K. (2007) "Beyond Legalism: Towards a Thicker Understanding of Transitional Justice", *Journal of Law and Society*, 34(4), pp. 411–440.

McEvoy, K. (2008) "Letting Go of Legalism: Developing a 'Thicker' Version of Transitional Justice", K. McEvoy, and L. McGregor (eds), *Transitional Justice From Below: Grassroots Activism and the Struggle for Change*, Oxford: Hart Publishing, pp. 15–47.

McEvoy, K., Anthony, G. and Mallinder, L. (2014) *Investigations, Prosecutions, and Amnesties under Articles 2 & 3 of the European Convention on Human Rights*, Belfast: Queen's University; Ulster University. http://amnesties-prosecution-public-interest.co.uk/

McEvoy, K. and McGregor, L. (eds) (2008) *Transitional Justice from Below. Grassroots Activism and the Struggle for Change*, London: Hart Publishing.

Mallinder, L. (2007) "Can Amnesties and International Justice be Reconciled?", *International Journal of Transitional Justice*, 1(2), pp. 208–230.

Mallinder, L. (2008a) *Human Rights and Political Transitions: Bridging the Peace and Justice Divide*, London: Hart Publishing, 2008.

Mallinder, L. (2008b) *Exploring the practice of states in introducing amnesties*, Belfast: Ulster University. http://uir.ulster.ac.uk/2265/1/Mallinder-NurembergchapterJune20081.pdf

Mallinder, L. (2010) "Global Comparision of Amnesty Laws", M. Ch. Bassiouni (ed.), *The pursuit of International Criminal Justice: A world study of conflicts, victimization and post-conflict justice*, Antwerp: Intersentia.

Mallinder, L. (2014) "Amnesties in the pursuit of reconciliation, peacebuilding and restorative justice", D. Philpott and J. Llewellyn (eds), *Restorative Justice, Reconciliation and Peacebuilding*, Oxford: Oxford University Press, pp. 138–173.

Mallinder, L. and McEvoy, K. (2011) "Rethinking Amnesties: Atrocity, Accountability and Impunity in Post-Conflict Societies", *Contemporary Social Science*, 6(1) pp. 107–128.

Mallinder, L., Moffett, L., McEvoy, K. and Anthony, G. (2015) *Investigations, Prosecutions, and Amnesties under Articles 2 & 3 of the European Convention on Human Rights*, Belfast: Queen's University; Ulster University.

Manjón-Cabeza Olmeda, A. (2012) "2012: Las posibilidades legales de la memoria histórica", *Revista Electrónica de Ciencia Penal y Criminología*, 14–12, pp. 1–42.

Maogoto, J. N. (2004) *War crimes and realpolitik. International justice from World War I to the 21st century*, Boulder: Lynne Rienner Publishers.

Martín, S. (2009) "Criminalidad política y peligrosidad social en la España Contemporánea (1870–1970)", *Quaderni Fiorentini per la storia del pensiero giuridico moderno*, 38, pp. 861–951.

Martín Beristáin, C. (2000) *Justicia y Reconciliación. El papel de la verdad y la justicia en la reconstrucción de sociedades fracturadas por la violencia*, Bilbao: Universidad del País Vasco/ Euskal Herriko Unibertsitatea.

Martín Pallín, J. A. (1992) "El derecho de gracia", *Ministerio Fiscal y sistema penitenciario. III Jornadas de Fiscales de Vigilancia Penitenciaria*, Madrid: Ministerio de Justicia, pp. 307–322.

Martín Pallín, J. (2008a) "La ley que rompió el silencio", J. A. Martín Pallín and R. Escudero Alday (eds), *Derecho y memoria histórica*, Madrid: Trotta, pp. 19–46.

Martín Pallín, J. (2008b) "Introducción", J. A. Martín Pallín and R. Escudero Alday (eds), *Derecho y Memoria Histórica*, Madrid: Trotta, pp. 9–18.

Martín Pallín, J. (2009) "De malas leyes, peores reglamentos: el desarrollo de la Ley de la memoria histórica", *Jueces para la Democracia*, 66, pp. 9–25.

Martín Pallín, J. (2011) "Amnistía", R. Escudero Alday (ed.), *Diccionario de memoria histórica: conceptos contra el olvido*, Madrid: Los Libros de la Catarata, pp. 57–63.

Martín Pallín, J. (2016) "Prólogo. La Justicia que luchó por la democracia", P. Díaz Sánchez (ed.) *Los jueces contra el franquismo: Justicia Democrática*, Madrid: Maia Ediciones, pp. 7–17.

Martín Pallín, J. A. and Escudero Alday, R. (eds) (2008) *Derecho y Memoria Histórica*, Madrid: Trotta.

Martín Pallín, J. A. and Escudero Alday, R. (eds) (2009) "De malas leyes, peores reglamentos: el desarrollo de la Ley de la memoria histórica", *Jueces para la Democracia*, 66, pp. 9–25.

Martínez Alcañiz, A. (2014) *El principio de justicia universal y los crímenes de guerra*, Doctoral Thesis directed by J. L. Rodríguez-Villasante y Prieto and A. Gil Gil, Madrid: Universidad Nacional de Educación a Distancia.

Mastromarino, A. (2016) "Memoria histórica del Estado y leyes de amnistía", *Revista de Investigaciones Políticas y Sociológicas*, 15(1), pp. 143–164.

Mate, R. (2003) *Memoria de Auschwitz. Actualidad moral y política*, Madrid: Trotta.

Mate, R. (2008) *La herencia del olvido*, Madrid: Errata Naturae.

Mate, R. (2011) "Deber de memoria", R. Escudero Alday (ed.), *Diccionario de memoria histórica: conceptos contra el olvido*, Madrid: Los Libros de la Catarata, pp. 27–33.

Mateos, A. (1993) *El PSOE contra Franco. Continuidad y renovación del socialismo español, 1953–1974*, Madrid: Fundación Pablo Iglesias.

Medina, F. (1996) *Las sombras del poder. Los servicios secretos de Carrero Blanco a Roldán*, Madrid: Espasa-Calpe.

Medina, F. (2004) *Memoria oculta del Ejército*, Madrid: Espasa-Calpe.

Méndez, J. (1997) "Accountability for Past Abuses", *Human Rights Quarterly*, 19(2), pp. 255–282.

Méndez, J. (2013) "Justicia de transición", R. Escudero Alday, and C. Pérez González (eds), *Desapariciones forzadas, represión política y crímenes del franquismo*, Madrid: Trotta, pp. 13–30.

Messuti, A. (2012) "La justicia argentina abre una causa para investigar los crímenes del franquismo", G. I. Anitua *et al.* (eds), *Derecho penal internacional y memoria histórica: desafíos del pasado y retos del futuro*, Buenos Aires: Fabián J. Di Plácido, pp. 276–297.

Messuti, A. (2013a) *Un deber ineludible. La obligación del estado de perseguir penalmente los crímenes internacionales*, Buenos Aires: Ediar.

Messuti, A. (2013b) "La querella Argentina: la aplicación del principio de justicia universal al caso de las desapariciones forzadas", R. Escudero Alday, and C. Pérez González (eds), *Desapariciones forzadas, represión política y crímenes del franquismo*, Madrid: Trotta, pp. 121–140.

Molinero, C. (2009) "La ley de amnistía de 1977: la reivindicación antifranquista y su lectura treinta años después", M. J. Espuny Tomás and O. Paz Torres (eds), *30 años de la ley de amnistía (1977–2007)*, Madrid: Universidad Autónoma de Barcelona; Dykinson, pp. 41–55.

Monferrer Tomàs, J. (2003) "La construcción de la protesta en el movimiento gay español: la Ley de Peligrosidad Social (1970) como factor precipitante de la acción colectiva", *Revista Española de Investigaciones Sociológicas*, 102, pp. 171–204.

Moreno, A. (1977) *Mujeres en lucha. El movimiento feminista en España*, Barcelona: Anagrama.

Moreno Gómez, F. (1985) *La Guerra Civil en Córdoba*, Madrid: Alpuerto.

Muniesa, B. (2007) *Dictadura y transición. La España lampedusiana. Vol. II. La Monarquía parlamentaria*, Barcelona: Universitat de Barcelona.

Muñoz Sánchez, A. (2012) *El amigo alemán. El PSOE y el SPD de la dictadura a la democracia*, Barcelona: RBA Libros.

Naqvi, Y. (2003) "Amnesty for war crimes: Defining the limits of international recognition", *International Review of the Red Cross*, 85, pp. 583–626.

Nash, M. (1986) "Ordenamiento jurídico y realidad social del aborto en España: una aproximación histórica", M. C. García-Nieto (ed.), *Ordenamiento jurídico y realidad social de las mujeres. Siglos XVI a XX: Actas de las IV Jornadas de Investigación Interdisciplinaria*, Madrid: Universidad Autónoma de Madrid, pp. 223–238.

Navarro, V. (2002) *Democracia incompleta, bienestar insuficiente. Sobre lo que no se habla en nuestro país*, Barcelona: Anagrama.

Noguera Fernández, A. (2013a) "Crisis y memoria: hacia una redefinición del concepto memoria histórica de la Ley 52/2007", *Anales de la Cátedra Francisco Suárez*, 47, pp. 249–271.

Noguera Fernández, A.(2013b) "Los usos de la memoria y la Ley 52/2007 de Memoria Histórica. De la memoria personal a una memoria colectiva de transformación", M. Criado de Diego (ed.), *El itinerario de la memoria. Derecho, historia y justicia en la recuperación de la memoria histórica en España. Vol. 1. El derecho y la memoria*, Madrid: Sequitur, pp. 83–104.

Núñez Díaz-Balart, M. (2010) "Una benevolencia contradictoria: los mecanismos de integración de los presos políticos en el franquismo", *Berceo*, 159, pp. 183–204.

O'Donnell, G., Schmitter, G. P. and Whitehead, L. (eds) (1986) *Transitions from Authoritarian Rule: Tentative Conclusions about uncertain democracies*, Baltimore: Johns Hopkins University Press, 4 vols.

O'Flaherty, M. (2004), "Sierra Leone's peace process: The role of the human rights community", *Human Rights Quarterly*, 26(1), pp. 30–62.

Office of the United Nations High Commissioner for Human Rights (2009) *Rule-of-law tools for post-conflict states: amnesties*, New York and Geneva: United Nations. HR/PUB/09/1.

Onaindía, M. (2001) *El precio de la libertad: Memorias, 1948–1977*, Madrid: Espasa.

Onaindía, M. (2004) *El aventurero cuerdo: Memorias, 1977–1981*, Madrid: Espasa.

Olivas Díaz, Amaya (2008) "La intervención del juez de instrucción en las diligencias de investigación seguidas por desapariciones forzadas en la dictadura franquista", *Jueces para la Democracia*, 63, pp. 86–102.

Oreja, M. (2011) *Memoria y esperanza: Relatos de una vida*, Madrid: La Esfera de los Libros.

Ortuño-Anaya, P. (1996) "El movimiento laborista británico y España (1974–1977)", *Espacio, Tiempo y Forma. Serie V. Historia Contemporánea*, 9, pp. 279–293.

Ortuño-Anaya, P. (2002) *European Socialists and Spain. The Transition to Democracy (1959–77)*, New York: Palgrave.

Otero, L. and Fortes, J. (1983) *Proceso a nueve militares demócratas*, Barcelona: Argos Vergara.

Otero Novas, J. M. (2015) *Lo que yo viví: Memorias políticas y reflexiones*, Barcelona: Prensa Ibérica.

Osiel, M. (1997) *Mass Atrocity, Collective Memory and the Law*, New Brunswick, NJ: Transaction Publishers.

Osorio García, A. (1980) *Trayectoria política de un ministro de la Corona*, Barcelona: Planeta.

Ott, L. (2011) *Enforced Disappearance in International Law*, Cambridge, Antwerp and Portland: Intersentia.

Patrone, I. (2000) "Un caso histórico de impunidad: la depuración del fascismo en Italia", I. Delgado (ed.), *Impunidad y derecho a la memoria: de Pinochet a Timor*, Madrid: Sequitur, pp. 109–117.

Parejo Alfonso, L. (2008) "Administración pública y memoria histórica", J. A. Martín Pallín and R. Escudero Alday (eds), *Derecho y Memoria Histórica*, Madrid: Trotta, pp. 127–184.
Payne, L. and Lessa, F. (eds) (2012) *Amnesty in the Age of Human Rights Accountability*, Cambridge: Cambridge University Press.
Pérez Amorós, F. (2009) "La amnistía sindical durante un trienio de la transición política (1976–1978): Llibertat, amnistía i estatut d'autonomia", M. J. Espuny Tomás and O. Paz Torres (eds), *30 años de la ley de amnistía (1977–2007)*, Madrid: Universidad Autónoma de Barcelona; Dykinson, pp. 71–165.
Pérez del Valle, C. (2001) "Amnistía, Constitución y justicia material", *Revista Española de Derecho Constitucional*, 61, pp. 187–206.
Pérez Francesc, J. H. (2009) "Amnistía, indulto e intencionalidad política", M. J. Espuny Tomás and O. Paz Torres (eds), *30 años de la ley de amnistía (1977–2007)*, Madrid: Universidad Autónoma de Barcelona; Dykinson, pp. 57–69.
Pérez González, C. (2013) "Derecho a la verdad y desapariciones forzadas durante la guerra civil y el franquismo: una perspectiva desde el desde el derecho internacional", R. Escudero Alday and C. Pérez González (eds), *Desapariciones forzadas, represión política y crímenes del franquismo*, Madrid: Trotta.
Peters, E. (1987) *La tortura*, Madrid: Alianza Editorial.
Peydro Cano, M. (1980) *Las escisiones del PSOE*, Barcelona: Plaza & Janés.
Pigrau Solé, A. (2009) *La jurisdicción universal y su aplicación en España: la persecución del genocidio, los crímenes de guerra y los crímenes contra la humanidad por los tribunales nacionales*, Barcelona: Generalitat de Catalunya. Oficina de Promoción de la Paz y de los Derechos Humanos.
Pinilla Martín, E. (2006) "La recuperación de la memoria histórica en España", F. Gómez Isa (ed.), *El derecho a la memoria*, Donostia/San Sebastián: Diputación Foral de Gipuzkoa; Universidad de Deusto, pp. 529–548.
Politi, M. and Nesi, G. (eds) (2001) *The Rome Statute of the International Criminal Court: A Challenge to Impunity*, Aldershot: Ashgate.
Poole, R. (2009) "Enacting oblivion", *International Journal of Politics, Culture and Society*, 22(2), pp. 149–157.
Pons Prandes, E. (1987) *Crónica negra de la transición española (1976–1985)*, Barcelona: Plaza & Janés.
Portell Manso, J. M. (1977) *Euskadi: Amnistía Arrancada*, Barcelona: Dopesa.
Poulantzas, N. and Mercado, T. (1976) *The crisis of the dictatorships: Portugal, Greece, Spain*, London: New Left Books and Humanities Press.
Preston, P. (2003) *Juan Carlos I. El rey de un pueblo*, Madrid: Plaza & Janés.
Preston, P. (2013) *El zorro rojo: La vida de Santiago Carrillo*, Madrid: Debate.
Raimundo, F. and Costa Pinto, A. (2014) "From ruptured transition to politics of silence: the case of Portugal", N. Wouters (ed.), *Transitional justice and memory in Europe (1945–2013)*, Cambridge: Intersentia, pp. 173–198.
Reig Tapia, A. (1984) *Ideología e Historia. Sobre la represión franquista y la Guerra Civil*, Madrid: Akal.
Remiro Brotóns, A. (2006) "La persecución de los crímenes internacionales por los tribunales estatales: el principio de universalidad", *XXXIII Curso de Derecho Internacional. El Derecho Internacional en las Américas: 100 años del Comité Jurídico Interamericano*, Río de Janeiro: Secretaría General de la OEA, pp. 491–516.
Requejo Pagés, J. L. (2001) "Amnistía e indulto en el constitucionalismo histórico español", *Historia constitucional. Revista electrónica de Historia constitucional*, 2, pp. 81–106.

Ripol Carulla, S. (2014) "La justicia de transición. Concepto y práctica española (selección de bibliografia y documentación) Transitional Justice: Concept and Practice in Spain", *Historiografías. Revista de Historia y Teoría*, 8, pp. 76–107.

Ripol Carulla, S. and Villán Durán, C. (eds) (2012) *Justicia de transición: el caso de España*, Barcelona: Institut Catalá Internacional per la Pau.

Rodríguez Arias, M. A. (2008) *El caso de los niños perdidos del franquismo: Crimen contra la humanidad*, Valencia: Tirant lo Blanch.

Rodríguez Gil, M. (1998) *Vice uxor: notas sobre el concubinato en España desde la recepción del derecho común*, Madrid: Universidad Complutense.

Rodríguez Jiménez, J. L. (2007) *De héroes e indeseables: la División Azul*, Madrid: Espasa.

Rodríguez Teijeiro, D. (2011) "Excarcelación, libertad condicional e instrumentos de control postcarcelario en la inmediata posguerra (1939–1945)", A. Barrio Alonso, J. de Hoyos Puente and R. Saavedra Arias (eds), *Nuevos horizontes del pasado. Culturas políticas, identidades y formas de representación. Actas del X Congreso de la Asociación de Historia Contemporánea*, Santander: Ediciones de la Universidad de Cantabria, pp. 1–15.

Roehrig, T. (2002) *The prosecution of former military leaders in newly democratic nations: the cases of Argentina, Greece and South Korea*, Jefferson, NC: McFarland.

Roht-Arriaza, N. (1995) *Impunity and Human Rights in International Law and Practice*, Oxford: Oxford University Press.

Roht-Arriaza, N. (2001) "The Role of International Actors in National Accountability Process", A. Barahona de Brito, C. González-Enríquez and P. Aguilar (eds), *The Politics of Memory. Transitional Justice in Democratizing Societies*, Oxford: Oxford University Press, pp. 40–64.

Roht-Arriaza, N. (2012) "The Spanish Civil War, Amnesty, and the Trials of Judge Garzón", *ASIL Insights*, 16(24). http://www.asil.org/pdfs/insights/insight120725.pdf

Roht-Arriaza, N. (2014) *Reparations and Economic, Social and Cultural Rights: Justice and Economic violence in Transition*, New York: Springer.

Roht-Arriaza, N. and Mariezcurrena, J. (eds) (2006) *Transitional Justice in the Twenty-First Century: Beyond Truth Versus Justice*, New York and Cambridge: Cambridge University Press.

Rubio Caballero, J. A. (2014) "¿Recordar o pasar página? 1936 en la(s) memoria(s) del nacionalismo vasco", *Cahiers de civilisation espagnole contemporaine*, p. 12. https://ccec.revues.org/5098

Sáez Valcárcel, R. (2009) "Justicia transicional y España. ¿Se puede juzgar la historia?", *Memoria histórica, ¿se puede juzgar la historia*, Madrid: Fundación Antonio Carretero, pp. 85–112.

Sáez Valcárcel, R. (2010) "Los jueces y el aprendizaje de la impunidad, a propósito de los crímenes del franquismo", *Mientras tanto*, 114, pp. 41–72.

Sáez Valcárcel, R. (2011) "Impunidad", R. Escudero Alday (ed.), *Diccionario de memoria histórica: conceptos contra el olvido*, Madrid: Los Libros de la Catarata, pp. 63–69.

Sáez Valcárcel, R. (2013) "Los crímenes de la dictadura y la negación de acceso a la jurisdicción", R. Escudero Alday and C. Pérez González (eds), *Desapariciones forzadas, represión política y crímenes del franquismo*, Madrid: Trotta.

Sainz Moreno, F. (1978) "Efectos materiales y procesales de la amnistía: responsabilidad penal de la Administración, devolución de sanciones pecuniarias, satisfacción extraprocesal de la pretensión", *Revista de Administración Pública*, 87, pp. 361–371.

Saiz del Moral, L. (1976) *Amnistía también para la derecha*, Móstoles: San Martín de Villagroy.

San Martín, J. L. (1983) *Servicio especial a las órdenes de Carrero Blanco (de Castellana a El Aaiun)*, Barcelona: Planeta.

Sánchez-Cervera Senra, J. M. (1978) "La amnistía laboral en la Ley 46/1977, de 15 de octubre", *Revista de Política Social*, 117, pp. 197–211.

Sánchez-Cuenca Rodríguez, I. and Aguilar Fernández, P. (2009) "Violencia política y movilización social en la transición española", S. Baby, O. Compagnon and E. González Calleja (eds), *Violencia y transiciones políticas a finales del siglo XX. Europa del Sur-América Latina*, Madrid: Casa de Velázquez, pp. 95–112.

Sancinetti, M. A. and Ferrante, M. (1999) *El Derecho penal en la protección de los derechos humanos*, Buenos Aires: Hammurabi.

Sarkin, J. (2004) *Carrots and sticks: TRC and the South African amnesty process*, Antwerp, Oxford: Intersentia.

Sartorius, N. and Alfaya, J. (1999) *La memoria insumisa*, Madrid: Espasa Calpe.

Sartorius, N. and Sabio, A. (1977) *El final de la Dictadura. La conquista de la democracia en España (Noviembre de 1975–Junio de 1977)*, Madrid: Temas de Hoy.

Sauca Cano, J. M. (2008) "El derecho ciudadano a la memoria histórica: concepto y contenido", J. A. Martín Pallín and R. Escudero Alday (eds), *Derecho y Memoria Histórica*, Madrid: Trotta, pp. 73–104.

Sauca Cano, J. (2011) "Derecho a la memoria", R. Escudero Alday (ed.), *Diccionario de memoria histórica: conceptos contra el olvido*, Madrid: Los Libros de la Catarata, pp. 21–27.

Schabas, W. A. (2002) "Punishment of Non-State Actors in Non-International Armed Conflict", *Fordham International Law Journal*, 26(4), pp. 907–933.

Schabas, W. (2006) *The UN International Tribunals: The Former Yugoslavia, Rwanda and Sierra Leone*, Cambridge, UK and New York: Cambridge University Press.

Schabas, W. (2010) *The International Criminal Court. A Commentary on the Rome Statute*, Oxford: Oxford University Press.

Schabas, W. A. and Darcy, S. (eds) (2004) *Truth Commissions and Courts: The Tension between Criminal Justice and the Search for Truth*, Dordrecht: Kluwer Academic Publishers.

Seibert-Fohr, A. (2003) "The Relevant of the Rome Statute of the International Criminal Court for Amnesties and Truth Commissions", *Max Planck Yearbook of United Nations Law*, 7, pp. 553–590.

Seibert-Fohr, A. (2009) *Prosecuting Serious Human Rights Violations*, New York: Oxford University Press.

Sempere Souvannavong, J. D. (2001) "Les pieds-noirs à Alicante", *Revue européenne des migrations internationales*, 17(3), pp. 173–198.

Sevillano Calero, F. (2003) "La construcción de la memoria y del olvido en la España democrática", *Ayer*, 52, pp. 297–319.

Silva, E. (2006) "El despertar de la memoria histórica en España: el papel de la sociedad civil", F. Gómez Isa (ed.), *El derecho a la memoria*, Bilbao: Diputación Foral de Gipuzkoa; Universidad de Deusto, pp. 571–580.

Silva, E. (2011) "Movimiento memorialista", R. Escudero Alday (ed.), *Diccionario de memoria histórica: conceptos contra el olvido*, Madrid: Los Libros de la Catarata, pp. 69–75.

Silva, E. and Macías, S. (2003) *Las fosas de Franco. Los republicanos que el dictador dejó en las cunetas*, Madrid: Temas de Hoy.

Skaar, E. (2012) "Reconciliation in a Transitional Justice Perspective", *Transitional Justice Review*, 1(1), pp. 54–103.

Skaar, E., Gianella Malca, C. and Eide, T. (2012) *A way out of violent conflict: the impact of transitional justice on peace and democracy*, Bergen: CMI.

Skaar, E., Gianella Malca, C. and Eide, T. (2015) *After Violence: Transitional Justice, Peace, and Democracy*, London: Routledge.

Soares, M. (1975) *Portugal's Struggle for Liberty*, London: Allen & Unwin.

Sobremonte Martínez, J. E. (1979) "Indulto general en España", J. R. Casabó Ruiz (ed.), *Escritos penales*, Valencia: Universidad de Valencia.

Sobremonte Martínez, J. E. (1980) *Indultos y amnistía*, Valencia: Universidad de Valencia.

Solé i Sabaté, J. M. (1985) *La repressió franquista a Catalunya, 1938–1953*, Barcelona: Edicions 62.

Soriano Gil, M. A. (2005) *La marginación homosexual en la España de la Transición*, Madrid: Egales.

Soriano Hernández, S. (2013) "El modelo español de impunidad de los crímenes franquistas de la Sentencia del Tribunal Supremo 101/2012, de 27 de febrero", M. Criado de Diego (ed.), *El itinerario de la memoria. Derecho, historia y justicia en la recuperación de la memoria histórica en España. Vol. 1. El derecho y la memoria*, Madrid: Sequitur, pp. 215–223.

Soto Carmona, A. (2009) "La transición a la democracia en el sur de Europa. La historia como instrumento para la comparación", *Estudios Internacionales*, 162, pp. 7–30.

Spyropoulos, P. K. and Fortsakis, T. F. (2009) *Constitutional Law in Greece*, New York: Wolters Kluwer Law.

Suárez Fernández, L. (2011) *Franco. Los años decisivos. 1931–1945*, Barcelona: Ariel.

Tamarit Sumalla, J. M. (2009) "Justicia transicional y Derecho Penal en España", *Memoria histórica, ¿se puede juzgar la historia?*, Madrid: Fundación Antonio Carretero, pp. 129–142.

Tamarit Sumalla, J. (2011) "Transition, Historical Memory and Criminal Justice in Spain", *Journal of International Criminal Justice*, 9(3), pp. 729–752.

Tamarit Sumalla, J. (2012) "Los límites de la justicia transicional penal: la experiencia del caso español", *Política Criminal: Revista Electrónica Semestral de Políticas Públicas en Materias Penales*, 7(13), pp. 74–93.

Tamarit Sumalla, J. (2013) *Historical Memory and Criminal Justice in Spain. A Case of Late Transitional Justice*, Cambridge: Intersentia.

Tamarit Sumalla, J. (2014) "Memoria histórica y justicia transicional en España: el tiempo como actor de la justicia penal", *Anuario iberoamericano de Derecho penal internacional*, 2, pp. 43–65.

Teitel, R. G. (2000) *Transitional Justice*, Oxford and New York: Oxford University Press.

Teitel, R. (2003) "Transitional Justice Genealogy", *Harvard Human Rights Journal*, 16, pp. 69–94.

Teitel, R. (2014) *Globalizing Transitional Justice*, Oxford: Oxford University Press.

Terradillos Basoco, J. M. (2010) "La revisión del pasado y la Ley de Memoria Histórica", *Revista Penal*, 25, pp. 151–166.

Thompson, J. (2002) *Taking responsibility for the past: reparation and historical injustice*, Cambridge: Polity.

Triffterer, O. (ed.) (1999) *Commentary on the Rome Statute of the International Criminal Court: Observers' Notes, Article by Article*, Baden-Baden: Nomos.

Tuñón de Lara, M. *et al.* (1985) *La guerra civil 50 años después*, Barcelona: Labor.

Tusell, J. (1988) *La dictadura de Franco*, Madrid: Alianza.

Tusell, J. (2003) "La reconciliación española", *Claves de Razón Práctica*, 132, pp. 32–39.

Tusell, J. (2005) "Dictadura franquista y democracia, 1939-2004," J. Lynch (ed.), *Historia de España*, Vol XIV, Barcelona: Crítica.

Urdánoz, J. (2014) *Veinte destellos de ilustración electoral (y una página web desesperada)*, Barcelona: Ediciones del Serbal.

Urdillo, U. (2011–2012) "Impunity for enforced disappearances in contemporary Spain. The Spanish Search for Truth", *Interdisciplinary Journal of Human Rights Law*, 6, pp. 41–60.

Uriarte, E. (2005) *Mirando hacia atrás: del proceso de Burgos a la amenaza permanente*, Barcelona: Ediciones B.

Valencia Villa, H. (2010) "Justicia transicional y acuerdos de paz: hacia una lex pacificatoria", C. Faleh Pérez and C. Villán Durán (eds), *Estudios sobre el derecho humano a la paz*, Madrid: Los Libros de la Catarata, pp. 155–166.

Valencia Villa, H. (2012) "La ley española de amnistía de 1977 en una perspectiva de justicia transicional", S. Ripol Carulla and C. Villán Durán (eds), *Justicia de transición: el caso de España*, Barcelona: Institut Catalá Internacional per la Pau, pp. 185–198.

Vallès Muñío, D. (2004) "Amnistía y responsabilidad civil", *InDret. Working Paper, n° 185*, Barcelona: InDret, pp. 1–45.

Vallès Muñío, D. (2014) "La amnistía laboral en la jurisprudencia del Tribunal Supremo", *IusLabor*, 3, pp. 1–14.

Vicente, L. (2009) "La obligación de investigar los crímenes del pasado y garantizar los derechos de las víctimas de desaparición forzada durante la guerra civil y el franquismo", *Memoria histórica, ¿se puede juzgar la historia*, Madrid: Fundación Antonio Carretero, pp. 143–171.

Vicente, L. (2012) "La responsabilidad penal individual por crímenes de genocidio, de guerra y de lesa humanidad. Derecho comparado y práctica española", S. Ripol Carulla and C. Villán Durán (eds), *Justicia de transición: el caso de España*, Barcelona: Institut Catalá Internacional per la Pau, pp. 148–171.

Vidal-Beneyto, J. (1981) *Diario de una ocasión perdida*, Barcelona: Kairós.

Villagrasa Hernández, F. and Alberola Suriñach, O. (2007) "Resumen histórico del Grupo pro revisión del proceso Granado-Delgado", *Hispania Nova*, 7, pp. 1–27.

Villán Durán, C. (2012) "La ley española de amnistía de 1977 en una perspectiva de justicia transicional", S. Ripol Carulla and C. Villán Durán (eds), *Justicia de transición: el caso de España*, Barcelona: Institut Catalá Internacional per la Pau, pp. 9–25.

Villán Durán, C. and Faleh Pérez, C. (2008) "Derecho a un recurso efectivo y a obtener una reparación justa y adecuada que corresponde a las víctimas de desapariciones forzadas, crímenes contra la humanidad y otras violaciones de los derechos humanos cometidas en España durante la Guerra civil y la dictadura", *Revista Electrónica de Estudios Internacionales*, 16. http://www.reei.org/index.php/revista/num16/notas/derecho-recurso-efectivo-obtener-una-reparacion-justa-adecuada-corresponde-victimas-desapariciones-forzadas-crimenes-contra-humanidad-otras-violaciones-derechos-humanos-cometidas-espana-durante-guerra-civil-dictadura

Villar, E. (2016) *Los espías de Suárez. La historia inédita de la Transición a través de los informes secretos de los espías rojos del Gobierno*, Madrid: Espasa Calpe.

Vinyes, R. (2004) *El daño y la memoria: las prisiones de María Salvo*, Barcelona: Plaza & Janés.

Vinyes, R. (2006) "Las desapariciones infantiles durante el franquismo y sus consecuencias", *International Journal of Iberian Studies*, 19(1), pp. 53–71.

Vinyes, R. (2009) *El Estado y la memoria: gobiernos y ciudadanos frente a los traumas de la historia*, Barcelona: RBA.

Vinyes, R. (2010) "Las políticas públicas de reparación y memoria en España", J. Babiano Mora (ed.), *Represión, derechos humanos, memoria y archivos: una perspectiva latinoamericana*, Madrid: GPS; Fundación Primero de Mayo, pp. 57–67.

Vinyes, R. (2011a) *Asalto a la memoria. Inmunidades y reconciliaciones, símbolos y éticas*, Barcelona: Los Libros del Lince.

Vinyes, R. (2011b) "Sobre víctimas y vacíos; ideologías y reconciliaciones; privatizaciones e impunidades", A. Domínguez Rama (ed.), *Enrique Ruano. Memoria viva de la impunidad del franquismo*, Madrid: Editorial Complutense, pp. 255–273.

Vinyes, R., Armengou, M. and Belis, R. (2003) *Los niños perdidos del franquismo*, Barcelona: Debolsillo.

Ysàs, P. (2009) "La transición española en la democracia: historia y mitos", M. J. Espuny Tomás and O. Paz Torres (eds), *30 años de la ley de amnistía (1977–2007)*, Madrid: Universidad Autónoma de Barcelona; Dykinson, pp. 19–40.

Wlasik, J. C. (2010) *Memoria, verdad y justicia en democracia: de la impunidad política a la impunidad técnica*, Mar del Plata: Editorial Universidad Nacional de Mar del Plata.

Wouters, N. (ed.) (2013) *Transitional Justice and Memory in Europe (1945–2013)*, Cambridge: Intersentia.

Zapico Barbeito, M. (2009) "La investigación de los crímenes del franquismo: entre el procesamiento por prevaricación abierto contra el juez Baltasar Garzón y la querella presentada en Argentina en virtud del ejercicio de la jurisdicción universal", *Anuario da Facultade de Direito da Universidade da Coruña*, 13, pp. 891–927.

Zapico Barbeito, M. (2010) "Investigating the Crimes of the Franco Regime: Legal Possibilities, Obligations of the Spanish State and Duties Towards the Victims", *International Criminal Law Review*, 10, pp. 243–274.

Zapico Barbeito, M. (2012) "La investigación penal de los crímenes del franquismo: ¿posible y/o deseable?", G. I. Anitua *et al.* (eds), *Derecho penal internacional y memoria histórica: desafíos del pasado y retos del futuro*, Buenos Aires: Fabián J. Di Plácido, pp. 437–475.

Zorrilla Ruiz, M. M. (1977) *Derecho del Trabajo y proceso de cambio social*, Bilbao: Universidad de Deusto.

Zúñiga Urbina, F. (1996) "Amnistía ante la jurisprudencia (Derechos humanos como límite al ejercicio de la soberanía)", *Revista de Derecho Político*, 42, pp. 371–422.

Newspapers and magazines

ABC (Madrid).

Egin (Hernani).

El Mundo (Madrid).

El País (Madrid).

Iraultza (San Sebastián).

La Hora (Santiago de Chile).

La Razón (Madrid).

La Vanguardia (Barcelona).

Mundo Obrero (Madrid).

Punto y Hora de Euskal Herria (Pamplona).

Unidad (Barcelona).

Websites

Amnistía Internacional. Sección española: https://www.es.amnesty.org/

Asociación de Expresos y represaliados políticos antifranquistas (AERPA): http://www.asocespresospoliticos.org/

Asociación Foro por la Memoria Democrática: http://www.foroporlamemoria.es/

Asociación para la Recuperación de la Memoria Histórica (ARMH): http://www.memoriahistorica.org/
Asociación por la Memoria Social y Democrática (AMESDE): http://amesde.org/
Asociación Pro Derechos Humanos de España: http://www.apdhe.org/
Centro Documental de la Memoria Histórica (Ministerio de Educación, Cultura y Deporte): http://www.mecd.gob.es/cultura-mecd/areas-cultura/archivos/mc/archivos/cdmh/portada.html
Convocatoria Cívica: http://convocatoriacivica.es/memoria-historica/
Coordinadora estatal de apoyo a la Querella Argentina contra crímenes del franquismo (CEAQUA): http://www.ceaqua.org/
Escola de Cultura de Pau: http://escolapau.uab.cat/
Federación Estatal de foros por la Memoria: http://www.foroporlamemoria.info/
Fundación Cultura de Paz: http://www.fund-culturadepaz.org/
Fundación Internacional Baltasar Garzón (FIBGAR): http://www.fibgar.org/
Fundación Transición Española: http://www.transicion.org/100materialInteres.php
Gobierno de España. Memoria histórica: http://www.memoriahistorica.gob.es/es-es/Paginas/index.aspx
Human Rights Watch: http://www.hrw.org/
Instituto de Derechos Humanos Pedro Arrupe (Universidad de Deusto): http://socialesyhumanas.deusto.es/cs/Satellite/socialesyhumanas/es/instituto-de-derechos-humanos
La Comuna. Presos del franquismo: http://www.lacomunapresxsdelfranquismo.org/
Memorial Democratic: http://memorialdemocratic.gencat.cat/cat/
Movimiento Político de Resistencia: http://movimientopoliticoderesistencia.blogspot.ie/p/transicion.html
Observatori del Sistema Penal i els Drets Humans (OSPDH) (Universidad de Barcelona): http://www.ub.edu/ospdh/
Plataforma contra la impunidad del franquismo: https://plataformacontralaimpunidad.wordpress.com/
Plataforma por la Comisión de la Verdad sobre los crímenes del Franquismo: https://comisionverdadfranquismo.com/
Rights International Spain: http://www.rightsinternationalspain.org/es/
The Amnesty Law Database, Queen's University: http://incore.incore.ulst.ac.uk/Amnesty/about.html
Transitional Justice and Memory in the UE (CSIC, Spain): http://www.proyectos.cchs.csic.es/transitionaljustice/home
United Nations: http://www.un.org

Interviews

Arzalluz, Xabier (2012) PNV deputy. Negotiator in representation of the Basque-Catalan Parliamentay Group in the 1977 Amnesty Law text (12 June 2012). Interview published in *Eleria, Euskal Herriko Legelarien Aldizkaria*, 23, pp. 119–124.
Campos, Josefina (2016) Pioneer in 1977 with regards to the recovery of the remains of those executed by Republicans (7 and 9 May 2016).
Castells Arteche, Miguel (2016) Lawyer. Founder of the Pro-Amnesty Associations in Gipuzkoa (6 May 2006).
Del Burgo, Jaime Ignacio (2016) UCD Senator. Second Secretary to the Senate (14 May 2016).

Herrero de Miñón, Miguel (2016) One of the authors behind the partial 1976 Amnesty Law, in his capacity as General Technical Secretariat in the Ministry of Justice, AP deputy in Parliament, and one of the "seven founding fathers" of the 1978 Constitution (21 May 2016).

Madariaga, Julen de. Lawyer (2016) Founding member of ETA. Granted amnesty by the 1977 Amnesty Law (15 June 2016).

Monreal, Gregorio (2016) Autonomous Front Senator in Parliament, member of this coalition in representation of ESEI (Socialist Unification of Euskadi) (10 April 2016).

Santos Itoiz, Eduardo (2017) Unidos Podemos Deputy in Congress (12 January 2017).

Serrano Izko, Bixente (2016) ETA prisoner amnestied by the 1977 Amnesty Law (14 June 2016).

Urroz, Javier (2016) Worker amnestied by the 1977 Amnesty Law (19 May 2016).

Index

For Product Safety Concerns and Information please contact our EU
representative GPSR@taylorandfrancis.com
Taylor & Francis Verlag GmbH, Kaufingerstraße 24, 80331 München, Germany

www.ingramcontent.com/pod-product-compliance
Ingram Content Group UK Ltd.
Pitfield, Milton Keynes, MK11 3LW, UK
UKHW020011200926
475702UK00014B/1818
* 9 7 8 0 3 6 7 2 3 2 3 6 8 *